A GENEALOGY OF BAMBOO DIPLOMACY

THE POLITICS OF THAI DÉTENTE WITH RUSSIA AND CHINA

A GENEALOGY OF BAMBOO DIPLOMACY

THE POLITICS OF THAI DÉTENTE WITH RUSSIA AND CHINA

JITTIPAT POONKHAM

ANU PRESS

ANU PRESS

Published by ANU Press
The Australian National University
Acton ACT 2601, Australia
Email: anupress@anu.edu.au

Available to download for free at press.anu.edu.au

ISBN (print): 9781760464981
ISBN (online): 9781760464998

WorldCat (print): 1285606289
WorldCat (online): 1285534030

DOI: 10.22459/GBD.2022

This title is published under a Creative Commons Attribution-NonCommercial-NoDerivatives 4.0 International (CC BY-NC-ND 4.0).

The full licence terms are available at
creativecommons.org/licenses/by-nc-nd/4.0/legalcode

Cover design and layout by ANU Press. Cover photograph courtesy of Ministry of Foreign Affairs, Thailand.

This book is published under the aegis of the Asia-Pacific Security Studies Editorial Board of ANU Press.

This edition © 2022 ANU Press

Contents

Preface		vii
1.	Introduction	1
2.	Cold War Discursive Hegemony: Anticommunism, Americanism and Antagonism	33
3.	Bending Before the Wind: The Emergence of 'Flexible Diplomacy' (1968–1969)	55
4.	Flexible Diplomacy: Thanat and the First Détente (1969–1971)	85
5.	Interregnum – 1971: A Coup against Diplomacy?	127
6.	A Diplomatic Transformation: Chatichai, Kukrit and the Second Détente (1975–1976)	173
7.	Equidistance: Kriangsak and the Third Détente (1977–1980)	233
8.	Conclusion: The End of 'Bamboo' Diplomacy? Back to the Future	291
Bibliography		307

Preface

This book is about the birth of bamboo diplomacy and the politics of Thai détente with Russia and China in the long 1970s. By 1968, Thailand was encountering discursive anxiety amid the disastrous catastrophe of the Vietnam War and the prospect of American retrenchment from the Indo-Pacific region. To cope with such anxiety, it was vital to the Thai state to develop a new narrative in order to make sense of rapidly changing world politics. The discourse of détente was an answer. It transformed Thai foreign policy away from the hegemonic discourse of anticommunism, and by doing so it created a political struggle between the old and new discourses. The book therefore also argues that bamboo diplomacy – previously seen as a classic tradition of Thai-style diplomacy – had its origins in Thai détente. It gradually emerged in the early 1970s and has become the metanarrative of Thai diplomacy since then. That said, the discourse of Thai détente and the birth of bamboo diplomacy are two sides of the same coin.

This book was gradually contrived and developed in the very first international relations department in the world, at Aberystwyth University. I am deeply grateful to Sergey Radchenko, whose intellectual insights on the Cold War's international history provided the building blocks for my initial project; Matt Phillips, whose historical expertise on Thailand in the Cold War was immensely invaluable and who enthusiastically put my thesis in the right direction as well as encouragingly believed in the main arguments of the thesis; and Charalampos Efstathopoulos (Haris), who professionally supported me as well as conceptually and theoretically strengthened my thoughts. Many thanks to the three of them, who diligently read through various drafts and provided me with very useful and insightful comments. I would also like to express my gratitude to Enze Han and James Vaughan, who critically engaged with my work as well as constructively sharpened and deepened the way in which this book was subsequently developed.

In Aberystwyth, I benefited greatly from my postgraduate fellows and professors, who provided an extremely critical (yet friendly) and stimulating dialogue over those two and a half consecutive years. Andrew Linklater, Mustapha Pasha and Milja Kurki served as my role models and wonderful sources of intellectual encouragement and inspiration. Thanks are also due to Dennis Rach and Thanapat Bekanan, who read the whole manuscript and provided helpful comments.

In Thailand, I am extremely indebted to all of my colleagues at the Faculty of Political Science, Thammasat University, most notably Chulacheeb Chinwanno and Kitti Prasirtsuk, for their generous and patient support, strong encouragement and intellectual companionship. Needless to say, without their endless support, this project would not have gotten far.

At my alma mater, Chulalongkorn University, I want to extend my special thanks to my former teachers, including Kullada Kesboonchoo Mead, Chaiwat Khamchoo, Supamit Pitipat and Soravis Jayanama, for their intellectual conversations, moral support and enduring inspiration. It was Kullada, my former supervisor and mentor, who first introduced me to critical international relations and archival research. In the mid-2000s, she and I conducted a research project on Thai–US relations during the Cold War at the National Archive in Maryland, United States. I am deeply grateful to her as well as Richard Mead, who also encouraged my academic pursuit.

Special thanks to Tej Bunnag, Surapong Jayanama, Sarasin Viraphol, Warnwai Phathanothai and Yodboon Lertrit, who kindly shared their firsthand experiences as well as political and diplomatic insights throughout our interviews.

I also owe a great debt to those archivists at Thailand's National Archive and the Ministry of Foreign Affairs as well as the librarians at Thammasat University, without whose help this book would not have been finished. Similarly, the book benefited immensely from those online published materials. I am thankful to Wahn, Kaem and Mohn for their invaluable technical and logistic assistance. Numerous conversations with my former and current students also stimulated a thoughtful commentary.

In the course of writing this book, I was invited to present various chapters as talks at Chulalongkorn University, the Yale-NUS College, National University of Singapore (NUS), Thammasat University, MGIMO (Moscow State Institute of International Relations) University and Lomonosov Moscow State University. Special thanks to my Russian colleagues and friends Victor Sumsky and Ekaterina Koldunova, for their academic comradeship and extraordinary generosity during my public lectures in Moscow. At Thammasat Institute of Area Studies, I wish to thank Suphat Supachalasai, for his generous hosting and hospitality for my inaugural public lecture, commemorating the 120th anniversary of Thai–Russian relations in 2017. At the NUS, I want to thank Naoko Shimazu, Tuong Vu and Yuexin Rachel Lin for their insightful and constructive engagement. At Chulalongkorn, I am grateful to Suthiphand Chirathivat, Rom Phiramontri and Natthanan Kunnamas for their invitation and support.

In addition, I would like to thank the editor of Asia-Pacific Security Studies series at ANU Press, Greg Raymond, for his generous encouragement and timely support of this book as well as the two anonymous reviewers for helpful and critical feedback. Many thanks to Beth Battrick for her astute and attentive copyediting.

Finally, I dedicate this book to my family: my late father for teaching me how to read; my mother for teaching me how to write; and my beloved aunt for teaching me how to care for details as well as for other human beings. Last, but not least, heartfelt thanks to Air for her companionship in life, unending patience, much-needed encouragement and immeasurable love.

1
Introduction

1.1. Puzzles

'Bamboo' or 'bending with the wind' diplomacy is a key concept frequently used in international relations (IR) and describes Thailand's diplomacy in particular. It alludes to the way in which the country has pursued a flexible, pragmatic policy, aimed at maintaining national survival and independence. In bamboo diplomacy, Thailand is blatantly playing one great power off against the others amid great power competition. The extant literature almost always treats this concept as universal, highlighting its historical continuity and heuristic tool of justification for appropriate foreign policy. For example, Pavin Chachavalpongpun sees bamboo diplomacy as a 'traditional' or 'classic' Thai diplomacy, which continued 'since Siam's old days up to Thailand's modern era'.[1] For Arne Kislenko, Thailand's diplomacy was 'a long-cherished, philosophical approach to international relations', which is 'always solidly rooted' but 'flexible enough to bend whichever way it had to in order to survive'.[2] These works largely neglect to ask the key question: when and how this strategic discourse came about. This is a puzzle of discontinuity or rupture, rather than continuity.

---

1 Pavin Chachavalpongpun, *Reinventing Thailand: Thaksin and His Foreign Policy* (Singapore: Institute of Southeast Asian Studies, 2010), 63–64, 274.
2 Arne Kislenko, 'Bamboo in the Wind: United States Foreign Policy and Thailand during the Kennedy and Johnson Administrations, 1961–1969' (PhD thesis, University of Toronto, 2000), 8.

The book is first and foremost a genealogy of bamboo diplomacy. Its purposes are twofold. One is to critically interrogate how the birth of 'bamboo' or 'flexible' diplomacy emerged and became the dominant or hegemonic discourse in Thai foreign policy. It should be noted here that Thailand in the pre-1968 period had sought to adjust relations with the Soviet Union and the People's Republic of China (PRC), the example of which was Field Marshal Plaek Phibunsongkhram (Phibun)'s attempt to work with Beijing between 1955 and 1957. However, these diplomatic practices were generally short-lived and merely tactical in the sense that they were used as a diplomatic tool in order to bargain with the US. Importantly, these diplomatic practices were not understood at that time as flexible or bamboo diplomacy. In particular, Phibun's 'brief encounter' with China was seen as part of a broader narrative of non-alignment.[3]

In other words, these previous diplomatic practices, despite their significant moves, were neither explicitly challenging the hegemonic discourse of anticommunism nor directly establishing the new discourse of détente par excellence. The book argues differently, that the term 'bamboo' diplomacy was discursively produced only by the late 1960s, when Thailand began to conduct a different set of diplomatic practices toward the USSR and China. In addition, as an epistemic knowledge, the term 'bamboo' diplomacy was not used before the 1970s. In order to justify contemporary diplomacy, many academic works retrospectively used this recently constructed concept to explain past diplomatic history. They anachronistically linked the new concept to the balance of power diplomacy of King Chulalongkorn, which will be subsequently discussed in this chapter.

In this sense, rather than following a conventional history in the study of Thai foreign policy, this book historically problematises the dominant knowledge and situates it within history. Therefore, my argument is that bamboo diplomacy was recently constructed as a new narrative in order to manage the anxiety instigated by the changing landscape of regional and world order – in particular, the prospect of American retrenchment from the region – as well as to make sense of how the world worked in the new era of détente.

---

3   Anuson Chinvanno, *'Brief Encounter': Sino–Thai Rapprochement after Bandung, 1955–1957* (Bangkok: Institute of Foreign Affairs, 1991).

This leads to the second purpose of the book, which is to investigate and reassess why and specifically how Thailand transformed its foreign policy towards the Soviet Union and the PRC in the long 1970s (1968–1980), when the country pursued détente with the Communist powers.

Détente, broadly defined as the relaxation of international tension, has been used particularly in relation to the Cold War politics, including the superpower détente of Richard Nixon, Henry Kissinger, Leonid Brezhnev, Mao Zedong, Charles de Gaulle and Willy Brandt. It was used, to a lesser extent, to describe small powers' détente and it was rarely used in literature on Thailand's diplomacy toward the Soviet Union and China in the 1970s. The book asserts that Thailand had its own conception of détente, culminating in so-called 'flexible diplomacy' (*karntoot yeutyun*) and 'triangular diplomacy' (*karntoot samsao*) with the Soviet Union and the PRC. In this book, Thai détente is studied in three main phases: (1) Thanat Khoman's (1969–1971); (2) MR Kukrit Pramoj's (1975–1976); and (3) General Kriangsak Chomanan's (1977–1980).

Détente marked a remarkable shift, from a discourse of 'enemy' toward that of 'friend' in Thai foreign relations with the Communist powers. Détente, in turn, intersubjectively constituted a new normal or common sense in the 1970s. In addition, it ultimately reflected power struggles within Thai politics. The emergence of Thai détente was not merely an ideational change or a change in norms, but represented a radical break in knowledge and political practices. It emerged out of a power contestation between different social forces at the top echelons of power, in particular between so-called détente proponents and détente opponents.

The former can be defined as those whose identities were intersubjectively shaped by Thai détente's discursive changes, and who enacted them in foreign policy thinking or decisions. The latter were those whose identities had not (yet) 'interpellated' or identified with the novel discourse and remained attached to the predominantly Cold War ideology, thereby envisaging the Soviet Union and China as 'Communist menaces'.

To achieve these two goals regarding the birth of bamboo diplomacy and détente with the Communist powers, the book employs a genealogical approach, which is a critical ethos for analysing and reinterpreting practice-based discourses of Thai diplomacy. This chapter is structured into four main sections. It begins with an examination of a historiographical literature of Thai détente. The second section elucidates a genealogical approach to Thai détente, which comprises a history of rupture, the discourse approach and a history of the present. The third section discusses sources of evidence, primarily newly declassified materials from Thai archives. The last section lays out the contribution and structure of the book.

1.2. The Narrative of 'Bamboo Diplomacy'

In this book, I take issue with two groups of literature on Thai foreign policy in the 1970s. Both groups explain Thai foreign policy in the détente era either by the continual narrative of bamboo diplomacy or by the motivations behind Thai foreign policy in specific periods of time and/or its bilateral relations.

The first group conceptualises Thai foreign policy through the conventional lens of 'bamboo' diplomacy, claiming that the history of Thai diplomatic relations has been interpreted as one of continuity. According to them, Thai diplomacy, at least since the reign of King Rama V, or King Chulalongkorn, in the late nineteenth century, has sought to balance one great power or a number of powers vis-à-vis the others.[4] By using a bamboo analogy, Thai diplomacy is flexible, pragmatic and even opportunistic. Given its status as a small power, Thailand strives for survival amid great power politics.[5] As Sarasin Viraphol sums up:

> Thailand is only a regional state with no desire for involvement in the great power rivalry; all that it desires is the maintenance and protection of its own national security.[6]

---

[4] See Likhit Dhiravegin, 'Thailand Foreign Policy Determination', *The Journal of Social Sciences* 11, no. 4 (1974); Likhit Dhiravegin, *Siam and Colonialism (1855–1909): An Analysis of Diplomatic Relations* (Bangkok: Thai Wattana Panich, 1975); Pensri Duke, *Karntangprated kub aekkarat lae attippatai kong thai* [Foreign affairs and Thailand's Independence and Sovereignty, since King Rama V to the Phibun Government] (Bangkok: The Royal Institute, 1999); Chulacheeb Chinwanno, *Siam, Russia, Thai: Karntootkarnmuang Karnmuangkarntoot, Aded pajupan anakod* [Siam, Russia, Thailand: Diplomatic Politics, Politics of Diplomacy, Past Present and Future] (Bangkok: Thammasat University Press, 2013).
[5] Sarasin Viraphol, *Directions in Thai Foreign Policy* (Singapore: Institute of Southeast Asian Studies, 1976); Wiwat Mungkandi and William Warren, eds, *A Century and a Half of Thai-American Relations* (Bangkok: Chulalongkorn University, 1982); Arne Kislenko, 'Bending with the Wind: The Continuity and Flexibility of Thai Foreign Policy', *International Journal* 57, no. 4 (Autumn 2002): 537–561. For literature on Thailand as a small power, see Astri Suhrki, 'Smaller-Nation Diplomacy: Thailand's Current Dilemmas', *Asian Survey* 11, no. 5 (May 1971): 438.
[6] Sarasin Viraphol, 'The Soviet Threat: Development of the Thai Perception', *Asian Affairs: An American Review* 11, no. 4 (Winter 1985): 69.

Wise (and mostly male) statesmen orchestrate the ability to bend with the wind, successfully maintaining Thailand's independence. Thailand, so the stories go, has had a cautious and calculated foreign policy, and avoided anything more than temporary entanglement with the great powers. The cases of Thailand's alignment with Japan during the Second World War, and its 'special relationship' with the US in the Cold War, are not portrayed as radical departures from the bamboo diplomacy paradigm.[7]

Corrine Phuangkasem suggests that Thailand's 'bamboo' or flexible diplomacy comprised three basic tenets.[8] First, Thailand pursues an accommodation policy with the great powers that are perceived as potential threats to national independence or survival. Second, Thailand plays off one power against another to provide a counterweight. Siddhi Savetsila, the former foreign minister, called it a 'balance of power policy'.[9] Third, Thailand seeks to befriend all great powers. Some might call this third tenet of Thai diplomacy an 'equidistant policy'.[10] Thai diplomacy is often criticised for a lack of firm principles, in that Thailand almost always aligns with the dominant or victorious power. As Likhit Dhiravegin has put it:

> The style of bending with the wind … means at a time when the dust is still not settled, the Thai leaders will be waiting on the wing … But as soon as the dust has settled, the Thai leaders will lean to the side which has risen in power.[11]

Corrine contends that the nature of Thai foreign policy during the Cold War remained 'bamboo diplomacy', in the sense of an alignment with the great powers.[12]

---

7   See Thamsook Numnonda, *Thailand and the Japanese Presence, 1941–1945* (Singapore: Institute of Southeast Asian Studies, 1977); Pensri, *Karntangprated kub aekkarat lae attippatai kong thai*.
8   Corrine Phuangkasem, *Thailand's Foreign Relations, 1964-80* (Singapore: Institute of Southeast Asian Studies, 1984); Corrine Phuangkasem, 'Thai Foreign Policy: Four Decades since the Second World War (1945–1989)', in *A Collection of Articles and Speeches on Thai Foreign Affairs from the Past to the Present*, eds Corrine Phuangkasem et al., vol. 1 (Bangkok: Faculty of Political Science, Thammasat University, 1999), 56, 70.
9   Siddhi Savetsila, *Pan Rorn Pan Nao* [Through Thick and Thin] (Bangkok, 2013), 78, 191.
10 Thanat Khoman, 'The Initiative of Establishing the Association of Southeast Asian Nations (ASEAN)', in Phuangkasem et al., *A Collection of Articles and Speeches*, 186–87.
11 Likhit Dhiravegin, 'Thailand's Relations with China, the US, and Japan in the New Political Environment', in Phuangkasem et al., *A Collection of Articles and Speeches*, 358.
12 Corrine, 'Thai Foreign Policy', 56.

Sarasin claims that in the 1970s, the Thai Ministry of Foreign Affairs followed bamboo diplomacy: it had pursued 'the traditional pattern of foreign diplomacy (prevalent in the late nineteenth and early twentieth centuries) which continually requires attention and wisdom in steering the nation through difficult times'. Unlike Corrine, Sarasin argues that this flexible diplomacy differed from 'the seemingly dogmatic and inflexible pattern of foreign relations as practiced by the previous military and other conservative elements'.[13]

Many, if not most, take the narrative of bamboo diplomacy for granted.[14] They tend to adopt this narrative, and concur that Thai foreign policy is governed by overarching ahistorical and persistent themes such as national interest and national survival.[15] Rarely have scholars asked how bamboo diplomacy came into being in the first place. Because these existing works refer back to the bamboo diplomacy narrative by way of explanation, they fail to ask when and how this style of diplomacy came about and became the dominant explanation, or a so-called 'tradition' of Thai foreign policy. The book argues that this narrative was epistemically constructed in the early 1970s, as the result of the changing practices of Thai détente. Bamboo diplomacy is not a natural or neutral tradition, but rather an invented tradition.[16]

---

13 Sarasin, *Directions in Thai Foreign Policy*, 52.
14 Even the latest works interrogate the bamboo diplomacy narrative without taking the birth of bamboo diplomacy into serious consideration. See, for example, Peera Charoenwattananukul, 'Beyond Bamboo Diplomacy: The Factor of Status Anxiety and Thai Foreign Policy Behaviors', in *Routledge Handbook of Contemporary Thailand*, ed. Pavin Chachavalpongpun (New York: Routledge, 2020), 408–19.
15 R Sean Randolph, *The United States and Thailand: Alliance Dynamics, 1950–1985* (Berkeley: Institute of East Asian Studies, University of California, 1986), 129; Sarasin, *Directions in Thai Foreign Policy*; Noranit Setabutr, *Kwam sampan tang prathet rawang Thai–Russia* [Thai–Russian Foreign Relations] (Bangkok: Sukhothai Thammathirat Open University Press, 1985 [2006]).
16 I borrow the term from Eric Hobsbawm and Terence Ranger, eds, *The Invention of Tradition* (Cambridge: Cambridge University Press, 1983).

1. INTRODUCTION

The second group of scholars include those who studied Thai foreign policy toward the Soviet Union and China in the 1970s. Although the literature on Thailand in the early Cold War is extensive, and widely researched,[17] the era of Thai détente is only sporadically and rarely addressed. The exception is Sarasin Viraphol, who mentioned the term 'détente' in passing. In surveying *Directions in Thai Foreign Policy* in the 1970s, he observed: 'after the loss of the American pivot, Thailand is trying to search for a new political alternative'. The Foreign Ministry had 'spearheaded détente' with the Soviet Union and the PRC. The 'acceleration of involvement by the Soviet Union and the People's Republic of China in Thailand', for Sarasin, needed a policy of equidistance. That is, 'the adoption of a balancing of interests policy, which has a mind toward keeping the two powers at arm's

---

17   The origins and development of Thailand's Cold War strategy and alignment with the United States can be classified into four main paradigms. First, the Cold War orthodox paradigm emphasises the international narratives and contestations, driven by either ideological or security imperatives: see Randolph, *The United States and Thailand*; Frank C Darling, *Thailand and the United States* (Washington DC: Public Affairs Press, 1965); Donald E Nuechterlein, *Thailand and the Struggle for Southeast Asia* (Ithaca: Cornell University Press, 1965); Apichart Chinwanno, 'Thailand's Search for Protection: The Making of the Alliance with the United States, 1947–1954' (PhD thesis, University of Oxford, 1985).

The second paradigm is domestic politics, focusing on the internal factors in Thailand – in particular the dynamics and interests of the military elites: see Thak Chaloemtiarana, *Thailand: The Politics of Despotic Paternalism* (Ithaca: Southeast Asia Program Publications, Cornell University, 2007); Daniel Fineman, *A Special Relationship: The United States and Military Government in Thailand, 1947–1958* (Honolulu: University of Hawai'i Press, 1997); John LS Girling, *Thailand: Society and Politics* (Ithaca: Cornell University Press, 1981); Surachart Bamrungsuk, *United States Foreign Policy and Thailand Military Rule, 1947–1977* (Bangkok: Duang Kamol, 1988); Sutayut Osornprasop, 'Thailand and the American Secret War in Indochina, 1960–1974' (PhD thesis, University of Cambridge, 2006).

The third paradigm is a revisionist one, which stresses the economic dimensions of the Cold War: see Arlene Becker Neher, 'Prelude to Alliance: The Expansion of American Economic Interest in Thailand during the 1940s' (PhD thesis, Northern Illinois University, 1980); Kullada Kesboonchoo Mead, *Kanmueng Thai yuk Sarit–Thanom phaitai khrongsang amnat lok* [Thai Politics during Sarit–Thanom Regimes under Global Power Structure] (Bangkok: 50 Years Foundation, The Bank of Thailand, 2007); Natthaphon Jaijing, 'Kanmueng Thai samai rattaban Chomphon Po Phibun Songkhram phaitai rabiap lok khong Saharat America (2491–2500) [Thai Politics under Field Marshal Phibun in US World Order (1948–1957)]' (PhD thesis, Chulalongkorn University, 1999).

Fourth, the cultural politics paradigm explicates the politics of 'truth', ideologies, and culture: see Benedict Anderson, 'Withdrawal Symptoms', in *The Spectre of Comparisons: Nationalism, Southeast Asia, and the World* (London and New York: Verso Books, 1998), 139–173; Kasian Tejapira, *Commodifying Marxism: The Formation of Modern Thai Radical Culture, 1927–1958* (Australia: Trans Pacific Press, 2001); Prajak Kongkirati, *And Then The Movement Emerged: Cultural Politics of Thai Students and Intellectuals Movements before the October 14 Uprising* (Bangkok: Thammasat University Press, 2005); Puangthong Pawakapan, *Truth in the Vietnam War: The First Casualty of War and the Thai State* (Bangkok: Kobfai, 2006). And yet there is an emerging 'cultural turn' in Cold War history, which discerns a broader range of topics such as popular culture, including film, songs, literature, fashion and so forth: see Matthew Phillips, *Thailand in the Cold War* (London and New York: Routledge, 2016).

length'.[18] A few scholars such as Wiwat Mungkandi directly link global détente with changing Thai diplomacy. They tend to agree that it was not easy for Thailand to adjust to changing global power relations.[19] However, most works do not conceptualise the long 1970s as the age of détente in Thai diplomacy.

That said, rather than spelling out and studying détente as a single entity, the existing literature on Thai foreign policy in the 1970s is compartmentalised into specific periods and overly focused on bilateral relations, either with the Soviet Union or the PRC. There is still no comprehensive work on Prime Minister Kriangsak's foreign policy toward the communist powers. This literature is preoccupied with the motivations or factors that determined Thai foreign policy. The literature can be organised into four distinct subgroups.

The first subgroup provides a 'security–ideology nexus' explanation. Thai détente with the communist powers happened largely due to the convergence of interests.[20] On Sino–Thai rapprochement, a deep and comprehensive study by Chulacheeb Chinwanno emphasises the security dimension. He argues that the diplomatic recognition established on 1 July 1975 was 'a strategic decision as Thai leaders were concerned with change in the international strategic environment, global as well as regional, especially the normalization between the US and China'.[21] MR Sukhumbhand Paribatra and Surachai Sirikrai also emphasise a convergence between Thailand and China's security interests during the

---

18   Sarasin, *Directions in Thai Foreign Policy*, 6–7, 52.
19   Wiwat Mungkandi, 'The Security Syndrome (1941–1975)', in *A Century and a Half of Thai-American Relations*, ed. Wiwat Mungkandi and William Warren (Bangkok: Chulalongkorn University, 1982), 61–114.
20   In one of the most illuminating works on the rise and decline of Thai–US relations, R Sean Randolph explains a change in Thai foreign policy in the long 1970s toward the US (from a divergence of interests between the two states), which originated from the internal and external pressures underlying the readjustment of Thai relations with the US. He claimed that its alteration was 'the critical problem of national survival'. Randolph, *The United States and Thailand*, 129.
21   Chulacheeb Chinwanno, 'Thai–Chinese Relations: Security and Strategic Partnership' (Working Paper No. 155, S Rajaratnam School of International Studies, Singapore, 2008: ii. See also Chulacheeb Chinwanno, *Sam sib pee kwam sampan tang karntoot thai-jin: kwam ruammue rawang kalayanamitr, 2518–2548* [Thirty Years of Diplomatic Relations between Thailand and China: Cooperation between Truthful Friends, 1975–2005] (Bangkok: Ministry of Foreign Affairs, 2005); Chulacheeb Chinwanno, *Sam sib har pee kwam sampan tang karntoot thai-jin, 2518–2553: Aded pajupan anakod* [Thirty-five Years of Diplomatic Relations between Thailand China, 1975–2010: Past Present and Future] (Bangkok: Openbook, 2010).

Third Indochina War, when Thailand formed a tacit alliance with the PRC and the US, with support for the Khmer Rouge as the main cause of their closer ties.[22]

On Thai–Soviet relations, although most of the literature provides an ideologically driven explanation,[23] Noranit Setaputr suggests that change in Thai foreign policy towards the Soviet Union came because of security interests.[24] I have previously argued that Thai–Soviet relations emerged and developed largely due to a synchronisation of economic interests between the two countries.[25]

The second subgroup focuses on threat perception. These writers explain Thailand's adjustment towards the communist powers as a transformation in threat perceptions in the 1970s. On the one hand, Sarasin Viraphol and Chantima Ongsuragz study Thai perceptions of the USSR, arguing that the Soviet Union remained a persistent threat to Thai national interests until the end of the Cold War. They do not see a change in Thai diplomacy.[26] As Chantima states:

> Since communism rejects monarchical government and religion and views them as impediments toward a classless society, Thailand is fundamentally anticommunist. The principal values and institutions of the Thai society make communism appear to be a natural enemy.[27]

On the other hand, Thailand's changing perceptions of the Chinese threat are examined by Naruemit Sodsuk and Surachai Sirikrai, who argue that by the late 1970s Thailand gradually changed its perceptions

---

22   Sukhumbhand Paribatra, *From Enmity to Alignment: Thailand's Evolving Relations with China* (Bangkok: Institute of Security and International Studies, Chulalongkorn University, 1987); Surachai Sirikrai, 'Sino–Thai Relations: A Thai Perception', in *China–ASEAN Relations: Political, Economic and Ethnic Dimensions*, ed. Theresa C Carino (Manila: De La Salle University, 1991).
23   See, for example, Paul R Shirk, 'Thai–Soviet Relations', *Asian Survey* 9 (September 1969): 682–93; Chulacheeb, *Siam, Russia, Thai: Karntootkarnmuang Karnmuangkarntoot, Aded pajupan anakod*.
24   Noranit, *Kwam sampan tang prathet rawang Thai-Russia*.
25   Jittipat Poonkham, *Withet Panid Sampan su Songkram Yen: Kwam sampan rawangprathet Thai–Russia (1897–1991)* [Foreign Economic Relations to the Cold War: Thai–Russian Foreign Relations (1897–1991)] (Bangkok: Chulalongkorn University Press, 2016).
26   Sarasin, 'The Soviet Threat', 61–70; Chantima Ongsuragz, 'Thai Perceptions of the Soviet Union and Its Implications for Thai–Soviet Relations', in *The Soviet Union and the Asia-Pacific Region: Views from the Region*, ed. Pushpa Thambipillai, and Daniel C Matuszewski (New York: Praeger, 1989), 122–33.
27   Chantima, 'Thai Perceptions of the Soviet Union', 122.

toward the PRC from enmity to friendship.[28] These works also consider the different perceptions of those communist powers among key actors within Thailand, such as the military and civilian elites.

The third subgroup of literature focuses on bureaucratic politics within Thailand. ML Bhansoon Ladavalya is the exemplar. Based on Graham Allison's bureaucratic politics approach, Bhansoon studies foreign policy decision-making in Thailand's normalisation with the PRC during the Kukrit Pramoj administration, claiming that this decision was the result of 'a long conflict between organizational interests and varying perceptions of national interests within the government', especially between the Ministries of Defence and Foreign Affairs.[29]

The last subgroup emphasises the internationalisation of the state. Drawing from the declassified documents in the US and UK, Kullada Kesboonchoo Mead highlights the role of US hegemony and its allies, or the so-called internationalised elites, in determining not only Thai foreign policy but also Thai domestic politics.[30] Similarly, Rapeeporn Lertwongweerachai studies the role of Thanat Khoman in Thai foreign affairs, by arguing that changes in Thanat's foreign policy, such as Sino–Thai rapprochement, followed the decline of US hegemonic power. These changes led to a direct conflict with the military elites, which ended in the military coup in 1971.[31]

All these significant works ostensibly approach the 1970s from historical and bilateral perspectives. Though some touch upon the domestic and international contexts within which Thai détente emerged, there is a huge gap in the literature that needs to be further explicated. First, despite their differing views on Thai foreign policy in the 1970s, the existing works are preoccupied with explaining the why-question or causation. They pay little attention to how détente emerged and became possible. That is, the process of diplomatic practice transformation, in which the new

---

28 Naruemit Sodsuk, *Sampantaparp tang karntoot rawang thai jeen* [Diplomatic Relations between Thailand and the People's Republic of China] (Bangkok: Thai Wattana Panich, 1981); Surachai Sirikrai, 'Thai Perceptions of China and Japan', *Contemporary Southeast Asia* 12, no. 3 (December 1990): 247–65.
29   Bhansoon Ladavalya, 'Thailand's Foreign Policy under Kukrit Pramoj: A Study in Decision-Making' (PhD thesis, Northern Illinois University, 1980), 4.
30   Kullada, *Kanmueng Thai yuk Sarit-Thanom phaitai khrongsang amnat lok*; Kullada Kesboonchoo Mead, 'The Cold War and Thai Democratization', in *Southeast Asia and the Cold War*, ed. Albert Lau (London and New York: Routledge, 2012), 215–40.
31   Rapeeporn Lertwongweerachai, 'The Role of Thanat Khoman in Thai Foreign Affairs during 1958–1971' (MA thesis, Chulalongkorn University, 2002).

discourse of détente transformed foreign policy thinking and practices of key actors. When and how did the discourse of détente come about? How was it possible that during the 1970s, the USSR and China shifted from being Thailand's foes towards friends and even tacit allies? How did this discourse become dominant? When did these discourses come undone? How and to what extent has détente become a discursive legacy in the Thai foreign policy tradition?

For example, when Thailand initiated the new approach of flexible diplomacy toward the communist powers, it deviated from dominant Cold War certainties. Many works tend to concur that it was largely due to the Nixon Doctrine, when US President Richard Nixon foreshadowed withdrawal from the region, under the rubric of 'Vietnamisation' in 1969.[32] As this book will indicate, Foreign Minister Thanat Khoman coined the term 'flexible diplomacy' in 1968, even before the promulgation of the Nixon Doctrine. Unlike the bamboo diplomacy narrative, Thailand was in fact bending before the wind had begun to shift.

In addition, failing both to recognise that the term 'détente' accurately conceptualises Thai foreign policy in the 1970s and to see Thai détente as a holistic practice transformation, previous scholarship largely neglects the fact that Thai détente occurred within a changing domestic context and configurations. First, the aforementioned works ignore the discursive struggle within Thai politics; namely how the dominant discourse of anticommunism was called into question, and how the new discourse of détente emerged and developed. This book argues that diplomacy and politics were not separable, and diplomacy was the contested site of domestic political contestation.

Second, the existing literature does not encompass Thailand's changing discourse and perceptions towards the communist powers. By the early 1970s, the Soviet Union and the PRC were no longer rendered as 'enemies', but rather 'friends' in Thai foreign policy discourses. Third, it overlooks a transformation in identity or subject position of those détente proponents, and in particular within the Ministry of Foreign Affairs (MFA). Through the détente process, the MFA became an increasingly independent institution that sought to conduct diplomacy in a more flexible and professional way.

---

32 Bhansoon, 'Thailand's Foreign Policy under Kukrit Pramoj'; Sarasin, *Directions in Thai Foreign Policy*.

In contrast to extant work, this book provides a direct, holistic and comprehensive discussion of the term 'Thai détente' to conceptualise changing diplomatic discourses and practices in the long 1970s. It does so for three reasons. First, the Thai elite, especially those in the Foreign Ministry, employed the globally recognised term 'détente' so as to communicate with the world about how Thailand intended to act diplomatically.[33] The practices of détente, such as back-channel, ping-pong and petro-diplomacy, continued throughout the 1970s. Second, the term 'détente' was also widely used by local and foreign newspapers at the time to capture Thailand's changing relationship with both the Soviet Union and the PRC.[34] Third, conceptualising Thai diplomacy in the long 1970s as détente situates the book within global studies of détente. The current state and status of Thai détente literature differs little from global détente studies more generally. Both are relatively understudied. This book aspires to fill this gap. It also indicates how the alternative strategy of small states in the Third World was able to contribute to Cold War superpower politics, and how successful that strategy was. In this sense, a study of Thai détente can be framed in terms of comparative and global dimensions of Cold War history.

In this book, the Thai conception of détente is defined as a new diplomatic discourse and practice to normalise relations with the communist powers in general and, specifically, the Soviet Union and the PRC. The terms 'détente' and 'flexible diplomacy' (*karntoot yeutyun*) were used interchangeably. In the process, the Thai state sought to pursue readjustment with the Soviet Union, and rapprochement with China. The other term, 'equidistant' relations with great powers, was also used, in particular during the Kukrit and Kriangsak administrations, as a state of flexible diplomacy that positioned Thailand in a more balanced and equal status vis-à-vis other great powers. All these key concepts were part and parcel of Thai détente. This diplomatic move was first and foremost a response to the prospect of American military disengagement from the region, and how to manage the changing international context. By the early 1970s, détente itself became a well-established norm in world politics of which Thai détente was a part.

---

33 Sarasin, *Directions in Thai Foreign Policy*.
34 See 'Thanat's Ostpolitik', *Far Eastern Economic Review*, 23 July 1973, 24–25; 'Beijing Ready for Détente with Thailand', *Bangkok Post*, 29 October 1973, 1.

The ultimate aim of the book, therefore, is to examine the emergence, development and transformation of détente discourse, and its concomitant narrative of 'bamboo diplomacy', in Thai foreign policy under the prospect of American retrenchment in 1968 until 1980, when the Third Indochina War gained momentum in the regional balance of power. Rather than seeing this as a continuation of Thai diplomacy, the process of détente was fundamentally a pivotal rupture in Thai foreign policy, and established the conditions of possibility for the present. In narrating the rupture in Thai foreign relations with the great powers, the book is methodologically committed to a genealogy of Thai détente.

1.3. A Genealogy of Thai Détente

1.3.1. Genealogy as Historical Problematisation

A genealogy is often supposed to connote a tracing of a pedigree or history back to its origins. For Michel Foucault, it is the opposite: a genealogy is an alternative approach that contentiously discards and disrupts (some commonly held beliefs about) a historical origin.[35] In his study of diplomacy, James Der Derian articulates this idea, which is worth quoting at length:

> [G]enealogy is a history of the present, not in the sense of tracing the seamless development of a phenomenon from some pristine origin, or projecting contemporary characteristics of it back into

---

35   In his seminal essay, 'Nietzsche, Genealogy, History', Foucault proposes a genealogical approach with two interrelated concepts: *descent* and *emergence*. First, rather than a search for an origin, genealogy is a search for descent, which 'is not the erecting of foundations: on the contrary, it disturbs what was previously considered immobile; it fragments what was thought unified; it shows the heterogeneity of what was imagined consistent with itself'. The analysis of descent dissolves the socially constructed unity of things, and discloses the dispersion, multiplicity and heterogeneity of events, which lie behind any historical beginnings.

Second, genealogy is the analysis of emergence. Historical emergence is conceptualised by Foucault as a temporary episode in 'a series of subjugations' or in 'the hazardous play of dominations', rather than the culminations of events or the end of a process of development. It is merely a momentary manifestation or a stage in the power struggle between different social forces. The emerging form of events is the (inter)play of dominations. Michel Foucault, 'Nietzsche, Genealogy, History', in *The Foucault Reader: An Introduction to Foucault's Thought*, ed. Paul Rabinow (London: Penguin Books, 1991 [1984]), 82–83. See also Michel Foucault, 'Lecture on Nietzsche: How to Think the History of Truth with Nietzsche without Relying on Truth', in *Lectures on the Will to Know: Lectures at the College de France, 1970–1971 and Oedipal Knowledge*, trans. Graham Burchell (Hampshire: Palgrave Macmillan, 2013), 202–23.

> the past, but rather in the sense of *discovering the transformations engendered by the instability and violent contests which diplomacy had mediated with discontinuous success.* We might say, then, that while history does not repeat itself, there are *historical confrontations of power and truth which recur and generate parallel sets of mediatory rules and practices.*[36]

A genealogical approach tells us a radically different story: a history of rupture and a history of the present. As Foucault argues, 'what is found at the historical beginnings of things is not the inviolable identity of their origin; it is the dissension of other things. It is disparity'.[37] In this book, the Thai conception of détente emerged as disparity or difference – the ubiquitous fear and estrangement from the domino theory, as the fall of Indochina and the prospect of American military disengagement from the region began to loom large on the horizon. This, in turn, generated a new 'system of rules' that helped mediate the ongoing conflicts and violence, thereby rendering détente with the communist powers possible. As a historical method and critical ethos, a genealogy differs from a conventional history in the sense that it historically problematises the political construction of knowledge.

In this book, a genealogy of Thai détente addresses three analyses: a history of rupture, the discourse approach and a history of the present. It closely examines the complex relationship and interplay between discursive and non-discursive meanings and practices, in particular the interaction between power/knowledge, discourses and subject positions in Thai foreign policy. Unlike Foucault, the book focuses on the 'macrophysics' of power: the study of Thai elites, especially those détente proponents.

The book argues that, first, Thai détente was a radical break with the hegemonic discourse of anticommunism. A genealogy of détente sees discursive anxiety in Thai diplomacy, and the power struggle between détente proponents and détente opponents. Second, rather than being simply viewed as an inevitable result of the objective qualities of bamboo diplomacy, as is often supposed, Thai détente is better understood as a political construction that occurred through a series of fortuitous historical events, and as the result of contingent political contestation. Knowledge of bamboo diplomacy was in fact produced by the changing practices of Thai détente.

---

36 James Der Derian, *On Diplomacy* (Oxford: Blackwell, 1987), 76. My emphasis.
37 Foucault, 'Nietzsche, Genealogy, History', 79.

1.3.2. A History of Rupture

First, a genealogy of Thai détente demonstrates a history of rupture. On the one hand, it engages with global détente studies with a different set of questions. Rather than explaining the motivations or factors that precipitated the rise and fall of Thai détente par excellence, a genealogy attempts to understand how and to what extent Thai détente was formed as a hegemonic project in Thai foreign policy.

On the other hand, in reassessing Thai détente, a genealogy negates the teleological historiography of Thai foreign policy, most of which focuses on the continuity of 'bamboo diplomacy'. This is because this conventional interpretation historically conflates the two. In fact, there was a critical rupture in the late 1960s when a new approach of 'flexible diplomacy' emerged. In other words, genealogy rejects history in its uninterrupted, continual, stable and essentialist form, as in fact it was constituted by historical contingency and complexity.

During the Cold War, Thai foreign policy was not ruled by a singular logic of strategy, but at least three logics. The first logic was anticommunism. Although 'anticommunism' had been introduced within the Thai state when various governments sought to eliminate their domestic political rivals, the narrative itself became a hegemonic discourse only after 1958. At the peak of the Asian Cold War, Thailand pursued a highly unbalanced and rigid strategy by deeply engaging with a Cold War narrative, closely forging an alliance, or 'special relationship', with the US, and antagonising the USSR and China.[38] For the US, Thailand became an invaluable anticommunist ally, and a forward base, or a so-called 'unsinkable aircraft carrier', especially during the Vietnam War.[39] The relationship was reflected in US commitments, such as military and economic aid given since 1950, Southeast Asia Treaty Organization (SEATO) membership between 1954 and 1977, and the Thanat–Rusk joint communiqué in 1962, all of which obliged the US to help Thailand in the event of a communist attack. Under the first logic of strategy, Thailand was extensively involved in the escalating conflicts, both in Vietnam and across the region. Benedict Anderson called the period the 'American Era'.[40] Similarly, this period sees

---

38 Fineman, *A Special Relationship*.
39 Girling, *Thailand: Society and Politics*, 231.
40 Benedict Anderson, *In the Mirror: Literature and Politics in Siam in the American Era* (Bangkok: Duang Kamol, 1985).

Thai foreign relations between late 1950s until 1960s not as 'bamboo', but as strictly tied to a rigid strategy dominated by the anticommunist discourse.[41]

The second logic of strategy, namely flexible diplomacy, appeared to emerge in 1968. American power and prestige globally and regionally had been challenged by events in Vietnam, precipitating the reversal of America's Vietnam policy. The US under Lyndon Johnson halted bombing in Vietnam, and then under Richard Nixon, introduced the doctrine of 'Vietnamisation' and the concomitant prospect of military retrenchment from the region in 1969. During this period, Thai foreign policy saw a radical departure from the first logic. Due to its strategic anxiety emerging out of American retrenchment from the region, Thailand initiated a truly balanced form of flexible diplomacy, or détente strategy. It pursued 'equidistance' with the great powers, and simultaneously began the processes of normalisation with the communist powers, by adopting rapprochement with China and readjustment with the Soviet Union. Thailand, therefore, deemphasised the role of the US in maintaining its own national security, and pushed the agenda of a demilitarisation of the American presence in Thailand. Girling calls this period a 'new course' in Thai foreign policy.[42] I can call it Thai détente.

The third logic of strategy began in the late 1970s after the Soviet-backed Vietnamese invasion of Cambodia in December 1978. Many scholars readily agreed that by the end of the decade, détente was in decline, and with respect to the communist powers, finally collapsed.[43] Despite the relative decline of triangular diplomacy, the discourse of détente remained and became the unfinished project of Thai diplomacy. What changed in the 1980s was the nature of strategic flexibility: the move to what might be described as unbalanced détente. By the end of the 1970s, triangular diplomacy between Thailand, the USSR and China was orientated toward one side. This is because Thailand formed a close association with a tacit ally, namely China, in the Third Indochina War. In its relationship with the Soviet Union, Thailand did not return to the pre-détente era of strategic rigidity and hostility. Instead, it still engaged with the Soviet Union, although from a distance and with scepticism. This was largely

---

41   Randolph, *The United States and Thailand*, 10.
42   John LS Girling, 'Thailand's New Course', *Pacific Affairs* 42, no. 3 (Autumn 1969): 346–59.
43   See Leszek Buszynski, 'Thailand: The Erosion of a Balanced Foreign Policy', *Asian Survey* 22, no. 11 (November 1982): 1037–55.

because of Soviet support for Vietnam and its increasing interest in the region in general. Consequently, in the 1980s Thailand under General Prem Tinsulanonda engaged deeply in regional conflicts and in particular joined an unlikely alliance with China and the US in support of the Khmer Rouge.

To conclude, a genealogy differs from a conventional history in the sense that it emphasises rupture in Thai foreign policy, in which détente became a separate logic in diplomatic practice. Although this book mainly focuses on the second logic, it highlights how détente emerged out of the declining anticommunist hegemonic discourse, while maintaining that the second and third logics of Thai strategy are not mutually exclusive.

1.3.3. The Discourse Approach: Discursive Anxiety and the Clash of Discourses

A genealogy also draws on the discourse approach to explicate Thai détente in three different episodes: Thanat Khoman's first détente (1969–1971); MR Kukrit Pramoj's second (1975–1976); and General Kriangsak Chomanan's third (1977–1980). The discourse approach is part and parcel of a genealogy, which closely examines both discursive and extra-discursive practices. Discourses can be broadly defined as ensembles of social practices, representations and interpretations through which certain regimes of truth, and their concomitant identities, are produced and reproduced in a particular historical context.[44] They are inseparably connected to social practices where meanings are given to subjects, objects and states' behaviours, such as diplomacy.

---

44 In this sense, the genealogical approach of discourse analysis is different from the constructivist approach of ideas, identity and norms, as follows. First, discourse is not purely an idea. Rather, it comprises both ideas and materiality. In other words, discourse is always already a discursive *practice* par excellence. Second, identity is not an a priori, inherently pre-given and objective entity, independent from social context. Rather, it is sociopolitically relational in the sense that it is constructed through discursive practices in representing foreign policy. Identity should be understood in terms of identification or subjectivation that produced and reproduced subjectivity or subject positions in temporal and spatial contexts. Third, a norm is not a standard or rule of appropriate behaviours. Rather, a norm is a normalising process. It defines what counts as 'normal' and 'abnormal', 'thinkable' and 'unthinkable', in social practices including foreign policy practices. See Lene Hansen, *Security as Practice: Discourse Analysis and the Bosnian War* (London and New York: Routledge, 2006); Charlotte Epstein, 'Who Speaks? Discourse, the Subject and the Study of Identity in International Politics', *European Journal of International Relations* 17, no. 2 (June 2011): 327–50; Maja Zehfuss, 'Constructivism and Identity: A Dangerous Liaison', *European Journal of International Relations* 7, no. 3 (September 2001): 315–48.

In order to narrate each and every episode in Thai détente, the discourse approach analyses how the elite's 'regime of truth' made possible 'certain courses of action' or a state's behaviour while 'excluding other policies as unintelligible or unworkable or improper'. Discourses are meaningful 'background capabilities that are used socially, at least by a small group of officials if not more broadly in a society or among different elites and societies'.[45] However, as Foucault notes, discourses are not simply 'groups of signs (signifying elements referring to contents or representations)', but rather 'practices that systematically form the objects of which they speak'.[46] Analysing discourses then is not simply a study of meanings but more importantly a study of 'sense-making' practices.[47] The discourse approach to foreign policy thus focuses on what policymakers actually say and do.

Diplomacy, as a set of social and discursive practices, depends on the representations and articulations of identities, including the representations of national identity and 'the others', such as 'friend' and 'enemy'. The formation of national identities was inseparable from the new representation of otherness. Through the process of foreign policymaking, identities are (re)produced.[48] In 1970s Thailand, two processes stood out: the subject formation of détente proponents and the representation of the Soviet Union and the PRC as 'friends'. Both marked how Thai détente proponents thought about, spoke of and acted on the communist powers anew, shifting foreign policy in a more flexible direction. Simultaneously, these new identities provided a justification for these emergent foreign policy orientations. In other words, a change in discourse ostensibly legitimised the process of rapprochement with China as well as readjustment with the USSR.

These double representations should be put into historical context. I introduce the concepts of 'the clash of discourses' and 'discursive anxiety' to understand how Thailand encountered diplomatic transformation throughout the 1970s. In general, anxiety is the existential state of feeling an uncomfortable disconnect with the self and disorientation from the

---

45 Jennifer Milliken, 'The Study of Discourse in International Relations: A Critique of Research and Methods', *European Journal of International Relations* 5, no. 2 (June 1999): 233, 236.
46 Michel Foucault, *The Archaeology of Knowledge*, trans. AM Sheridan Smith (London and New York: Routledge, 1972), 49.
47 Charlotte Epstein, *The Power of Words in International Relations: Birth of an Anti-Whaling Discourse* (Cambridge, Massachusetts: MIT Press, 2008).
48 David Campbell, *Writing Security: United States Foreign Policy and the Politics of Identity* (Minneapolis: University of Minnesota Press, 1992).

world.⁴⁹ In international politics, discursive anxiety, including diplomatic anxiety, happens when states experience changing international contexts that make national understandings about the world problematic. As Ned Lebow suggests, these states suffer deep-seated anxiety 'when these routines are disrupted by novel or critical situations'.⁵⁰ Discursive anxiety also brings about uncertainty and unpredictability in diplomatic relations.

This condition of uncertainty not only causes divided selves within the state, but also affects foreign policy toward other states.⁵¹ This kind of anxiety is not simply ontological (about the sense of the self in the world) but discursive (about the understanding and expectation of the world). As anxious actors, states attempt to reduce or relieve discursive anxiety by seeking new discourses or narratives as well as developing coherence and consistency in their understanding of the world. In particular, they will adapt the narratives they have told about who they are, and who their 'friends' and 'foes' are in international politics. As Epstein argues, the function of discourse is to provide 'important principles of coherence for statehood', which are reflected in both 'the everyday language used to describe international politics', and 'the practice of diplomacy'.⁵² Discourse brings narrative coherence to events that seem contingent. In particular, the discourse of a 'friend' reduces discursive anxiety and paves the way for international recognition.⁵³ This book argues that in a changing and contingent international context, states do not simply aim to pursue physical or existential security,⁵⁴ but rather seek to have secure discourses that help them make better sense of the world and adjust their diplomatic practices toward other countries.

---

49   Unlike fear, anxiety is a 'presupposition' of despair about nothing. It is the self's encounter with its own nothingness, or a 'lost object', that makes it anxious. See Soren Kierkegaard, *The Concept of Anxiety*. Translated by Reidar Thomte (Princeton: Princeton University Press, 1981); Martin Heidegger, *Being and Time*, trans. J Macquarrie and E Robinson (New York: Harper and Row, 1967); Jacques Lacan, *Anxiety: The Seminar of Jacques Lacan, Book X*, trans. AR Price (Cambridge: Polity Press, 2014).
50   Richard Ned Lebow, *A Cultural Theory of International Relations* (Cambridge: Cambridge University Press, 2008), 25.
51   I adopt the term 'divided selves' from RD Laing, *The Divided Self: An Existential Study in Sanity and Madness* (New York: Penguin, 1990).
52   Epstein, 'Who Speaks?', 341–42.
53   See Felix Berenskoetter, 'Friends, There Are No Friends? An Intimate Reframing of the International', *Millennium: Journal of International Studies* 35, no. 3 (2007): 647–76.
54   This is the theoretical stance of ontological security framework, see Brent Steele, *Ontological Security in International Relations: Self-Identity and the IR State* (London and New York: Routledge, 2008); Marco A Vieira, 'Understanding Resilience in International Relations: The Non-Aligned Movement and Ontological Security', *International Studies Review* 18 (2016): 290–311; Trine Flockhart, 'The Problem of Change in Constructivist Theory: Ontological Security Seeking and Agent Motivation', *Review of International Studies* 42, no. 5 (2016): 799–820.

For social agents in Thailand, discursive anxiety emerged in the late 1960s when the dominant discourses of pro-Americanism and anticommunism became increasingly meaningless for making sense of world politics. Discursive anxiety, and its concomitant lack of relative consistency in diplomacy, brought about a change in discourse. Thai détente proponents spoke the discourse of détente, and their subject positions were produced by this new discourse. A change in discourse in turn translated into novel diplomatic practices toward the communist powers, such as ping-pong diplomacy.

Furthermore, discursive anxiety set the conditions for the clash of discourses in politics, whereby the prevailing discourse was deeply delegitimised and challenged by the emerging one. Different social forces, attached to both old and new discourses, were profoundly anxious about their respective status and position within the changing power structure. In this sense, a genealogy emphasises that history is irreducibly based upon a constant struggle, or even warfare, between different power blocs attempting to impose their own systems of domination and rules.[55]

I argue that discursive anxiety and the clash of discourses shed light on both ontological and epistemological dimensions of diplomacy as well as the power relationships of foreign policy. First, discursive anxiety saw a new social ontology: new kinds of social agents, or new subject positions, which in turn brought new social relations into being. These social agents held subject positions, or positions within a discourse.[56] In doing so, they were establishing themselves as the subjects speaking that particular discourse, such as détente discourse, and thereby identifying themselves as détente proponents. The discourse they spoke and acted upon not only marked who they were, but also provided them with narratives on how to make sense of the world they lived in. The agents were, strictly speaking, socially and discursively embedded actors with particular subject positions in the foreign policymaking process.

In this book, Thai détente proponents were mainly linked to new social forces, mostly civilians, such as Thanat Khoman (foreign minister, 1959–1971) and MR Kukrit Pramoj (prime minister, 1975–1976), or progressive military leaders, such as General Chatichai Choonhavan (deputy foreign minister, 1973–1975, and later foreign minister, 1975–1976) and General

---

55 Quoted in Barry Smart, *Michel Foucault* (Sussex: Ellis Horwood, 1985), 57.
56 Epstein, *The Power of Words*, 15.

Kriangsak Chomanan (prime minister, 1977–1980). Détente opponents or Cold Warriors, on the other hand, were mostly military leaders or conservative civilians, most notably Thanin Kraivichien (prime minister, 1976–1977). Later, I argue that some ardent détente opponents gradually and implicitly embraced détente discourse, as evidenced in the late Cold War and the Third Indochina War in particular.

The second, and related, issue is that during the period of discursive anxiety, a discursive struggle is unavoidable, if not inevitable. It is evident through a series of sociopolitical showdowns, such as student demonstrations, civil protests, revolutions and coups d'état. These discursive struggles illustrate that foreign policy discourses have never been absolutely hegemonic, but are subject to challenges, rearticulations and resistances. As Foucault notes:

> discourse is not simply that which translates struggles or systems of domination, but is the thing for which and by which there is struggle, discourse is the power which is to be seized.[57]

In each episode, Thai détente challenged the hegemonic discourse of anticommunism, and brought about a discursive struggle, which manifested in a contestation with the Thai establishment. While détente proponents gained discursive momentum due to the decline of American power in the region, successive episodes of détente were historically contingent and relatively short-lived, resulting in either a military coup d'état or a downfall of the government. Opponents, who held the Cold War ideological hegemony and were strongly supported by conservatives, still dominated Thai politics. In this period, a coup can be equally seen as a coup about/against foreign policy.

Third, epistemologically, discursive anxiety requires a newly formed consensus in terms of knowledge about diplomacy so as to justify the new diplomatic practices, and reinstate the secure representations of national identity and interest. To create successful and effective diplomatic practices, new discourses required knowledge production. Like every social struggle in history, this new diplomatic knowledge informed who the state was and determined what its foreign policy looked like. In the case of Thai détente

---

57 Michel Foucault, 'The Order of Discourse', in *Language and Politics,* ed. Michael J Shapiro (New York: New York University Press, 1984), 110.

that knowledge was bamboo diplomacy, which will be discussed in the next section. In other words, there was a transformation in diplomatic practices at the same time as new knowledge was invented and produced.

In sum, a genealogy in this case concerns the discursive politics of Thai foreign policy. The diplomatic discursive framework can problematise a conventional history in Thai studies, which takes the discourses and practices of diplomacy for granted. Following Foucault, the discourse approach is not only the study of discursive and knowledge formation, but also sheds light on subject formation as well as power contestation between different subject positions. It also illustrates that international politics is the contested realm of friend–enemy relationships.[58] This book further examines how discursive politics in Thai foreign policy shaped the way in which the discourse of 'friend' changed Thailand's diplomatic perception and practices toward the communist powers.

1.3.4. A History of the Present: The Birth of Bamboo Diplomacy

Last but not least, a genealogy of Thai détente exposes the making of 'bamboo' diplomacy which, I argue, only emerged as accepted and legitimate knowledge in the early 1970s. This section examines how knowledge of bamboo diplomacy was disseminated through discursive practices of détente and academic narratives in the early 1970s. The latter historiography began to explain many episodes of Thai foreign policy in the past, as well as in the present, through this new lens. More importantly, both academic and policymaking practices rendered bamboo diplomacy an ahistorical 'truth' or conventional wisdom of Thai foreign policy. This section begins with tracing the descent and emergence of a 'flexible diplomacy' discourse in elite perspectives. Then it indicates how this new discourse has shaped and constituted knowledge production within Thai academia.

First of all, changing practices produced the new narrative of 'bamboo diplomacy'. In the early 1970s, the narrative challenged the anticommunist discourse, which had dominated during the early Cold War. Some people

---

58   See Carl Schmitt, *The Concept of the Political* (Chicago and London: University of Chicago Press, 1996).

termed this new discourse 'flexible diplomacy', while others called it 'bamboo diplomacy'. Regardless of the name, this emerging discourse rendered a rupture with the hegemonic discourse of anticommunism.

This book argues that it was Foreign Minister Thanat Khoman who coined the term 'flexible diplomacy' in the late 1960s.[59] He suggested that foreign policy 'should be flexible in a world of changing conditions. A rigid policy is dangerous, especially for a small country'.[60] However, it was in fact Pridi Phanomyong, the former Thai prime minister in exile, who juxtaposed this 'flexible diplomacy' with the conceptual lexicon of 'bamboo' diplomacy.

In his interview with *The Nation*'s special correspondent in Paris in August 1971, Pridi claimed that China was ready to establish relations with Thailand if the Thai Government 'changes her hostile policy'. During his exile in Beijing for many years, he became quite familiar with high-ranking Chinese officials. Consequently, he said that the crucial issue for rapprochement with China was about motives:

> If Thailand had good motives towards them, they would certainly reciprocate. Let bygones be bygones. I don't think there are any problems with Communist China. It would be a noble thing if two hostile persons can patch up their quarrels.

Like Thanat, Pridi strongly urged a *'flexible'* foreign policy with the objective of ensuring Thailand's survival amid changing global and regional dynamics. He traced this policy back to the reign of King Rama V in the late nineteenth century:

---

59 After obtaining a PhD in law from Paris in 1940, Thanat Khoman returned to Thailand and joined the Ministry of Foreign Affairs. From 1941 to 1943, he was stationed as a second secretary at the Thai Embassy in Tokyo. During the Second World War, Thanat disagreed with Phibun's foreign policy of alignment with Japan and a so-called virtual Japanese occupation of Thailand, which made him a member of the Seri Thai ('Free Thai') resistance movement. His pro-Americanism and anticommunism were gradually formed during his various diplomatic posts, most of which were based in the US. From 1952 to 1957, Thanat served as the deputy to the Permanent Representative from Thailand to the UN before becoming the Thai Ambassador to the US in 1957.

Thanat was promoted to the position of Foreign Minister in 1959 under the Sarit regime and became a strong voice in pro-American and anticommunist policies in the critical time of the Asian Cold War. However, since the late 1960s, Thanat's foreign policy ideationally shifted and thereafter he became a strong détente proponent until he was ousted from the foreign ministry following the coup in 1971.

60 'Thanat urges contact with China', *Bangkok Post*, 7 January 1973, 1.

> Just look back at the example set down by King Rama V. We followed a neutral policy and that saved our country. There was a balance of powers. We must accept that while all other neighboring countries fell into the hands of foreign countries, King Rama V saved Thailand from imperialism because His Majesty followed a flexible policy.

'Whenever we took a different line set down by His Majesty King Rama V', Pridi continued, 'we always had troubles such as when we sided with Japan during World War II'.[61]

Pridi also suggested that Thailand should trade with every country without taking their political regimes or ideologies into consideration. As he puzzled:

> What kind of Chinese are we talking about? Look at those Chinese merchants in the country. Why are they so rich? If we trade with Communist China, it should be on a government-to-government basis. They hold two trade exhibitions every year. When foreign merchants visit them and sign trade contracts, they sign on behalf of their governments. The government can also choose to allow some particular organizations to deal with Communist China – not private merchants.[62]

Trade with China, for him, was inevitable. Commenting on President Nixon's visit to Beijing, he asserted that: 'the United States simply cannot afford to ignore a country with 800 million people. It's a big market'.[63]

While Pridi shared the discourse of flexible diplomacy with Thanat Khoman, and strongly supported détente with the communists, there is no evidence of direct collaboration. Later on, Prime Minister Thanom admitted that both Foreign Minister Thanat Khoman and Deputy Foreign Minister Sa-nga Kittikachorn had met separately with Pridi at the Royal Thai Embassy in Paris in 1971. He denied that Pridi was asked to serve as a middleman in contacting China. As he told Thai reporters, 'I have never assigned Pridi to do anything'. Both Cabinet members did

---

61   Somrit Intaphanti, 'Pridi: China Ready for Thailand Ties', *The Nation,* 16 August, 1971.
62   Somrit, 'Pridi: China Ready for Thailand Ties'.
63   Somrit, 'Pridi: China Ready for Thailand Ties'.

not discuss any political issues with Pridi. Thanom said that 'Pridi talked about his life in Beijing'.[64] Pridi himself also denied that he was a 'third party' making contact between the two countries.[65]

The concept of 'bamboo diplomacy' only became ubiquitous from the 1970s. In July 1972, Boonchu Rojanastein, the leading and influential director of the Bangkok Bank, gave a speech before the American Chamber of Commerce in Bangkok that later became famous. He spoke about the need to 'bend with the wind':

> As Americans, you see us as corrupt, trafficking in drugs, full of bureaucratic red tape, alien bills, etc. On our part, we complain about your military bases, your hippies, your Americanization of our culture, your arrogance. But whatever dissatisfactions there are with each other, America has been the closest friend and ally of Thailand for the past 20 years. For the past 20 years you have served us well, and we have served you well. But the time, I think, of America being our closest friend and ally is coming to an end. Perhaps not of our own choosing, it's more of yours. When the time comes and we shall have to part, let it not be said that Thailand broke away, but rather that the national interests of both our countries made it undesirable for the United States to have exclusive rights over Thailand's relationship. But let us remain good friends.[66]

Boonchu continued:

> For example, we are grateful that the U.S. has given us a protective umbrella for many years. How can we now refuse your request to open up an air base, say at Takli? The Thai nature would allow this even if it were against our better judgment. Yet in giving in to such a request, we have virtually allowed the U.S. to bind us to her, and taken away the opportunity of greater flexibility in our foreign policy. The more you want to get out of Vietnam, the more you tie up Thailand. And when the time comes for you to withdraw, we will be blamed for 'flexibility' again. Is this really fair to us?[67]

Subsequently, Anand Panyarachun, former ambassador to the US and the UN, gave a speech by asking 'What is diplomacy?' He said that 'diplomacy is the art of the possible', and compared Thai diplomacy with a 'bamboo'

---

64 'PM Says Ministers Met Pridi in Paris', *Bangkok Post*, 22 July, 1971, 1.
65 Theh Chongkhadikij, 'Pridi: Recognize China now', *Bangkok Post*, 7 November, 1971, 1.
66 Quoted in Randolph, *The United States and Thailand*, 164.
67 Quoted in Randolph, *The United States and Thailand*, 164.

that 'bent with the wind'. Anand disregarded those who charged that Thailand was a country with no firm principles. Rather, he claimed, Thailand pursued 'flexible' diplomacy. 'If international politics or foreign policy of any country did not have flexibility', Anand went on, 'the tree would have broken … when the storm is coming'. He highlighted the difference between 'slippery' [*kalon*] and 'flexible' [*yeutyun*] diplomacy. For Anand, the former did not 'accept the truth', 'wish to know the truth' or 'seek the truth'. On the contrary, 'the aim of flexibility is to know the certain truth, find a right fact … and how to deal with the fact'. During the high time of the Cold War, 'Thailand lacked this flexible diplomacy. This was partly because we were a victim in the Cold War'.[68]

This so-called 'bamboo' diplomacy only became the metanarrative in historiography and theory of Thai foreign policy in the 1970s. This kind of knowledge is the result of Thai détente.

Bamboo diplomacy also became a metanarrative in academia during the mid-1970s. This followed the transformation of détente discourse and its diplomatic practices. If we are to understand the emergence of the 'bamboo diplomacy' narrative, we should begin with an analysis of the historiography, which only emerged during the 1970s. Three renowned scholars in Thailand, namely Likhit Dhiravegin, Sarasin Viraphol and Thamsook Numnonda, narrated Thai foreign policy by employing the lens of 'bamboo' diplomacy.[69] I argue that this was the first time that this conceptual lexicon was employed, not only to justify Thai foreign policy in the present, but also explicate Thai diplomacy in the past. This has included explanations of Siamese foreign policy during the nineteenth century, and Thai foreign policy during the Second World War.

In his 1974 oft-cited article, entitled 'Thailand Foreign Policy Determination', Likhit Dhiravegin conceptualised Thai foreign policy as 'bamboo diplomacy'. He contended that:

---

68 Anand Panyarachun, 'Negotiating Readjustment in Thai–Vietnam Diplomatic Relations' (presented at seminar 'Thai–Vietnam Relations in the contemporary decade and towards cooperation in the future', Faculty of Political Science, Thammasat University, 2 August 1996).
69 Likhit, 'Thailand Foreign Policy Determination'; Likhit, *Siam and Colonialism (1855–1909)*; Sarasin, *Directions in Thai Foreign Policy*; Thamsook, *Thailand and the Japanese Presence, 1941–1945*.

the basic foreign policy of the country is to watch the 'direction of the wind' and bend accordingly in order to survive … The present writer would like to term this Thai national style as 'bamboo diplomacy'.[70]

In his 1975 book, Likhit extends this conceptual lexicon to explain Siam's survival amid colonialism during the nineteenth century. Siam survived the imperialist threat and colonisation because of the 'flexible' diplomacy that the Thai kings diligently mastered.[71]

In his 1976 book, Sarasin Viraphol also used the narrative of 'bamboo diplomacy' to explicate contemporary Thai foreign policy.[72] In 1977, Thamsook Numnonda reinterpreted Phibun's foreign policy during the Second World War in line with this flexible diplomacy. As she put it, 'the Thai art of [bamboo] diplomacy had once again saved the country. And this, of course, has always been the way the Thais have met and overcome every crisis'.[73]

While such studies were expertly argued, the lens itself is anachronistic, in the sense that scholars have used this very recent concept to universalise or essentialise Thai foreign policy. It is also tautological in the sense that the scholars reproduced knowledge of Thai foreign policy while appearing to be unaware of the power/knowledge production of 'bamboo diplomacy'. Since the 1970s, scholars have repeatedly adopted and shared this powerful narrative. A genealogy of Thai détente then renders this 'bamboo diplomacy' narrative highly problematic.

To sum up, a genealogy of Thai détente is a historical problematisation in double senses: in the first place, it explicates the descent and emergence of Thai détente in the long 1970s. We can call it a history of rupture. Through the analysis of discourse, it saw discursive anxiety and tussles within this historical rupture. In the second place, a genealogy calls into question the conventional history of 'bamboo diplomacy' and asserts the constructedness of this narrative. We call it a history of the present. In other words, such genealogy aims to historically situate diplomacy, to interrogate what is deemed as conventional wisdom, and to show how knowledge functions as a power relationship.

---

70 Likhit , 'Thailand Foreign Policy Determination', 48.
71 Likhit , *Siam and Colonialism (1855–1909)*.
72 Sarasin, *Directions in Thai Foreign Policy*.
73 Thamsook, *Thailand and the Japanese Presence, 1941–1945*, vi.

1.4. Archives

In this book, 'archives' – including collections of writings, speeches and works as well as other related documents of key policymakers – are closely studied as a 'set of texts' in order to understand the overlapping discourses within Thai elite circles, especially the discourse of détente. The book also analyses the 'intertextuality' of such sources, meaning the interconnectedness among texts and meanings through reference to other texts, in order to observe what practices were performed in diplomacy. These archives are not simply 'a register of statements' but also 'constitute evidence of ways of thinking and ways of relating to the world'. In this sense, archives can be understood as 'sites of interrogation', which reflect evidence of imaginaries and 'power relations involved in deciding what to store, how, where and the design of systems of retrieval of material'. As Luis Lobo-Guerrero put it:

> the imaginaries of the researcher meet, if willing, the imaginaries of those who classified and stored the material, of those who recorded the facts and designed the recording systems … and of the actors involved in the narratives there contained.[74]

Following the Foucauldian way, archives are not merely 'the mass of texts gathered together at a given period, those from some past epoch that have survived erasure', but rather 'the set of rules which at a given period and for a given society define' what the sayable (and unsayable) statements are, how these sayings are circulated (or prohibited), who has access to them and on what terms, and, importantly, who is permitted to speak of them in the first place.[75] By interrogating the archives, the discourse of détente produced not only diplomatic practices but also conventional wisdom of society at large.

To understand the transformation of Thai foreign policy in the 1970s, the book draws on a number of sources including primary materials such as newly available archival materials, collected volumes, newspapers, memoirs, private correspondence and other related writings, coupled with in-depth interviews and secondary literature. It is largely based

---

74 Luis Lobo-Guerrero, 'Archives', in *Research Methods in Critical Security Studies: An Introduction*, ed. Mark B Salter and Can Mutlu (London and New York: Routledge, 2012), 121–24.
75 Michel Foucault, 'Politics and the Study of Discourse', in *The Foucault Effect: Studies in Governmentality*, ed. Graham Burchell, Colin Gordon and Peter Miller (Chicago: University of Chicago Press, 1991), 59–60.

1. INTRODUCTION

on newly declassified archival documents from Thai sources, including those from the National Archives of Thailand (TNA) and Library and Archives Division at the Ministry of Foreign Affairs (MFA) in Bangkok. The former contains related documents, most of which are a variety of newspapers and a number of official documents from the late 1960s and the early period of the 1970s, while the latter provides a number of official documents from the whole period of the 1970s. Some Chinese sources are available at the Thai MFA. Regarding the Russian sources, Thailand and Russia have closely cooperated in the exchanges and translation of archival documents, all of which are from the Archive of the Foreign Ministry of the Russian Federation (AVPRF). Recently, four volumes on Thai–Soviet relations have been published commemorating the 120th anniversary of diplomatic relations in 2017. The first volume covers the early Cold War until 1970 while the other three volumes cover the periods between 1971 and 1991.[76]

The book also consults foreign archival documents, most of which have been published online, including the US State Department's *Foreign Relations of the United States* (FRUS), and the National Archives and Records Administration (NARA) and Central Intelligence Agency (CIA) online databases.

This book has thus attempted to conduct multiarchival research, with an emphasis on Thai sources. This is largely because it studies Thai détente from a Thai perspective. It focuses mainly on Thailand's shifting discursive perceptions of, and practices toward, such communist powers as the USSR and China, not the other way round. However, I use foreign sources both for cross referencing and for 'imaginary interviewing': in the sense that, as these sources prevailed, these international diplomats and officials directly engaged with and talked to Thai elites as well as pursued a kind of participatory observation during the particular period. I, therefore, use these foreign archives with the aim of being able to 'correct national bias, to measure influence, impact and effect, to monitor perception and misperception and even to learn what cannot be found in the archives at home'.[77]

---

76   Thailand's Ministry of Foreign Affairs, *Collected Volume of Soviet Archival Documents, 1941–1970* (Bangkok: Ministry of Foreign Affairs, 2016); Thailand's Ministry of Foreign Affairs, *Collected Volumes of Declassified Documents on Thai–Russian Relations, 1970–1991*, Vols 1–3 (Bangkok: Ministry of Foreign Affairs, 2017).
77   Zara Steiner, 'On Writing International History: Chaps, Maps and Much More', *International Affairs* 73, no. 3 (1997): 541.

1.5. Contribution and Structure

The book makes a contribution to at least three fields of study. First, and most obviously, it theoretically and empirically contributes to Thai studies, especially to the study of Thai foreign policy. The reinterpretation and reassessment of Thai diplomatic practices in the 1970s and their concomitant narrative of 'bamboo diplomacy' call into question the dominant historiography within Thai studies. One key finding is that the conception of Thai détente is inextricably linked to the knowledge and political construction of bamboo diplomacy as well as to the formation of new subject positions. Diplomatic practices were a result of power contestation within Thailand, and Thai détente happened in the long 1970s as a historical rupture in Thai foreign policy. The genealogical break marks the moment when the unthinkable – the normalisation of diplomatic relations with the communists – began to become thinkable, and shaped the way in which Thai foreign policy has been conducted in the present. The second finding is that a genealogy problematises the continuation of 'bamboo' diplomacy and asserts that knowledge itself was constituted as the metanarrative in Thai diplomacy in the early 1970s.

Second, the book aspires to contribute to Cold War international history, especially global détente studies, in the sense that it provides an insight into the case studies of Thai détente, which indicates how small powers, such as Thailand, initiated alternative strategies beyond superpower politics, and how successful these strategies were. Although the success of diplomatic détente in part depended on the receptivity of the great powers, this book shows that Third World or non-Western states were no longer passive agents in global politics, and had an impact upon the global Cold War. Cold War international history should pay much greater attention to the agency of small powers, and their strategies of détente with the communist powers. Third, this book makes a contribution to international relations (IR) as a discipline, in particular critical IR theories. It takes issue with a genealogy and the discursive formation of bamboo diplomacy – how and in what ways was knowledge discursively constituted by change in diplomatic practices such as détente? In addition, the book might also reassess the way in which we can conduct research on Cold War international history by using alternative approaches, especially genealogy.

The remainder of the book is organised as follows. Chapter 2 provides the historical background of the Cold War discursive hegemony and its discontents between 1958 and 1968. The next two chapters examine the first episode of détente, discussing Thanat Khoman's discourse of 'flexible diplomacy' (Chapter 3), and Thailand's changing diplomatic practices with the Soviet Union and the PRC under the context of American withdrawal from the region (Chapter 4). Chapter 5 is an interregnum of the 1971 military coup, which at first sought to lessen détente, but in fact continued it. Détente culminated in ping-pong and trade diplomacy with the PRC.

Chapter 6 examines the second détente under Kukrit Pramoj's and Chatichai Choonhavan's foreign policy of rapprochement with China and, to a lesser extent, normal relations with the USSR between 1975 and 1976. Chapter 7 explores the third détente under Kriangsak Chomanan, whose foreign policy of 'equidistance' with great powers between 1977 and 1980 culminated in balanced détente. Chapter 8 concludes by reflecting on the significance of a genealogical approach to Thai diplomacy. First, a genealogy as a history of rupture reveals the zenith of détente's discursive practices, rather than their decline, in the 1980s. What changed due to, or despite, the Third Indochina War was merely the unbalanced side of flexible diplomacy – closer alignment with China. In other words, while there was a decline in triangular diplomacy, the discourse of flexible diplomacy with the great powers persisted. Second, a genealogy as a history of the present asserts that détente epistemically produced the novel knowledge or narrative of 'bamboo diplomacy', which in turn has politically constituted the conditions of possibility for the present representations of identities and foreign policy. In other words, it explicates how and why the practice-based discourse of détente has significantly influenced, and had an impact on, Thai foreign policy thinking and implementation until the present day. In general, Thai détente was a long-term process of diplomatic transformation that not only shaped the practices of Thai foreign relations with the communist powers but also produced knowledge of bamboo diplomacy itself.

2
Cold War Discursive Hegemony: Anticommunism, Americanism and Antagonism

> Communism can be worse than the Nazis or fascists. In practice, it is more terrible than dictatorship.
>
> – King Bhumibol Adulyadej (1967)[1]

> We in Thailand want to coexist with everyone including Communist countries, but the trouble is that some Communist countries do not want to coexist with us. They want to wipe us out of our existence, or they want to control us as you may have seen. Beijing has started to say that they declared guerrilla war on Thailand. Well, this is not coexistence. This is the opposition to coexistence ... God should condemn us to make accommodation with the Communists.
>
> – Thanat Khoman, foreign minister (1967)[2]

---

1   King Bhumibol, interview, *Look* magazine, 1967, quoted in Jim Algie, et al., *Americans in Thailand* (Singapore: Editions Didier Millet, 2014), 189.
2   Thanat Khoman, 'Interview given by Foreign Minister Thanat Khoman to Japanese Pressmen', at the Ministry of Foreign Affairs, Bangkok, 10 July 1967, in *Collected Interviews of H.E. Dr. Thanat Khoman, Minister of Foreign Affairs of the Kingdom of Thailand, Vol. 1: 1967* (Bangkok: Department of Information, Ministry of Foreign Affairs, 2014), 52–53; Thanat Khoman, 'Interview given by Foreign Minister Thanat Khoman to Mr. Walker Stone, Editor-in-Chief of the Scripps-Howard Newspapers', Bangkok, 27 September 1967, in *Collected Interviews of H.E. Dr. Thanat Khoman, Vol. 1: 1967,* 111.

A GENEALOGY OF BAMBOO DIPLOMACY

It is impossible to understand the emergence of 'bamboo' diplomacy in the long 1970s without first tracing how anticommunism became hegemonic in the late 1950s. This chapter examines how anticommunist discourse emerged out of a discursive struggle within Thai politics and foreign policy formation; it is divided into two main parts. The first part discusses the struggles and clash between four contradictory and competing discourses – or myths – of Thai diplomacy: discourses of independence, lost territory, anticommunism and flexible diplomacy. It elucidates the power struggle between royal nationalism and military nationalism, which set the context for the emergence of anticommunist discourse in the Cold War, as well as the countervailing discourse of flexible diplomacy. The second part specifically examines the descent and emergence of anticommunism, from the late nineteenth century until the military regimes under Field Marshals Sarit Thanarat (1958–1963) and Thanom Kittikachorn (1963–1968). It argues that although the concept of anticommunism predated the rise of active communism in Thailand; it was merely used as a tactic to hinder antiradical discourses, to destroy political enemies and to justify the status quo. It was only from the coup in 1958 that anticommunism became a hegemonic discourse. This discourse not only demonised the communist threat but also shaped anticommunist identity and practices. Thai foreign relations with the communist powers including the USSR and the People's Republic of China (PRC) were largely framed by this Cold War discursive hegemony.

2.1. Discursive Struggles in Thailand

The discourse of anticommunism was one among many foreign policy discourses in Thailand. Since the formation of the modern Thai state in the nineteenth century, Thailand had at least four faces, or myths, upon which diplomacy was based, namely the discourses of independence, lost territory, anticommunism and flexible diplomacy. These four myths shaped the way in which Thailand perceived itself in the world as well as how a 'threat' was constructed in different periods of time. Discursive hegemony happened when one discourse became dominant at a particular time. It defined conventional wisdom and marginalised other understandings. However, this does not mean that one discourse totally replaced another. On the contrary, new discourses tended to emerge alongside, and in contradiction with, older ones. Sometimes old discourses faded away, sometimes they discredited the new one.

During the Cold War, Thailand encountered the discursive struggle between these consecutive myths. The first discourse is that of independence. This is a royal nationalist narrative of Thai diplomacy that emerged out of the late nineteenth century. It asserts that Thailand is a unique or exceptional country in Southeast Asia in two senses: first, Thailand, unlike others in the region, was never colonised by Western imperialist powers. Second, Thailand cannot be compared with other countries.[3] This discourse of independence remains a dominant discourse. The narrative goes that Thailand was a 'victim' of Western imperialism/colonialism and it interprets French imperialism during the Franco–Siamese crisis of 1893 as a 'threat' that was defeated by the Thai establishment. In other words, the monarchy is portrayed as an institution that helped save the country from imperialist expansionism and should be considered saviour of the nation.[4] The discourse of independence has thus empowered royal hegemony.[5] It also forms the national status and identity of Thailand as an independent state, which means not being colonised.

The second discourse is that of the lost territory or 'national humiliation'. The royalist discourse of independence was not directly challenged until after the 1932 Revolution, which ended the absolute monarchy. The discourse of lost territory emerged during the first administration of Field Marshal Plaek Phibunsongkhram, aka 'Phibun' (1938–1944). This saw a shift from royal nationalism to military nationalism. This discourse was a 'tool for delegitimizing state leadership', particularly the monarchy, and 'an effective way to discredit political opponents'.[6]

---

3   See David Wyatt, *Thailand: A Short History* (New Haven: Yale University Press, 1984); Pensri Duke, *Karntangprated kub aekkarat lae attippatai kong thai* [Foreign Affairs and Thailand's Independence and Sovereignty, since King Rama V to the Phibun Government] (Bangkok: The Royal Institute, 1999). Benedict Anderson bluntly observes that 'what damn good is this country – you can't compare it with anything'. See his 'Studies of the Thai State: The State of Thai Studies', in *Exploration and Irony in Studies of Siam over Forty Years* (Ithaca: Cornell University, 2014), 15–46.
4   See Patrick Tuck, *The French Wolf and the Siamese Lamb: The French Threat to Siamese Independence, 1858–1907* (Bangkok: White Lotus Press, 1995). Thongchai Winichakul critically interrogates this metanarrative. See his *Siam Mapped: A History of the Geo-Body of a Nation* (Honolulu: University of Hawai'i Press, 1994).
5   Thongchai Winichakul terms it 'rachachatniyom' [royalist nationalism]. See his *Prawatisat thai baep rachachatniyom: Jak yuk ananikhom amphrang su rachachatniyom mai rue latthi phor khong kradumphi thai nai patchuban* [Royalist Nationalist History: From the Colonial Era to the New Royalist Nationalism], *Silapawatthanatham* 23, no. 1 (November 2001): 43–52.
6   Shane Strate, *The Lost Territories: Thailand's History of National Humiliation* (Honolulu: University of Hawai'i Press, 2015), 3.

In *The Lost Territories,* Shane Strate elegantly argues that Phibun's nationalist diplomacy heavily depended on the discourse of '*lost territory* while reassigning [the discourse of] *never colonized* to a subordinate role':

> In order to construct an anti-imperialist discourse that would mobilize an entire nation, the government downplayed Siam's legacy of independence and instead interpreted the Franco–Siamese crisis of 1893 as a defeat that robbed the nation of both its territory and its honour. The leaders of Thailand provoked the 1941 war with French Indochina because they felt confident that avenging the loss from a half century earlier would allow the military to replace the monarchy in the role of national saviour.[7]

The crisis of 1893 was redefined as a collective 'trauma' and loss of sovereignty, while the alliance with Japan, and the 1941 war with France in Indochina, was portrayed as redemption. In turn, the military, instead of the monarchy, was presented as the national 'hero'. However, the Japanese (coupled with Thai) defeat at the end of the Second World War delegitimised, yet did not end, this second discourse. The latter persists as a powerful discourse.[8] Throughout the history of Thai diplomacy, both independence and lost territory discourses have been in a state of discursive tension.

The third discourse is anticommunism. Although this discourse began in the late nineteenth century to discredit any radical discourses and support the status quo,[9] it emerged as a dominant narrative or knowledge only after the 1958 coup of Field Marshal Sarit Thanarat, when he became the prime minister himself. Following his visit to Washington DC, Sarit installed a new military regime and unquestionably aligned with the US. Within this discourse, the communists – which included the powers of the Soviet Union and the PRC – were demonised as vital threats to national interest and survival. While Thailand had diplomatic relations with the USSR since 1941 and no formal relations with the PRC, Thai foreign relations with both powers were mutually antagonistic. The anticommunist discourse also positioned Thailand as an inviolable part of the Free World, where the US led and promised to guarantee its independence.

---

7   Strate, *The Lost Territories*, 4.
8   This discourse was revivified during the losing Preah Vihear incident in 1962, which has persisted in Thai politics until recently.
9   Kasian Tejapira, *Commodifying Marxism: The Formation of Modern Thai Radical Culture, 1927–1958* (Australia: Trans Pacific Press, 2001).

The last discourse is that of flexible diplomacy. This is the idea that Thai foreign policy is firmly grounded in a basic pragmatism that 'bends with the wind'. The ultimate objective is Thailand's survival and independence, and it is therefore described as 'bamboo' diplomacy.[10] In conventional historiography, the monarchs were portrayed as gifted leaders who saved the country from external threats.[11] Thamsook Numnonda also reinterprets Phibun's foreign policy as inherently flexible. As she puts it, 'the Thai art of [bamboo] diplomacy had once again saved the country. And this, of course, has always been the way the Thais have met and overcome every crisis'.[12] This discourse of flexible diplomacy is powerful in the sense that, first, it conveniently blends the discourses of independence and lost territory, and second, it demonstrates continuity in Thai diplomacy since the nineteenth century. This book argues differently, claiming that this discourse emerged out of the détente strategy and a concomitant historiography in the 1970s. Moreover, it was a discourse of diplomats.

To sum up, each discourse constituted a historical narrative as well as the national identity and interest at different times, which in turn determined who or what was treated as a 'threat' from within and without. Different discourses heralded the transformation of domestic subject positions. By the late 1950s, the anticommunist discourse, coupled with the anticommunists, started to dominate Thai politics and foreign affairs.

2.2. The Emergence of Anticommunism

2.2.1. Anticommunism as a Tactic (Before 1958)

This section argues that the idea of anticommunism predated the emergence of active communism in Thailand. It emerged in the late nineteenth century as a reaction of Thai royalism to any anti-royalist, radical discourses. Anticommunism was fundamentally employed during both the absolutist and early democratic eras as a political tool to curb or combat local enemies. In Cold War Thailand, while communism was

---

10   See Likhit Dhiravegin, 'Thailand Foreign Policy Determination', *The Journal of Social Sciences* 11, no. 4 (1974): 37–65; Arne Kislenko, 'Bending with the Wind: The Continuity and Flexibility of Thai Foreign Policy', *International Journal* 57, no. 4 (Autumn 2002): 537–61.
11   See Likhit Dhiravegin, *Siam and Colonialism (1855–1909): An Analysis of Diplomatic Relation* (Bangkok: Thai Wattana Panich, 1975).
12   Thamsook Numnonda, *Thailand and the Japanese Presence, 1941–1945* (Singapore: Institute of Southeast Asian Studies, 1977), vi.

highlighted as a red menace during the second Phibun administration (1948–1957), the idea of anticommunism before 1958 was first and foremost a tactic in bargaining with the US for military aid. That is, anticommunism was an idea without any genuine communists.

The origin of anticommunism in Thailand can be traced back to the late nineteenth century. In 1881, King Chulalongkorn reportedly told American Consul-General John A Halderman that all rulers in the world would someday be saved by Providence from 'those based classes Socialist, Nihilist, Communists etc'.[13] In 1912, his son, King Vajiravudh, alarmed by domestic (the attempted coup in March 1912) and international (Chinese Republican Revolution in October 1911 and subsequent abdication of the Manchu emperor in February 1912) factors, wrote diary entries on a critique of what he called 'the doctrine of socialism' (*latthi khong sochialist*). The latter was preached as impractical and unrealistic.[14] From then, the terms 'communism' and 'socialism' were used interchangeably. Both were counted as equivalent forms of radical discourses.[15]

Nevertheless, only a few Thai students were influenced by Western radical or progressive discourses (such as Pridi Phanomyong and Prince Sakol Wannakon Worawan, alias the 'Red Prince'). Communism, on the other hand, was strictly limited to Chinese and Vietnamese immigrants. For Kasian Tejapira, their main aim was 'externally oriented and anti-imperialist'. The spectre of communism was thus 'less menacing' but 'more alien' to the Thais.[16] From the outset, it was an un-Thai ideology. However, after the collapse of the Kuomintang–Chinese Communist Party alliance in 1927 and a shift in the Comintern's strategy toward the so-called 'Third Period' of ultra-leftism in 1928, an increase in communist activities in Thailand precipitated the severe crackdown by the Thai Government in 1929. The latter led to a series of deportations

---

13 Quoted in Benjamin Batson, *The End of the Absolute Monarchy in Siam* (Oxford: Oxford University Press, 1985), 165.
14 Quoted in Kasian, *Commodifying Marxism*, 13–14.
15 On the emergence of radical and republican discourses, see Craig J Reynolds and Hong Lysa, 'Marxism in Thai Historical Studies', *Journal of Asian Studies* 43, no. 1 (1983): 77–104; Craig J Reynolds, *Thai Radical Discourse: The Real Face of Thai Feudalism Today* (Ithaca: Cornell Southeast Asia Program Publications, 1987); Patrick Jory, 'Republicanism in Thai History', in *A Sarong for Clio: Essays on the Intellectual and Cultural History of Thailand*, ed. Maurizio Peleggi (Ithaca: Cornell Southeast Asia Program Publications, 1987, 2015): 97–117.
16 Kasian, *Commodifying Marxism*, 18.

and imprisonments. At the same time, this event triggered a new turn to communism in Thailand and the Communist Party of Siam was established in 1930.[17]

After the 1932 Revolution – which ended Thai absolutism – anticommunism and, particularly, anti-Chinese policies continued under successive People's Party governments. During this period, communism was mainly used as a political tool to delegitimise political opponents in Thai politics. In his royal critique, or so-called *Samud pokkhao,* King Rama VII himself attacked Pridi, leader of the civilian wing of the People's Party, and his Economic Plan (*Samud pokleuang*) as 'Communist'. He was quoted as saying:

> I do not know whether Stalin copied [Pridi] or whether [Pridi] copied Stalin ... the only difference is that one is Russian, the other Thai ... This is the same program that has been used in Russia. If our government adopted it, we would be assisting the Third International to achieve the aim of world Communism ... Siam would become the second Communist state after Russia.[18]

Eventually, Pridi went into exile, whereas the first Anti-Communist Act was enacted on 2 April 1933. The definition of 'Communism' in the Act was vague and extremely broad. According to Kasian, it was 'veritably not anticommunist at all, but anti-socialist, or more specifically, anti-Pridi, anti-left wing of the People's Party, and anti-Economic Plan'.[19]

The definition of communism was revised after the second military coup in 1933. The 1935 Amendment to the Anti-Communist Act was instead to exclude socialist reformists, including Pridi and his left-wing fellows. It continued to target the communists. Communist activities in Thailand drastically faded away when the Communist Party of Siam declined in 1936. Then, from 1938, the Phibun Government pursued nationalist policies.

---

17 See Christopher E Goscha, *Thailand and the Southeast Asian Networks of the Vietnamese Revolution, 1885–1954* (London and New York: Routledge, 1999); Eiji Murashima, *The Early Years of Communism in Thailand (1930–1936)* (Bangkok: Matichon, 2012).
18 Quoted in Judith Stowe, *Siam Becomes Thailand: A Study of Intrigue* (Honolulu: University of Hawai'i Press, 1991), 37–38.
19 Kasian, *Commodifying Marxism*, 39.

During the Second World War in the Pacific, the rise of anti-Japanese, anti-Phibun movements provided new opportunities for communist activities in Thailand. However, the number of Thai communists in the post–Second World War era remained very small and their influence marginal.[20] In addition, with the active domestic support of Pridi, the Anti-Communist Act was repealed in September 1946 in order to gain Soviet endorsement for Thailand's membership in the United Nations.

When Phibun returned to power in early 1948, anticommunism was not his primary agenda. Phibun was indifferent to ideology, which was explicit in his policy toward local Chinese and communists. 'Anticommunist' repression happened only when the US subsequently pushed the agenda on the Thai elite.[21] As Fineman puts it, ideology 'maintained only *a minor role* in the Thai political system' in the 1950s.[22]

What changed Phibun's foreign policy orientation was the quest for military aid from the US, which he considered as imperative for the fate of the military regime. At first, the US opposed the Phibun Government and rendered military aid politically undesirable.[23] But by early 1949, US policymakers came to concur that foreign aid would be a tool to strengthen Thailand's will to resist communism.[24] It heralded Thailand's increasing importance to America's anticommunist policy in the region.

Phibun's shift toward a pro-American stance was shown in his (at least rhetorically) self-portrayal as a hardline anticommunist. Following the victory of Chinese communism in October 1949, he supported the Bao Dai and Korean War decisions in 1950. Despite the initiation of Military Assistance Agreement in October 1950, US military assistance

---

20 Kasian, *Commodifying Marxism*, 26.
21 Daniel Fineman, *A Special Relationship: The United States and Military Government in Thailand, 1947–1958* (Honolulu: University of Hawai'i Press, 1997); Soymook Yingchaiyakamon, 'Thailand's Foreign Policy towards the People's Republic of China during Field Marshal P. Phibulsonggram's Government (1948–1957)', (MA thesis, Chulalongkorn University, 2001).
22 Fineman, *A Special Relationship*, 75. Historiographically, Fineman transcends the predominant Cold War paradigm, or what he called 'international-relations-oriented studies' (5), which explains the alliance from an ideological perspective, namely anticommunism. This paradigm 'fails to explain the role of the military and military-controlled governments in the alliance' (4). Fineman asserts instead that 'rather than considering Thailand's alliance with the United States as separate from internal politics and driven by the novel and imported ideology of anticommunism, as the Cold War model assumes, we should view the country's domestic politics and foreign policy, as the Thais themselves did, as closely connected' (4).
23 See Edwin F Stanton, *Brief Authority: Excursions of a Common Man in an Uncommon World* (New York: Harper, 1956), 209.
24 Frank C Darling, *Thailand and the United States* (Washington DC: Public Affairs Press, 1965), 70.

to Phibun's regime remained 'limited and uncertain', 'significant but modest'. In other words, Thailand still occupied a 'distant place' in US foreign policy thinking.[25]

By the mid-1950s, when the Americans had increased their involvement in Indochina following the French defeat at Dien Bien Phu, Thailand gradually became an American 'bastion' against communism in Southeast Asia. Military aid for Thailand rose dramatically, and the commitment to fight for Thailand's survival was strengthened via the establishment of the Southeast Asia Treaty Organization (SEATO) in September 1954. As the military regime consolidated power over the next five years (1950–1954), Thailand and the US became increasingly close allies.[26]

Following incessant pressures from the US, the Thai military-dominated regime pursued a harsher policy toward communists and dissidents, as well as the Soviet Union and the PRC. In 1952, Phibun banned a Soviet publication named *Tass Bulletin*, reduced quotas on Chinese immigration and imposed an embargo on all trade with Communist China.[27] The PRC reacted by announcing the establishment of a Thai Autonomous People's Government in the southern province of Yunnan in 1953. By now, therefore, it was clear that Thailand's pro-American stance was negatively impacting its relations with both the USSR and the PRC.[28]

In domestic politics, the military regime developed a 'triumvirate politics', including such three rivalling strongmen as Phibun, Police General Phao Siyanon and Field Marshal Sarit Thanarat of the Royal Thai Army.[29] In brief, Thai authoritarianism rose in tandem with American influence in the region. However, during the democratic interlude between 1955 and 1957, proceeding with elections, Phibun allowed political parties to form, lifted restrictions on the press and free speech, revived leftists and dissidents, and intensified the power struggle at the top of the state. This, in turn, saw a deterioration of the Thai–US alliance and the rise of anti-Americanism became ubiquitous in public debate.

---

25 Fineman, *A Special Relationship*, 131, 128.
26 Matthew Phillips, *Thailand in the Cold War* (London and New York: Routledge, 2016), 92–93.
27 Paul R Shirk, 'Thai–Soviet Relations', *Asian Survey* 9, no. 9 (1969): 690.
28 Anuson Chinvanno, *Thailand's Policies towards China, 1949–54* (Hampshire: Macmillan, 1992).
29 Thak Chaloemtiarana, *Thailand: The Politics of Despotic Paternalism* (Ithaca: Southeast Asia Program Publications, Cornell University Press, 2007).

Moreover, in foreign affairs, Phibun started to veer toward neutrality and engagement with Beijing. This manifested in the emerging concept of non-alignment, which had developed globally following the Afro-Asian Conference at Bandung in 1955. Phibun sent his foreign minister, Prince Wan Waithayakon, to attend the Bandung Conference, where the latter made an acquaintance with the Chinese Premier, Zhou Enlai.[30] Phibun also initiated secret diplomacy with the PRC, by sending his unofficial emissary to Beijing. Then he sent two children of Sang Phathanothai, his close confidante, to Beijing as part of a tributary diplomacy. Warnwai, aged 12, and Sirin, aged 8, were raised under the tutelage of Premier Zhou.[31]

It can be stressed that at that time, flexible or bamboo diplomacy was not the formal policy of the country. Phibun's brief moment to engage with China was part of the spirit of Bandung. Neither non-alignment nor neutralisation were epistemically conceived as flexible diplomacy. Furthermore, Thailand's 'China card' was primarily designed by Phibun to pressure the Americans for more aid.[32] According to Anand Panyarachun, '[Thai foreign policy] during the Phibun administration toward China was not serious. It was merely an insurance policy with fear'.[33]

The Thai non-alignment orientation was short-lived and ended in the military coup in 1957, led by Phibun's own protégé, Field Marshal Sarit Thanarat. The first coup in 1957 was deemed essential because, as a cable to Washington reported, the Phibun Government had 'allowed secret contacts with Communist circles in China'. As US Ambassador to Bangkok, Edwin Stanton, put it, the Thai foreign policy of anticommunism was 'to run with the hare, and hunt with the hounds'.[34]

---

30 Anuson Chinvanno, *'Brief Encounter': Sino–Thai Rapprochement after Bandung, 1955–1957* (Bangkok: Institute of Foreign Affairs, 1991).
31 See Aree Pirom, *Buanglang kan sathapana samphanthaparp yukmai thai-jeen* [Background to the Establishment of Sino–Thai Relations in the Modern Period] (Bangkok: Mitnara Press, 1981); Warnwai Phathanothai, *Zhou Enlai: Pupluek maitri Thai-jeen* [Zhou Enlai, The Man Who Planted Thai–Chinese Friendship], 2nd edn (Bangkok: Prakonchai, 1976 [2001]); Sirin Phathanothai, *The Dragon's Pearl* (New York and London: Simon & Schuster, 1994).
32 Fineman, *A Special Relationship*.
33 Anand Panyarachun, 'Patakata pised' [Special Lecture], in *Kwam sampan thai-jin* [Sino-Thai Relations: Past and Future Prospects], ed. Khien Theeravit and Cheah Yan-Chong (Bangkok: Chualolongkorn University, 2000), 12–13.
34 Quoted in Fineman, *A Special Relationship*, 244, 66.

In other words, Phibun was not staunchly anticommunist. For him, anticommunism was a means to obtain American military aid and sustain his political survival. Phibun's era in the 1950s was then a prolegomenon to the genuine 'revolution' under the Sarit Government.[35] Especially after his second coup in 1958, Sarit abruptly ended his 'democratic' experiment in Thailand, and became strongly committed to anticommunist discourse.

In sum, the term 'anticommunism' was introduced much earlier to Thai political discourse when the Thai monarchy attempted to discredit radical discourses. It served as a political tool to battle domestic political opponents and to justify the political status quo. The demonisation of communism was done even before the existence of Thai communists. Anticommunism was by and large repressive in the sense that Thai governments fought those alleged communists. However, without any genuine communists, they did not and could not produce the new subjects of politically committed anticommunists in the country.

2.2.2. Anticommunism as a Hegemonic Knowledge (1958–1968)

This section examines the descent and emergence of anticommunist discourse during the Sarit and Thanom administrations. After 1958, anticommunism began to be the dominant knowledge in Thailand. In turn, the new subject positions of anticommunists, such as the military elites and civilian conservatives, were discursively constructed. By then, anticommunists emerged only when individuals made a strong commitment to this hegemonic discourse of anticommunism and defended it to a hilt. Thailand's close alignment with the US and its involvement in the Vietnam War further deepened this discourse.

---

35 On the contrary, Fineman claims that the year 1950 was a 'revolution' in Thai diplomacy towards pro-American alignment and anticommunism. I argue differently, that it was merely a 'prelude to revolution', rather than a revolution in itself. This period brought about a transition toward what can be called a 'Cold War discursive hegemony' in the 1960s (specifically, the period after the Sarit coup in 1958 through to 1968). See Daniel Fineman, 'Phibun, the Cold War, and Thailand Foreign Policy Revolution of 1950', in *Connecting Histories: Decolonization and the Cold War in Southeast Asia, 1945–1962*, ed. Christopher E Goscha and Christopher F Ostenmann (Washington DC and Stanford: Woodrow Wilson Center Press with Stanford University Press, 2009), 275–300.

After his return from medical treatment at Walter Reed Military Hospital in Washington DC, Field Marshal Sarit Thanarat (1958–1963) launched a second coup in 1958. He then assumed absolute power domestically.[36] The coup was endorsed by the king, who was considered by the US State Department as pro-Western and strongly anticommunist. Sarit cited the communist threat as one of the justifications for the coup. He often called the communists 'trouble-makers', and 'our worst enemy, which poses an internal as well as external danger'.[37]

Discursively, communism was demonised as a menace in Thai politics.[38] Sarit himself rendered it a 'dirty plague'.[39] Foreign Minister Thanat Khoman (1959–1971) pathologised communism as 'spring fevers, call it red or pink', or 'Asian flu'. By so doing, he used the analogy of a 'doctor' that tried to cure this 'rather vicious virus':

> I am glad that one of our doctors has said that the Thais are perhaps the most immune people from the Asian flu, and I wish that I can apply our immunity to that kind of Asian flu.[40]

As Thanat put it:

> We are not going to allow the Asian flu to affect us, in the sense that the students in Paris, or Rome, not to speak of Berkeley or Michigan, who are less immune than we are, and who have been affected by what they euphemistically call the Cultural Revolution.

---

36   The role of the US in the 1958 coup is debatable. Fineman claims that the US had no role in the coup; however, from Surachart Bamrungsuk we now know that during his medical visit to the US, Sarit had a chance to meet with President Eisenhower and Secretary of State Dulles to discuss a 'free world defense against Communist pressure' as well as the means of strengthening closer ties between Thailand and the US. In contrast, Kullada argues that the US was behind the 1958 coup. Sarit was 'lectured' by the high-ranking US officials, especially US Under-Secretary of State for Economic Affairs, Douglas Dillon, to adopt the 'development' agendas and programs. Surachart Bamrungsuk, *United States Foreign Policy and Thailand Military Rule, 1947–1977* (Bangkok: Duang Kamol, 1988), 77; see also Fineman, *A Special Relationship*; Kullada Kesboonchoo Mead, *Kanmueng Thai yuk Sarit-Thanom phaitai khrongsang amnat lok* [Thai Politics during Sarit-Thanom Regimes under Global Power Structure] (Bangkok: 50 Years Foundation, The Bank of Thailand, 2007).

37   Thak, *Thailand*, 127, 136.

38   The anticommunist discourse was mutually shared among Thai elite and public. MR Kukrit Pramoj, a well-renowned royalist and publisher of *Siam Rath* newspaper, was an ardent advocate of this discourse. See Saichon Sattayanurak, *Kukrit kap praditthakam 'Khwam pen Thai', lem 2* [Kukrit and the Construction of 'Thainess', Book 2] (Bangkok: Silapawatthanatham, 2007).

39   Quoted in Puangthong Pawakapan, *Truth in the Vietnam War: The First Casualty of War and the Thai State* (Bangkok: Kobfai, 2006), 42.

40   Thanat Khoman, 'Statement by Foreign Minister Thanat Khoman to Members of the Foreign Correspondents' Club of Thailand', Bangkok, 28 August 1968, in *Collected Interviews of H.E. Dr. Thanat Khoman, Minister of Foreign Affairs of the Kingdom of Thailand, Vol. 2: 1968* (Bangkok: Department of Information, Ministry of Foreign Affairs, 2014), 254–55.

> How can you conceive that the Cultural Revolution can spread from the Empire of the Middle Kingdom [China] to the confines of Europe and America? And how the influence of the Cultural Revolution has surpassed us and bypassed us to go directly to Paris, or to California or to New York, it is beyond my conception. But that is the kind of things that we have to face and perhaps because we keep our eyes firmly on the horizon, scrutinizing openings for future settlement, and keeping our feet firmly on the ground we can escape the nefarious effects of those viruses. We can keep our minds, our hearts and our bodies healthy.[41]

For him, 'we are sick of Communist imperialism'.[42] And 'if anyone were to think that the Communists have abandoned the scheme of world domination, he is not of the sane mind'.[43] The spectre of communism was then metaphorically framed as a medical problem that required a series of therapeutic interventions. That was the pathologisation of the other – the foreign body perceived to threaten the body politic. To deal with this 'Communist' flu or virus, said Thanat, 'there is no alternative! We prefer to spend money and keep the Communist out rather than have the Communists in'. Thailand fought the 'war against Communist expansion in Southeast Asia' in order to 'eradicate the Communist terrorists'.[44]

Sarit believed that Thailand needed a stable military regime in order to simultaneously suppress communism and attract foreign investment. Upon his consolidation of power, he dissolved the National Assembly, closed down many newspapers that were accused of supporting communist activities and banned political organisations and labour unions. The Sarit Government also arrested communist suspects and those who were labelled as communist sympathisers, many of whom included political opponents, journalists, writers and political activists.[45] In particular, Sarit considered Chinese immigrants a major source of communist

---

41 Thanat Khoman, 'Statement by Foreign Minister Thanat Khoman to Members of the Foreign Correspondents' Club of Thailand', Bangkok, 28 August, 1968, in *Collected Interviews of H.E. Dr. Thanat Khoman, Vol. 2: 1968*, 254–55.
42 Thanat Khoman, 'Interview given by Foreign Minister Thanat Khoman to Takashi Oka, The Christian Science Monitor', at the Ministry of Foreign Affairs, Bangkok, 20 January 1967 in *Collected Interviews of H.E. Dr. Thanat Khoman, Vol. 1: 1967*, 19.
43 Thanat Khoman, 'Interview given by Foreign Minister Thanat Khoman to Mr. Rafael Steinberg from the Saturday Evening Post', at the Ministry of Foreign Affairs, Bangkok, 25 September 1967, in *Collected Interviews of H.E. Dr. Thanat Khoman, Vol. 1: 1967*, 104–5.
44 Thanat Khoman, 'Interview given by Foreign Minister Thanat Khoman to a Group of Scandinavia's Newspapermen', Bangkok, 9 November, 1967, in *Collected Interviews of H.E. Dr. Thanat Khoman, Vol. 1: 1967*, 126.
45 Thak, *Thailand*.

infiltration. In May 1959, for instance, his government restricted Chinese immigration in order to curb the domestic communist insurgency. It also arrested a group of Thai actors who went to Beijing. They were charged with being involved in communist activities. Four of them were accused of being communist leaders, and executed by the special powers under Article 17 of the Interim Constitution of Thailand (1959).[46] Henceforth, the military regime took a strong anticommunist policy.

Deeply embedded in anticommunist discourse, Sarit's foreign policy was a major shift from Phibun's. He abruptly ended the latter's attempted strategy of neutrality and accommodation with the PRC. For Sarit, neutrality or non-alignment was vulnerability to the communist threat. Foreign Minister Thanat said, in retrospect, that the idea of non-alignment became a 'bankrupt concept' because the communists were 'not willing to uphold the original concept of peaceful coexistence', which was 'a necessary premise or a necessary foundation for the policy of non-alignment'.[47] By 1958, the spirit of Bandung faded away in Thailand temporarily and Thai state actors advocated a close alliance with the US. Thanat justified the necessity of a 'protective umbrella' by claiming that there

> are only two umbrellas in the world, either the Soviet or American umbrella. We cannot hope to have the Soviet umbrella. So, we shall have to use the only one available, the American umbrella.[48]

Sarit's foreign policy was based on the following characteristics. First, it strengthened Thai–US relations. The year 1958 marked a historical watershed because it restored and consolidated the Thai–US special relationship. As Fineman has put it, in 1958:

> the question was whether the Americans would stand firmly behind the democratic process or selectively intervene on behalf of the elected government's opponents. They chose the latter, and democracy paid the price.[49]

---

46 Surachart, *United States Foreign Policy and Thailand Military Rule*, 106–7.
47 Thanat Khoman, 'Interview given by Foreign Minister Thanat Khoman to a Group of New Zealand Reporters', at the Ministry of Foreign Affairs, Bangkok, 7 September 1967, in *Collected Interviews of H.E. Dr. Thanat Khoman, Vol. 1: 1967*, 69.
48 Thanat Khoman, 'Interview given by Foreign Minister Thanat Khoman to Mr. Tom Wicker, Washington Bureau's Chief of the New York Times', Bangkok, 8 February 1967, in *Collected Interviews of H.E. Dr. Thanat Khoman, Vol. 1: 1967*, 33.
49 Fineman, *A Special Relationship*, 13.

'The Americans had not embraced military dictatorship in Thailand in 1958 because they had no other choice', rather, the Americans enthusiastically embraced military authoritarianism because it aligned with their strategic interests.[50] This was the foundation of the so-called 'special relationship' between Thailand and the US throughout the Cold War. Both countries were intimately interdependent. While, on the one hand, Thai military stability and survival largely relied on American military and economic aid, the US, on the other hand, depended on Thailand's congenially strong, stable and pro-American military regime. This was not a coincidence, but a mutual construction. However, this alliance was a 'tragedy' for Thai democratisation.[51]

For Thailand, an alliance with the US was rooted in a number of assumptions: their shared belief in the domino theory; the US commitment to defend Thailand from communism; and US military assistance and aid in supporting counterinsurgency warfare. The US started to develop air bases and military facilities, thereby using Thailand as forward defence stations in the region.[52] Sarit's pro-American strategy was a pretext for an ever-closer alliance during the Vietnam War in the 1960s.

Second, the Sarit regime reaffirmed Thailand's commitment to SEATO. However, the alliance was significantly tested during the deteriorating situation in Laos in 1960–1962. The crisis began when the right-wing government, led by Phoumi Nosavan, who was also Sarit's cousin, was overthrown by communist forces, or the *Pathet Lao*, in August 1960. The Sarit Government expressed its dissatisfaction with SEATO and the US Government, which were reluctant to use military force to support the anticommunist factions. Sarit reportedly began to negotiate with the Soviet ambassador on trade and cultural exchanges as a bargaining tool vis-à-vis the US.[53] Sarit even threatened to withdraw from SEATO before President John F Kennedy agreed to promulgate the Thanat–Rusk joint communiqué in March 1962. The communiqué was aimed to reaffirm

---

50   Fineman, *A Special Relationship*, 262.
51   Fineman, *A Special Relationship*, 8. See also Kullada Kesboonchoo Mead, 'The Cold War and Thai Democratization', in *Southeast Asia and the Cold War*, ed. Albert Lau (London and New York: Routledge, 2012), 215–40.
52   See Surachart, *United States Foreign Policy and Thailand Military Rule*.
53   Jittipat Poonkham, *Withet Panid Sampan tung Songkram Yen: kwam sampan rawangprathet Thai-Russia (1897–1991)* [Foreign Economic Relations to the Cold War: Thai–Russian Foreign Relations (1897–1991)] (Bangkok: Chulalongkorn University Press, 2016), 92–94.

the US military commitment to Thailand. It stated that the US would protect Thailand from 'Communist aggression and subversion' by giving full support under 'its constitutional process'.[54]

While the Thanat–Rusk communiqué was in fact a 'bilateralization of SEATO' without any clear substance,[55] the military regime viewed it as a significant assurance. After that, the US supplied Phoumi's right-wing troops and trained the indigenous Hmong tribes under Vang Pao. In May 1962, the US ordered a carrier task force of the 7th Fleet into the Gulf of Thailand, and deployed 5,000 US troops, US jet bombers and 1,800 US marines in Thailand.[56]

The crisis in Laos obviously indicated a divergence of perceptions and strategies between Thailand and the US.[57] First, the Laotian crisis was perceived as an immediate threat to Thailand. If the Phoumi's faction in Laos collapsed, Thailand would become a 'frontline state'. In turn, Laos would provide a support base for the Communist Party of Thailand (CPT). Furthermore, the Thai military advocated a forward defence strategy, by fighting outside the country. As Field Marshal Thanom Kittikachorn later explained: 'It is better for Thailand to fight the enemy away from home than wait for him to arrive at one's door.'[58]

The third characteristic of Sarit's foreign policy was its antagonism towards the Soviet Union and the PRC. On the one hand, the Sarit Government continued to be sceptical of Soviet activities in Bangkok. In 1959, it declared the Soviet attaché 'persona non grata' and expelled the Russian news agency Tass journalist. However, Sarit also used the 'Soviet' card as leverage with the Americans when Thai–US relations turned sour. During the Laotian crisis, he talked about the possibility of trade relations with the Russians, and even exchanged formal Trade Notes.[59] Yet, it did not come to any concrete outcomes.

---

54 Quoted in R Sean Randolph, *The United States and Thailand: Alliance Dynamics, 1950–1985* (Berkeley: Institute of East Asian Studies, University of California, 1986), 41.
55 Surachart, *United States Foreign Policy and Thailand Military Rule*, 103.
56 Surachart, *United States Foreign Policy and Thailand Military Rule*, 105.
57 On the Laotian crisis, see Sutayut Osornprasop, 'Thailand and the American Secret War in Indochina, 1960–1974' (PhD thesis, University of Cambridge, 2006).
58 *New York Times*, 2 June 1970, quoted in Sutayut, 'Thailand and the American Secret War', 230.
59 Jittipat, *Withet Panid Sampan tung Songkram Yen*, 92–94.

On the other hand, Sarit terminated Phibun's initial accommodation with China. He issued Revolutionary Proclamation No. 53 in 1959, which banned trade with China. Sarit also strengthened the Anti-Communist Act, thereby pursuing a repressive crackdown upon domestic communist insurgents, or even communist sympathisers.[60]

His anticommunist and anti-Beijing policies were affirmed by a reversal of the PRC's stance in 1957–1958, and the increasingly proactive role of the CPT. By the end of 1957, Beijing resumed a militant, aggressive international policy. It increased the level of Chinese anti-Thai propaganda. In 1962, with Chinese support, the Voice of the People of Thailand Radio began to operate from Yunnan in southern China.

In addition, the CPT began to undertake a clandestine insurgency in rural Thailand. In 1960, it proclaimed that 'for Thailand there can never be any peaceful path, but only the way of armed struggle'.[61] In 1962, CPT's 'Prediction for BE2505' was distributed in Thailand, calling for the establishment of a united front in order to oust the US and overthrow the Sarit military regime.[62] For the Thai military, these changes precipitated an actual threat of communist insurgency in Thailand, which was supported and funded by foreign communists, especially the Chinese.

Fourth, Sarit pursued an American model of socio-economic 'development' in order to gain foreign investment and to fight communism. Sarit thus rescinded Phibun's economic nationalism and resuscitated liberalisation. Shortly after the coup, his government initiated Revolutionary Proclamation No. 11 as a plan to modernise the country, and Revolutionary Proclamation No. 33 to implement liberalism as economic policy. Sarit subsequently set up the National Economic Council in July 1959, and launched the first Six-Year National Economic Development Plan (1961–1966) in October 1960. He also cancelled import tax on all machinery for five years, which was enshrined in the Investment Promotion Act of 1962. In turn, the US increasingly provided Thailand with more economic aid. Most of it was used for military objectives,

---

60 Thak, *Thailand*.
61 Patrice de Beer, 'History and Policy of the Communist Party of Thailand', *Journal of Contemporary Asia* 8, no. 1 (1978): 164.
62 Surachart, *United States Foreign Policy and Thailand Military Rule,* 107.

such as building the 450-mile Friendship Highway between Bangkok and Nong Khai near Laos.[63] In other words, by adopting the concept of 'development' (*karn pattana*), Sarit promoted capitalism in Thailand.

Fifth, in the foreign policymaking process, Sarit monopolised power within the military group and thereby marginalised the roles of civilians – in particular, in the Ministry of Foreign Affairs (MFA). Although he appointed a civilian, Thanat Khoman, as foreign minister, Thanat's role was relatively marginal.[64]

In brief, the military regime of Sarit oversaw a major transformation in Thai politics and foreign affairs. His regime committed Thailand to an authoritarian road and a close alliance with the US. Most importantly, it established the discourse of anticommunism and, unlike his predecessors, linked the ideology inextricably with both Thai nationalism and royalism. By 1958, the Cold War discursive hegemony, including discourses of Americanism, anticommunism and antagonism with communist powers, was fully established and implemented in Thailand.

After Sarit's death in December 1963, his successor, Field Marshal Thanom Kittikachorn, continued the anticommunist discourse. By that time, Thailand perceived the communists, particularly the Chinese and North Vietnamese, as genuine 'threats' to national security. As Arne Kislenko put it:

> [Thanom] was profoundly anticommunist, believing firmly that the threat [Beijing] and Hanoi posed to Thailand was real, immediate, and unyielding. Trying to accommodate communism was useless, and so too was a return to a more neutral foreign policy.[65]

While the nature of their relationship was unequal, Thailand and the US were increasingly dependent upon each other. Thanom saw the US as the guarantor of Thai security. The Tonkin Incident in 1964, which led to direct American involvement and escalation in the Vietnam War, made

---

63   Kullada Kesboonchoo Mead, 'A Revisionist History of Thai–US Relations', *Asian Review* 16 (2003): 59–60; Ukrist Pathmanand, 'Saharat America kap nayobai sethakit Thai' [The US and Thai Economic Policy] (MA thesis, Chulalongkorn University, 1983).

64   John Funston, 'The Role of the Ministry of Foreign Affairs in Thailand: Some Preliminary Observations', *Contemporary Southeast Asia* 9, no. 3 (December 1987): 236.

65   Arne Kislenko, 'Bamboo in the Wind: United States Foreign Policy and Thailand during the Kennedy and Johnson Administrations, 1961–1969' (PhD thesis, University of Toronto, 2000), 175.

Thailand an invaluable anticommunist ally, or an 'unsinkable aircraft carrier'.[66] Benedict Anderson called this period the 'American Era' of Thai history.[67]

After stepping up the air war (in late 1964) and ground war (in July 1965) against Hanoi, the US Government under President Lyndon Johnson led the Thais to believe that the US would make a strong military commitment to protect Thai security and independence. Both countries concluded a secret military agreement, called the Contingency Plan of 1964. From then, the Thanom Government permitted the US to deploy its troops in the country, allowing for covert operations throughout Indochina to steadily expand, including the so-called 'secret war' in Laos.[68] In order to support the bombing of North Vietnam, Thailand allowed the US access to strategic air bases across the country. American airplanes flew out of Thai bases, with 25,000 bombing flights in 1965, 79,000 in 1966, and 108,000 in 1967. Until 1967, the Thai Government publicly denied that the Americans bombed North Vietnam from Thai air bases.[69] In 1967, both governments signed the Joint Use and Air Defense Operations Agreement. In return, the US increased economic and military aid to the Thai military government. It provided the Thai Army with military hardware and advisors, while developing security programs, and launching counterinsurgency programs at the village level. Thailand also became an R&R (rest and recreation) centre for the US personnel in the region.

---

66 John LS Girling, *Thailand: Society and Politics* (Ithaca: Cornell University Press, 1981), 231.
67 Benedict Anderson, *In the Mirror: Literature and Politics in Siam in the American Era* (Bangkok: Duang Kamol, 1985).
68 In fact, there were actually more Thai 'boots on the ground' in the secret war in Laos than in Vietnam during the Vietnam War. See Sutayut, 'Thailand and the American Secret War'.
69 Randolph, *The United States and Thailand*, 76. During his visit to Washington DC in October 1965, Foreign Minister Thanat Khoman gave an interview to the *Washington Post*, acknowledging that US military involvement in Vietnam represented a strong commitment to the defence of Southeast Asia. He openly attacked those who advocated a policy of neutrality, suggesting that it was a concession to the communists. More interestingly, Thanat conceded that Thailand did not need 11,000-foot runways in the north-east for its own air force. He implicitly admitted Thai involvement with the American air war in Vietnam. As one summed up, 'It was a very Thai way of announcing Bangkok's commitment to Washington, and given the emphasis placed in plausible denial, it was clearly designed to elicit more support from the US'. Thanat Khoman, interview with Robert Eastabrook, *The Washington Post*, 11 October 1965, in Kislenko, 'Bamboo in the Wind', 216.

A GENEALOGY OF BAMBOO DIPLOMACY

Thailand's increasing involvement in Vietnam had some of the following characteristics. First, the Thai military firmly monopolised Thai foreign and security policymaking decisions. This marked the waning power of Foreign Minister Thanat and the MFA, which were almost entirely excluded from the country's foreign policy.

Second, with the exception of U-Tapao Air Base and Ramasun Radio Station, the stationing of US forces in Thailand was dealt with on an informal basis, with no written agreements.[70] This was to avoid Congressional investigations for the US and difficult questions regarding sovereignty for the Thais.

Third, Thailand's close alignment with the US increased communist activities inside the country. In fact, the first official attack by the communist insurgents on Thai military forces in the rural areas only occurred in 1965.[71] That is, anticommunist counterinsurgency programs began long before there was any serious communist threat in Thailand.

Fourth, Thailand's involvement with the Vietnam War weakened its foreign relations with the communist powers. In 1965, the Soviet Union denounced Thailand's pro-Americanism. When Soviet Premier Alexei Kosygin visited Hanoi in January 1965, he pledged to provide military aid and supplies to North Vietnam. Thai–Soviet relations further worsened and when the Association of Southeast Asian Nations (ASEAN) was established in August 1967, the Soviet Union complained about the anticommunist nature of the organisation.[72]

Also, since 1965, the PRC responded to the expanding influence of the US in the region, including Thailand, by providing direct support to the CPT and repeatedly attacking the Thai military government. It called on the CPT to step up its armed struggle to overthrow 'the reactionary Thanom government'. In 1965, Chinese Foreign Minister Marshal Chen Yi allegedly declared the 'hope to have a guerrilla war going in Thailand before the year is out'.[73] Likewise, Liao Chengzhi, Chair of the Overseas Chinese Affairs Commission, announced that Beijing had 'unshirkable

---

70   Randolph, *The United States and Thailand*, 73.
71   Katherine A Bowie, *Rituals of National Loyalty: An Anthropology of the State and the Village Scout Movement in Thailand* (New York: Columbia University Press, 1997), 63.
72   Ganganath Jha, *Foreign Policy of Thailand* (New Delhi: Radiant Publishers, 1979), 75–77.
73   Quoted in John Wong, *The Political Economy of China's Changing Relations with Southeast Asia* (London: Macmillan Press, 1984), 164.

obligations' to support 'the struggles of the people' of Thailand.[74] The revival of communist insurgency, with Chinese sponsorship, alarmed the Thai military. In December 1965, the Thai Government, with American assistance, established the Communist Suppression Operations Command (CSOC) in order to oversee and coordinate anticommunist activities among different agencies.[75]

Fifth, Thailand at first provided military facilities for the US in the Vietnam War, then sent its own special forces to fight in Vietnam. This was in exchange for a huge amount of military assistance. The first unit deployed to Vietnam in the late 1960s was the Royal Thai Army Volunteer Force, or the so-called 'Black Panthers', consisting of 11,000 troops.[76]

Sixth, a vested interest in the US military presence grew among the higher echelons of the military elite, who became caught up in the intricate web of corruption. Their mutual demands and expectations also rose.

Lastly, as the Vietnam quagmire worsened and antiwar student protests and popular movements emerged across the world, including in Thailand, the promulgation of the February 1968 election and the return to a parliamentary system meant that Thai foreign and security policy was opened to more public scrutiny.[77]

Thus, by the 1960s, the discourse of anticommunism was arguably at its most deeply embedded in Thai politics and foreign affairs, inseparable from both pro-Americanism and antagonism with the communist powers.

However, the Tet Offensive, when South Vietnam was surprised by an attack by the North Vietnamese forces on the Vietnamese New Year in January 1968, led to new pressure in American politics. President Johnson declared he would not stand in the next election, and began to negotiate an end to the war. Subsequently, he halted the aerial bombings in Vietnam. Thailand had not been given any prior warning of this announcement, which infuriated many Thai leaders. Foreign Minister Thanat said that he did not fear 'the cessation of the bombing' itself, but 'the cessation of the hostilities'. For him, Thailand was

---

74   Quoted in Kislenko, 'Bamboo in the Wind', 219.
75   Saiyud Kerdphol, *The Struggle for Thailand: Counter-insurgency, 1965–1985* (Bangkok: S. Research Center, 1986).
76   Randolph, *The United States and Thailand*, 79–80.
77   Kullada, 'The Cold War and Thai Democratization', 225.

not opposed to the halting of the bombing of North Vietnam as such. But we would oppose the cessation of the bombing if it were to put the aggressive side in a position that will help them strike at us, at our soldiers, at our people, at the people in Vietnam, at the American and South Vietnamese soldiers who are fighting so bravely and also the Thai soldiers in South Vietnam.[78]

It was this shifting American policy that instigated discursive anxiety for the MFA, led by Thanat Khoman, which in turn started to conduct a more flexible diplomacy.

2.3. Conclusion

This chapter has traced a genealogy of the anticommunist discourse within the discursive context of Thai diplomacy. Although anticommunism was mentioned throughout diplomatic history, it became a hegemonic narrative only in the late 1950s. Thai governments under Sarit and Thanom, along with a military elite, became strongly attached to the anticommunist discourse and a pro-American stance during the Vietnam War. The identities of the military and conservatives were constructed as staunch anticommunists. The communists were discursively denounced and demonised as imminent 'threats' and Thailand's foreign relations with the USSR and the PRC became mutually antagonistic. In general, Thai diplomacy in the Cold War was neither flexible nor 'bending with the wind' at all. Rather, it was rigid and confrontational. This only began to change in the late 1960s as a consequence of an emergent discursive struggle. It was this struggle which will be explored through the rest of this book.

---

78 Thanat Khoman, 'View from Thailand', an ABC interview with Foreign Minister Thanat Khoman, 7 October 1967, in *Collected Interviews of H.E. Dr. Thanat Khoman, Vol. 1: 1967*, 100–101.

3

Bending Before the Wind: The Emergence of 'Flexible Diplomacy' (1968–1969)

> We claim we have been practicing the Nixon Doctrine even before it was announced.
>
> – Thanat Khoman, foreign minister[1]

If the year 1968 was an annus horribilis for the discourse of anticommunism, it was also an annus mirabilis for Thai détente. The prospect of American retrenchment from the region following the Tet Offensive, when the North Vietnamese forces launched surprise attacks against South Vietnam on 30 January, placed pressure on the anticommunist discourse. This raised discursive anxiety for Thailand's security and diplomacy. The former Cold Warrior and long-serving foreign minister Thanat Khoman, seeing the changing international dynamic, initiated the concept of 'flexible diplomacy' to meet the anxiety. Initially, this concept comprised three main characteristics: anti-Americanism, regionalism and détente with the communist powers. By the end of 1968, flexible diplomacy and détente were used interchangeably. This chapter argues that Thailand's changing discourse occurred even before the Nixon Doctrine.[2] We can say that Thailand was bending before the wind.

---

1 'FM: We back China's entry', *Bangkok Post*, 18 September 1971.
2 It should be noted that détente with the Soviet Union had earlier been attempted by the US administrations prior to Nixon, such as John F Kennedy's failed détente in 1963. See Jennifer W See, 'An Uneasy Truce: John F. Kennedy and Soviet–American Détente, 1963', *Cold War History* 2, no. 2 (2002): 161–94.

This chapter traces the discursive descent of flexible diplomacy by first closely analysing Foreign Minister Thanat Khoman's speeches between 1968 and 1969. It then examines a change in institutional practices within the Ministry of Foreign Affairs, exemplified in the training programs of the newly established Devawongse Varopakarn Institute of Foreign Affairs (DVIFA). Both discursive and non-discursive practices rendered the formation of détente proponents possible.

3.1. Discursive Practices: Discourse of 'Flexible Diplomacy'

Prominent narratives of the changing trajectory of Thai foreign policy often posit the Nixon Doctrine as an important milestone.[3] The doctrine arose when, on 25 July 1969, newly elected US president Richard M Nixon signalled the American retreat from Vietnam and the prospect of withdrawal from the region, including Thailand.[4] Amid the prospect of a communist takeover of Indochina, the possibility of US retrenchment aroused anxiety among the Thai political elite. What would be the security arrangement with the US, and how would it ensure Thailand's national survival? However, while Thailand's decision to establish relations with the communist powers undoubtedly followed a transformation of US foreign policy, it was not directly caused or influenced by the US. In fact, the discourses and practices of détente *preceded* the American decision to demilitarise and deescalate the Vietnam War.[5] In other words, Thailand was bending even *before* the wind began to blow.

The new course began shortly after President Lyndon Johnson dramatically reversed his Vietnam policy in March 1968. After the Tet Offensive, Johnson ordered a halt to the surgical bombing of Indochina, and began peace talks with the North Vietnamese. By that time, Thanat Khoman, Thailand's long-serving and astute foreign minister since 1958, and other

---

3   See Sarasin Viraphol, *Directions in Thai Foreign Policy* (Singapore: Institute of Southeast Asian Studies, 1976); Wiwat Mungkandi and William Warren, eds, *A Century and a Half of Thai–American Relations* (Bangkok: Chulalongkorn University, 1982); Chulacheeb Chinwanno, 'Thai–Chinese Relations: Security and Strategic Partnership' (Working Paper No. 155, S Rajaratnam School of International Studies, Singapore, 2008).
4   See John LS Girling, 'The Guam Doctrine', *International Affairs* 46, no. 1 (January 1970): 48–62.
5   R Sean Randolph, *The United States and Thailand: Alliance Dynamics, 1950–1985* (Berkeley: Institute of East Asian Studies, University of California, 1986), 136; Leszek Buszynski, 'Thailand: The Erosion of a Balanced Foreign Policy', *Asian Survey* 22, no. 11 (November 1982): 1037–55.

like-minded diplomats began to realise that Thailand's former diplomacy of strategic dependence on the US was no longer tenable. He declared that: 'The United States has tried to raise doubts in our minds and it has succeeded. It has succeeded in raising doubts in its own mind.'[6] Thanat sought to find Thailand's own response to the changing international and regional circumstances. By 1968, Thanat started to call for a reduction of the US military presence in Thailand, and more nuanced and more balanced relations with other great powers, particularly the Soviet Union and the People's Republic of China (PRC). He proposed a so-called 'flexible diplomacy'. By 1969, the Thai Foreign Ministry had decided to reconsider the situation as 'the old era passes and the new one comes'.[7]

3.1.1. Thanat Khoman's Foreign Policy Options

The events of 1968 situated Thailand in a rapidly changing world, leading to a paradigmatic rupture in its foreign policy. Thanat Khoman was a leading voice in this newly emerging discourse of 'flexible diplomacy'. With great uncertainty about the role of the US in Southeast Asia, Thanat began to reassess policy options in case of American retrenchment. He came up with five possible options that can be described as: non-alignment, bandwagoning, neutralisation, bipolarisation and regional cooperation.

The first option was non-alignment or non-involvement. For Thanat, a 'policy of not being involved with one side or another' was 'not very easy', and:

> not a cure all, it is not even a safe device, because those who chose to follow a non-aligned policy have been the first to be subject to attacks and also to threatening dangers.

In his historical understanding, those non-aligned countries were 'those who suffered most' from their non-alignment strategy.[8] This was because the great powers were 'not willing to recognize that you are in the middle

---

6   Press release No. 52, Permanent Mission of Thailand to the United Nations, New York, 8 July 1968, quoted in Frank C Darling, 'Thailand: De-escalation and Uncertainty', *Asian Survey* 9, no. 2 (February 1969): 115.
7   'Thanat Khoman's Speech at Thammasat University', July 1969, in *China and Thailand, 1949–1983*, ed. RK Jain (New Delhi: Radiant Publishers, 1984), 161.
8   Thanat Khoman, 'Statement by Foreign Minister Thanat Khoman to Members of the Foreign Correspondents' Club of Thailand', Bangkok, 28 August 1968, in *Collected Interviews of H.E. Dr. Thanat Khoman, Minister of Foreign Affairs of the Kingdom of Thailand, Vol. 2: 1968* (Bangkok: Department of Information, Ministry of Foreign Affairs, 2014), 250.

and that they should come to trample upon you'. According to Thanat, the non-aligned countries were 'under boots, under the threat, under the guns, or right in the middle of the danger'. They were 'right in the firing line'.[9] As such, for Thanat non-alignment policy was not a suitable option.

The second option was bandwagoning, meaning a policy of coming to terms with the sources of danger themselves, especially the PRC. In Thanat's words, this option was to 'win their favors' and while equivalent to détente, Thanat at the time did not see it as such. In relation to this course of action, he questioned why Thailand should go 'straight to the sources of danger and try to reason with, argue with them, and to come to terms with them'. According to Thanat, while this offered a practical solution, from his recent experience, it was not yet possible. As a small state, he puzzled

> who are we … to dare to go direct to the source of danger? What result can we expect from having direct discussion, heart to heart discussions, and try to come to terms with the possible source of danger.[10]

For the time being, this option was not viable. However, Thanat still kept this policy option open for the future. As he succinctly asserted:

> We do not lose hope. If tomorrow, there are straws in the wind, and if the wind begins to blow and if the straws begin to fly, we may decide to go directly and face the dangers, and try to talk and see what is going to happen. But so far there has been no indication … There have been no straws and no winds.[11]

As a result, Thanat concluded:

> I don't expect that in the case of Thailand, we can produce the straws and make the wind blow. But we keep our fingers crossed and we keep in the back of our mind the possibility.[12]

---

9   Thanat, 'Statement by Foreign Minister Thanat Khoman to Members of the Foreign Correspondents' Club of Thailand', 250.
10 Thanat, 'Statement by Foreign Minister Thanat Khoman to Members of the Foreign Correspondents' Club of Thailand', 251.
11 Thanat, 'Statement by Foreign Minister Thanat Khoman to Members of the Foreign Correspondents' Club of Thailand', 251.
12 Thanat, 'Statement by Foreign Minister Thanat Khoman to Members of the Foreign Correspondents' Club of Thailand', 251.

This possibility was the option for détente with the communist powers in the near future, which would be the bedrock of his flexible diplomacy.

The third option was neutralisation, where the state officially declared its nonparticipation in any conflicts or wars. Thanat condemned 'liberals' in the West, who suggested that those Southeast Asian nations threatened by communist encroachments should 'bow to such threats and neutralize themselves'. In an address to the University of Minnesota on 22 October 1968, Thanat stated:

> The authors of neutralization plan who do not call for similar neutralization on the part of the Marxist regimes, contend that the actual and potential aggressors may grant them a lease of free national life. The least one can say is that such a proposal is entirely one-sided and does not take into account the realities of life in Southeast Asia where bitter struggles are going on between the expansionist forces and those which staunchly resist Communist expansion and conquest.[13]

For Thanat, this unilateral neutralisation policy was a worst-case scenario that he ruled out from the outset. He said that

> even if you join them because you cannot lick them, even if you join them, you are also licked. Even if you join them, you have to expect tanks, guns and troops to come to your doors. So it does not solve the problems … If you join them, you have to bow your heads very low, you have to follow the dogmas strictly to the letters and spirit. If you try to move a little bit away, you are either a revisionist or deviationist, with all the risks that accompany such qualifications.

Thanat admitted that, 'Of course you can survive; for how long, you don't know'.[14]

Thus, 'If you want to survive as free men, free nations', contended Thanat, 'neither of these solutions, non-alignment, win their favors, or even join them, will enable you to enjoy life as free peoples and free nations'.[15] The fourth option was what Thanat termed the 'bipolarisation' policy, which was predicated upon

---

13   'Address by Foreign Minister Thanat Khoman at the University of Minnesota, USA', 22 October 1968, in Jain, *China and Thailand*, 142.
14   Thanat, 'Statement by Foreign Minister Thanat Khoman to Members of the Foreign Correspondents' Club of Thailand', 253.
15   Thanat, 'Statement by Foreign Minister Thanat Khoman to Members of the Foreign Correspondents' Club of Thailand', 251.

the coexistence of two centers of powers, one respecting the other and one allowing the other to exert its rights and influence without undue interferences. If such a situation is not recognized and one side even goes so far to seek the destruction of the other, such a proposition becomes wholly impractical.[16]

In a Southeast Asian context, this policy of 'bipolarisation' meant that there should be two poles or centres of power – namely the US and the PRC. Both would be obliged to guarantee peaceful coexistence among secondary or small states. However, for Thanat, this 'bipolarisation' policy 'didn't work, because China didn't play the game'.[17] Elsewhere, he contended:

neither a neutralization plan nor even a bipolarization policy has been able to guarantee [small states] a peaceful and free existence, because some parties have shown themselves to be unwilling to play the game.[18]

Thanat's fifth, and perhaps most reasonable, option – and what Thailand was 'trying to perform now' – was regional cooperation and regional solidarity in Southeast Asia.[19] Thanat said that Thailand was at the forefront of developing regional organisations such as the Association of Southeast Asian Nations (ASEAN) – which was established by the Bangkok Declaration on 8 August 1967 – in Southeast Asia, and also the Asian Pacific Council (ASPAC) in the Asia-Pacific region. These groupings could offset the risks of 'the withdrawal of the United States from this part of the world'.[20] Thanat suggested:

we are doing this to enable us to deal more effectively and more adequately, not only with our foes, potential and actual, but also with our friends … We can deal on a more equal footing and more equal basis with our friends.

---

16 'Address by Foreign Minister Thanat Khoman at the University of Minnesota, USA', 22 October 1968, in Jain, *China and Thailand*, 141.
17 Thanat Khoman, 'Transcript of H.E. Thanat Khoman, Ministry of Foreign Affairs, interviewed by Edwin Newman of WNBC Television', New York, 2 November 1968, in *Collected Interviews of H.E. Dr. Thanat Khoman, Vol. 2: 1968*, 294.
18 'Address by Foreign Minister Thanat Khoman at the University of Minnesota, USA', 22 October 1968, in Jain, *China and Thailand*, 143.
19 Thanat, 'Statement by Foreign Minister Thanat Khoman to Members of the Foreign Correspondents' Club of Thailand', 251.
20 Thanat Khoman, 'Transcript of an Interview given by H.E. Thanat Khoman, Ministry of Foreign Affairs of Thailand to Mr. Friedhelm Kemna, Southeast Asia Correspondent of the Die Welt of Hamburg and Berlin at the Foreign Ministry', Bangkok, 29 November 1968, in *Collected Interviews of H.E. Dr. Thanat Khoman, Vol. 2: 1968*, 308.

Thanat claimed that this possibility was 'the practical and pragmatic policy'.[21]

In his other interviews and speeches, Thanat also included the second option of détente with communist powers as one of the practical and pragmatic policies as well.[22] Both policies – regional cooperation and détente – would be mutually constitutive and inextricably intertwined. However, subsequently, the former was less strategically and discursively important than the latter. Above all, these foreign policies required Thailand to rely on itself, and to work with other nations in Asia-Pacific. As he put it in December 1968:

> Now we in Asia do not want to rely on outside powers. We want to rely on ourselves and that is why Thailand for instance has been developing its own national strength in many fields, political, economic, social, cultural fields also. Thailand … has been making strenuous efforts to develop regional solidarity not only in Southeast Asia but in the Asian and Pacific region with Japan for instance.[23]

To put it differently, by 1968 Thanat attempted to lay out the basis for individual and regional self-reliance, thereby replacing excessive dependence on external powers. Thanat repeatedly claimed that this was a change in Thai foreign policy, and we can agree that the salience of these policy options was part and parcel of the new discourse of flexible diplomacy from 1968 on.

The chapter now turns to examine 'flexible diplomacy', a concept that Thanat coined in 1968. At the outset, flexible diplomacy comprised three main characteristics or discourses: increasing doubts on Americanism, regional cooperation and cohesiveness, and détente with the great powers. As Thanat Khoman summarised:

> There are three big question marks. One is the uncertainty of the future attitude and policy of the US, which has been created by the Americans themselves through their mass-media, academic

---

21 Thanat, 'Statement by Foreign Minister Thanat Khoman to Members of the Foreign Correspondents' Club of Thailand', 254.
22 Thanat Khoman, 'Interview given by Foreign Minister Thanat Khoman to Miss Frances Starner of the Far Eastern Economic Review and to Mr. Donald Kirk of the Washington Star', Bangkok, 23 August 1968, in *Collected Interviews of H.E. Dr. Thanat Khoman, Vol. 2: 1968*, 245.
23 Thanat Khoman, 'Transcript of an Interview given by H.E. Thanat Khoman to Mr. Yasuo Hozumi, an NHK Correspondent of Japan at his Residence', Bangkok, 10 December 1968, in *Collected Interviews of H.E. Dr. Thanat Khoman, Vol. 2: 1968*, 314.

and political channels ... The second question mark was what will be the future policy of Communist China. And the third question mark was what we are trying to do to fill the power vacuum created by the withdrawal of western colonial powers to try to forge a new working relationship in order to prevent the Asian Communist powers from filling that vacuum with their own authority. We have had many set-backs with ASA [the Association of Southeast Asia][24] and ASEAN. What will be the outcome of our efforts to create regional solidarity and cooperation? All these questions should be dealt with together.[25]

3.1.2. Discourse of Anti-Americanism

The first discourse involved increased scepticism of American policy. Thanat began to identify the danger of being drawn into a highly dependent relationship with a single world power. An architect of the Thai–US security alliance in the 1960s, he had originally believed the US presence to be beneficial. The objectives of the US and Thailand were aligned during the Vietnam War. That is, containing communism. Thanat said that he had advocated 'close cooperation with the United States because our objectives were similar. I did not want, and still do not want, Thailand to be swamped by Communism'. But in 1968, for Thanat:

> the United States, for domestic reasons, was no longer able to pursue that objective ... It became obvious that the objective to resist [the communists], under which Thailand had joined with the United States, was no longer there. The objective was changed on the part of the US. *It was not we who changed; it was the US that changed.* I felt that the presence of American forces in Thailand had lost its justification.[26]

---

24 ASA was a nascent regional organisation formed by the Philippines, Thailand and the Federation of Malaya (nowadays Malaysia) on 31 July 1961. It was the predecessor to ASEAN.
25 Thanat Khoman, 'Interview given by Foreign Minister Thanat Khoman to Beryl Bernay of the Westinghouse Broadcasting Company, Derek Davies of the Far Eastern Economic Review, Joonghee Park of the Central Daily News of South Korea, Jung Suk Lee of the Dong-a Ilbo of South Korea and Kim Willenson of UPI', Bangkok, 26 March 1969, in *Collected Interviews of H.E. Dr. Thanat Khoman, Minister of Foreign Affairs of the Kingdom of Thailand, Vol. 3: 1969* (Bangkok: Department of Information, Ministry of Foreign Affairs, 2014), 490.
26 Thanat Khoman, interview, *The Bangkok Post,* 21 July 1976. My emphasis.

In early March 1968, Thanat responded to possible US disengagement or withdrawal from Vietnam and the region with irritation. 'Some people in the United States are advocating that the United States should get out', he exclaimed, 'I think those people, who talk so loudly about withdrawal, are not quite realistic'.[27] He said that:

> the recent experience that we have got from our friends … opened our eyes … We here in Thailand, and I should say in Asia in general, have been rather innocent and naïve. We have had a rather simple or simpleton approach that peoples are either friends or foes. That is not so. There may be foes among our friends [by which Thanat meant some senators and congressmen as well as various media].[28]

Furthermore, between 1968 and 1969, Thanat emphatically complained that the prospect of American retrenchment from Southeast Asia was not compatible with the image, status, prestige and responsibility of the US as a superpower. For him, this would inevitably lead to an erosion of American power and credibility, both in Southeast Asia and in the international system in general. First and foremost, the effects would be directly felt by the US itself. In August 1968, he argued that:

> [the] US remains a great power. But if the domestic public opinion in the United States should force the administration to forsake its responsibilities in other parts of the world, then of course the effects will be felt by none other than the United States itself, and the American people. Because then, the US will not be able to perform the role of a great power. Because if you are a great power, whether you like it or not, you will have to bear certain

---

27 Thanat Khoman, 'Interview given by Foreign Minister Thanat Khoman to Mr. Shackford Howards, Reporter for Scripps papers at the Ministry of Foreign Affairs', Bangkok, 6 March 1968, in *Collected Interviews of H.E. Dr. Thanat Khoman, Vol. 2: 1968*, 192. In an interview with a United Press International reporter in March 1968, Thanat answered:

> the people who should feel concerned in the first place, are not the Thais or the Southeast Asians, but the American people because they are well developed enough intellectually, morally and physically to understand what such a decision would mean for the United States. We are a small people around here; we are not the defeated people of the great powers. Quite frankly, I do not see much choice before the United States or before us: either keep on doing what we all have started doing or else call it quit and leave the whole place to the Communists, just to satisfy certain senators, certain newspapers and radio and television commentators. That is all there is to it.

Thanat Khoman, 'Interview given by Foreign Minister Thanat Khoman to Mr. Arnold Dibble of U.P.I. at the Ministry of Foreign Affairs', Bangkok, 11 March 1968, in *Collected Interviews of H.E. Dr. Thanat Khoman, Vol. 2: 1968*, 195–96.
28 Thanat, 'Statement by Foreign Minister Thanat Khoman to Members of the Foreign Correspondents' Club of Thailand', 252.

responsibilities. You cannot shake off your responsibilities and remain a great power or otherwise your influence, image, your presence will be eroded.[29]

On another day, he again stressed the requirements of great power responsibility:

> As a leading power in the non-Communist camp, if the United States were to say well, alright, we decided to retrench ourselves and recoil into our own hell, in 'our fortress America', the major effect will be felt by the United States and by the American nation, even more than by the rest of the world … If that were to be the case, then the United States will have relinquished its role as a major power, a world power, to become only a regional power … Would that be advantageous or disadvantageous to the United States' position as a world power?[30]

Even after Richard Nixon won the presidential election, Thanat warned of the degenerating effects of 'neo-isolationism' in the US. In December 1968, for example, he stated emphatically:

> a world power like the United States in my opinion can afford to isolate itself only if it renounces its role as a world power. I don't think a world power can retreat into Fortress America.[31]

Although he had discerned that the Nixon administration would reduce military involvement in Vietnam, Thanat still wanted to believe that the reduction would be gradual. In his opinion:

---

29 Thanat Khoman, 'Interview given by Foreign Minister Thanat Khoman to Murray Fromson of CBS News', Bangkok, 22 August 1968, in *Collected Interviews of H.E. Dr. Thanat Khoman, Vol. 2: 1968*, 240.
30 Thanat, 'Interview given by Foreign Minister Thanat Khoman to Miss Frances Starner of the Far Eastern Economic Review and to Mr. Donald Kirk of the Washington Star', 243.
31 Thanat Khoman, 'Transcript of an Interview given by Foreign Minister Thanat Khoman to Mr. William Pinwill, a staff correspondent for the Australian Broadcasting Commission', Bangkok, 9 December 1968, in *Collected Interviews of H.E. Dr. Thanat Khoman, Vol. 2: 1968*, 312; see also Thanat, 'Transcript of an Interview given by H.E. Thanat Khoman, Ministry of Foreign Affairs of Thailand to Mr. Friedhelm Kemna, Southeast Asia Correspondent of the Die Welt of Hamburg and Berlin at the Foreign Ministry', 308; Thanat, 'Transcript of an Interview given by H.E. Thanat Khoman to Mr. Yasuo Hozumi, an NHK Correspondent of Japan at his Residence', 313–14; Thanat Khoman, 'Transcript of an Interview given by H.E. Thanat Khoman to Mr. Wortelboer, Representative of KRO Television of Holland', Bangkok, 16 December 1968, in *Collected Interviews of H.E. Dr. Thanat Khoman, Vol. 2: 1968*, 316.

American troops will be withdrawn from South Vietnam in proper time. The question is to withdraw them in a gradual and appropriate way and not in a sudden massive pull-out because then all the efforts and sacrifice which have been made for many years with the cost of so much money and so many lives may be lost.[32]

Subsequently, Thanat suggested that Thailand could no longer rely on America's protecting presence, and should pursue self-reliance. In his speech on Tokyo television on 25 February 1969, Thanat said:

> there must be a recognition and perhaps acknowledgement of the fact that the intervention of outside powers in dealing with Asian problems may not be the most effective nor the most desirable device for their settlement. Either those powers may become tired of the exacting ordeals or their domestic public opinion may find the burden of responsibility too heavy for their taste … We would do well, therefore, to acknowledge this new mood and prepare ourselves accordingly.[33]

In July 1969, Thanat relayed the same concept of self-reliance at Thammasat University:

> Thailand must consider the situation as the old era passes and the new one comes and above all we must strengthen ourselves to meet possible dangers from all sides. For with the possibility that the US would withdraw from the region, we must not continue to rely on others. We should be as self-reliant as we can. However, we must cooperate with all nations on an equal basis and status.[34]

In light of talk of American disengagement, put forward in the Nixon Doctrine in July 1969, Thanat stressed a policy of self-reliance and the need for an American military withdrawal. He said 'Thailand has been practicing this policy of self-reliance for many years already'.[35] When President Nixon visited Bangkok after his famous declaration of the Nixon Doctrine at Guam on 28 July 1969, he reassured the Thai Government

---

32 Thanat, 'Transcript of an Interview given by H.E. Thanat Khoman to Mr. Wortelboer, Representative of KRO Television of Holland', 316.
33 Quoted in John LS Girling, 'Thailand's New Course', *Pacific Affairs* 42, no. 3 (Fall 1969): 349.
34 'Thanat Khoman's Speech at Thammasat University', July 1969, in Jain, *China and Thailand*, 161.
35 Thanat Khoman, 'Interview given by H.E. The Minister of Foreign Affairs to a Group of Newspapers' Editors from Australia at the Ministry of Foreign Affairs', Bangkok, 30 July 1969, in *Collected Interviews of H.E. Dr. Thanat Khoman, Vol. 3: 1969*, 562.

of America's commitment to protect Thailand's security, as promised in the SEATO obligation (1954) and the Thanat–Rusk joint communiqué of 1962:

> We will honor our obligations under that treaty. We will honor them not simply because we have to, because of the words that we have signed, but because we believe in those words, and particularly believe in them in association with a proud and a strong people, the people of Thailand. We have been together in the past, we are together in the present, and *the United States will stand proudly with Thailand against those threaten it from abroad, or from within.*[36]

In response to Nixon's pledge, which seemed to be in contradiction to the Guam Doctrine, Thanat proclaimed:

> We told President Nixon that Thailand is not going to be another Vietnam. We told him that we never asked for American soldiers to come and fight in defense of Thailand. We pledged that we will not ask for American soldiers to come and fight in defense of Thailand in an insurgent war. This includes even a covert invasion of the kind North Vietnam is carrying out against South Vietnam.[37]

He constantly repeated that the existence of American troops in Thailand were specifically intended for the Vietnam War, rather than for a local fight against communist insurgencies in Thailand.[38]

Thanat, first of all, had raised doubts about the US's commitment to Thailand. As he told members of the Foreign Correspondents' Club of Thailand on 19 August 1969:

---

36 Quoted in Randolph, *The United States and Thailand*, 138. My emphasis.
37 *New York Times*, 20 August 1969.
38 For example, Thanat said that:

> The purpose for the American forces stationed here in Thailand has been linked with the Vietnam War. American forces in Thailand … are not here to help Thailand defend itself against Communist activities. American forces are here in Thailand to fight the war in Vietnam from Thailand and not to engage physically in fighting Communist activities here in Thailand.

Thanat Khoman, 'Interview given by H.E. Thanat Khoman Foreign Minister of Thailand to Bernard Kalb of CBS', Bangkok, 17 July 1969, in *Collected Interviews of H.E. Dr. Thanat Khoman, Vol. 3: 1969*, 551.

> The partners to the Treaty will carry out that treaty obligation only if their national interests are concordant with us, but not otherwise. There are many escape clauses, called by such names as 'constitutional processes' and so on and so forth. So, we believe that we can rely on ourselves, and only when our national interests are concordant with the national interests of others can we expect other nations to carry out, to implement, their obligation, not otherwise.[39]

Consequently, 'relations between Thailand and the United States', Thanat suggested, 'will evolve toward a more selective basis'.[40]

Secondly, Thanat began to press for the pullout of American forces. On 20 August 1969, he formally proposed to US ambassador Leonard Unger that the process of 'immediate evacuation' of 49,000 US military personnel stationed in Thailand had to commence.[41] Two days later, he announced that negotiations on American withdrawal would start soon. This idea was not so appealing to the military elites who did not want US troops to leave the country, and felt that the security of the regime was inextricably linked to the US military presence. The military government, led by Prime Minister Field Marshal Thanom Kittikachorn disagreed with the urgency of the issue, and instead suggested a mutually agreed-upon 'gradual reduction'. On 25 August, Prime Minister Thanom said that the discussions had not yet got underway: 'a mutual agreement must be reached first'. The next day, a joint Thai–American statement stated that 'talks to arrange for a gradual reduction of level of United States forces in Thailand consistent with the assessment of both governments of the security situation would be held in the near future'.[42] On 3 September, Thailand and the US began a series of bilateral negotiations, led by Thai Foreign Minister Thanat and US Ambassador Leonard Unger, to discuss this gradual reduction of US troops in Thailand. During the talks, Thanat pulled back from his initial position towards a more gradualist position.

By 8 September, Thanat declared that the Thai Government was 'willing to discuss the prolongation of the presence of US forces in Thailand as desired by the US government'.[43] The first pullout of troops, which was

---

39 Quoted in Randolph, *The United States and Thailand*, 127.
40 Thanat's speech, American Chamber of Commerce address, 15 July 1970, *Foreign Affairs Bulletin* 9 (June-July 1970): 507. Quoted in Randolph, *The United States and Thailand*, 137.
41 Louis Heren, 'US and Thailand to Discuss Troop Withdrawals', *Times* (London), 23 August 1969.
42 Quoted in Randolph, *The United States and Thailand*, 140.
43 Quoted in Alessandro Casella, 'US–Thai Relations', *The World Today* 26, no. 3 (March 1970): 123.

essentially a symbolic gesture, was proclaimed on 30 September 1969, stating that 6,000 US military personnel were to be withdrawn from Thailand by July 1970. They were to be pulled out 'as expeditiously as possible consistent with the operational requirements related to the Vietnam conflict'.[44] Nevertheless, there was no mention of any schedule for the withdrawal of the remaining 42,000 American forces. Another 10,000 were withdrawn the following year, reducing the total US forces in Thailand to 32,000 by June 1971.

While the Thai military elites attached to the Cold War discursive hegemony preferred the preponderance of American troops in Thailand, Thanat consistently pushed for the withdrawal of American military forces from Thailand. As he summed up, the Thailand-initiated withdrawal program for the American forces had 'improved Thailand's position and given Thailand greater freedom in the conduct of its foreign policy for its own national interests and the interests of the region'.[45] By 1968, the discourse of scepticism of Americanism, or even anti-Americanism, was widening and deepening in Thai politics.

3.1.3. Discourse of Regional Cooperation

The second discourse was regional cooperation and cohesiveness. From 1968, Thanat proposed that if the US were to withdraw from the region, a power vacuum would open up. In addition to the policy of national self-reliance, he forcefully recommended regional cooperation, solidarity and cohesiveness as an attempt to avoid any contending powers filling the strategic gap or seeking their own domination in the region. As he stated on television in December 1968:

> this is why Thailand has been in the forefront in advocating greater cooperative efforts among the nations of this area, to work together, to think together, to join together in common endeavours, to preserve peace and to safeguard our national and regional interests in this part of the world.[46]

---

44 Clark D Neher, 'Thailand: The Politics of Continuity', *Asian Survey* 10, no. 2 (February 1970): 166.
45 'FM Softens Line on Red Bloc', *Bangkok Post*, 29 December 1970, 1.
46 Thanat, 'Transcript of an Interview given by H.E. Thanat Khoman to Mr. Wortelboer, Representative of KRO Television of Holland', 317.

In other words, efforts to build such regional groupings as ASEAN and ASPAC were meant to 'outweigh the withdrawal of the United States' from Southeast Asia. As he pointed out, 'whether the US stays around here or not, it is in our interest to develop regional cooperation'.[47] To a certain extent, the prospect of American disengagement, according to Thanat, provided a 'sense of urgency' as well as 'a greater sense of responsibility' for countries in the Asia-Pacific region to shape their own destinies, and to protect their own security and national interests.[48] The ultimate aim of regional cohesiveness was to obtain a negotiating position vis-à-vis the great powers. Although still 'very young, very tender, very soft, and perhaps very inefficient', a regional grouping was for Thanat an 'entity of respectable size' – with more than 200 million people. As he explained:

> We are doing this to enable us to deal more effectively and more adequately, not only with our foes, potential and actual, but also with our friends. If one is better organized, our friends will respect one more. They will not trample upon your foot, step on your toes, they will listen to your voices and your opinions, and they will respect your interests. If you are separated … you do not count much. But if you are joined together, becoming a respectable and sizable entity in terms of population of resources, and also of prestige, then you become somebody … We are doing this so that we can cope with foes and we can deal on a more equal footing and more equal basis with our friends.[49]

Thus, by working together, the region could build a larger or cohesive 'power base' which would 'afford us an entity which can cooperate more closely with friendly and like-minded nations on a more equal footing, to ensure peace and stability in the region'.[50] Due to its respectable size and influence, a regional grouping could also have a greater say in global

---

47 Thanat, 'Transcript of an Interview given by H.E. Thanat Khoman, Ministry of Foreign Affairs of Thailand to Mr. Friedhelm Kemna, Southeast Asia Correspondent of the Die Welt of Hamburg and Berlin at the Foreign Ministry', 308; Thanat Khoman, 'Interview given by Foreign Minister Thanat Khoman to Terrence Smith of the New York Times', Bangkok, 18 September 1968, in *Collected Interviews of H.E. Dr. Thanat Khoman, Vol. 2: 1968*, 267.
48 Thanat, 'Interview given by Foreign Minister Thanat Khoman to Murray Fromson of CBS News', 240.
49 Thanat, 'Statement by Foreign Minister Thanat Khoman to Members of the Foreign Correspondents' Club of Thailand', 254.
50 Thanat Khoman, 'Interview given by Foreign Minister Thanat Khoman to the Nishi-Nippon Shimbun, the Chunichi Shimbun, the Tokyo Shimbun, and the Hokkaido Shimbun', Bangkok, 4 October 1968, in *Collected Interviews of H.E. Dr. Thanat Khoman, Vol. 2: 1968*, 280. See also Thanat, 'Transcript of H.E. Thanat Khoman, Ministry of Foreign Affairs, interviewed by Edwin Newman of WNBC Television', 291.

politics and deal adequately with the great powers. For Thanat, his idea of 'collective political defense' was not, and could not be, a military organisation. As he reiterated:

> none of us in Southeast Asia can be considered a military power: no military potential, no industry to support a military power. Therefore, we must use other means than military means to shore up our positions, our independence and our security. The only available means are diplomatic and political ones, political consultations, political and economic cooperation.

'Anyone who has any sense', Thanat concluded, 'can see very well that ASEAN cannot and will not be turned into a military organization'.[51]

In contrast to a collective defence system like SEATO, a new regional grouping would be based on a system that Thanat termed 'collective political defense', not military, but political, economic, socio-cultural and technical cooperation with the neighbouring countries. As Thanat observed:

> I do not think that military alliance is an answer to the problems ... Because we in this part of the world, we are smaller nations, we have no military potential, and even if we were to pull together our military resources, it will not be sufficient to stop or to prevent military incursions by big nations like Communist China. Therefore, we believe that we should try to deter the other side, the aggressive regimes, from taking military actions through political means, through building up of regional solidarity and regional cohesiveness rather than expecting results from military means.[52]

Thus, from 1968 Thanat sought an alternative to the former policy of dependence on the American security alliance by trying to build up a non-communist counterweight in Southeast Asia through 'regional cooperation'. Nevertheless, over time, he grappled with the pressing question of American retrenchment by attempting to lessen the hostility of the communist powers, particularly Communist China. In March 1969, while Thanat still discerned that the PRC had aggressive intentions

---

51 Thanat Khoman, 'Press Interview at Singapore Airport given by Foreign Minister Thanat Khoman', 8 August 1968, in *Collected Interviews of H.E. Dr. Thanat Khoman, Vol. 2: 1968*, 234.
52 Thanat, 'Transcript of an Interview given by H.E. Thanat Khoman to Mr. Wortelboer, Representative of KRO Television of Holland', 321–22.

against Thailand, he was shifting the discourse of regional cooperation to help 'induce Communist China to come out and work with us'. He said the PRC might even agree upon true peaceful coexistence.[53]

Crucially, therefore, Thanat suggested détente with the communist powers before the promulgation of the Nixon Doctrine. That is to say, from early 1969 the discourse of regional grouping was already signposting and anticipating a future détente with the communists. In February 1969, Thanat said:

> the key to a lasting peace in Asia rests in cooperation among the non-Communist nations. Only if we succeed in working together among the non-Communist nations will the Communist nations come and talk to us. The Communist nations will never agree to discuss and build peace unless they know that the other nations of Asia want peace and that they are organized to preserve and maintain it.[54]

In the *Times* article in August 1969, titled 'Withdrawal and a New Era', Thanat wrote:

> Thus far there has been no dialogue with and no change of heart on the part of the Asian Communists. Nevertheless, renewed efforts must be made to establish, at least in the initial stage. Such efforts can hope to meet with success only if the Asian nations organize themselves in a constructive manner. They will thus be in a better position to persuade the Communist reactionaries to forsake war for a more productive and mutually beneficial collaboration.[55]

This required 'some readjustment' of attitudes within Thailand to 'envisage a further widening of collaboration. This would include cooperation with the Marxist regimes if they should relinquish their policy of expansion and domination'.[56] Thus, the practical and pragmatic discourse of détente with the USSR and the PRC loomed larger than the more aspirational discourse of regional cohesiveness and solidarity.

---

53 'Thanat Khoman's Address at a Luncheon hosted by the American Management Association in Bangkok', March 1969, in Jain, *China and Thailand*, 156.
54 Thanat Khoman, 'Interview given by Foreign Minister Thanat Khoman to Choi Ho of the Chosan Daily of South Korea', Bangkok, 27 February 1969, in *Collected Interviews of H.E. Dr. Thanat Khoman, Vol. 3: 1969*, 450.
55 Thanat Khoman, 'Withdrawal and a New Era', *Times* (London), 18 August 1969.
56 Thanat, 'Withdrawal and a New Era'.

3.1.4. Discourse of Détente

The third discourse was détente with the communists. Between 1968 and 1969, Thanat began to rethink how Thailand should choose to live with the communists. One of his policy options was détente. While this was not deemed an option at the time, he believed that it would be a 'practical and pragmatic policy' in the future. He noted that any mention of opening dialogue with the Soviet Union and the PRC tended to be misinterpreted as a Thai foreign policy moving toward a neutralist position. He contended that this was a 'complete mistake'. It was 'not inevitable that the Communist aggressors would continue to be aggressive'.[57] Thanat suggested that Thailand should prepare a policy to deal with the communist powers and that it would be better if Thailand adopted a 'practical and pragmatic policy'. In particular, this meant being 'more flexible in its policy towards China'. To date, Thanat admitted that it was the Chinese who showed no desire to meet. Yet, 'if Beijing were to show any indication that it is approachable, I myself would recommend my Government to sit with them, to talk with them. But there has been no such sign'.[58] In the future, he continued:

> when Communist China should come back to its senses, and would want to deal with other nations on an intelligent, reasonable basis, Southeast Asia shall not and should not be caught unprepared to deal with it, to preserve peace and strengthen our national independence.[59]

By late 1968, Thanat had reassessed Thai foreign policy in order to best deal with the communist powers, and decided that Thailand could pursue two separate approaches. On the one hand, Thailand could pursue regional cohesiveness in order to establish collective negotiating powers vis-à-vis the communists. On the other hand, Thanat began to contemplate a bilateral approach of détente with the communists.

On 26 February 1969, at a press conference in Tokyo, Thanat Khoman spoke of Thailand's willingness to have 'serious talks' with the communist countries, especially the PRC. This was the first time Thanat advocated

---

57 Thanat, 'Transcript of H.E. Thanat Khoman, Ministry of Foreign Affairs, interviewed by Edwin Newman of WNBC Television', 290.
58 Thanat Khoman, 'Interview given by Foreign Minister Thanat Khoman to Peter Kumpa of the Baltimore Sun, Ian Wright of the Guardian (London) and John Sterling of the London Observer', Bangkok, 10 February 1969, in *Collected Interviews of H.E. Dr. Thanat Khoman, Vol. 3: 1969*, 428.
59 Thanat, 'Interview given by Foreign Minister Thanat Khoman to Miss Frances Starner of the Far Eastern Economic Review and to Mr. Donald Kirk of the Washington Star', 245.

the opening of an unprecedented Thai–Chinese dialogue. Though it was not directly aimed at paving the way for diplomatic relations, this was a 'peace offensive' towards the PRC. Thanat asserted that Thailand was not 'anti-Communist or anti-Chinese'. The objective of the negotiations was to find out 'what we can do to live in peace'. 'To show that Thailand is not anti-Communist and anti-Chinese', Thanat stressed, 'we are prepared to sit down and talk – and have meaningful discussion – with Beijing to establish peaceful coexistence'.[60] He contended that 'Thailand wants a dialogue and expect China to respond to a dialogue'. In Bangkok, when he was asked by the foreign press, Thanat replied:

> By saying that we are willing to sit down and meet them – enter into contact with them – we want to show that we are willing to take responsibility in our hands and try to deal with the problem ourselves, not depend on the other nations to try to solve the problem for us.[61]

The foreign minister also reassured foreign reporters that Thai foreign policy was not anti-Chinese. On the contrary, it was the Chinese who were 'anti-Thai', as illustrated by the alleged declaration of Foreign Minister Marshal Chen Yi that the PRC would launch a guerrilla war against Thailand. Thanat said that he wanted to know what China's genuine intentions and motivations were. Indeed, for him, this was the ultimate purpose of the decision to engage with the Chinese – to clarify exactly what they meant by declaring war on Thailand. 'We want to know whether that was what they intended to do, whether they intend to pursue that, and what were their motivations.'[62] Thanat wanted to sound out what possibilities there might be for peaceful coexistence between the two countries.

Thai foreign policy towards communism should thus become 'more flexible'.[63] In March, in a television interview, he strenuously urged that he was:

---

60 Thanat Khoman, 'Interview given by Foreign Minister Thanat Khoman to the Press', Bangkok, 26 February 1969, in *Collected Interviews of H.E. Dr. Thanat Khoman, Vol. 3: 1969*, 619; 'Foreign Minister Thanat Khoman's Statement at a Press Conference in Tokyo, 26 February 1969', in Jain, *China and Thailand*, 155.
61 Thanat, 'Interview given by Foreign Minister Thanat Khoman to Choi Ho of the Chosan Daily of South Korea', 452–53.
62 Thanat, 'Interview given by Foreign Minister Thanat Khoman to Choi Ho of the Chosan Daily of South Korea', 453.
63 Thanat, 'Interview given by Foreign Minister Thanat Khoman to Peter Kumpa of the Baltimore Sun, Ian Wright of the Guardian (London) and John Sterling of the London Observer', 428.

> willing to meet a representative of Beijing at any place, at any time, if such a meeting would help bring peace in Asia. It was necessary to draw China out of her isolation so that she could become a member of the Asian family.[64]

In other words, by early 1969, Thanat made a public offer to meet with the representatives of the PRC at international venues.

Thanat also said he would be prepared to send an emissary to Beijing, and hypothetically suggested that MR Kukrit Pramoj, a well-renowned politician and influential publisher of the *Siam Rath* newspaper, or Klaew Norapati, a key socialist member of the Parliament, might be suitable emissaries to Beijing. However, Kukrit abruptly dismissed the whole idea of talking with the PRC as utterly useless:

> If the purpose of talking with China is to ask China questions on why they want to destroy Thailand, then it is a waste of time, since we clearly know the answers, that is, that Thailand is on the American side.[65]

Thanat repeatedly denied any change in Thai foreign policy in the media. He said that the goal of foreign policy, which remained the protection of Thailand's independence and survival, had never changed. However, he argued that the means to that particular end needed to be adapted to cope with the changing global contexts. As he put it:

> realizing the present situation, the changes in world powers' positions and policies, we had to adopt a more direct approach in our policy. It does not mean that we have changed our policy. Our policy remains the same. We shall never depart from the principles underlying our moral and intellectual stand.

What was different now however was that

> a defensive policy is no longer possible. We have no other choice but to go ahead and face the trouble as it comes, to go to the source and try to meet the contingencies which may arise.[66]

---

64 'Thanat Khoman's Statement in a Television Interview, 2 March 1969', in Jain, *China and Thailand*, 155.
65 *Siam Rath,* 19 March 1969.
66 Thanat Khoman, 'Post-Vietnam Period – A New Era for Asia?, An Address by Foreign Minister Thanat Khoman to Member of the Thai-American Technical Cooperation Association', Bangkok, 31 March 1969, in *Collected Statements of H.E. Dr. Thanat Khoman, Minister of Foreign Affairs of the Kingdom of Thailand, Vol. 5: November 1968–October 1969* (Bangkok: Department of Information, Ministry of Foreign Affairs, 2014), 490–91.

In other words, Thailand had to go:

> [to] the source of the danger and try to argue, to reason with them, and to find out whether there can be any possibility for them to relent in their militant policies or to have peaceful coexistence and cooperation with us.[67]

He termed it a more 'forward approach'. Suppose the Chinese Government were to respond in kind, Thanat argued that the Thai Government would not hesitate to meet with the Chinese to end the hostile situation and to return to 'the status of 1954–55 when, at the Bandung Conference there was an attempt to create a certain sense of solidarity and peaceful coexistence'; he reaffirmed that this change is not a 'personal policy of the Foreign Minister but the official policy of the Government of Thailand'.[68] Asking what would happen if the Communist Chinese asked Thailand to recognise them, Thanat replied that 'the question of the recognition of either Beijing or Taiwan as the legitimate government is not a question for outside powers to resolve but for the Chinese to resolve themselves'.[69] For Thanat, the main point at the moment was to find out whether there were any possibilities for peaceful coexistence between Thailand and the PRC. Thanat publicly proclaimed that Thailand was willing to talk with the communists, by hoping that 'in our lifetime we may see the change of policy *from enmity to a more friendly cooperation*'.[70]

In brief, the recurring discourse of flexible diplomacy that Thailand embarked upon in the late 1960s was how to act upon in a so-called post-American world. It sought to deal with the communist powers in a more balanced and flexible diplomacy in a rapidly changing global–regional complex. As Thanat had suggested provisionally in September 1968:

---

[67] Thanat, 'Interview given by Foreign Minister Thanat Khoman to Beryl Bernay of the Westinghouse Broadcasting Company, Derek Davies of the Far Eastern Economic Review, Joonghee Park of the Central Daily News of South Korea, Jung Suk Lee of the Dong-a Ilbo of South Korea and Kim Willenson of UPI', 487.
[68] Thanat, 'Interview given by Foreign Minister Thanat Khoman to Beryl Bernay of the Westinghouse Broadcasting Company, Derek Davies of the Far Eastern Economic Review, Joonghee Park of the Central Daily News of South Korea, Jung Suk Lee of the Dong-a Ilbo of South Korea and Kim Willenson of UPI', 489.
[69] Thanat, 'Interview given by Foreign Minister Thanat Khoman to Beryl Bernay of the Westinghouse Broadcasting Company, Derek Davies of the Far Eastern Economic Review, Joonghee Park of the Central Daily News of South Korea, Jung Suk Lee of the Dong-a Ilbo of South Korea and Kim Willenson of UPI', 488.
[70] Thanat, 'Post-Vietnam Period – A New Era for Asia?, An Address by Foreign Minister Thanat Khoman to Member of the Thai-American Technical Cooperation Association', 491. My emphasis.

> What we are trying to do is to have political cooperation not only between the countries of Southeast Asia but between the countries of Southeast Asia and *the outside powers, like the US, like the Soviet Union and in the future, I don't know when, with Communist China.* This is what we are working at. We hope that within our life time, we will be able to see a new basis of cooperation first between the countries of Southeast Asia, next between the countries of Southeast Asia and the outside world on a more equal footing than it is the case now.[71]

This reappraisal of policy discourses brought about a reassessment of Thailand's relations with the communist powers in the 1970s. While Thanat constantly said that there was no change in the direction of Thai foreign policy, this new course sought to shift toward diplomatic flexibility and resilience. This unwittingly contributed to a new discourse of flexible diplomacy or détente with the communist powers.

3.2. Institutional Practices: Institute of Foreign Affairs and the Emergence of Détente Proponents

> Old diplomats never die they give way to the young ones.
> – Thanat Khoman, foreign minister[72]

The discourse of détente also had a non-discursive, institutional dimension. This section examines the institutional practices of diplomatic training, through the newly established Institute of Foreign Affairs at the Foreign Ministry. As one of the key sites and process of subject formation, the institute was central to constructing the identities of those of détente proponents in Thailand.

In the literature, there are two broad interpretations regarding the role of the Ministry of Foreign Affairs (MFA). The first is what I call a personal(ised) politics paradigm. Many scholars claim that the Foreign

---

71 Thanat, 'Interview given by Foreign Minister Thanat Khoman to Terrence Smith of the New York Times', 268. My emphasis.
72 Thanat Khoman, 'An Address by Foreign Minister Thanat Khoman to Junior Chamber International (JCI)', Bangkok, 12 June 1968, in *Collected Statements of H.E. Dr. Thanat Khoman, Minister of Foreign Affairs of the Kingdom of Thailand, Vol. 4, October 1967–October 1968* (Bangkok: Department of Information, Ministry of Foreign Affairs, 2014), 431.

Ministry had a relatively minor institutional role and influence in foreign policy formulation throughout the Cold War. The key foreign policy decisions were made by the military government and the foreign minister himself. As the Thai political scientist Suchit Bunbongkarn put it:

> foreign policy formulation has been dominated by the cabinet, particularly the Foreign Minister. The military, long dominating the political scene in Thailand, has also been a powerful force in setting the course of the country's foreign relations. The MFA has been left to be merely a policy implementation mechanism of the government.[73]

Some scholars traced the marginalisation of civilians from the foreign policymaking process to the military authoritarian regime of Field Marshal Phibun in the 1950s.[74] However, from 1958 on, when Thanat Khoman was an influential and (over)confident foreign minister (1958–1971) under the Sarit and Thanom regimes, the MFA increasingly became *his* ministry. Some scholars suggest that Thanat's decision in foreign affairs, with his authoritarian style, was paramount:

> Thanat seldom used the Ministry's staff for advice and consultation before reaching his decision. Most of the major issues and policies were decided by Thanat himself and the Ministry's departments concerned were usually asked just to provide justifications for the adopted policies.[75]

The second interpretation is a bureaucratic politics paradigm. This position claims that, despite his discreetly personalised leadership, Thanat had a small group of trustworthy and loyal diplomats, who acted on his behalf.[76] Thanat's close aides included, among others, Anand Panyarachun, Sompong Sucharitkul, ML Pirapongse Kasemsri, Arsa Sarasin, Manaspas Xuto and Pracha Gunakasem. With degrees from English-speaking universities, they helped draft Thanat's policy statements as well as speeches. According to one study, Thanat preferred policy recommendations by Anand and Sompong to those of

---

73 Suchit Bunbongkarn, 'The Role of Social Science in Foreign Policy Making of Thailand', in *Social Sciences and National Development: The Southeast Asian Experience*, ed. Shou-sheng Hsueh (New Delhi: Abhinav Publications, 1977), 123.
74 Daniel Fineman, *A Special Relationship: The United States and Military Government in Thailand, 1947–1958* (Honolulu: University of Hawai'i Press, 1997).
75 Suchit, 'The Role of Social Science', 118.
76 See, for example, Asadakorn Eksaengsri, 'Foreign Policy-Making in Thailand: ASEAN Policy, 1967–1972' (PhD thesis, State University of New York, 1980).

Manaspas.[77] Anand, after serving as a personal aide to Thanat, became Thai Ambassador to Canada (1968–1971), and Ambassador to the US (1971–1974). During the same time, he concurrently held a position as Ambassador to the United Nations (UN) (1969–1973). Pirapongse was a gatekeeping Secretary to the Foreign Minister while Sompong was the Director-General of the Economic Department (1966–1970) and Thai Ambassador to the Netherlands (1970–1974).

Beyond these two paradigms, this chapter suggests that flexible diplomacy can be understood in terms of institutionalised practices and power/knowledge. In the late 1960s, Thanat's Foreign Ministry established the Institute of Foreign Affairs – which was later known as Devawongse Varopakarn Institute of Foreign Affairs (DVIFA). Its role was to professionalise and depoliticise diplomats through technocratic training in line with the newly emerged discourse of flexible diplomacy.[78] Since then, diplomats have been trained to be 'docile' bodies that followed the rules and norms of diplomatic discourses and practices.[79]

In Thailand, diplomatic training was initially aimed at enhancing the capacity of diplomats in terms of knowledge, skills and competence, attitude and appropriate manners to reckon and grapple with the changing international situation. At first, the training was by nature temporary and ad hoc. Learning was achieved by doing, or on-the-job training, as well as through an informal system of apprenticeship whereby senior diplomats would pass tacit knowledge to junior diplomats.[80] In 1962, proper training began with occasional in-service training, including practice-oriented seminars on drafting official letters (in both Thai and English languages), official rules and regulations, and diplomatic protocols, as well as other practical and tacit knowledge. There was no permanent curriculum. The MFA also invited former ambassadors and distinguished experts to give talks on various topics.[81] In 1963 and 1964 it trained junior

---

77 Asadakorn, 'Foreign Policy-Making in Thailand', 141.
78 Chantipa Phutrakul, '25 Years Past and Next Step in Future', in *Devawongse-sarn* [Devawongse Journal] (Bangkok: Ministry of Foreign Affairs, 2010), 286–99.
79 See Michel Foucault, *Discipline and Punish: The Birth of the Prison*, trans. Alan Sheridan (London: Vintage Books, 1995).
80 'A History of Devawongse Varopakarn Institute of Foreign Affairs', Ministry of Foreign Affairs, Thailand, accessed on 9 September 2019, available at: dvifa.mfa.go.th/en/page/79143-a-history-of-devawongse-varopakarn-institute.
81 For example, in 1966, it invited Puay Ungpakorn, the governor of the Bank of Thailand, to give a lecture on economics, Phraya Anuman Ratchathon on religion, and Prince Wan Waithayakon, former Foreign Minister, on his ambassadorial experiences in the US. 'A History of Devawongse Varopakarn Institute of Foreign Affairs', Ministry of Foreign Affairs, Thailand, accessed on 9 September 2019, available at: dvifa.mfa.go.th/en/page/79143-a-history-of-devawongse-varopakarn-institute.

diplomats who were about to hold positions abroad (20 and 40 diplomats, respectively), and in 1966, it extended the program to include those civil servants in other ministries who would be positioned abroad (53 in total). Diplomatic training continued in 1968 (for 60 third secretaries), and in 1969 (two courses for new diplomats – 28 and 20 respectively – and another for 31 first secretaries).[82]

The Institute of Foreign Affairs was officially approved on 12 December 1967, to become part of the Personnel and Training Division within the MFA. It was Thanat's desire that diplomatic training should be 'routinized and permanent'.[83] His aim was to systematically and effectively train and educate diplomats at every level – from junior to senior. Civil servants from other ministries were also welcome. Five training curricula were set, covering: (1) orientation of new diplomats; (2) junior diplomats who would hold positions abroad; (3) attachés and third secretaries; (4) second and third secretaries; and (5) the English language. Between 1970 and 1973, five formal training programs for new diplomats, totalling 209, were provided annually. Additional training occurred twice in 1971.[84] The Institute of Foreign Affairs was officially opened during the foreign ministership of Charunpan Isrankul na Ayuthaya on 14 February, 1974, and diplomatic training has continued ever since.

In general, diplomatic training involved education, seminars, formal training and development, coaching, mentoring, on-the-job training and rotation. The point, to use Thanat's words, was to transfer a stock of tacit knowledge, or know-how, and practices (acquired through experiences) from 'old diplomats' to 'the young ones'. Arguably, however, the knowledge that diplomats, particularly Thanat and his associates, passed on to other diplomats in the MFA was not the old knowledge, but in fact the new emerging discourse of détente.

Like Thanat, many of these 'experts' – most notably Anand Panyarachun, Sompong Sucharitkul and ML Pirapongse Kasemsri – had previously been attached to the Cold War hegemonic discourse, especially during the Sarit

---

82 'Background of Training, Ministry of Foreign Affairs', Institute of Foreign Affairs, Ministry of Foreign Affairs (MFA), Library and Archives Division, MFA POL2/PM2517/9, MFA, Thailand, 1–11.
83 'Background of Training, Ministry of Foreign Affairs', Institute of Foreign Affairs, MFA, Library and Archives Division, MFA POL2/PM2517/9, MFA, Thailand, 3.
84 28 diplomats attended the first training program between 3 August and 12 October 1970; 22 diplomats between 2 August and 29 September 1971 and 51 diplomats between 1 November and 29 December 1971; 37 diplomats between 21 February and 24 March 1972; 71 diplomats between 30 April and 20 June 1973. See 'Background of Training, Ministry of Foreign Affairs', Institute of Foreign Affairs, MFA, Library and Archives Division, MFA POL2/PM2517/9, MFA, Thailand, 3.

and Thanom regimes, but gradually became détente proponents in the early 1970s. They changed their identities and subject positions, largely due to the new discourse of détente. In other words, subject positions emerged only in and through diplomatic practices. Anand's speeches at the UN provided good examples. In November 1969, he gave a harsh statement at the UN General Assembly proclaiming that Communist China still maintained 'hostile behaviour and inflexible policy', and had not given up its 'aggressive proclivities and expansionist tendencies' towards the neighbouring countries in Southeast Asia, including Thailand.[85] But his view began to change following the Chinese entry into the UN in 1971 (see Chapter 4), and Anand soon became one of the key figures in negotiating a rapprochement with the PRC. As Director-General of the ministry's Economic Department, Sompong also played a key role in concluding the trade agreement with the Soviet Union in 1970.

Outside the close circle of Thanat, others, such as Major General Chatichai Choonhavan, then Ambassador to Switzerland, were pro-détente. In 1971, Chatichai was asked by Thanat to go to Rome with him to make contact with the Chinese. Between 1972 and 1974, he became deputy foreign minister, during which time he conducted so-called 'petro-diplomacy' with the PRC, which began to sell petroleum to Thailand at reduced prices. Chatichai subsequently served as foreign minister (1974–1975) during the Kukrit Pramoj Government, overseeing the normalisation of formal diplomatic relations with the Chinese in 1975 (see Chapter 5). Détente proponents who shared knowledge of flexible diplomacy thus emerged in and through emerging diplomatic practices of détente.

3.2.1. Diplomacy as Power/Knowledge

Taking diplomacy seriously as power/knowledge addresses the shortcomings of the paradigms of wise and competent leaders and of bureaucratic tussles. It sheds light on power in and through diplomatic practices in five ways.[86]

---

85 'Statement by Thai representative Anand Panyarachun in the UN General Assembly on Chinese representation in the UN', 10 November 1969, in Jain, *China and Thailand*, 163–66.
86 This part has been inspired by not only Foucault's genealogy in general but also the 'practice theory' of multilateral diplomacy. See, for example, Emanuel Adler and Vincent Pouliot, 'International Practices', *International Theory* 3, no. 1 (2011): 1–36; Rebecca Adler-Nissen and Vincent Pouliot, 'Power in Practice: Negotiating the International Intervention in Libya', *European Journal of International Relations* 20, no. 4 (2014): 889–911; Vincent Pouliot, *International Pecking Orders: The Politics and Practice of Multilateral Diplomacy* (Cambridge: Cambridge University Press, 2016).

First, diplomacy as power/knowledge was socially productive and constitutive. Through training and exercises, it established and constituted diplomatic subject positions. Diplomacy individually reconfigured social agents into 'docile' diplomats as a part of a specific historical bloc/group in the diplomatic site of the Ministry of Foreign Affairs. In this case, the 'docile' diplomats produced since the late 1960s were détente proponents. Like disciplinary power, institutionalised diplomatic power via diplomatic training involved not only bodies but also actions – or their potential actions (what they can or cannot do) – as its main targets.[87] This kind of power was individualising power in the sense that training positively developed and harvested diplomats' capacities. Diplomatic discipline led to a less centralised, but much more economical and effective, power over individual bodies through institutional training.

Second, diplomacy had a practical character. It positioned career diplomats as competent players, with a specific set of tacit knowledge and competent skills, for making sense of and dealing with the changing international situation. Diplomatic competence was a 'socially recognized attribute', rather than an individual attribute, whereas the struggle for competence was never-ending and inseparable from the struggle for recognition within the diplomatic site.[88] As Foucault put it, 'a body is docile that may be subjected, used, transformed and improved'.[89]

Third, diplomacy was deeply relational. Diplomatic training, in either informal or formal forms, was a system of apprenticeship that emphasised the master–apprentice relationship. For Thanat, it was about the relationship between old and young diplomats. Skilful or competent diplomats were not measured according to their individual attributes. Rather, they were competent because they were locally situated in a hierarchical order of the Foreign Ministry, as well as immersed in the emerging patterns of diplomatic discourse. The practice of apprenticeship provided the condition of possibility for this hierarchical structure and social stratification to dominate in the MFA. This was a 'sense of place' that diplomats embody,[90] while a community of Thai diplomats, despite their heterogeneous and dispersed nature, also gradually emerged.

---

87 Jeffrey T Nealon, *Foucault Beyond Foucault: Power and Its Intensification since 1984* (Stanford: Stanford University Press, 2008), 31.
88 Adler-Nissen and Pouliot, 'Power in Practice', 896.
89 Foucault, *Discipline and Punish*, 136.
90 See Pouliot, *International Pecking Orders*, Chapter 3.

Fourth, diplomatic power was effective in the sense that it installed and produced a certain regime of truth, namely the knowledge of flexible diplomacy. Diplomacy was constructed as a sphere of expertise that required a particular kind of knowledge and a particular kind of 'expert', namely trained diplomats, rather than amateurs, including military elites or politicians. This new knowledge of flexible diplomacy shaped the way of doing things, particularly in regard to pursuing diplomacy with the communist powers. They also legitimised the dominant roles of the MFA over this emerging area of expertise.

Last but not least, diplomacy was highly political. Diplomacy as power/knowledge was inseparable from the struggle for authority or influence in the contestation of power. Diplomats sought to establish their mastery of the diplomatic game by framing particular issues as 'diplomatic' ones, and positioning themselves as technocratic, professionalised and depoliticised 'experts'. In other words, there was a *'diplomatisation'* of political issues, which can be read as a depoliticisation or technocratisation of diplomatic issues. In this sense, the struggle for diplomatic competence was fundamentally the struggle for hegemony in the foreign policymaking process and in the public spheres in general.

In sum, reconceptualising flexible diplomacy as a technique of power and knowledge formation helps understand those diachronic changes of subject positions – from Cold Warriors toward détente proponents. The incremental intensification of détente practices was in turn an emergence of a new mode of control and surveillance in Thai diplomacy. Through diplomatic schooling, a group of individuals were trained to be diplomats as well as docile bodies. However, the role of social agents was significant and irreducible to languages or discourses in the sense that they performed, as well as were performed, in and through diplomatic discourse. Agents with specific subject positions were not purely rational actors, but socially and institutionally embedded actors performing within the field and relationship of power. Diplomatic practices are then an institutionally and socially embedded way of doing things diplomatically.

3.3. Conclusion

International uncertainty, in particular the worsening situation in Vietnam and the prospect of American disengagement from Southeast Asia, brought about discursive anxiety within the minds of many Thai foreign policymakers, most notably Foreign Minister Thanat Khoman during the late 1960s. This chapter has examined the emergence of détente or 'flexible diplomacy' with the communist powers, as a new paradigmatic and pragmatic discourse in order to manage this rising anxiety. It argues that this discourse, which challenged the anticommunist one, predated the enunciation of the Nixon Doctrine. In the process, the discourse of détente, coupled with a change in institutional practices, formed a new subject position in Thai politics: that of détente proponents in the Ministry of Foreign Affairs and beyond. Thailand's perceptions of the Soviet Union and the PRC were incrementally transformed from 'enemies' to 'friends'. The next chapter will examine the first episode of détente with the Soviet Union and the PRC between 1969 and 1971, and the roles of those détente proponents, especially of Thanat Khoman.

4

Flexible Diplomacy: Thanat and the First Détente (1969–1971)

4.1. 1969 as a *Volte-Face*?

'Escape from a tiger only to happen upon a crocodile' is a famous Thai proverb. This is similar to the fish, in Aesop's fable, that jumps from the frying pan into the fire. In 1969, Thai Foreign Minister Thanat Khoman used this allegory to describe a state of discursive anxiety in Thailand:

> If you avoid a tiger [China] and come to face a crocodile [the Soviet Union], it is not much of a change … If we do not have any other alternative, may be we will have to live with the crocodile … This is exactly the international pattern that may emerge if and when the United States has to yield to the pressure of completely withdrawing from this part of the world … because we cannot claim that our regional grouping is powerful enough … We hope that you will be understanding and that you will discreetly support the efforts of the nations of the area who are trying to form a cohesive grouping.[1]

The year 1969 marked a watershed in Thai politics and diplomacy. In domestic politics, it was an experimental transition from authoritarianism towards (semi-)democracy. After the promulgation of

---

1 Thanat Khoman, interview with *Los Angeles Times* correspondent, Bangkok, 6 November 1969. Quoted in Astri Suhrki, 'Smaller-Nation Diplomacy: Thailand's Current Dilemmas', *Asian Survey* 11, no. 5 (May 1971): 438.

the new Constitution in June 1968, there was a parliamentary election on 10 February 1969. The result did not see a total victory for the pro-military United Thai People's Party (UTPP), but immediately after the election, the UTPP recruited independents into the party and thereby gained a parliamentary majority. The largest opposition party was the Democrat Party, led by former prime minister MR Seni Pramoj.[2] Field Marshal Thanom Kittikachorn retained his position as Prime Minister and Minister of Defense. His close associate, General Praphas Charusathien, remained Deputy Prime Minister and Minister of Interior. The most prominent Cabinet members included Pote Sarasin, Minister of National Development, Air Chief Marshal Dawee Chullasapya, Minister of Communications, and Thanat Khoman, Foreign Minister. While the Cabinet and Parliament were still dominated by the military and civilian bureaucrats, democracy provided for new voices, new advocacy, new factionalism and new criticism. Détente also became a contentious domestic political issue as distinct groups began to contest both whether and how to deal with the communist powers.

In foreign affairs, Thailand encountered the prospect of American retrenchment from the region, culminating in the Nixon Doctrine in July 1969. This was a serious challenge to Thailand's hegemonic discourse of pro-Americanism and anticommunism. Coupled with the deterioration of the Vietnam War, the Thai communist insurgency, supported by the Chinese, loomed larger while the survival of the Thai state was at stake. Many commentators designated Thailand 'another Vietnam'.[3] Both internal and external challenges brought about niggling anxieties in the Thai body politic. The greatest puzzle for Thailand was how to deal with these new transformations.

A 'Thai version of détente' was proposed by Foreign Minister Thanat Khoman as a thoroughgoing attempt to end antagonism with the communist powers. As one put it, Thanat was not 'advocating a piecemeal adjustment to pressures, but a coming-to-terms with reality'.[4] While he regarded détente and the US military presence as an either/or situation, his

---

2   See Clark D Neher, 'Thailand: The Politics of Continuity', *Asian Survey* 10, no. 2 (February 1970): 161–68.
3   See Bernard Gordon, 'Thailand: Its Meaning for the US', *Current History* 52, no. 305 (1967): 16–21, 53–54; Kenneth Young, 'Thailand's Role in Southeast Asia', *Current History* 56, no. 330 (1969): 94–99, 110–11.
4   Harvey Stockwin even envisions Thanat's détente as an equivalent of Willy Brandt's Ostpolitik. See 'Thanat's Ostpolitik', *Far Eastern Economic Review*, 23 July 1973, 24–25.

approach was rather gradualist on both issues. That is, Thanat supported a cautious step-by-step process of de-Americanisation from Thailand while advocating a gradual road of détente with the People's Republic of China (PRC) and the Soviet Union. Overall, what Thanat aimed for was an independent foreign policy of détente.

This chapter examines Thailand's changing diplomatic practices towards the communist powers between 1969 and 1971. It explicates the ways in which the discourse of détente worked in and through diplomatic practices. The first section discusses how the Thai Government pursued closer trade relations with the USSR, culminating in the bilateral trade agreement of 1970 and air transport agreement of 1971. The second section elucidates the way in which Thailand attempted to contact the Chinese through back-channel diplomacy via third parties in order to explore possibilities of rapprochement. Thanat's 'hope' – a discursive change of communist powers from 'enemies' to 'friends' – was rendered possible through new practices of détente. The chapter concludes by highlighting the politics of discursive contestation in Thai foreign policy, which ended in the 1971 coup d'état.

4.2. Living with the 'Crocodile': Thai–Soviet Relations

The Soviet Union had maintained formal diplomatic relations with Thailand since 12 March 1941 and the two countries first exchanged their ambassadors after the end of the Second World War.[5] However, during the Cold War, the Thai state was sceptical of Soviet activities in the country. The tension between the two countries rose with the Laotian crisis and Vietnam War in the 1960s. Both countries had condemned and levelled charges against each other, leading to the notorious deportation of Soviet trade representative Leonid Mamurin on espionage charges in September 1969.[6]

---

5   Noranit Setabutr, *Kwam sampan tang prathet rawang Thai–Russia* [Thai–Russian Foreign Relations] (Bangkok: Sukhothai Thammathirat Open University Press, 1985 [2006]); Chulacheeb Chinwanno, *Siam, Russia, Thai: Karntootkarnmuang Karnmuangkarntoot, Aded pajupan anakod* [Siam, Russia, Thailand: Diplomatic Politics, Politics of Diplomacy, Past Present and Future] (Bangkok: Thammasat University Press, 2013); Jittipat Poonkham, *Withet Panid Sampan tung Songkram Yen: kwam sampan rawangprathet Thai–Russia (1897–1991)* [Foreign Economic Relations to the Cold War: Thai–Russian Foreign Relations (1897–1991)] (Bangkok: Chulalongkorn University Press, 2016).
6   Paul R Shirk, 'Thai–Soviet Relations', *Asian Survey* 9 (September 1969): 691.

From a Thai perspective, the Soviet Union, unlike the PRC, did not directly support North Vietnam and the communist insurgency in Thailand. Therefore, the Thai Government did not regard the USSR as a hostile state. As Foreign Minister Thanat Khoman claimed, Thailand was friendly with the Soviet Union because, unlike communist China, the USSR was not directly engaged in any hostile acts against it.[7] With the grudging approval from the government of Thanom Kittikachorn, the Ministry of Foreign Affairs led by Thanat demonstrated a willingness to respond favourably to Soviet involvement in the region and take trade relations into consideration. In the early 1970s, two significant changes in Thai–Soviet relations occurred. First, the Soviet Union launched a diplomatic offensive in Southeast Asia which culminated in Brezhnev's idea of so-called 'Collective Security system in Asia'. The second was increased Soviet interest in expanding trade and technical cooperation with Thailand. One was regional in nature, the other bilateral.

4.2.1. Brezhnev's Collective Security in Asia: Thailand's Views

From 1969, the USSR increasingly 'pivoted' to Southeast Asia. While the US was increasingly bent on retrenchment, the Soviet Union was reasserting its presence and influence. At the end of his speech given to the International Meeting of Communist and Workers Parties in Moscow on 8 June 1969, Leonid Brezhnev proposed the idea of 'a system of Collective Security in Asia':

> For us, the burning problems of the present international situations do not push into the background more long-range tasks, especially the creation of a system of Collective Security in those parts of the world where the threat of the unleashing of a new world war and the unleashing of armed conflicts is centred. Such a system is the best substitute for the existing military-political groupings … We think that the course of events also places on the agenda *the task of creating a system of Collective Security in Asia.*[8]

---

7   RK Jain, ed., *China and Thailand, 1949–1983* (New Delhi: Radiant Publishers, 1984), lvi.
8   Quoted in Soo Eon Moon, 'Importance of ASEAN in Soviet Foreign Policy: An Evaluation of Soviet Policy Toward Southeast Asia in the Post-Vietnam War Era' (PhD thesis, Claremont Graduate School, 1984), 57. My emphasis.

Brezhnev's idea was vague, if not superficial, and this inevitably triggered doubts and speculation about Soviet motives. Most observers tended to focus on Sino–Soviet border conflicts, highlighted by the clashes at Damansky Island on the Ussuri River in March 1969.[9] Brezhnev's proposal was believed to be mainly directed toward the PRC, as described by Vikenty V Matveyev (pseudonym)'s article in *Izvestiya* a few days before Brezhnev's enunciation. The article warned of Chinese expansionist designs on some Asian countries in response to American retrenchment. To counter this threat, the American withdrawal

> should pave the way for the laying of the foundation of collective security, in which case the countries that have gained their freedom would, by pooling efforts, consolidate peace and repulse all machinations of imperialist expansionist forces.

Matveyev pledged that the Soviet Union and other socialist countries would be prepared 'to contribute to every effort helping to insure firm, dependable peace in Asia'.[10]

In September 1969, Soviet Foreign Minister Andrei Gromyko told the United Nations (UN) General Assembly that international events in the past few years 'proved the need for a system of Collective Security in Asia': 'Many countries in Asia are seeking possibilities to ensure peace and security by collective effort'. He claimed that the Soviet Union was 'ready to take part in consultation and exchanges of views on all questions concerning a Collective Security system in Asia'.[11] Rather than clarifying the term, Gromyko merely toyed with Brezhnev's concept at the UN. One scholar argues that this vague concept of a Collective Security system in Asia and its lack of substance was deliberately aimed at testing the waters among Asian countries, and eliciting 'reactions from potential members of the "system" before going further'. In short, it was fundamentally a 'club in search of members'.[12]

---

9   Alexander O Ghebhardt, 'The Soviet System of Collective Security in Asia', *Asian Survey* 13, no. 12 (December 1973): 1075–91.
10 Vikenty V Matveyev, *Izvestiya*, 29 May 1969, quoted in Arnold L Horelick, 'The Soviet Union's Asian Collective Security Proposal: A Club in Search of Members', *Pacific Affairs* 47, no. 3 (Autumn 1974): 271.
11 'Russia Ready for Asian Pact', *Bangkok Post*, 21 September 1969, 12.
12 Horelick, 'The Soviet Union's Asian Collective Security Proposal', 271, 269.

Thailand saw Brezhnev's idea of a Collective Security system in Asia as the Soviet Union preparing to move into the power vacuum in the region.[13] In an interview with *The Asia Magazine*, Thanat Khoman believed that the USSR wanted a collective defence alliance in Asia in order to protect its interests after the US military withdrew from the region, and more importantly, to contain Communist China. Thanat also said that Thailand was ready to consider Soviet engagement in Southeast Asia as part of a new balance.

In other words, Thailand did not react unfavourably to Brezhnev's Asian Collective Security proposal. As Thanat noted:

> the Soviet Union realizes better than the West that a (military) vacuum would not be in its national interest because there will be some other power that will try to fill the gap with its own authority.

'Asian countries', Thanat added, would have to 'look after their own interests and see who should fill the gap when the United States withdraws'.[14] However, he disagreed with any military alliance in Asia, partly because he realised that the countries in the region were not military powers or potential military powers. As he put it, 'there is no use setting up new military alliances just on paper'.[15] Thanat argued:

> if it were to be a threatening power which showed itself to be hostile to nations in Asia, they may find the Soviet move more in conformity with their interests, rather than allow that large Asian power to fill the gap.[16]

However, at the time, the trouble, according to Thanat, was that

> we do not know what shape or form the so-called Soviet suggestion of an Asian Collective Security has. They do not want to spell it out or to elaborate on their suggestion. So many nations, Asian

---

13 Thanat Khoman, 'Questions Posed by Members of the Republic of China's National Defense College to Foreign Minister Thanat Khoman', Bangkok, 15 July 1969, in *Collected Interviews of H.E. Dr. Thanat Khoman, Minister of Foreign Affairs of the Kingdom of Thailand, Vol. 3: 1969* (Bangkok: Department of Information, Ministry of Foreign Affairs, 2014), 546.
14 'Thanat: Soviets Want to Fill Power Gap', *Bangkok Post*, 31 December 1969, 12.
15 Thanat Khoman, 'Interview Given by Foreign Minister Thanat Khoman to Noel Norton of the Australian Broadcasting Commission', Bangkok, 9 September 1969, in *Collected Interviews of H.E. Dr. Thanat Khoman, Vol. 3: 1969*, 584.
16 'Thanat: Soviets Want to Fill Power Gap', 12. See also Thanat Khoman, 'Interview Given by Foreign Minister Thanat Khoman to Suman Dubey, Associate Editor of The Asian Magazine', Bangkok, 31 October 1969, in *Collected Interviews of H.E. Dr. Thanat Khoman, Vol. 3: 1969*, 606.

or non-Asian, have been asking this question, but so far we have received no elucidation. It is very vague just to throw out the idea that Asian nations should develop their own security.[17]

Later, Thanat asked the Soviet Ambassador to Bangkok to elaborate on what Brezhnev had in mind by collective Asian security. He explained:

> the reply that we got was that [the Soviet leaders] would like to hear the reaction from Asian nations about this idea. So we said that to be in a position to offer a reaction, we must first know what it is all about and what we can expect.[18]

Brezhnev did not specifically explain the project until 1972. In his address at the Fifteenth Congress of the Soviet Trade Unions in March 1972, Brezhnev asserted:

> It is becoming increasingly clear that the real road to security in Asia is not the road of military blocs and groupings, not the road of opposing some states against others, but the road of good-neighbourly cooperation by all interested states. Collective Security in Asia, as we see it, should be based on such principles as renunciation of the use of force in relations among states, respect for sovereignty and inviolability of borders, noninterference in internal affairs, extensive development of economic and other cooperation on the basis of full equality and mutual advantage.[19]

At that time, Brezhnev's idea of a 'Collective Security system in Asia' was largely ignored by Asian countries, including Thailand. However, many countries in the region started to accommodate the more assertive Soviet power and its presence in the form of military aid, a naval presence and bilateral relations, specifically trade relations.[20]

---

17 Thanat, 'Interview Given by Foreign Minister Thanat Khoman to Noel Norton of the Australian Broadcasting Commission', 584.
18 Thanat Khoman, 'Interview Given by Foreign Minister Thanat Khoman to Welles Hangen, NBC TV', Bangkok, 28 August 1969, in *Collected Interviews of H.E. Dr. Thanat Khoman, Vol. 3: 1969*, 601.
19 Quoted in Moon, 'Importance of ASEAN in Soviet Foreign Policy', 60.
20 Also, the Soviet Union readjusted relations with the region in general as part of its foreign policy of détente. It established diplomatic relations with Malaysia in 1967, Singapore in 1968, and the Philippines in 1976. Particularly in the case of Malaysia, Nikolai S Patolichev, Minister of Foreign Trade, visited Kuala Lumpur in 1969, concluding the Soviet import of 240,000 tons of Malaysian rubber, which rendered Malaysia the most important trading partner in the region. In October 1972, Malaysian Prime Minister Tun Abdul Razak paid an official visit to the Soviet Union, and signed economic and technical agreements as well as a science and cultural cooperation agreement. Charles B McLane, *Soviet–Asian Relations* (London: Central Asian Research Center, 1973), 107.

4.2.2. Trade Relations

The USSR accelerated its trade relations with Thailand from 1968, beginning with the Soviet Government wanting its ambassador in Bangkok to push Thai–Soviet commercial cooperation and agreement.[21] Conversations between the Soviet leaders, the Thai Ambassador to Moscow, Police Major Pramote Chongcharoen (1963–1967) and Yuad Lertrit (1968–1971) show this. For example, Pramote concurred with his Soviet counterpart that despite their political differences, both countries should begin with trade and cultural relations to strengthen their ties.[22] Yuad agreed that Thailand was determined to expand trade with the Soviet Union. However, in the views of the Soviet leaders, they had pushed proposals for trade agreement with Thailand for at least seven years with no response. The Soviet Ambassador to Bangkok, Mikhail M Volkov (1965–1969), said that both sides needed to first determine what agendas and issues would be negotiated so as to successfully achieve a trade agreement.[23]

The Thai Government responded positively to the Soviets because it felt that the USSR did not pursue 'hostile' policies and practices towards Thailand. In his conversation with Soviet Ambassador Volkov in early 1968, Air Chief Marshal Dawee Chullasapya said that Thai–Soviet relations were 'normal, but not close friends'. Dawee respected the USSR in the sense that the Soviet Union, unlike the PRC, did not use force to expand its ideology in the region.[24] The present trend of improving relations with the USSR, as Foreign Minister Thanat subsequently asserted, was because the Soviet Union did not pose a direct threat to

---

21 Record of conversation held between Chairman of the Presidium of the Supreme Soviet of the Soviet Union Nikolai V Podgorny and Thai Ambassador to Moscow Police Major Pramote Chongcharoen, 22 November 1967, in Thailand's Ministry of Foreign Affairs, *Collected Volume of Soviet Archival Documents, 1941–1970* (Bangkok: Ministry of Foreign Affairs, 2016), 265.
22 Record of conversation held between Soviet Foreign Minister Andrei Gromyko and Thai Ambassador to Moscow Police Major Pramote Chongcharoen, 20 November 1967, in Ministry of Foreign Affairs, *Collected Volume of Soviet Archival Documents, 1941–1970*, 263–64.
23 Record of conversation held between the Soviet Ambassador to Bangkok MM Volkov and Thai Ambassador to Moscow Yuad Lertrit, 15 February 1968, in Ministry of Foreign Affairs, *Collected Volume of Soviet Archival Documents, 1941–1970*, 271–72.
24 Record of conversation held between the Soviet Ambassador to Bangkok MM Volkov and Air Chief Marshal Dawee Chullasapya, 15 January 1968, in Ministry of Foreign Affairs, *Collected Volume of Soviet Archival Documents, 1941–1970*, 268–70.

Thailand's existence and the improved relations were 'part of the policy of widening our horizons', in a search for the possibility of 'consolidating peace through commercial relations and cultural exchanges'.[25]

In 1968, Prime Minister Thanom asked the new Ambassador to Moscow, Yuad Lertrit, to convey a message to the Soviet Government that Thailand wished to strengthen and further develop friendly relations with the Soviet Union and Eastern Europe, and would send a delegation of Thai business representatives in the near future. He also encouraged the Soviet Trade Organization to buy more rubber from Thailand.[26] With regards to the proposed trade agreement, meetings were held once a week between the Economic Department of the Ministry of Foreign Affairs, led by its Director-General Sompong Sucharitkul, and EA Dmitriev, the chargé d'affaires of the Soviet embassy in Bangkok, together with Russian Commercial Counsellor, Nikolai P Karpov. The pact was delayed considerably because of the Thai refusal to give in to Russia's demands to accord full diplomatic privileges, including immunity, to its trade representation to Thailand, as well as to attach a navigation agreement to the trade agreement.[27] Sompong strongly defended the position, by insisting that navigation would be negotiated only after concluding and signing the trade agreement.[28]

Thanat commented in August 1968 that a trade agreement with the Soviet Union was mentioned 'for many years, but no formal agreement has been reached'.[29] This was due to many factors. First, bilateral trade was not in great volume. Second, the two economic systems were seemingly too different. As Thanat put it:

---

25 Thanat Khoman, 'Interview Given by Foreign Minister Thanat Khoman to Shin-Il Park of the Kyunghyang Shinmoon of the Republic of Korea', Bangkok, 6 August 1969, in *Collected Interviews of H.E. Dr. Thanat Khoman, Vol. 3: 1969*, 596.
26 Record of conversation held between Soviet Deputy Foreign Minister Nikolai Feryubin and Thai Ambassador to Moscow Yuad Lertrit, 10 June 1968, in Ministry of Foreign Affairs, *Collected Volume of Soviet Archival Documents, 1941–1970*, 273.
27 'USSR Trade Pact Being Drafted', *Bangkok Post*, 13 December 1969, 5.
28 Record of conversation held between Soviet Charge d'Affaires EA Dmitriev, and Director-General of the Economic Department, Ministry of Foreign Affairs, Sompong Sucharitkul, 7 May 1969, in Ministry of Foreign Affairs, *Collected Volume of Soviet Archival Documents, 1941–1970*, 282.
29 Thanat Khoman, 'Interview Given by Foreign Minister Thanat Khoman to Miss Frances Starner of the Far Eastern Economic Review and to Mr. Donald Kirk of the Washington Star', Bangkok, 23 August 1968, in *Collected Interviews of H.E. Dr. Thanat Khoman, Minister of Foreign Affairs of the Kingdom of Thailand, Vol. 2: 1968* (Bangkok: Department of Information, Ministry of Foreign Affairs, 2014), 245.

> Trade on our side is free. The Soviet Union can buy what it wants here and also tries to sell what it can, but there is a very competitive market. Of course, trade on the other side is not free, it is a state monopoly; we do not have a socialist system; therefore, the state doesn't engage in controlling the merchants. Private firms not the governments are engaged in trade. Therefore, it is very difficult. And we in Thailand do not believe in the barter system.[30]

However, he emphasised that Thailand had been prepared to discuss trade with the USSR 'for many many years'.[31]

Despite faltering negotiations on a trade agreement, the Thai Government expressed willingness to widen the scope of relations with Moscow. In 1968, Prime Minister Thanom sent a Thai trade mission to Eastern Europe to seek new markets for Thai products, especially agricultural goods such as rice, jute and rubber. Pramote, who was promoted to Permanent Secretary of the Foreign Ministry after his five-year turn as Ambassador to Moscow, informed Soviet Ambassador Volkov that the purpose of this delegation, which would last one month, was to explore trade opportunities, both export and import. He asked the Soviet Union to take this trade delegation seriously.[32]

In May 1969, Prime Minister Thanom stated that 'we already export many products to the free world, but now we wish to expand our trade with Eastern Communist countries': 'It is to the benefit of our international trade if we can expand markets for our products in these countries'.[33] A 26-member Thai trade delegation was led by Vicharn Nivatwongse, the Director of the Commercial Intelligence Department, and included two government officials and another 23 prominent business representatives. Over the course of the month, delegates visited the Soviet Union, Hungary, Czechoslovakia, Poland, Bulgaria, Romania and Yugoslavia.[34]

---

30   Thanat, 'Interview Given by Foreign Minister Thanat Khoman to Miss Frances Starner of the Far Eastern Economic Review and to Mr. Donald Kirk of the Washington Star', 245.
31   Thanat, 'Interview Given by Foreign Minister Thanat Khoman to Miss Frances Starner of the Far Eastern Economic Review and to Mr. Donald Kirk of the Washington Star', 245.
32   Record of conversation held between the Soviet Ambassador to Bangkok MM Volkov and Thai Permanent Secretary, Ministry of Foreign Affairs, Police Major Pramote Chongcharoen, 20 November 1968, in Ministry of Foreign Affairs, *Collected Volume of Soviet Archival Documents, 1941–1970*, 279–80.
33   'Thanom: Seek New Marts in E. Europe', *Bangkok Post*, 9 May 1969, 13.
34   The itinerary for the trade delegation was: Finland (12–15 May), Denmark (15–17 May), the Soviet Union (17–26 May), Hungary (26–30 May), Czechoslovakia (30 May – 3 June), Poland (3–8 June), Bulgaria (8–11 June), Romania (11–14 June), Yugoslavia (14–19 June) and Italy (19–20 June). The mission returned to Bangkok on 21 June. 'Thanom: Seek New Marts in E. Europe', 13.

Economic Affairs Minister, Bunchana Atthakorn, asked the mission to study ways and means of promoting the direct sale of Thai products to East European countries. Before his departure, Vicharn told the press that 'the mission has absolutely nothing to do with politics. All we want to succeed is to sell our raw materials and agricultural products to them'.[35] By the end of the trip, Thailand exchanged goodwill missions with Yugoslavia, and established commercial relations with Poland, Romania and Czechoslovakia.

The symbolic gesture of Thai trade delegation to a certain extent rendered the bilateral trade agreement unavoidable. But Russia's demand for (a) a 'Most Favoured Nation' clause; (b) full diplomatic privileges, including immunity, to its trade representation based in Thailand; and (c) a navigation agreement, delayed agreement. The Soviet Union wished to negotiate both trade and air agreements together. Thailand suggested that both agreements should be considered separately.

By the end of 1969, an agreement was in place that regulated imports and exports between the two countries, but that did not fix a trade balance figure. It excluded air and navigation agreements. The draft also stated that all trade transactions would have to be made on a government-to-government basis, through the Thai Chamber of Commerce or through the Ministry of Economic Affairs, thereby prohibiting private Thai exporters from dealing directly with the Russians.[36] In March 1970, the new Soviet Ambassador to Thailand, Anatoly A Rozanov (1970–1974), arrived in Bangkok and presented his letter of credentials to the king.

On 25 December, Thanat and Rozanov signed the first Thai–Soviet trade agreement, marking a pivotal moment in their relations. The pact was aimed at improving and developing closer commercial relations between the two countries. It identified a means of international payment, facilitation of trade and transportation, and lists of tradable commodities. The Soviet Union was determined to import rice and rice products, natural rubber, mineral products (especially fluorites), maize, millet, leather, precious stones and jewellery, while Thailand would import metals and metal parts, machinery products and their components, electrical equipment and parts, cars and car parts, tractors and polymers.[37]

---

35 'Trade Group Leaves for E. Europe', *Bangkok Post*, 12 May 1969, 1.
36 'USSR Trade Pact Being Drafted', 5.
37 Alexander A Karchava, *Kaewsip pee kwam sampan tang karntoot Russia–Thai* [Ninety-Year Russian–Thai Diplomatic Relations] (Bangkok: Bapith Printing, 1988), 102.

The Soviet Union would establish trade representation with a residence in Bangkok. Ambassador Rozanov wrote a related letter to Thanat on the day of signing the agreement, specifically emphasising the importance of trade representation. Due to that fact that the state had a monopoly on foreign economic relations in the Soviet Union, the ambassador claimed that the Soviet Government needed trade representation in Bangkok. As he elaborated:

> The trade representation shall have the following functions to perform:
> a. to promote the development of trade relations between the Union of Soviet Socialist Republics and the Kingdom of Thailand;
> b. to represent the interests of the Union of Soviet Socialist Republics in the Kingdom of Thailand in all matters relating to foreign trade of the Union of Soviet Socialist Republics;
> c. to effect trade between the Union of Soviet Socialist Republics and the Kingdom of Thailand.

Rozanov insisted that the trade representation, which was an integral part of the Soviet embassy in Thailand, had full diplomatic privileges and immunity equivalent to diplomatic representatives.[38]

With the signing of the trade agreement, Thanat expected greater cooperation with the USSR. Likewise, Deputy Foreign Minister Police Major General Sa-nga Kittikachorn observed that in general the improved relations with the communist bloc had led to an increased opportunity to export goods. The former policy of enmity toward the communist powers would be now 'very risky'. Due to Thailand's easing of relations with the Soviet Union and East European countries, Sa-nga claimed, 'our foreign policy has made possible the reduction of the Communist threat'. 'This will mean that we can devote more of our budgetary funds to economic development than to military defence'.[39] In relation to the trade agreement specifically he stated that the Soviet Union 'has already brought about an improvement in the price of fluorite'. Previously, Japan had been the sole market, and, as a monopoly, this had depressed the price for many years. Sa-nga thus asked Thai exporters not to sell all fluorites to the Japanese,

---

38 A letter from Soviet Ambassador to Bangkok Anatoly A Rozanov to Foreign Minister Thanat Khoman, 25 December 1970, in Ministry of Foreign Affairs, *Collected Volume of Soviet Archival Documents, 1941–1970*, 305.
39 'Govt's Foreign Policy "Eases Red Threat"', *Bangkok Post*, 1 March 1971, 3.

but to also sell to the Russians, which helped them bid at higher prices.[40] To reporters who asked him whether the US would object to the proposed closer trade relations with the USSR, Sa-nga markedly replied that

> we don't care. We mean to maintain our good relations with the United States. But through Russia we may reach an agricultural commodities agreement involving countries in the Soviet bloc. We may sell tapioca and animal foodstuffs.[41]

According to Thai trade statistics, the percentage of bilateral trade with the Soviet Union rose exponentially in the 1970s, though with relatively small volume compared to Thailand's trade with other major partners. For example, in 1970, Thailand for the first time sold almost 35,000 tons of maize to the USSR.[42] The overall volume of bilateral trade with the USSR in 1971 amounted to 6.6 million roubles. This increased to 17.3 and 173.1 million roubles in 1975 and 1980, respectively. In 1971, Thai exports to Moscow were 4.1 million roubles, whereas Thai imports were 2.5 million roubles (see Table 4.1). Between 1971 through the end of the Cold War, Thailand had a surplus in trade with the Soviet Union. In the year 1981, out of all the Association of Southeast Asian Nations (ASEAN) countries, Thailand was the Soviet Union's largest trade partner.

Table 4.1: Thailand's trade volume with the USSR (million roubles).

Year	Volume	Export	Import	Trade balance
1970	3.4	2.6	0.8	+
1971	6.6	4.1	2.5	+
1975	17.3	13.3	4.0	+
1979	33.9	26.3	7.6	+
1980	173.1	164.5	8.6	+
1981	320.4	312.4	8.0	+
1982	141.8	132.9	8.9	+
1983	62.5	54.7	7.8	+
1984	73.9	62.6	11.3	+
1985	67.9	54.5	13.4	+
1986	90.9	80.7	10.2	+

Source: Thai Ministry of Commerce.

---

40   Police Major-General Sa-nga Kittikachorn, interview given to the press, 23 December 1970, Ministry of Foreign Affairs, Bangkok, Ministry of Foreign Affairs Documents, (9) MFA 1.1/107, the National Archives of Thailand (TNA), 21.
41   'FM Softens Line on Red Bloc', *Bangkok Post*, 29 December 1970, 1.
42   *Bangkok Post*, 25 December 1970, 2.

At the same time, the Soviet Union pushed for an air transport agreement with Thailand, which was drafted by the Soviets in early February 1970. The Soviet airline, Aeroflot, which had recently begun to expand its flights and develop new routes in Southeast Asia to locations such as Singapore and Cambodia, asked the Thai Government for flyover rights to Phnom Penh and landing rights in Bangkok.[43] The negotiations officially started in May, when a Russian air team, led by aviation chief AV Besedine, went to Bangkok to discuss the air transport agreement with Thai officials headed by Sirilak Chandrangsu, Permanent Secretary of Communications. Thailand and the Soviet Union readily agreed in principle to allow each other's national airlines to fly to their respective capitals and four points beyond. Thailand would grant Aeroflot rights to fly to Bangkok, and connect to Phnom Penh, Kuala Lumpur, Singapore and Jakarta. In return, Thai Airways International hoped to have stopovers at Tashkent and Moscow, and connect with Copenhagen, London, Paris and New York, which would provide the shortest route service from Southeast Asia to Europe and America. The exchange of rights would be incorporated into the air transport agreement. Sirilak pointed out that the agreement would be fair to both countries. However, he said the USSR may have more benefits 'because it has a larger company and will be able to make use of its rights much before THAI [Airways International]'.[44]

However, the first meeting ended in a stalemate. Officials on both sides conceded that no agreement had been reached, and their governments had to be consulted before further negotiations could be carried out. Sirilak said that 'there are many important obstacles that have to be looked into by the Cabinet'. He claimed that both sides had 'mostly differences in attitudes and ideologies'.[45]

In fact, the differences mainly concerned the stationing of Aeroflot's sales officers and mechanical personnel in Bangkok, which the Soviets demanded as necessary to facilitate its air operations. Earlier, the Thai Government had ruled that Thailand would not allow the Russians to station those personnel in Bangkok. The Thanom Government then decided to relax the restrictions, provided the offices were not used for political purposes. Thanom was also willing to speed up the discussion of

---

43 Record of conversation held between the Soviet Ambassador to Bangkok MM Volkov and Thai Permanent Secretary, Ministry of Foreign Affairs, Police Major Pramote Chongcharoen, 6 February 1969, in Ministry of Foreign Affairs, *Collected Volume of Soviet Archival Documents, 1941–1970*, 281.
44 'Russian Team due to Discuss Air Pact', *Bangkok Post,* 10 May 1970, 5.
45 'Thai, USSR Air Talks End in Stalemate', *Bangkok Post,* 20 May 1970, 3.

4. FLEXIBLE DIPLOMACY

other details with the Russians. Soviet Commercial Counsellor, Nikolai P Karpov, expressed optimism, saying that the decision was a 'good sign'.[46] The negotiators returned to the meetings and settled any difficulties.

On 6 May 1971, the air transport agreement was signed by Deputy Foreign Minister Police Major General Sa-nga Kittikachorn, and the Soviet ambassador, Anatoly A Rozanov, in Bangkok. The agreement was based on the principle of a 'fair and equal opportunity' for the designated airlines of the two countries to operate agreed services on their respective routes. On the one hand, Thai Airways International was entitled to operate its services from Thailand via New Delhi, Karachi, Kabul and Teheran to Tashkent and/or Moscow, and beyond to Copenhagen, Paris, London and New York, and vice versa. On the other hand, Aeroflot was entitled to operate its services from the Soviet Union via Tehran, Karachi, New Delhi and Rangoon to Bangkok, and beyond to Kuala Lumpur, Singapore, Manila, Jakarta and Australia, and vice versa. After the signing of the agreement, Sa-nga expressed the hope that the direct air services would serve to 'further strengthen the cordial relations between the two nations'. Ambassador Rozanov assured Sa-nga that Aeroflot would begin its air services to Bangkok within a few months, following approval from the Thai Government for its Bangkok-based personnel.[47] The inaugural Aeroflot flight arrived in Bangkok in November 1971.[48]

On 15 May 1971, the Thanom Government dispatched the second trade team, led by Economic Affairs Minister Bunchana Atthakorn, to the USSR and the East European countries, including Poland, Czechoslovakia, Hungary, Yugoslavia, Bulgaria and Romania. Three days before the departure, the 34-person Thai trade and economic delegation was instructed by Deputy Prime Minister General Praphas Charusathien to remember that the Thai Government wished to trade with any country that maintained a friendly attitude towards Thailand. Praphas expressed his support for Thailand's more extensive trade relations with the Soviet Union: 'Russia has shown her good attitude towards us and has not

---

46 Karpov claimed that he knew about the Thai decision to allow Aeroflot to set up offices in Bangkok from the *Bangkok Post* newspaper. As he put it, 'I don't know where we are. We haven't got any news for the Thais. We have no information whatsoever'. 'Soviets Happy with Air Talks', *Bangkok Post*, 27 June 1970, 2.
47 'Russians Jets May Land by August', *Bangkok Post*, 7 May 1971, 1.
48 Thai Ambassador to Moscow Yuad Lertrit and his wife, coupled with their two daughters, were guests of honour of Aeroflot who arrived in Bangkok with this historic flight. 'Govt Sets Out Rules for USSR Air Service', *Bangkok Post*, 25 May, 1971, 3; 'Envoy to Propose Thai-Soviet Move', *The Nation*, 4 November 1971.

involved itself in causing political problems for Thailand'.[49] The mission, which lasted for three weeks, aimed at exploring the possibilities of expanding trade relations between Thailand and those countries.[50] The mission was the first to be led by a Cabinet minister, and the largest ever to be sent to the communist bloc by the Thai Government. According to Bunchana, 'Russia has expressed its willingness to open broader trade relations with Thailand and the visit of our mission would help achieve this'. The mission listed 35 items to export to those countries, including rice, rubber, sugar, timber and mineral ores.[51]

When the Thai trade delegation reached Moscow on 19 May, Bunchana initiated talks with the Soviet Deputy Minister of Foreign Trade, Ivan Grishin. The talks were aimed at improving the trade agreement of 1970. One important issue was whether trade should be conducted between the governments or between a government agency and private firms. He said that trade between the USSR and Thailand was worth 3.4 million roubles last year, and wished to increase the volume of export and import.[52] The most interesting item was fluorite, which the USSR had begun to import from Thailand in 1970. The USSR wanted a five-year fluorite deal with Thailand. This presented an economic opportunity for Thai producers to diversify their markets, especially from the Japanese ones. The business representatives responded favourably to the Russian offer.[53] One of them, Major General Pramarn Adireksarn, an influential politician and the President of the Association of Thai Industries, revealed later that throughout the mission, chambers of commerce in those communist countries complained over restrictions on the entry of their people into Thailand. First, he suggested that 'if the government lifted its restrictions on visas, we'll see that trade relations between Thailand and those countries would move up very fast'. Second, Pramarn also recommended that the government form a single organisation to trade with communist countries because their foreign trade was undertaken by their governments.[54]

---

49 'Trade Team to USSR Will Represent Government', *Bangkok Post*, 13 May 1971, 13.
50 Infodept News, 17 May 1971, Ministry of Foreign Affairs Documents, (2) MFA 1.2/35, TNA, Bangkok, 119.
51 'Trade Team to USSR Will Represent Government', 13.
52 Infodept News, 17 May 1971, Ministry of Foreign Affairs Documents, (2) MFA 1.2/35, Bangkok, TNA, 119; 'Thai, USSR Talks Begin', *Bangkok Post*, 20 May 1971, 13.
53 'USSR-Thai Fluorite Trade Move Welcomed', *Bangkok Post*, 12 June 1971, 11.
54 'Pramarn Expects Large Growth in Red Trade', *Bangkok Post*, 15 June 1971, 11.

The trade agreement facilitated increasing commercial contacts between Thailand and the USSR in the 1970s. For instance, in 1971, the USSR made an approach to buy an additional 150,000 tons of maize, worth approximately 270 million baht. The proposal came from the new Commercial Counsellor of the USSR embassy, Victor I Ocheretin, who had direct contact with Vicharn Nivatwongse, Director-General of the Foreign Trade Department. Ocheretin informed Vicharn that the Russian buyers wished to import between 20,000 and 30,000 tons per month. Vicharn guaranteed that Thailand would be in a position to supply the Russians.[55] Overall, according to Yuad Lertrit, the Ambassador to Moscow, there was good potential for Thailand to export maize, tin, fluorite, rubber and tobacco to the Soviet Union despite some residual issues.[56]

In sum, Thailand since 1969 established 'closer but correct and careful ties' with the Soviet Union, which began to seek greater involvement in the region.[57] For Thailand, the Soviet Union was no longer considered an enemy. The Thai Government performed diplomatic practices of détente with the Soviet Union in the realms of regional receptivity toward the Soviet Union as well as bilateral trade and air transport agreements, thereby increasing their mutual contact. Readjustment with the Soviet Union was still an ongoing and unfinished project in the 1970s, yet it was much further ahead than any rapprochement with China, which will be discussed in the next section.

4.3. Facing the 'Tiger': Back-Channel Diplomacy with China

> I don't see why, if the United States can meet with the representatives of Beijing in Warsaw, we cannot meet with them somewhere in Asia, such as Japan or Hong Kong.
>
> – Thanat Khoman, foreign minister[58]

---

55 'USSR Wants 150,000 Tons Maize', *Bangkok Post*, 28 October 1971, 13.
56 For example, there were reports that Thai fluorite ore shipped to the USSR in early 1971 did not measure up to Soviet standards. Yuad also mentioned two other obstacles which needed to be overcome, namely poor Thai export control and the lack of a regular shipping service to the Soviet Union. He recommended that should the Thai government develop the potential, it would establish a group consisting of Thai exporters and government representatives dealing specifically with each item: 'Envoy to Propose Thai-Soviet Move'.
57 Theh Chongkhadikij, 'Thailand 1971: A Year for Adjustments of Political Alignments', *Bangkok Post*, 27 December 1970, 19.
58 Thanat Khoman, interview, 'Strategy for Peace', *Bangkok Post*, 30 March 1969.

From early 1969, Thanat Khoman publicly offered a dialogue with the PRC. Between 1970 and 1971, Thailand's Ministry of Foreign Affairs (MFA) tried to establish greater contact with the PRC via third parties such as Albania, Sweden, France and Italy, respectively. After China's entry to the UN in October 1971, Thanat directly contacted Chinese representatives at the UN in New York. This section is divided into two parts. The first part discusses back-channel diplomacy with China. The second examines Thailand's position and practices regarding China's admission to the UN. These processes were not mutually exclusive.

4.3.1. Contact via Third Parties

The Thai MFA made incessant attempts to contact Chinese representatives via third parties at international venues. While there is no official memorandum available documenting the specific detail of back-channel diplomacy, we can deduce the practices from what Thanat and high-ranking diplomats said and did throughout the periods of 1969 and 1971. We now know that Prime Minister Thanom authorised and closely supervised the process himself.[59] The absence of official documents suggests that the operation was diplomatically covert and secretive. Almost all these conversations were conducted verbally, rather than written. The anxiety of the Thai state in general, and the ambiguity of Chinese intentions toward Thailand, rendered diplomatic contact with the Chinese largely secret, if not politically dangerous. Minimising documentation, to an extent, provided a deniability clause for the Thai military elite. Nonetheless, despite the behind-the-scenes diplomatic missions, the indirect contacts with the PRC were leaked, both intentionally and unintentionally.

Since early 1969, Thanat had consistently engaged in a 'peace offensive' with China. He said that Thailand was 'ready to sit down and talk with Red China, to seek genuine peace for the sake of Asia'.[60] In March 1969, in a speech to Parliament, Thanat reiterated that he was willing and ready to carry 'the offensive for peace and stability to Beijing', and if possible, to negotiate a trade pact with China. However, diplomatic relations were not contemplated for the time being.[61] Because of Beijing's stance, Thanat knew that the peace offensive was complicated. Beijing, he said, was

---

59 Ministry of Foreign Affairs Documents, (2) MFA 1.2/35, TNA, Bangkok, 141–43; 'Thanat Makes a Verbal Détente', *Bangkok Post*, 15 May 1971.
60 *Bangkok Post*, 27 February 1969.
61 *Bangkok Post*, 25 March 1969.

conservative. The Communist Chinese are petrified in their position. They have not changed their policy of supporting terrorist activities in many Asian countries, including Thailand. They have shown no flexibility whatsoever in their attitude towards peaceful coexistence.[62]

But for Thailand, this was a matter of national survival as well as peace and security in the region. Therefore, Thanat stated:

> we must be more flexible in our approach. We cannot simply stay behind an imaginary Maginot Line. If they [Chinese Communist leaders] do not respond to this peaceful initiative, they will be seen in an unfavourable light by the outside world.[63]

Thanat suggested that if talks with China were held, it would be 'open talks', something similar to those that took place at the Bandung Conference in 1955. He emphasised that there would be no 'secret mission' by any Thais to Mainland China.[64] In 1969, Thanat's main idea was to end the hostile situation so that both countries could return to the 'spirit of Bandung' when there was 'an attempt to create a certain sense of solidarity and peaceful coexistence'.[65] In early 1970, Thanat specifically called for a 'revival of the Bandung formula with necessary modifications'. He stated that 'if the smaller nations could cooperate, they might convince China at such a meeting to come to terms with its neighbors'.[66]

By the end of the 1960s, the Chinese had not responded to Thanat's various offers in kind. As Thanat put it in June 1969:

> so far there has been no reply or reaction on the part of Beijing. I suppose that is the general attitude of Beijing for the time being. Beijing has declined to meet with other nations; the only visible contact which Beijing has is with Albania and perhaps with Sweden. But so far I am not aware that any progress has been achieved.[67]

---

62 *Bangkok Post*, 25 April 1969.
63 *Bangkok Post*, 25 April 1969.
64 *Bangkok Post*, 11 June 1969.
65 Thanat Khoman, 'Interview Given by Foreign Minister Thanat Khoman to Beryl Bernay of the Westinghouse Broadcasting Company, Derek Davies of the Far Eastern Economic Review, Joonghee Park of the Central Daily News of South Korea, Jung Suk Lee of the Dong-a Ilbo of South Korea and Kim Willenson of UPI', Bangkok, 26 March 1969, in *Collected Interviews of H.E. Dr. Thanat Khoman, Vol. 3: 1969*, 489.
66 *Strait Times*, 26 February 1970.
67 Thanat Khoman, 'Interview Given by Foreign Minister Thanat Khoman to Mass Media Representatives at Kawana Japan', 10 June 1969, in *Collected Interviews of H.E. Dr. Thanat Khoman, Vol. 3: 1969*, 542.

Throughout 1970, Chinese reactions to Thailand were mixed. China continued its aggressive gestures and policies against Thailand. For example, it built a road in northern Laos near the Mekong River, which the Thai Government perceived to be a vital threat to its territorial sovereignty.[68]

The idea of meeting with the Chinese, nevertheless, remained open. In September 1970, Thanat reiterated that there remained a 'public offer' by the Thai Government to 'sit down and meet with Beijing representatives'. Thanat presumed that the Chinese Government had not yet responded to his offer because it wanted secret talks.[69] Separately, a spokesman for the Government's United Thai People's Party and representative, Yuang Iamsila (Udon Thani), proposed trade with Communist China through third countries. He said: 'Why not trade through Hong Kong or Singapore?' In this issue, Thanat suggested that 'whether we trade directly or through third countries, we have to first find out if we stand to gain or lose'.[70]

In 1970, Thanat and his close associates at the Foreign Ministry began to make contact with the Chinese. Discussions with Chinese officials were conducted through Pridi Phanomyong, the former Thai prime minister who had previously been exiled in China for more than 20 years, and since 1970 remained in exile in Paris,[71] and Étienne Manac'h, the new French Ambassador to Beijing (1969–1975).[72] Manac'h was a personal acquaintance of Thanat and had passed through Bangkok in 1969 before he took up his ambassadorial post in Beijing.[73]

In an interview with *The Nation*'s special correspondent in Paris in August 1971, Pridi claimed China was ready to establish relations with Thailand if the Thai Government 'changes her hostile policy'. His exile in Beijing made him quite familiar with some high-ranking Chinese officials and he said that the crucial issue for rapprochement with China was about motives:

---

68   *Bangkok Post*, 5 July 1969.
69   *Bangkok Post*, 10 September 1970.
70   *Bangkok Post*, 29 December 1970.
71   Maynard Parker, 'Untying Thailand', *Foreign Affairs*, January 1973, 334.
72   *Bangkok Post*, 22 May 1969.
73   Suthichai Yoon, 'Thai-China Talks Likely', *The Nation*, 6 September 1971.

> If Thailand had good motives towards them, they would certainly reciprocate. Let bygones be bygones. I don't think there are any problems with Communist China. It would be a noble thing if two hostile persons can patch up their quarrels.[74]

Like Thanat, Pridi strongly urged a *'flexible'* foreign policy – with the objective of ensuring Thailand's survival amid the changing global and regional dynamisms. He traced this policy back to the reign of King Rama V in the late nineteenth century:

> Just look back at the example as that set down by King Rama V. We followed a neutral policy and that saved our country. There was a balance of powers. We must accept that while all other neighbouring countries fell into the hands of foreign countries, King Rama V saved Thailand from imperialism because His Majesty followed a flexible policy.

'Whenever we took a different line set down by His Majesty King Rama V', Pridi continued, 'we always had troubles such as when we sided with Japan during World War II'.[75]

Pridi also suggested that Thailand should trade with every country without taking their political regimes or ideologies into consideration. As he queried:

> What kind of Chinese are we talking about? Look at those Chinese merchants in the country. Why are they so rich? If we trade with Communist China, it should be on a government-to-government basis. They hold two trade exhibitions every year. When foreign merchants visit them and sign trade contracts, they sign on behalf of their governments. The government can also choose to allow some particular organizations to deal with Communist China – not private merchants.[76]

---

74 Somrit Intaphanti, 'Pridi: China Ready for Thailand Ties', *The Nation*, 16 August 1971; Ministry of Foreign Affairs Documents, (2) MFA 1.2/36, TNA, Bangkok, 175.
75 Somrit, 'Pridi: China Ready for Thailand Ties'; Ministry of Foreign Affairs Documents, (2) MFA 1.2/36, TNA, Bangkok, 175.
76 Somrit, 'Pridi: China Ready for Thailand Ties'; Ministry of Foreign Affairs Documents, (2) MFA 1.2/36, TNA, Bangkok, 175.

Trade with China, for him, was inevitable. Commenting on the possibility that President Nixon could visit Beijing in the near future, Pridi asserted that: 'the United States simply cannot afford to ignore a country with 800 million people. It's a big market'.[77]

Later, Prime Minister Thanom admitted that both Foreign Minister Thanat and Deputy Foreign Minister Sa-nga Kittikachorn had met separately with Pridi at the Royal Thai Embassy in Paris in 1971, but denied that Pridi was asked to serve as a middleman in contacting China. As he told Thai reporters, 'I have never assigned Pridi to do anything'. Thanom said the Cabinet members did not discuss any political issues with Pridi, who spoke 'about his life in Beijing'.[78] Pridi himself also denied that he was a 'third party' in making contact between the two countries.[79]

However, Thanat continued to make appeals for dialogue with the Chinese. On 13 January 1971, in an interview with Columbia Broadcasting Corporation (CBS) Television, he reemphasised his 'peace offensive' with China, despite the fact the Chinese had failed to respond. He said that time would be needed for the Chinese leaders to realise the benefits of peaceful coexistence with Thailand and other Asian countries. Thanat added:

> As Asians, we are patient. If they want to play ball with us, we in Asia are always ready to join in the game. If, on the contrary, they want to create disturbances and insurgencies in our lands, we will fight them as indeed we are doing.[80]

The absence of any Chinese response was largely due to the domestic politics of the Cultural Revolution. When the Cultural Revolution ended in the early 1970s, the Chinese Government began to look outward, and normalise its diplomacy with other countries, thereby opening a window of opportunity for Thailand. The first sign, or turning point, was Sino–US détente, beginning with 'non-political' events like a table tennis, or ping-pong, tournament in April 1971, and followed by the relaxation of the

---

77 Somrit, 'Pridi: China Ready for Thailand Ties'; Ministry of Foreign Affairs Documents, (2) MFA 1.2/36, TNA, Bangkok, 175.
78 'PM Says Ministers Met Pridi in Paris', *Bangkok Post*, 22 July 1971.
79 Theh Chongkhadikij, 'Pridi: Recognize China Now', *Bangkok Post*, 7 November 1971.
80 Thanat Khoman's interview with CBS Television in Bangkok, 13 January 1971 (extracts), in Jain, *China and Thailand*, doc. 183; see also 'Govt Launches Asian Peace Offensive', *Bangkok Post*, 14 January 1971.

American trade embargo with the PRC.⁸¹ The Thai Government officially welcomed this détente. As Prime Minister Thanom said, if the Chinese leaders 'stop giving us trouble, we can be friends'. Thanat observed that 'the Chinese, clever and chauvinistic, have now opened a window to the rest of the world'. He went on:

> Communist China has undergone internal convulsions and has isolated itself. It is now realizing that times have changed and that isolation is costly in terms of economic development. It cannot keep up with modern technology and it cannot compete with the United States, Japan and Europe.⁸²

Thanat said that China had moved in 'a rather clever way' because they used non-political ping-pong diplomacy to allow them to take steps toward the relaxation of relations with Washington.⁸³ Nevertheless, for Thanat, China 'continues to constitute a danger' to Thailand and other Southeast Asian countries. He expressed hope that China would renounce its sponsorship and support of 'national liberation movements' in those countries, including Thailand. As Thanat put it, 'if the Chinese Communist leaders change their attitude, we will change ours'.⁸⁴

Another good sign was the decrease in Red Radio attacks on the Thai Government. In March 1971, General Saiyud Kerdphol, Director of the Communist Suppression Operations Command, announced that communist propaganda and attacks against the Thai Government via the clandestine radio station, Voice of the Thai People, had been reduced to a certain extent over the past 30 days. He attributed the ebbing of such attacks to improved trade relations between Thailand and other Eastern European countries. However, Saiyud said that communist activities, which were intent on winning the hearts and minds of local villagers and undermining Thailand's national security, remained ongoing.⁸⁵

Despite some good signs, the Thanom Government made it clear that Thailand would refrain from automatically following the American move, which was using ping-pong diplomacy to kick-start the normalisation

---

81   'American Sportsmen to Visit Red China', *Bangkok Post*, 8 April 1971. See Margaret MacMillan, *Nixon in China: The Week That Changed the World* (New York: Random House, 2007), 173–81.
82   'We Can be Friends, PM Tells China', *Bangkok Post*, 17 April 1971.
83   Thanat Khoman, interview, *The New York Times*, 21 April 1971 found in the Ministry of Foreign Affairs Documents, (2) MFA 1.2/35, TNA, Bangkok, 141.
84   'We Can be Friends, PM Tells China'.
85   'Attacks by Red Radio Lessen', *Bangkok Post*, 4 March 1971.

of Sino–US relations. Foreign Minister Thanat stressed that Thailand had its own independent policy to follow in order to protect its own national interests. He claimed he had anticipated the American move 'for quite some time': 'We knew that the United States would change its attitude towards Communist China and reopen trade links. Therefore, we are not surprised'.[86] Thanat remarked:

> We watch developments with great interest. If the new smiles [from the Chinese] were to be followed by measures to ease the situation in Southeast Asia, so much the better. What we would like to know is what exactly is the meaning and import of those new smiles. Was it to pave the way toward recognition by more countries or to prevent what Beijing itself has called 'hostile collusion' between the United States and the Soviet Union? Was it a move to join the Big-Powers club? Was there a real change of attitude or policy … a reversal to the Bandung policy? No one knows exactly.[87]

According to Thanat, there could be at least two possible tests of China's real intention:

> The first important test … is the Vietnam War. If there were a real change, then we should see a new mood or atmosphere reflected in the attitudes of North Vietnam and the Viet Cong at Paris … The second important test is the situation in Southeast Asia, especially Beijing's attitude toward Thailand and other countries in the region. If Beijing were to adopt a more peaceful approach with less doctrinaire support to 'wars of national liberation', then there would be a real change in Chinese attitude.

Thanat contended that 'these two tests will be sufficient to gauge the reality of the new smile … But if nothing happens, then it would be just a superficial, tactical move, and not a real change of direction'.[88]

Thai foreign policy was thus forging a wait-and-see approach. As Thanat put it, 'at present there are no changes. I cannot say now the Government will make any changes in the future'.[89] In addition, the Thanom

---

86   'Thailand hails US China Move', *Bangkok Post*, 16 April 1971.
87   Thanat Khoman, interview, *The New York Times*, 21 April 1971 found in the Ministry of Foreign Affairs Documents, (2) MFA 1.2/35, TNA, Bangkok, 141.
88   Thanat Khoman, interview, *The New York Times*, 21 April 1971 found in the Ministry of Foreign Affairs Documents, (2) MFA 1.2 35, TNA, Bangkok, 141.
89   'Thailand Hails US China Move'.

4. FLEXIBLE DIPLOMACY

Government took a cautious attitude towards the question of trade with China. The option of trade, without prior diplomatic recognition, was left open, should the Chinese renounce their aggressive and hostile policies. Mentioning that a number of European countries had begun to trade with the Chinese without having first set up formal diplomatic relations, Thanat said that Thailand could trade with China without prior diplomatic relations if it deemed to be economically advantageous to conduct such commerce.[90] Legally, trade with China would also infringe the Revolutionary Party Announcement No. 53, prohibiting the sale of goods to China. Deputy Minister of Economic Affairs, Prasit Kanchanawat, recommended that the law be abolished as a step to further establish trade relations with China. If the government repealed the law, trade would become possible.[91]

At the MFA, Thanat set up a China-watching committee to study the pros and cons of trading with Communist China, as well as to monitor the developments in China and its external relations.[92] Other Cabinet members also gave their opinions. Deputy Prime Minister Praphas Charusathien said that China, like any other country, should purchase rice and other products directly from Thailand. Pote Sarasin, Minister of National Development, insisted that Thailand would begin trading if China separated 'her trade from political issues'. However, according to Pote, the opening up of trade would not directly lead to diplomatic relations.[93]

Support for trade with Communist China was growing not only in the government but also among other members of the political and business community. Some opposition parties' members, such as Pichai Rattakul (Democrat, Bangkok) and Somkid Srisangkhom (Social Democrat), agreed with Thanat's proposal to establish dialogue with the Chinese but cautioned that it must be carried out with extreme care and planning. As Pichai said, 'unlike the countries in the West, Thailand is within easy reach of Red China geographically'.[94] Even the well-renowned proprietor of the *Siam Rath* newspaper, MR Kukrit Pramoj, who had previously disregarded Thanat's ideas, now began to show support for the discourse

---

90 'We Can be Friends, PM Tells China'.
91 'Abolish China Trade, Says Prasit', *Bangkok Post*, 18 April 1971.
92 Theh Chongkhadikij, 'Pressure Grows to Trade with China', *Bangkok Post*, 26 April 1971.
93 Statement by Pote Sarasin, 18 May 1971, and Deputy Prime Minister Praphas Charusathien's interview with the *Bangkok Post*, 26 May 1971, in Jain, *China and Thailand*, 178.
94 'MPs Back Thanat on Dialogue', *Bangkok Post*, 24 May 1971.

of flexible diplomacy with China. He said that Thailand had to admit the existence of the PRC: 'China is a big country, and being an enemy will not be beneficial to Thailand'.[95]

Similarly, in the business community, Charoon Sibunruang, the President of the Thai Chamber of Commerce and of the Board of Trade, favoured the opening of trade with China. He suggested that the government should abrogate the laws and regulations to permit trade with China, by explaining that 'Thailand will gain a lot from trading with Communist China, since it is a huge market'. However, Charoon opposed direct trade with Communist China because 'we are uncertain of what the Chinese Communists are up to'. For the present, trade should be conducted through a third country, preferably Hong Kong.[96] Some business representatives, such as Major General Pramarn Adireksarn, the President of the Association of Thai Industries, disagreed. Pramarn claimed that Thailand was not yet ready for trading with Beijing because of the vulnerability to communism and the danger of developing a large trade deficit with Communist China.[97]

Following the establishment of Sino–US rapprochement, Chinese leaders led by Premier Zhou Enlai opened up normal diplomacy with other countries. In May 1971, Thanat sounded optimistic about Sino–Thai relations, and accordingly used the term 'People's Republic of China' for the first time. He claimed that Beijing had responded favourably to Thailand. Communist China, he added, 'have shown interest in contacting us and are watching our attitude'.[98] Having appealed to Chinese leaders for an open dialogue two years ago, Thanat disclosed that a number of 'third parties' had since approached Beijing on behalf of Thailand.[99] He revealed:

> after our announcement that we would like open dialogue with Beijing ... some friendly 'third parties' offered to make approaches for us. Tensions have been relaxed. Disturbances along the border have been reduced.[100]

---

95 'M.R. Kukrit Backs Thanat on China', *Bangkok Post*, 11 June 1971.
96 'Charoon Backs Beijing Trade', *Bangkok Post*, 4 May 1971.
97 *Bangkok Post*, 5 May 1971.
98 'Thanat Makes a Verbal Détente'.
99 An anonymous foreign ministry official told the *New York Times* that Thanat had opened the door to better relations with China in a speech in Tokyo in 1969, even before Beijing invited the US ping-pong team to China in April 1971. He claimed that Thailand had received encouraging indications from Beijing through third parties. Henry Kamm, 'Thailand Cites own China Moves', *New York Times*, 16 May 1971.
100 'Thanat Makes a Verbal Détente'.

At that time, Thanat said he could not identify the 'third parties' because of the delicate nature of their missions. As Thanat said: 'Even if you asked for ten hours, I would not tell.' Above all else, Thanat believed 'the Beijing leaders have shown interest because we have made an open offer for a dialogue with them'.[101] We now know that Thanat wanted to establish more contact with China via third parties such as Albania, Sweden, France and Italy. Among them, France was the principal one.[102]

These indirect exchanges had, he explained, achieved a 'better understanding between the two countries. Our differences have narrowed. The situation has improved. Beijing leaders have begun to understand us [Thailand]. It may well lead to a real dialogue'.[103] Asked when a real dialogue would take place, he said:

> it's not up to us alone. Diplomatic contacts have to be made quietly, discreetly. Participants and subjects of negotiations could never be disclosed. We have to be patient and careful, keeping the national interests in mind.[104]

For Thanat, the ultimate aim of state-to-state dialogue with the Chinese was to dampen the communist insurgency in Thailand. As he put it, 'the idea is to stop the killing. We want to stop being the enemy'.[105] However, Thanat warned against rushing willy-nilly into setting up an embassy, due to the risk of propaganda and subversion in Thailand: 'we will deal with the Chinese Communists only on a basis of mutual trust and equality'.[106]

Meanwhile, the Thai Government officially ordered Radio Thailand to cease propaganda attacks against Communist China. In May 1971, Deputy Prime Minister Praphas gave an interview, saying that the government had cut down on 'polemics against Communist China over Radio Thailand in order to find out if China would make a friendly response'. He emphasised that Thailand had a policy of being friendly with

---

101 'Beijing "Wants our Opinions" – Thanat', *Bangkok Post*, 9 May 1971.
102 Kamm, 'Thailand Cites own China Moves' found in the Ministry of Foreign Affairs Documents, (2) MFA 1.2/36, TNA, Bangkok, 83.
103 Theh Chongkhadikij, 'Beijing Dialogue a Step Nearer', *Bangkok Post*, 14 May 1971.
104 'Thanat Makes a Verbal Détente'.
105 'FM Explains Move to Cut Insurgency', *Bangkok Post*, 20 May 1971.
106 'FM Explains Move to Cut Insurgency'.

all countries, including communist states, which were friendly to Thailand.[107] Thanat agreed with Praphas, stating that the halt in radio attacks was 'a way to reduce tensions'.[108]

However, this early Thai détente with China inflamed public debate, and in particular generated discontent against Thanat specifically, discussed in more detail in the next chapter. One consequence of this heated debate was that by the end of May 1971, Thanom made a decision to slow the rate of contact with China until such a time that China ceased supporting the insurgent movements in Thailand: moving the process to what was described as 'go-slow' (*pai-cha*) diplomacy.[109] The Thai Government also decided against opening trade relations with Communist China for the present. Thanom was concerned that China would not separate trade from politics.[110]

The Minister for National Development, Pote Sarasin, asserted:

> if China can treat its economic relations with other countries separately from political considerations, there will not be problems in trading with other countries. The question is whether or not Red China can do that.[111]

Consequently, it would be better for Thailand to be cautious in its development of economic relations with China and to open such relations only 'when Red China separates her trade from political issues'. Economic Affairs Minister Bunchana Atthakorn echoed the same concern. Trading with China would not be 'safe' as long as that country continued attacking Thailand through Radio Beijing and carried on its 'subversive infiltration' of the kingdom. Thailand would not, therefore, change its 'policy before that country changed its attitude towards us'.[112] In brief, the government's 'go-slow, wait-and-see attitude to ensure minimum safety replaced a quickened pace to seek better understanding with Communist China'.[113]

---

107 Deputy Prime Minister Praphas Charusathien's interview with the *Bangkok Post*, 26 May 1971, in Jain, *China and Thailand*, 178–79.
108 'Thanat Makes a Verbal Détente'.
109 Theh Chongkhadikij, 'Govt Orders Slowdown in Beijing Thaw', *Bangkok Post*, 24 May 1971 found in the Ministry of Foreign Affairs Documents, (2) MFA 1.2/36, TNA, 366.
110 'Thanom Halts Contact with Beijing', *Bangkok Post*, 5 July 1971.
111 Quoted in Shee Poon Kim, 'The Politics of Thailand's Trade Relations with the People's Republic of China', *Asian Survey* 21, no. 3 (March 1981): 314.
112 Quoted in Shee Poon Kim, 'The Politics of Thailand's Trade Relations with the People's Republic of China', *Asian Survey* 21, no. 3 (March 1981): 314–15.
113 Theh, 'Govt Orders Slowdown in Beijing Thaw'; Ministry of Foreign Affairs Documents, (2) MFA 1.2/36, TNA, Bangkok, 366.

However, 'go-slow' diplomacy was partially undone by the US National Security Advisor Henry Kissinger's secret visit to Beijing between 9 and 11 July 1971 and the subsequent announcement that Nixon would visit Beijing in February 1972. Kissinger had visited Bangkok en route and one early morning in July 1971, US Ambassador to Bangkok Leonard Unger invited a group of Thais, including Sulak Sivaraksa, a leading Thai public intellectual, and Tej Bunnag, a young Foreign Ministry official, to a working breakfast with Kissinger. The topic of discussion was 'how to end the Vietnam War'. Tej recalled that at the meeting:

> Sulak Sivaraksa said 'the key to resolving the Vietnam War is China'. Kissinger was dumbstruck, but said nothing … we later learned that he went on a secret trip to Beijing.[114]

The Beijing visit surprised many in the Thai establishment, including Prime Minister Thanom. He told the reporters that 'Dr. Kissinger was in Bangkok, and then he left to return to the United States. Now, we learn that he had not gone home but made a side trip to Beijing'. Asked for the Thai attitude toward this Sino–US rapprochement, Thanom replied that 'we have not yet done anything about this, but our policy is that we will be friendly to all countries which are not hostile to us'.[115] A day later, Thanom said 'we will wait and see how other nations react towards the latest development'. Yet, he also insisted that if the other side eased its hostile attitude, Thailand would reciprocate.[116]

In his initial response, Thanat expedited contacts with China via third parties to ascertain the possibility of establishing diplomatic relations. In August, Prime Minister Thanom again denied that Thanat had asked former prime minister Pridi Phanomyong to be a middleman to contact with the Chinese leaders.[117] Thanom acknowledged that Thanat met Pridi in Paris 'because they used to know each other and had once worked together'. While the prime minister reassured the press that Thailand had not asked any government to establish contact with Communist China, he admitted that 'several countries with good intentions offered to inform Beijing of our policy and to inform us about the attitude of the Chinese Communists'.[118]

---

114 Quoted in Supalak Ganjanakhundee and Wiraj Sripong, 'How Sino-Thai Relations Were Sparked Off 40 Years Ago', *The Nation*, 29 June 2015.
115 'Nixon's Beijing Visit Comes as Surprise', *Bangkok Post*, 17 July 1971.
116 'Govt Talks on Nixon Visit Tomorrow', *Bangkok Post*, 19 July 1971.
117 He had also denied the Pridi connection earlier in July.
118 'Thanom Defends FM', *Bangkok Post*, 11 August 1971.

Despite previous attempts to open up back channels for Thailand to approach the Chinese, there was no response until October 1971. According to Ross Terrill, an Australian professor at Harvard University who spent some time in China, it was only in October 1971 that Beijing signalled a readiness to open a dialogue with Thailand.[119] Secret reciprocal contacts facilitated by France, in particular the new French Ambassador to Beijing Étienne Manac'h, had advanced to the point where China was now prepared to open talks with Thailand in order to begin the process of establishing formal relations between the two countries.[120] Despite his attempt to hide the identification of the third party, Thanat reluctantly admitted that particular third country was 'a country which is friendly to us and has a representative in Beijing'.[121] Also, the French embassy in Bangkok had reportedly been using its 'good offices' to bring about an 'understanding' between Thailand and China. Officials of the embassy told *The Nation* newspaper that although the Thai Government had not requested the embassy to contact China and nor had the embassy offered the service, 'it does not mean that things don't take place'. They admitted that since France had an embassy in Beijing, it would only be normal for French officials to discuss Thai–Chinese relations when 'chances arise'.[122]

In early October, Thanat disclosed in an interview with a foreign correspondent that Communist China had begun to respond to the suggestion of a dialogue with Thailand via a third country. He claimed that Thailand had realised the role which Communist China would play on the international scene for many years and this led to Thailand approaching the possibility of a dialogue. As he put it, 'it will be easier for Thailand to get in touch with the People's Republic of China after its admission to the United Nations'.[123] According to Terrill, the Chinese expected to enter into such a relationship on the condition that, following

---

119 Earlier, in an interview on 30 July, Terrill told Thanat that 'the Chinese are interested in your proposal for a dialogue with them and in particular your personal proposal'. However, Terrill believed that nothing had come of this proposal perhaps because 'there have sometimes come different voices from Thailand'. Thanat agreed that there were different views on the question of China. See 'We can Give a "Friendly" China our Cooperation – Thanat', *Bangkok Post*, 18 September 1971.
120 There was some speculation in Bangkok that Pridi Phanomyong was an intermediary between Thanat and the Chinese. See Parker, 'Untying Thailand', 334. Terrill suggests otherwise, that it was through a French envoy to Beijing who knew Thanat very well and visited him on his way to take up the China post. Thanat did have a meeting with Pridi at an Embassy reception in Paris. However, Pridi was unable or unwilling to act as a go-between. Ross Terrill, 'Reports and Comment – Thailand', *The Atlantic Monthly*, October 1972, 7–8.
121 'Beijing Responds to "Dialogue" Plan', *Bangkok Post*, 6 October 1971.
122 Suthichai, 'Thai-China Talks Likely'.
123 'Beijing Responds to "Dialogue" Plan'.

Thanat's claims, American troops would withdraw from Thailand with the peace settlement of the Vietnam War. In return, China was to stick strictly to its Five Principles of Coexistence and a policy of noninterference in Thailand, thereby ending its support of insurgencies.[124] By that time, the beginning of a breakthrough in Thai–Chinese relations emerged. Critically, on 25 October 1971, the PRC was given Taiwan's seat at the UN. Thailand could now make direct contact with the Chinese at the UN, rather than via third parties.

4.3.2. The PRC's Entry into the UN

The admission of the PRC to the UN was a vital moment in the development of Thai–Chinese relations. At the outset, the Thai Government had had a strong position against Mainland Chinese representation. Giving a statement at the UN General Assembly in November 1969, Anand Panyarachun, Thai Ambassador to the UN, said that Communist China still maintained its 'hostile behavior and inflexible policy', and had not given up its 'aggressive proclivities and expansionist tendencies' towards the neighbouring countries in Southeast Asia, including Thailand. As he put it:

> Since its assumption of the reins of Government on the Chinese Mainland, the Beijing regime has conducted a continuing and vicious campaign against this world body. It has defied the United Nations by acts which contravene the latter and the spirit of the Charter. The People's Republic of China has, by word and deed, demonstrated its unwillingness to refrain in its international relations from the threat or use of force against the territorial integrity or political independence of any State.[125]

In November 1970, Anand reiterated this narrative at the UN General Assembly, by asserting that 'we have seen no evidence that would qualify the People's Republic of China as a peaceloving State'. 'In our view', he claimed, 'the People's Republic of China has so far not shown that it was willing or able to accept the obligations as contained in the Charter of our Organization', in particular no respect for the principle of nonintervention

---

124 Terrill, 'Reports and Comment – Thailand', 7–8.
125 Statement by Thai representative Anand Panyarachun in the UN General Assembly on Chinese representation in the UN, 10 November 1969, in Jain, *China and Thailand*, 163–66.

in the domestic affairs of other states. Accordingly, Thailand continued to hold the view that the Republic of China, or Taiwan, was entitled to retain its seat in the UN.[126]

By the mid-1971, a changing global balance of power, in particular the prospect of Sino–US rapprochement, revived the debate regarding China's UN membership among many countries, including Thailand. The Thai Government could not afford to stand idly by, and developed a 'two-China' policy. Thailand, it was decided, would not oppose the admission of the PRC into the UN, yet would vote to retain Nationalist China, or the Republic of China (ROC), in the international organisation.[127] As Thanom told Parliament in August:

> [if] there is a majority vote for Communist China to enter the United Nations, we will not protest. But we cannot support the ouster of Nationalist China because we are old friends.[128]

However, in official discourses, Thailand did not subscribe to a 'two-China' policy because the policy was rejected by both the Communist China and Nationalist China. There was only one China.[129] In a statement at the UN General Assembly in September 1971, Thanat asserted:

> It is indeed a fact that both Beijing and Taiwan firmly adhere to the concept of 'one China'. Other countries, such as Thailand, likewise believe in the unity and integrity of all sovereign states, and it is hoped that time will bring an accommodation to the conflicting claims of the parties concerned.[130]

In brief, though acknowledging de jure One-China policy, Thailand de facto shifted its position towards the dual representation in the UN.

On 10 September 1971, the Thai National Security Council chaired by Prime Minister Thanom made an official decision that Thailand would vote for Beijing's admission to the UN while voting to retain Taiwan inside the world body.[131] According to Thanat, the council realised that

---

126 Statement by Thai representative Anand Panyarachun in the UN General Assembly on Chinese representation in the UN, 19 November 1970, in Jain, *China and Thailand*, 172–74.
127 'China Policy "to Suit Thailand" ', *Bangkok Post*, 7 August 1971.
128 *Bangkok Post*, 27 August 1971.
129 'Beijing Attacks Govt Stand', *Bangkok Post*, 19 September 1971.
130 Statement by Thai representative Thanat Khoman in the UN General Assembly, 30 September 1971, in Jain, *China and Thailand*, 182.
131 'Big Decision on China: Thailand to Vote for Beijing in UN', *Bangkok Post*, 11 September 1971; 'FM Hints at China Ties', *The Nation*, 15 September 1971.

Communist China's admission into the UN would ease world tensions as Beijing would be offered the opportunity to observe the UN Charter. For Thailand, moreover, Beijing's entry to the UN would provide an opportunity for direct dialogue without the necessity of back-channel diplomacy via third parties. With Communist China in the UN, Thailand would be able to get a better sense of Chinese attitudes and be provided with opportunities for ending a Chinese-sponsored 'war of national liberation' in Thailand. The council concluded that Thailand, regardless of its vote for Communist China in the UN, would not follow up with either trade or diplomatic relations with China in the immediate future.[132] It also banned any individual visits or travel to China.

With regard to the dual representation of the Chinese at the UN, Thanat said that it was a Chinese problem, which both Communist and Nationalist China needed to settle on their own. Thanat saw Taiwan's UN membership as a moral question. As he put it, 'we feel morally bound to support Taiwan membership due to our good relationship since the end of the war'.[133] Before Thanat left for the UN in New York, Thailand had not yet decided whether it would co-sponsor the American resolution for admission of Communist China into the UN and the retention of the Nationalist China in the international body.[134]

Parenthetically, at the UN General Assembly sessions, there were two resolutions regarding the Chinese representation. One was the Albanian resolution, which proposed to seat Beijing in the UN and oust Taiwan. The Chinese Communist Government showed clearly that it wanted to enter the UN on the terms of the Albanian resolution, which meant 'restoration to China of its rightful place in the UN'.[135] The second resolution was the American dual representation resolution, which called for the admission of Communist China in the UN and for consideration of the expulsion of the ROC as an 'important question' requiring two-thirds majority vote in the General Assembly.

A Thai delegation headed by Thanat left to attend the UN General Assembly, which began on 21 September. This included Thai Ambassador to the UN, Anand Panyarachun; Thai Ambassador to the Netherlands,

---

132 'Big Decision on China: Thailand to Vote for Beijing in UN'; 'Talks in House First: Opposition Backs China Policy', *Bangkok Post*, 12 September 1971.
133 'FM: We Back China's Entry', *Bangkok Post*, 18 September 1971.
134 'Gen Sa-nga Explains Policy', *Bangkok Post*, 16 September 1971.
135 'Beijing Attacks Govt Stand'.

Sompong Sucharitkul; Deputy Secretary-General of the Cabinet, Dusit Boontham and Secretary to the Foreign Minister, ML Pirapongse Kasemsri.[136] While in New York, Thanat decided to co-sponsor the American dual representation resolution and vote for China's UN membership, while at the same time reaffirming his support for the continued membership of Taiwan in the UN.[137] According to Deputy Prime Minister Praphas Charusathien, Thailand decided to co-sponsor the American resolution because:

1. Communist China has a population of over 700 million people and should not be kept out of the UN. Because of its size, it should sit in the Security Council.
2. Thailand has diplomatic and friendly relations with Nationalist China, which is a founder member of the UN.[138]

Speaking at the UN General Assembly on 22 October 1971, Thanat as the Thai representative said that the question and reality of Chinese representation was felt more by Thailand due to its proximity. As he put it:

> We are, in fact, dealing with something that touches upon tenuous threads of Asian political life as well as the precarious balance of forces both within the Asian and Pacific region and in the outside world.

He emphasised the principle of universality in his speech, noting that the principle had been invoked to justify the seating of Beijing. Thanat stressed that the same principle should be applied with equal force to the 14 million people of Taiwan. As he asserted:

> any proposal which would result in the denial of representation of that entity in the UN is an unavoidable infringement of the very same principle and will not bring us any nearer to the goal of universality of membership of the UN.[139]

---

136 Deputy Foreign Minister Sa-nga Kittikachorn joined the team later to serve as head of the delegation when the Foreign Minister returned to Bangkok before the end of the UN session. 'Thais to Key UN Meet in 9 Days', *The Nation*, 5 September 1971.
137 'Govt Will Back US Stance', *Bangkok Post*, 24 September 1971.
138 'Thailand to Keep Taps on China', *Bangkok Post*, 28 September 1971. See also 'Praphas Opts for Beijing Seat in UN', *The Nation*, 1 September 1971.
139 'FM Thanat Appeals for Two Chinas', *Bangkok Post*, 24 October 1971. See also Statement by Thai representative Thanat Khoman in the UN General Assembly on Chinese representation in the UN, 22 October 1971, in Jain, *China and Thailand*, Doc. 193.

4. FLEXIBLE DIPLOMACY

Beijing's entry, even on its own terms, could not undo the reality of Nationalist China. For Thailand, dual representation was the only logical solution, at least in the short term, until the Chinese people could resolve the question for themselves. As Thanat put it:

> That is why my Government has decided to support the representation of the People's Republic of China in both the Assembly and the Security Council. If, however, we also support the continued representation of the Republic of China in the Organization, it is because Thailand has had friendly and normal relations with [Taiwan] and there is no valid justification to do away with them.[140]

Thanat stated:

> ultimately it should be recognized that divergence between the Republic of China and the People's Republic of China is strictly a Chinese affair and must and can only be resolved by the Chinese people themselves, certainly not by outsiders or even the UN.

Finally, he expressed the hope that the peoples of the UN 'will live as one world united under the sign of universality'.[141] Thailand thus supported China's UN admission despite wanting the representation of Taiwan to continue.

On 25 October, following the defeat of the American resolution, the General Assembly voted overwhelmingly to admit the PRC into the UN and expel Taiwan under the Albanian resolution, by a historic 76–35 vote. Sino–US rapprochement – most notably, Henry Kissinger's second and public visit to Beijing in October during the UN sessions and the announcement of Nixon's impending visit to Beijing – was one of the key factors in securing the vote. Rather than voting against the Albanian resolution, Thailand abstained.[142] Thanat explained Thailand's decision by claiming that, first, this was a prearranged government decision to record an abstention if the US 'important question' resolution was

---

140 Statement by Thai representative Thanat Khoman in the UN General Assembly on Chinese representation in the UN, 22 October 1971, in Jain, *China and Thailand*, 184.
141 'FM Thanat Appeals for Two Chinas'. See also Statement by Thai representative Thanat Khoman in the UN General Assembly on Chinese representation in the UN, 22 October 1971, in Jain, *China and Thailand*, Doc. 193.
142 'Beijing's Victory: Drama at the UN', *Bangkok Post*, 27 September 1971; *Bangkok World*, 26 October 1971.

defeated.¹⁴³ Second, he also claimed that the abstention was not a signal of opposition to Communist China's entry, but an objection to the expulsion of Taiwan.¹⁴⁴ As he put it later, 'if we had voted against the resolution, we would have been down on record as against admission of the PRC to the UN'.¹⁴⁵ On a practical level, following China's UN entry, Thailand would have to allow Mainland Chinese delegations into Bangkok for meetings of the UN Economic Commission for Asia and the Far East (ECAFE) and other UN bodies.

China's admission to the UN brought forth increased pressure on the Thai Government to readjust its foreign policy towards Mainland China. Thai public opinion clamoured for improved relations with Beijing.¹⁴⁶ Meanwhile, three Members of Parliament, including Khaisaeng Sooksai (Peoples Party; Nakhon Phanom), Sanam Thirasirichote (Socialist Economic Front; Khon Kaen) and Somkid Srisangkhom (Social Democratic Party; Udon Thani) sent a cable to Chairman Mao Zedong congratulating him on the PRC's admission.¹⁴⁷

Shortly after the UN meeting in late October, Thanat had a stopover in Rome on his way back to Bangkok where he was granted an audience with Pope Paul in the Vatican. One Thai newspaper, *Phim Thai*, claimed that Thanat, accompanied by Major General Chatichai Choonhavan, Ambassador to Switzerland and Yugoslavia, would make a secret trip to Beijing to negotiate with the Chinese leaders.¹⁴⁸ Thanat denied the rumour that he would make a trip like Kissinger's secret trip, to Beijing on his return to Thailand.¹⁴⁹ When asked by reporters whether it was true that Foreign Minister Thanat had some talks with the Chinese trade delegation in Rome, Thanom replied, 'Such a report was unfounded and Thailand would not take the initiative to trade with China in the immediate future'. Questioned about what decision his government would make if China wished to open trade relations, Thanom replied that such trade would be certainly be beneficial to the country, but the government was not sure that China had the intentions to trade with

---

143 'Govt Calls Meet on China', *Bangkok Post*, 1 November 1971.
144 'US Move "Too Late" – Thanat', *Bangkok Post*, 27 October 1971.
145 'China Ready to Begin Talks', *Bangkok Post*, 13 November 1971.
146 'Three MPs Send Cable to Mao', *Bangkok Post*, 30 October 1971; 'MPs who Cabled Mao may Face Charges', *Bangkok Post*, 2 November 1971.
147 'Three MPs Send Cable to Mao'; 'MPs who Cabled Mao may Face Charges'.
148 'Thailand Negotiates Red China: Thanat Flies to Beijing', *Phim Thai*, 26 October 1971; 'Thanat Flies to Rome – Meet Chatichai', *Phim Thai*, 27 October 1971.
149 'Govt Calls Meet on China'.

Thailand. He insisted that a 'wait and see' attitude would be accurate in dealing with China for a time being.[150] Due to the urgency of the changing international situation, Thanom asked Thanat to cut short his stay in Rome.[151]

Upon his return, a historic meeting of the Thai National Security Council (NSC) was held on 3 November 1971 to discuss the Chinese admission. While Thailand continued to maintain friendly relations with Taiwan, Prime Minister Thanom raised doubts on China: 'Red China has just been made a member of the United Nations and we still do not know whether she will respect the spirit of the UN Charter'.[152] Nonetheless, the NSC decided to establish friendlier relations with the Chinese. The Council agreed in principle to consider removing the ban on trade with Beijing by abolishing the Revolutionary Party Announcement No. 53; to relax existing anticommunist laws; and to allow visits to Communist China of invited sports and cultural missions. The council reportedly approved of Thanat's efforts to ascertain the Chinese Government's position – either indirectly or through third parties. It identified the UN ECAFE annual convention, to be held during 15–27 March 1972 in Bangkok, as an opportunity for the first official talks between Thai and Chinese representatives.[153]

However, the NSC ruled out diplomatic relations with Beijing in the near future, and did not allow individual and political figures to visit Beijing.[154] As Thanom proclaimed, 'the softening of the government attitude toward Mainland China is aimed at paving the way for further relations with that country after it has been admitted to the United Nations'.[155] He said that trade with China would only be allowed on a government-to-government basis in the initial stages. Trade relations between private groups continued to be banned. Thanom confirmed that the government would continue to fight communist infiltration and insurgency, but would no longer consider China as the '*enemy of the nation*'.[156] Although the NSC, led by the military elite, had signalled the necessity of foreign policy transformation, its ultimate aim remained the same: cautious, 'go-slow' diplomacy.

---

150 'Thanom Denies Report', *Bangkok World*, 26 October 1971.
151 Suthichai Yoon, 'Thailand's New Approach Towards China', *The Nation*, 3 November 1971.
152 'Too Early to Open Ties with Beijing', *Bangkok Post*, 30 October 1971.
153 'Official Contact with China only in March', *The Nation*, 4 November 1971. See Kanchit Kumragse, 'China and ECAFE', *The Nation*, 3 November 1971.
154 'China Trade Ban to Go', *Bangkok Post*, 4 November 1971.
155 'PM Confirms China Decision', *Bangkok Post*, 5 November 1971.
156 'Thanom Paves Way for China Trade', *Bangkok Post*, 10 November 1971. My emphasis.

Many military leaders vocally echoed this stance, and indeed some publicly contradicted the NSC's recommendations, especially on trade. General Praphas Charusathien, Deputy Prime Minister, stressed that there could be no friendly diplomatic relations unless the 'war of national liberation against Thailand' was renounced: 'We have not shown any hostility towards Beijing. But the Chinese Communists have been supporting the insurgents here'.[157] He commented that the admission of Communist China into the UN did 'not mean that Thailand should at once set up diplomatic relations with Beijing'. On the contrary, resuming diplomatic relations 'should be taken calmly, as a matter of course'.[158] Praphas said that the Thai Government would move towards a 'status of relations on a basis of equality' in a stage-by-stage strategy. In its step-by-step plan, the Thai Government would first permit social contacts between Thai diplomats and Communist Chinese officials. Evaluating Beijing's attitude from the response of the Chinese officials at informal meetings, the government would then consider the next move, namely the exchange of sport teams, such as table tennis. Subsequently, it would discuss other cultural exchanges. Praphas said that when the development of informal relations proved satisfactory, the government would consider the advantages and disadvantages of trading with Mainland China. At the outset, he would not allow any private companies to trade with Beijing directly, but through government agencies. As he put it, 'we will not plunge into trade with any country if it looks like we are going to import much more than export'.[159] Only when the government considered it time to trade with Mainland China would it take the necessary legislative measures to abrogate Revolutionary Party Announcement No. 53. There were, for Praphas, 'two kinds of people', who wanted Thailand to immediately establish diplomatic relations with Beijing: 'those who are panicky and those who are ignorant'. Both these people 'want Thailand to go to Beijing and kowtow to the Chinese leaders'.[160]

---

157 'Govt Sanctions China Dialogue', *Bangkok Post*, 11 November 1971.
158 'Govt Sanctions China Dialogue'.
159 'Govt Sanctions China Dialogue'.
160 'Govt Sanctions China Dialogue'. Similarly, despite his attempt to make contact with the Chinese delegation to the UN General Assembly, Deputy Foreign Minister Sa-nga admitted that there was no need to expedite diplomatic links with Beijing because, 'the Chinese people are also interested in having friendly relations with us, we do not have to hurry up such relationship'. He even threatened to resign if Thailand exchanged diplomatic relations with the PRC: 'Sa-nga to Contact Beijing at UN', *Bangkok Post*, 9 November 1971; 'Govt Won't Rush into Beijing Links – Sa-nga', *Bangkok Post*, 16 November 1971.

4. FLEXIBLE DIPLOMACY

Thanat, on the other hand, now sought to expedite diplomatic talks with the Chinese. Having been informed by French intermediaries of China's readiness and willingness to enter a dialogue with Thailand, Thanat declared humorously, 'we will meet the Beijing representatives any place mutually convenient except, perhaps, the North and the South Poles'. Instead of contact via third parties, the direct dialogue would be conducted on an ambassadorial level, which was 'the most appropriate level of contact at the moment'.[161]

Thanat continued:

> We will inform the People's Republic of China that we wish to live in a peaceful, neighbourly fashion with all countries. We would like to see peace in the neighbourhood and no interference from the outside.

With regard to the Chinese demand on Thailand to sever diplomatic relations with Taiwan, Thanat said, 'we will have to find out how categorical, absolute, relative, inflexible or flexible the Chinese Communists are on this matter'.[162] He hoped that rapprochement with China would decrease its support of the communist insurgents in Thailand.[163]

However, referring to reports that Mainland China had begun to show interest in a dialogue with Thailand, Thanom remained unsure of Beijing's real attitude because the response was mainly made through a third party.[164] In short, the military leaders remained sceptical about the emerging discourse of détente with China. On 17 November 1971, Thanom launched a coup d'état against his own government, ousting Thanat from the MFA. Heightened discursive anxiety ended with the pre-existing Cold War hegemonic discourse asserting its dominance over détente.

The military coup in November 1971 put an end to the three-year secret diplomacy led by Thanat Khoman, whose aim was to contact the Chinese and ascertain the conditions of possibility for détente.[165] For the military

---

161 'China Ready to Begin Talks'.
162 'China Ready to Begin Talks'.
163 'Beijing & Peace in Asia', *Bangkok Post*, 18 November 1971.
164 'Thanom Paves Way for China Trade'.
165 According to the American documents, Nixon's reaction to the 1971 coup was relatively positive. One reason for US endorsement of the coup was that Kissinger did not want Thanat to pre-empt him in establishing relations with Mao. Shortly after the coup, Kissinger reported Thanat's dismissal to Nixon, who replied that 'this is what matters'. Quoted in Kullada Kesboonchoo Mead, 'The Cold War and Thai Democratization', in *Southeast Asia and the Cold War*, ed. Albert Lau (London and New York: Routledge, 2012), 227.

elite, it was unnecessary to hasten diplomatic ties with Communist China. However, as the following chapter will demonstrate, the process of Sino–Thai dialogue was only deferred, not deterred. One significant discursive shift emerged: détente with China. That is, Thailand began to regard China not as the 'enemy of the nation', as Premier Thanom himself put it. Personal contacts between Thai and Chinese diplomats also began and increased at the UN.

4.4. Conclusion

In an interview in the *Bangkok Post* in early November 1971, Pridi Phanomyong said in Paris that he urged the Thai Government to recognise the PRC immediately. He was quoted as saying 'the period of wait-and-see has ended. The time has come for a decision'. Thailand, he believed, 'has already waited too long'.

> Now that People's Republic of China has been voted into the rightful place in the United Nations by the overwhelming majority. It is placed in an advantageous position over us in any negotiations on diplomatic or any other relations.

Because China was recently recognised as a de facto and de jure big power, Thailand, as 'a small nation', could 'exercise the balance of power by close friendly relations with all the big powers' and 'all nations, irrespective of ideological differences'. 'We must be friends of all and foes of none', he argued. Pridi contended that 'let us remember the ancient Thai saying about going into the jungle with the courage to face a tiger'.[166]

This chapter has shown how the diplomatic practices of flexible diplomacy with the two communist powers were gradually introduced by détente proponents, especially Foreign Minister Thanat Khoman. Thanat's efforts shaped critical events and improved the international situation between Thailand and the communist powers. The work of Thanat and his protégés in establishing new diplomatic practices set a condition of possibility for a more comprehensive détente. In other words, détente rendered many practices, which had previously been unthinkable, possible. This included trade and air transport relations with the Soviet Union and back-channel contacts with the PRC. Détente marked the beginning of a shift from

---

166 Theh, 'Pridi: Recognize China Now'.

a logic of enmity to a logic of friendship. The next chapter will situate Thai détente within the domestic context of a power struggle. It was a clash of discourses, between the hegemonic discourse of Cold War militarism and the emergent discourse of détente. This clash precipitated the coup of 1971 which, as this chapter argues, in the long run only deferred, rather than deterred, flexible diplomacy.

Before proceeding to the next chapter, the different natures and characteristics of Thai–Soviet and Thai–Chinese relations should be noted. First, the Thai state in the Cold War considered the Soviet Union and the PRC as posing differing degrees of threat. That is, Thai elites generally perceived the PRC as a primary threat to its national interests, while seeing the USSR as a lesser one. This was largely because the Chinese directly supported the communist insurgency in Thailand. Second, the USSR and China had different diplomatic histories with Thailand. On the one hand, Communist China did not have diplomatic relations with Thailand, and, more importantly, Thailand had established and maintained close relations with another China, namely Taiwan. On the other hand, despite a brief interruption after the Bolshevik Revolution, Thailand had maintained continual and business-as-usual diplomatic relations with the Soviet Union from 1941, with the exchange of their ambassadors since the end of the Second World War. Third, in Thailand, there were very few Russians, while there were a large number of ethnic Chinese who had long been present, and to an extent had assimilated with the local Thai people. In this sense, relations with China were perceived both as an opportunity (a cultural and commercial interconnectedness) and danger (a threat of communist infiltration). These differences between these two bilateral relations in large part explain why Thailand's diplomatic practices toward the Soviet Union and China proceeded at different paces, at least at the beginning: rapprochement with China was far slower than readjustment with the Soviet Union. The discourse of détente emerged within the context of these historical complexities and legacies.

5

Interregnum – 1971: A Coup against Diplomacy?

> The decision to send Prasit [Kanchanawat] and the ping-pong team to China [in 1972] is a major turning point in the process of redirecting Bangkok's policy toward Beijing that was inaugurated by former foreign minister Thanat in 1968.
>
> – Central Intelligence Agency (CIA)[1]

On 17 November 1971, the Thai military junta, led by Field Marshal Thanom Kittikachorn, launched a coup d'état against itself, ending the short-lived democracy. One of the first acts of the new regime was to oust Foreign Minister Thanat Khoman from the Ministry of Foreign Affairs (MFA). Over the previous three years, an emerging discourse of détente had challenged the existing hegemony of Cold War rhetoric. The military and conservative elite remained deeply committed to the certainties provided by pro-Americanism, anticommunism and antagonism towards the Soviet Union and China. Proponents of détente, led by Thanat, questioned these certainties. Adjusting to a shift in global and regional power relations, they sought alternative diplomatic practices. Both within the elite, and through popular channels, they spoke openly about a new 'flexible diplomacy' and in doing so instigated what might be described as a series of 'discursive struggles'. While existing scholarship has tended to

---

1 Central Intelligence Agency, *Central Intelligence Bulletin,* 4 August 1972, 5.

characterise the 1971 coup as a coup against democracy, this chapter sees it equally as a coup against diplomacy.² The dismissal of Thanat as foreign minister was a clear attempt to pull back from the move toward détente.

However, by early 1972, Thailand risked being left behind. Détente was becoming an international phenomenon driven largely by the US, China and the Soviet Union. In February 1972, US President Richard Nixon made his famous visit to China, and formally established a course toward Sino–US rapprochement. By then, the authority of new discursive practices within Thailand was already partially secured. This chapter demonstrates how the post-1971 military regime was, implicitly if not explicitly, hemmed in by the discursive practices established prior to the coup. What began as an attempt to halt the progress of détente saw 'flexible diplomacy' continue but at a reduced pace. While a more formalised approach toward normalising relations was put on the backburner, developments such as ping-pong and economic diplomacy ensured it continued to smoulder. In truth, the coup only deferred rather than deterred Thai détente. By 1972, the process of Sino–Thai rapprochement was, therefore, already well established.

This chapter begins by reviewing the discursive struggle that preceded the 1971 coup. It then moves to looking at the coup itself, and after that discusses how, despite the coup attempting to preserve hegemonic discourse, small moves toward détente diplomacy continued in the shape of the famous 'ping-pong' diplomacy and the relaxation of trade restrictions. The chapter considers how diplomatic practice continued to evolve in this period.

5.1. Discourses at War

This section situates the newly emerging discourse of détente within the discursive struggles of Thai politics between 1969 and 1971. In particular, it focuses on the tussles that took place within the Cabinet, between Thanat and the House of Parliament, and between Thanat and the press.

---

2   See Thak Chaloemtiarana, *Thailand: The Politics of Despotic Paternalism* (Ithaca: Southeast Asia Program Publications, Cornell University, 2007), 228. The exception includes Kullada Kesboonchoo Mead, *Kanmueng Thai yuk Sarit–Thanom phaitai khrongsang amnat lok* [Thai Politics during Sarit–Thanom Regimes under a Global Power Structure] (Bangkok: 50 Years Foundation, The Bank of Thailand, 2007); Rapeeporn Lertwongweerachai, 'The Role of Thanat Khoman in Thai Foreign Affairs during 1958–1971' (MA thesis, Chulalongkorn University, 2002).

It argues that these struggles were not simply between détente proponents and opponents but between those who championed a cautious approach to détente, compared with those who sought rapid progress, especially within Parliament. I argue that these discursive struggles set the conditions that made the November 1971 military coup possible.

The discourse of détente with the communist powers, initiated by Thanat, triggered policy debates and contestations among the Thai elite. This was particularly true within the military, who remained largely committed to the existing discourse of anticommunism. The general perspective of the Thai ruling elite on rapprochement with China was one of scepticism, largely due to lingering suspicion over Chinese support for the Communist Party of Thailand (CPT). Deputy Prime Minister General Praphas Charusathien stated in January 1971 that 'as long as I remain in office, I would follow the present policy towards Beijing', and 'would not stand on two boats'.[3] For him, Thailand would not recognise both the People's Republic of China (PRC) and Taiwan at the same time. The government's position was further expounded by Thanom's younger brother and Deputy Foreign Minister Sa-nga Kittikachorn, who said that 'as long as Beijing pursues a hostile policy towards Thailand it would be "too early" to plan any change in the existing policy'.[4]

The emerging discourse of détente was also further complicated by the new domestic context of democratisation. The promulgation of the eighth Constitution in June 1968, and its concomitant parliamentary election, held on 10 February 1969, unleashed political debate and free speech both within political parties and the public sphere. While the military-dominated United Thai People's Party (UTPP), coupled with other pro-military parties, controlled Parliament, other political parties that had been banned in 1958 were extremely active in questioning and criticising various areas – including foreign affairs. Regarding détente, 'the most important problem', as one local newspaper put it, was 'that rapprochement with Red China remains ambiguous. So far it was not understandable. Some say this and some say that. It is hard to apprehend'.[5] In part, it was the confused and mixed messages of the government's stated policies on the PRC that brought about the debate in the first place.

---

3   Quoted in Shee Poon Kim, 'The Politics of Thailand's Trade Relations with the People's Republic of China', *Asian Survey* 21, no. 3 (March 1981): 314.
4   *Far Eastern Economic Review*, 22 May 1971.
5   'Thailand in One Week', *Daily News,* 13 June 1971.

The main target of this debate was Foreign Minister Thanat, who reacted and responded to those who criticised détente in a temperamental manner, exacerbating an already fierce debate. This was no doubt made worse by the fact that in a semi-democratic regime, Parliament was more comfortable attacking the military regime's foreign minister than the military leaders themselves.

Moreover, the debate was not about Thanat per se, but rather was underpinned by discursive struggles concerned with how Thailand should respond to the provocative question of the communist powers, and in particular the PRC. This can be represented in three sets of struggles: those between Thanat and the press, Thanat and the parliamentarians, and struggles within the Cabinet itself.

The first struggle, the debate between Thanat and the press, had begun with the promulgation of détente policy towards the communist countries, described in the previous chapter. The latest and perhaps harshest confrontation came to a head in May 1971 when Thanat alleged that certain journalists might have taken bribes from foreign sources or embassies to attack his flexible foreign policy towards Communist China. Some reporters claimed the foreign minister linked the *Siam Rath* newspaper to his allegation.[6] This prompted *Siam Rath's* publisher, MR Kukrit Pramoj, to write a front-page statement demanding Thanat to name the 'corrupt journalist or journalists'. He ended by saying that *should* the foreign minister fail to come up with the identification, 'the people would not have confidence in Thanat Khoman as the Foreign Minister'.[7]

The situation deteriorated when Thanat appeared on TV Channel 4 on 19 May, and attacked some journalists who had repeatedly criticised him. As he put it, 'these newspapermen have become the instruments of the aliens and have written reports antagonistic to government policy especially that of the Ministry of Foreign Affairs'.[8] The four press associations – including the Press Association, the Reporters Association, the Journalists Association and the Regional Press Association of Thailand – issued

---

6 Suthichai Yoon, 'Thanat Versus the Press', *The Nation*, 15 June 1971 found in the Ministry of Foreign Affairs Documents, (2) MFA 1.2/35, the National Archive of Thailand (TNA), Bangkok, 21.
7 Quoted in Suthichai, 'Thanat Versus the Press'; Ministry of Foreign Affairs Documents, (2) MFA 1.2/35, TNA, Bangkok, 21.
8 'Press Group Refutes Thanat's remarks', *Bangkok Post*, 23 May 1971.

a joint statement demanding that Thanat should name the 'misbehaving journalists' while describing his speech as 'an act of temper from a person unfit to hold the post of foreign affairs minister'.⁹

This prompted Thanat to meet with the presidents of the four press associations in order to ease tensions. A 'joint communiqué' was issued, following their luncheon meeting, stating the foreign minister's faith in the press. The supposed compromise nevertheless backfired when many reporters angrily claimed that the communiqué had been made without first consulting the associations' members. Some local newspapers maintained their criticism against Thanat's policy towards China as well as his 'hot-headed' personality. Some even charged Thanat with having been bribed by the Chinese communists.¹⁰

In response, Thanat reportedly put strong pressure on the Thanom Government to make charges against three journalists. On 7 June 1971, the police department arrested Nopporn Bunyarit, editor of *Siam Rath*; Kampol Vajarapol, director of *Thai Rath*; and Prasarn Meefuengsart, a *Thai Rath* columnist on charges of 'defaming the character of a government official on duty'. Prasarn, alias 'Krashae',¹¹ described Thanat as a very 'temperamental person', who was 'unsuited for a position which requires a cool-headed person', and pledged to fight for the freedom of the press to the end. Also, the four press associations immediately held a meeting and decided to boycott Thanat in all newspapers by banning publication of all interviews with, and pictures of, the foreign minister until the controversy was settled or the foreign minister's term complete.¹²

This controversy dragged on for months until the coup in November. Despite the personal nature of the public wrangling between Thanat and the press, it was clear that the underlying tensions concerned the ongoing debate on Thai foreign policy towards China.

---

9   'Press Group Refutes Thanat's Remarks'. See also 'Press Statement on Thanat', *Bangkok Post* 25 May 1971.
10 For example, Prasarn Meefuengsart, a prominent *Thai Rath* columnist, claimed in his column that Thanat trusted Communist China too easily and that he had received bribes from that country. After his arrest, he disclosed that 'the first comment I copied from a *Straits Times*' editorial and the second is my own'. 'Newsmen Move Against Thanat', *Bangkok World*, 8 June 1971; *Thai Rath*, 19 May 1971.
11 'Krashae' in Thai connotes homemade liquor or spirit. '"Krashae" – Thai Rath's Columnist Extraordinary', *Bangkok Post*, 8 June 1971.
12 'Journalists Free on 50,000 Baht Bail', *Bangkok Post*, 8 June 1971.

The second debate was between Thanat and Parliament. Coupled with the press, many Members of Parliament attacked Thanat's temperamental personality, and urged the Thanom Government to dismiss him. Once again, the underlying conflict was in regard to his policy toward China. Some members of Parliament remained sceptical of the thaw in relations. Leader of Democrat Party, MR Seni Pramoj, for example, said that 'you offer the Communists a hand and they grab your whole body. They don't understand us'. However, at the same time he conceded that 'China is there whether we like it or not, like the moon. Her entry into the community of nations is inevitable'.[13]

In August, Thanat was questioned by MP Praseng Nuengchamnong (Independent, Chon Buri), who asked whether the government intended to 'take action against the Foreign Minister for having explicitly supported Communism through his declaration that he will open diplomatic relations with a Communist country (Communist China), without governmental authority'.[14] Thanat made the observation that the question would violate the House Meeting Rules and Regulations, which precipitated a protest by a number of MPs who demanded Thanat formally withdraw his observation. Dissatisfied by Thanat's replies, a group of over 40 MPs, including those from the UTPP, walked out. They also sought to pressure the prime minister to remove Thanat from the Cabinet.[15] The motion was withdrawn shortly after Thanom defended Thanat during a meeting with the UTPP. He claimed that Thanat had

> carried out his functions and duties according to the government's policy with the interests of the nation in mind. Every time before he leaves for an official trip, he always comes to me for policy.

Several MPs continued to argue that Thanat's temper was an obstacle to better outcomes in diplomacy.[16]

However, many MPs in both government and opposition parties supported opening a dialogue with China. This second discursive struggle was primarily, therefore, concerned more with both the extent and speed with which the Thai Government should pursue the policy. One group of parliamentarians put pressure on the Thanom Government to

---

13 'Seni: We're unprepared', *Bangkok Post*, 16 May 1971, 2.
14 'Question to be Asked about Foreign Minister', *The Nation*, 5 August 1971.
15 'MPs Demand Cabinet Changes', *Bangkok Post*, 6 August 1971, 1.
16 'Thanom Defends FM: Minister Fights Off Crisis', *Bangkok Post*, 11 August 1971, 1, 3.

expedite the Sino–Thai rapprochement in the form of commercial and diplomatic ties with the Chinese. In August 1971, 70 MPs called on the prime minister to repeal the trade ban on China on the grounds that the Revolutionary Proclamation No. 53, banning trade with all communist countries, especially China – initiated by Field Marshal Sarit Thanarat in 1959 – was not effective due to the unstoppable inflow of Chinese goods into Thailand.[17]

MP Yuang Iamsila (UTPP, Udon Thani) went further, suggesting that the prime minister should visit Beijing. He said the Thai Government should not send anybody 'like Dr. Kissinger' to Beijing to 'fish' for an invitation, but wait for the Chinese prime minister to send one: 'When we get an invitation, we, the UTPP, will ask the Prime Minister to make the trip himself'. 'Our Prime Minister should even visit Beijing ahead of President Nixon. We are closer'. He added, 'we should not wait-and-see, as advocated by some government and opposition leaders, but get moving'.[18] Another MP also asked the government to allow him to visit China, though Thanom told Parliament that he could not allow any MPs to go on a fact-finding mission there.[19]

Parliamentarians found the way in which Thanat and the MFA were dealing with the Chinese neither fast nor efficient. In other words, Parliament favoured a 'go-fast' (*pai-rew*) diplomacy as opposed to the 'go-slow' 'wait-and-see' attitude of the military regime. Unfortunately, Thanat's form of détente was considered to be in the middle of these two diplomatic practices.

After the Albanian resolution passed in the United Nations (UN) General Assembly on 25 October 1971, three MPs cabled congratulations to Mao Zedong on China's admission to the UN.[20] Some parliamentarians now called for the resignation of Foreign Minister Thanat due to his failure to vote with the international community. MP Sanam Thirasirichote (Socialist Economic Front, Khon Kaen) proposed an urgent session of Parliament to discuss foreign policy in light of the Chinese entry to the UN, stated that 'Thanat should have already resigned because he

---

17 Some Chinese products were illegally imported into Thailand mainly through Hong Kong. *Bangkok Post*, 5 November 1971.
18 'Pressure on for PM to Visit Beijing', *Bangkok Post*, 26 July 1971.
19 'Thanom Bars MPs from China Visit', *Bangkok Post*, 27 August 1971, 1.
20 'Three MPs Send Cable to Mao', *Bangkok Post*, 30 October 1971, 1; 'MPs who Cabled Mao may Face Charges', *Bangkok Post*, 2 November 1971, 1.

blundered and should not be given the opportunity to continue doing so'. The motion also criticised Thailand's support for the US resolution of the two Chinas in the UN, asserting that it was against world opinion. The motion suggested that Parliament should be consulted before the government formulated a foreign policy. It was supported by many members from both the government and opposition parties.[21]

What made the debates in Parliament relatively distinct, therefore, was that rather than being concerned with whether détente should be pursued, they were more preoccupied with the speed of the process. It can be argued that criticism from Parliament was simultaneously both anti-Thanat and pro-détente. In this sense, strong voices in the Thai Parliament were generally *pro-Chinese*.

The last and arguably most important struggle was within the Cabinet itself. This was much more contested than is normally acknowledged. For Thanat, a high degree of confidence in his position, coupled with Thanom's 'green light' signals and gestures of support, fuelled the progress of a cautious rapprochement with the PRC. Well aware of the Cold War discursive hegemony, Thanat recognised the need to be discreet and to move cautiously within the military-led government. He routinely asserted that Thailand should not recognise the PRC until they had indicated their intention to curtail support for communist insurgencies in Thailand.

Nonetheless, the foreign minister provoked public debate and strong criticism of Thai foreign policy toward the communist powers. The military saw this policy as unnecessary and potentially reckless and dangerous to Thailand's security and economic interests. By the end of May 1971, Cold Warriors like Thanom and Praphas, who were much more hesitant about the haste with which Thanat expedited the diplomatic process, specifically ordered the MFA to follow 'go-slow' (*pai-cha*) diplomacy. They claimed that any contacts with China would not be possible until such a time that China ceased supporting insurgent movements in Thailand.[22]

---

21   'MPs Calls for Thanat to Quit FM Post', *Bangkok World,* 28 October 1971.
22   Theh Chongkhadikij, 'Govt Orders Slowdown in Beijing Thaw', *Bangkok Post,* 24 May 1971; Ministry of Foreign Affairs Documents, (2) MFA 1.2/36, TNA, Bangkok, 366.

5. INTERREGNUM – 1971

The Thai National Security Council, chaired by Thanom, decided against opening trade relations with Communist China.[23] The council was concerned that China would not separate trade from politics. Pote Sarasin, the Minister for National Development, asserted:

> if China can treat its economic relations with other countries separately from political considerations, there will not be problems in trading with other countries. The question is whether or not Red China can do that.

Consequently, for Pote, it would be better for Thailand to be cautious in developing economic relations with China and only consider closer ties 'when Red China separates her trade from political issues'.[24] The government's go-slow diplomacy, as the *Bangkok Post* put it, 'replaced a quickened pace to seek better understanding with Communist China'.[25]

In early November 1971, when asked by reporters whether it was true that Foreign Minister Thanat Khoman had discussed establishing trade relations with a Chinese delegation in Rome, Thanom replied, 'such a report was unfounded and Thailand would not take the initiative to trade with China in the immediate future'. Questioned about what decision his government would make if China wished to open trade relations with Thailand, Thanom said that such trade would certainly be beneficial, but added that the government was not sure that China had such intentions. He insisted that a 'wait and see' attitude would be most appropriate in dealing with China for the time being.[26]

This chapter argues that the target of these triple struggles was primarily Foreign Minister Thanat Khoman and his version of détente. Discursively, there were struggles between three forms of discourse, namely anticommunism, a gradual détente and a rapid détente. The discourse of anticommunism was spearheaded by military leaders while a rapid

---

23 Theh, 'Govt Orders Slowdown'; Ministry of Foreign Affairs Documents, (2) MFA 1.2/36, TNA, Bangkok, 366.
24 Likewise, Economic Affairs Minister Bunchana Atthakorn, echoed the same concern: trading with China would not be 'safe' as long as that country continued attacking Thailand through Radio Beijing and carried on its 'subversive infiltration' of the kingdom. Thus, Bunchana emphasised that if Beijing changed 'its attitude towards us', Thailand would change its policy. Quoted in Kim, 'The Politics of Thailand's Trade Relations', 314–15.
25 Theh, 'Govt Orders Slowdown'; Ministry of Foreign Affairs Documents, (2) MFA1.2/ 36, TNA, Bangkok, 366.
26 Quoted in Kim, 'The Politics of Thailand's Trade Relations', 315–16.

détente was supported by several factions in Parliament and a portion of public opinion. Thanat, who supported a gradual détente, was in the midst of these discursive struggles.

By the early 1970s, Suthichai Yoon of *The Nation* could identify two broad rival 'schools of thought', regarding Thailand's policy toward the PRC. One school clung to an existing Cold War hegemony and sought to 'make clear to China that Thailand cannot possibly establish some sort of relations with her and sacrifice Taiwan, which has been a staunch ally for more than a decade'.[27] Another school sought to consolidate a discourse of détente, which required 'a total overhaul of the country's approach towards China'.[28] Given Thailand's changing attitude toward China, which had not only been admitted into the UN but had shown 'signs of willingness to establish some dialogue with Thailand' through third parties, this approach asserted the need for a more flexible diplomacy with China.[29] This discourse consisted of Thanat and the MFA, who preferred a cautious rapprochement, and a number of Members of Parliament who urged for a rapid rapprochement.

5.2. 1971: A Coup against Détente?

On 17 November 1971, Field Marshal Thanom Kittikachorn staged a coup d'état against his own government, established military rule under the National Executive Council (NEC), and appointed himself foreign minister. This section argues that the 1971 coup was not only a coup against democracy but also, more significantly, a coup against diplomacy. It also asserts that while initially Thanom sought to freeze Sino–Thai rapprochement, changes in international circumstances, especially Nixon's trip to Beijing in February 1972, made Thai détente inevitable. Détente continued, if reluctantly, on the same course.

Upon seizing power, the military junta justified the coup on both domestic and international grounds. Domestically, the coup was to restore order and stability as well as efficient government: to 'set our house in order again'.[30] The underlying reason was to end the criticism from

---

27 Suthichai Yoon, 'Thailand's New Approach towards China', *The Nation*, 3 November 1971.
28 Suthichai, 'Thailand's New Approach towards China'.
29 Suthichai, 'Thailand's New Approach towards China'.
30 'NEC to Rule 5 Years', *Bangkok Post*, 21 November, 1971, 1.

Parliament. The junta claimed that politicians were demanding economic development budgets for their local provinces, which in turn meant they sought to slash military budgets. Some members of the government's UTPP were threatening to vote against the latter unless their development projects were allocated.[31]

The criticism and obstacles of the parliamentary system annoyed the military.[32] As Thanom stated in a press conference two days after the coup, 'never, in my long political career have MPs caused such trouble to government administrators as in these recent times. Some of them even attacked me over my private affairs'. He blamed the country's troubles on those 'self-seeking politicians who had interfered too much in the government to the point where it could not function smoothly and properly'. Thanom came to the conclusion that 'if there were no MPs, government administrators would certainly work more smoothly and efficiently, like the days during the time of the late Field Marshal Sarit [Thanarat]'.[33] In other words, authoritarian impatience prevailed over democratic process.

Thanom also cited the communist threat as justification for the coup. He warned that closer relations with China posed a threat, due to the large number of ethnic Chinese living in Bangkok who may have communist sympathies. As he stated, 'the situation in the country could be turmoil because it will aggravate the existing terrorist infiltration that exists in every part of the country'.[34] While abrogating the Constitution, the military junta declared war on crime, pollution and late-night drinking. They issued 47 major decrees, including dissolving political parties, abolishing local elections and prohibiting strikes.

On foreign policy, Thanom cited the need to forestall leftist pressure from MPs for immediate relations with China.[35] His task was to 'build up a stable government in full control of the country', and to 'negotiate from a position of strength with the Chinese Communists'. The NEC

---

31 David Morell, 'Thailand: Military Checkmate', *Asian Survey* 12, no. 2 (1972): 156–67. See also Michael L Mezey, 'The 1971 Coup in Thailand: Understanding Why the Legislature Fails', *Asian Survey* 13, no. 3 (1973): 306–17.
32 Thak, *Thailand*, 228.
33 Thanom said that King Bhumibol, informed of the reasons for the coup, 'agreed that it was necessary to remedy the situation'. *Bangkok World*, 19 November 1971; *Times* (London), 20 November 1971.
34 'Why Marshall Thanom overthrew the Thai Government', *Times*, 19 November 1971.
35 *New York Times*, 21 November 1971.

A GENEALOGY OF BAMBOO DIPLOMACY

did not consider relations with China to be an urgent matter and believed there was no necessity for trade or diplomatic relations in the near future.[36] General Praphas, Deputy Chairman of the NEC, echoed these sentiments. He claimed that before the seizure of power, a small but growing number of people were advocating a pro-Beijing diplomatic policy, and to move 'quickly' to establish diplomatic and trade relations with the Chinese communists.[37]

It can be argued that the coup was intended to end the discursive struggles in Thai politics. The coup was an attempt to take absolute control over the direction of Thai foreign policy, especially towards the Communist great powers. While Thanom had given the green light to Thanat's détente, he was still reluctant to pursue détente with China. That is, he was constantly oscillating between the new discourse and a defence of Cold War discursive hegemony. He was clearly uncomfortable about the switch from an anticommunist strategy to a more flexible diplomacy.

However, the change in US foreign policy paradoxically exacerbated discursive anxiety for the Thai military junta. On the one hand, Nixon's 'peace with honor' in the Vietnam War meant, first, an increase in US troops in Thailand. By the spring of 1972, the number of US troops in Thailand had increased to 45,000. Second, the US used Thai air bases to expedite large-scale and secret bombing in Vietnam.[38] But, on the other hand, Nixon and Henry Kissinger pursued détente with the Soviet Union and rapprochement with the PRC as leverage both in its triangular diplomacy and vis-à-vis Hanoi. While the former actions seemed to reassure Cold Warriors, who were considered to be détente opponents, the latter raised doubts, complicating Thai foreign policy and the existing discourse of anticommunism.

Nixon's historic visit to Beijing in February 1972 was a watershed event. After the long secret diplomacy and back channels spearheaded by Kissinger and his Chinese counterpart, Zhou Enlai, Sino–US rapprochement was

---

36 'NEC Shelves Beijing Relations', *Bangkok Post*, 25 December 1971, 1; 'NEC to Rule 5 Years', 1.
37 'No Rush Towards China', *Bangkok Post*, 29 December 1971, 2.
38 *Far Eastern Economic Review*, 2 April 1976, 13. See Surachart Bamrungsuk, *United States Foreign Policy and Thailand Military Rule, 1947–1977* (Bangkok: Duang Kamol, 1988); R. Sean Randolph, *The United States and Thailand: Alliance Dynamics, 1950–1985* (Berkeley: Institute of East Asian Studies, University of California, 1986), Chapter 5.

looking increasingly inevitable.[39] These changing contexts continued to push the Thai military junta toward improving their relations with China. A few months after the coup, the military junta announced, 'if China is not hostile to us, we are ready to be friends and we will respond to them'.[40]

Domestic developments on both sides in 1972 also made rapprochement increasingly feasible. On the Chinese side, the most radical period of the Cultural Revolution came to an end and domestic politics returned to normality. Zhou Enlai's peaceful coexistence strategy towards Southeast Asian states was restored. This change from the Chinese side helped facilitate a fundamental reassessment of the prospect of a Sino–Thai rapprochement.[41]

On the Thai side, while the military regime under Thanom and Praphas had dismissed détente proponents such as Thanat, it implicitly followed a détente discourse. Though developing formal diplomatic relations with China remained a way off, due to lingering suspicion over Chinese support for communist subversion and insurgency in Thailand, the junta did agree to non-political engagement such as sports and cultural exchanges. At the same time, the Thai business community urged the government to permit trade with China.[42] For example, Charoon Sibunruang, President of Thai Chamber of Commerce, said that 'Thailand will gain a lot from trading with Communist China, since it is a huge market'.[43] The junta agreed to this as well.

By 1972, some Thai elite who had once been against détente with China started to change their position. This was an unnerving position for Cold Warriors, including Thanom and Praphas. Faced with the new normal of global détente, they hesitantly continued with Thai détente. One of the key leaders, Pote Sarasin, signalled in June 1972 that 'Thailand welcomes mutual friendly relations with China, including exchange of visits by sports

---

39   Margaret MacMillan, 'Nixon, Kissinger, and the Opening to China', in *Nixon in the World: American Foreign Relations, 1969–1977*, ed. Fredrik Logevall and Andrew Preston (Oxford: Oxford University Press, 2008), 107–25. See also Margaret MacMillan, *Nixon in China: The Week That Changed the World* (New York: Random House, 2007); Evelyn Goh, *Constructing the US Rapprochement with China, 1961–1974: From 'Red Menace' to 'Tacit Ally'* (Cambridge: Cambridge University Press, 2005).
40   'Thai Coup Brings Few Changes', *Washington Post,* 23 January 1972.
41   See Frank Dikotter, *The Cultural Revolution: A People's History, 1962–1976* (London: Bloomsbury, 2016).
42   Chulacheeb Chinwanno, 'Thai-Chinese Relations: Security and Strategic Partnership' (Working Paper No. 155, S Rajaratnam School of International Studies, Singapore, 2008), 6.
43   'Charoon Backs Beijing Trade', *Bangkok Post*, 4 May 1971, 11.

teams and trade'.[44] In brief, the coup that at the outset had strived for halting détente switched to going along with Sino–Thai rapprochement. Harnessed by the global transformation, détente discourse was resilient in Thai diplomacy.

5.3. Détente Continued

This section explores the ways in which the military regime continued the process of détente through sports and economic diplomacy. When Chinese leaders invited the Thai ping-pong team to visit Beijing, the military junta readily dispatched a team. They also sent Prasit Kanchanawat as a special envoy to initiate a rapprochement with the PRC in late August 1972. Further sports and economic diplomacy followed. The section argues that though the military reluctantly accepted détente, the MFA remained strongly committed to the détente discourse.

5.3.1. Ping-pong Diplomacy: Prasit Kanchanawat as 'Thailand's Kissinger'

> The small ping-pong ball has moved the big earth ahead.
> – Zhou Enlai[45]

The preliminary process of Sino–Thai rapprochement began with ping-pong diplomacy in 1972. The PRC invited Thailand to send a ping-pong team to the first Asian Table Tennis Union Championships in Beijing on 2–13 September 1972. After a highly contentious debate within the Thai National Security Council, Thanom made a decision to accept the invitation and dispatch a 20-member ping-pong team headed by Police Lieutenant General Chumpol Lohachala, Deputy Police Chief on Special Affairs and Chairman of the Badminton Association of Thailand.[46] The total team included 13 sportspeople and seven officials, including Dr Veekij Viranuvat, a team doctor. One of the sportspeople, Prachan

---

44 'NEC Says Beijing Contacts Welcome', *Bangkok Post*, 8 June 1972, 1.
45 Cheng Rui-sheng, 'Karntoot ping-pong thai-jin' [Sino-Thai Ping-pong Diplomacy], trans. Vasin Ruengprathepsang, *Saranrom Journal* 63 (February 2006): 106.
46 'Beijing: Contacts Begin – NEC Approves Ping-Pong Visit', *Bangkok Post*, 3 August 1972, 1.

Kunachiva, told the *Bangkok Post* that 'I have been told what [China] is like, now I would like to see for myself'. Most of them were anxious to see the 'real' Communist China.[47]

Following initial footsteps toward US–China rapprochement, Thanom and Praphas wished to use 'ping-pong diplomacy' to sound out China's attitudes and intentions towards Thailand. In particular, they sought to question China's alleged support for the CPT, and discuss the prospect of trade relations. Praphas, a staunch anticommunist, gradually warmed to the idea of Thai–Chinese rapprochement. As Maynard Parker explained in 1973, Praphas sensed 'the importance of the China question to Thailand's future as well as the personally lucrative aspects of trade', and therefore 'set about placing the reins of Thailand's China policy in his own hands'.[48]

Praphas appointed Prasit Kanchanawat, a Deputy Director of Economic Affairs under the NEC, as an adviser to the team.[49] Better known by his original name Hsu Tun-Mao, Prasit was born in Thailand to Chinese parents and briefly educated in Shanghai. He was a leading Chinese Thai business figure, Director of the Bangkok Bank, and above all, one of Praphas's closest confidantes. Both the Thais and Chinese knew perfectly well that Prasit would act as a de facto special envoy from Thailand to launch a Sino–Thai rapprochement. Prasit was preparing for the possibility of informal talks with Chinese leaders on many major issues affecting Sino–Thai relations, including China's support for communist insurgency in Thailand, dual nationality of the Chinese in Thailand, Taiwan, trade and Chinese representation at the Economic Commission for Asia and the Far East (ECAFE) Headquarters in Bangkok. He was also expected to inform Chinese leaders that Thailand welcomed peaceful coexistence, and sought to resurrect the Bandung spirit of 1955.[50] Praphas also presented ping-pong team leader Chumpol, and adviser Prasit, to King Bhumibol at Chitrlada Palace. The king expressed his approval of

---

47 '13 Sportsmen Picked for Beijing Trip', *Bangkok Post*, 9 August 1972, 1.
48 Maynard Parker, 'Untying Thailand', *Foreign Affairs*, January 1973, 334.
49 According to Prasit, his trip to Beijing was a surprise for him. He said that after his visit to Indonesia, he met Pote Sarasin, then Director of Economic Affairs at the NEC, who told him that 'General Praphas wished you to go to China'. Prasit Kanchanawat, 'Sumphantamaitri Thai-Jeen korn por sor 2518' [Sino–Thai Friendship before 1975], *Warasan Asiatawanoak suksa* [East Asian Studies Journal] 3, no. 1 (July 1990): 13.
50 Theh Chongkhadikij, 'Beijing Offers Thai Ping-Pong Players a Tour of China After Match,' *Bangkok Post*, 16 August 1972, 1.

ping-pong diplomacy as 'social contacts between fellow human beings'. However, he advised his audience to remain aware of the fundamental political and ideological differences.[51]

Before leaving for Beijing, Prasit asked Warnwai Phathanothai to act as personal contact with the Chinese. Warnwai, the son of Sang Phathanothai who was a prominent politician during the Phibun Government, had been sent to Beijing in the mid-1950s at the age of 12, together with his eight-year-old sister, Sirin. Both were brought up under Zhou Enlai's patronage as a symbolic part of Field Marshal Phibun's 'secret diplomacy' with China. At Warnwai's insistence, Praphas had put his consent in writing, authorising Prasit and Warnwai to contact Chinese leaders. Prasit's letter advised:

> so that my mission may achieve, in the best way, the results which are expected, I would like to ask Mr. Warnwai Phathanothai to go to Beijing ahead of me, in order to make initial contact, explain the nature of our mission and to arrange the necessary meetings with Chinese authorities.[52]

This letter served as a guarantor for Warnwai's security. Due to the changing political situation in Thailand, where the anticommunism act remained intact, Warnwai feared that he might be labelled a 'communist' and thrown into jail, as his father, Sang, had once been.[53]

On 12 August 1972, Warnwai was sent to the United Kingdom to make contact with the Chinese Government through the Chinese embassy in London. He also sought to confirm the arrangements for Prasit's trip. Warnwai's younger sister, Sirin Phathanothai – who had stayed in London with her British husband after fleeing Beijing during the Cultural Revolution – arranged the meeting.[54] Just 10 days before the ping-pong

---

51   'HM Favors "Contacts"', *Bangkok Post*, 9 August 1972, 1.
52   Warnwai Phathanothai, *Zhou Enlai: Pupluek maitri Thai-jeen* [Zhou Enlai, The Man Who Planted Thai–Chinese Friendship], 2nd edition (Bangkok: Prakonchai, 1976 [2001]), 154.
53   Warnwai Phathanothai, interview by author, 17 June 2016, Bangkok.
54   See Sirin Phathanothai, *The Dragon's Pearl* (New York and London: Simon & Schuster, 1994). At the height of Mao Zedong's Cultural Revolution, Sirin was forced to publicly denounce her father and brother, and sever all ties to her family back in Bangkok. She later recalled:

> My friends and I suffered greatly at the hands of Mao and his policies. Despite our privilege, we were also very much victims of the Cultural Revolution. I was part of the hundreds of thousands that suffered. I was lucky to be alive … Despite all this though, I had no hatred for Mao – he still felt like my grandfather.

Sirin Phathanothai, interview, 'A Childhood Spent in the Dragons' Den', *Bangkok Post*, 19 July 2015.

team travelled to Beijing,[55] Sirin made contact with Yu Enguang, chief of Xinhua News Agency in London, who helped arrange the meeting with Ambassador Song Zhiguang. After she explained Prasit's trip, Ambassador Song said he would convey the message to Premier Zhou Enlai. In the meantime, Warnwai discussed the proposal in detail with Pei Jiangzhang, the Chinese embassy counsellor.[56]

Warnwai informed Pei that the Thai Government was sending Prasit to sound out Chinese attitudes toward Thailand and seek to develop contacts. He asked if there might be an opportunity for Prasit to meet with Chinese leaders and, if so, whether Prasit would be able to discuss mutual problems as well as build mutual understanding for the future. Given that Prasit's trip was not a normal sports exchange, but political, Pei then asked why General Praphas had given an interview in which he had claimed that this visit had nothing to do with political negotiations. Warnwai responded that Thailand did not know the precise nature of Chinese intentions, and feared that should things go wrong, Praphas would lose face. He affirmed that this trip was definitely about political negotiations, 'because everyone in Thailand knew well that Prasit had no particular duty in the Thai Table Tennis Association and seemingly could not play ping-pong at all'.[57]

The Chinese had only one reservation: the status of Taiwan. As Pei told Warnwai:

> China has only one vital condition in establishing relations with foreign countries, namely, that they recognise the government of the People's Republic of China as the sole government of one China. Taiwan is an inseparable part of China, and governments must be ready to sever any diplomatic relations they have with Taiwan.[58]

He then asked what the Thai Government's attitude on this matter was. Warnwai replied that he had not been authorised to express an opinion but assured Pei that Prasit would be empowered to discuss further details.

---

55 Warnwai, *Zhou Enlai: Pupluek maitri Thai-jeen*.
56 Sirin, *The Dragon's Pearl*, 300.
57 Warnwai, *Zhou Enlai: Pupluek maitri Thai-jeen*, 157.
58 Sirin, *The Dragon's Pearl*, 300.

In her memoir, *The Dragon's Pearl*, Sirin recalled that, 'a couple of days later, Yu Enguang called. From his voice I knew the news was positive'.[59] On 18 August, Warnwai was invited to the Chinese embassy in London, and met Ambassador Song Zhiguang. The latter conveyed a message from the Chinese Government:

> The government of the People's Republic of China wishes to inform the royal government of Thailand that it warmly welcomes Mr. Prasit Kanchanawat and his advisers Warnwai and Sirin Phathanothai as special guests of the Chinese government.[60]

Song also told Warnwai that he was 'delighted to see better and friendly Sino–Thai relations, starting with ping-pong diplomacy'.[61]

Prasit led the ping-pong team to Beijing between 24 August and 10 September 1972, and was well received as a special state guest, despite there being no formal diplomatic relations between the two countries. According to Cheng Rui-sheng, then Deputy Director of Southeast Asian Division of the Chinese Foreign Ministry – who would be a liaison and personal contact with Thai Foreign Ministry officials in developing Thai–Chinese relations in the years to come – the Chinese Government treated Prasit as a 'special envoy'.[62] In Beijing, Prasit was accompanied by Cheng Rui-sheng, as well as Warnwai and Sirin Phathanothai, who served as sole translator in all official meetings.[63] The Chinese also provided Prasit with the same 'Hongqi' car that had carried US President Nixon in early 1972.[64]

Prasit met with Prime Minister Zhou Enlai and other Chinese leaders, including Deputy Foreign Minister Han Nianlong, Deputy Minister of Economic Affairs Li Qiang and Director of the World Peace Committee Liao Chengzhi.[65] Though fluent in Mandarin, Prasit spoke in Thai while Sirin translated into Chinese. The first meeting was between Prasit and Liao on 1 September at 16:00. Prasit began the conversation by stating:

---

59   Sirin, *The Dragon's Pearl*, 301.
60   Warnwai, *Zhou Enlai: Pupluek maitri Thai-jeen*, 158.
61   Warnwai, *Zhou Enlai: Pupluek maitri Thai-jeen*, 159.
62   Cheng, 'Karntoot ping-pong thai-jin', 107.
63   It seemed to be the first time that the Chinese leaders allowed the non-Chinese to act as a sole translator throughout every official meeting.
64   'Beijing Peace "Hinges on Reduction of Red Support"', *Bangkok Post*, 16 September 1972, 3.
65   Liao Chengzhi worked in various positions heavily involved in foreign affairs, most prominently, President of the Sino-Japanese Friendship Society, and Minister of the Office of Overseas Chinese Affairs. According to Warnwai, Liao was like his and Sirin's father, as she called him 'Papa Liao', raising them in China, and they retained a close relationship until his death in 1983. Warnwai Phathanothai, interview by author, 17 June 2016, Bangkok.

there is an old Thai saying 'Chinese and Thais are not strangers to each other but brothers'. From this point of view, there should be no problem in our relations.

'If there was any problem', said Prasit, it was because sometimes it was 'necessary for Thailand to link itself with other countries, especially with the United States and Taiwan after World War Two. Perhaps it is best not to discuss that so as not to arouse antagonisms'.[66]

Liao said that 'the international situation had been changing rapidly. US President Nixon had visited Beijing'. He also provided the example of Sino–Japanese relations, which had taken 20 years to establish in the postwar period. He said he wished Sino–Thai rapprochement would be quicker. Moreover, he stated that it was 'not quite correct to say that Thailand had no relations with China. In fact, during the Phibun administration we had initiated contact for a while'. Pointing to Warnwai and Sirin, 'once, with Prime Minister Phibun, we had good people-to-people relations. They came to China when they were children in 1956, they studied, and they grew up here'. 'We had trading contacts', Liao continued, 'and many Thai delegations paid visits to China'.[67]

Prasit said Thailand was not yet ready to normalise relations with China. First, the Thai alliance with the US made it difficult. Second, Thailand was still afraid of Chinese ideological promotion and support for communist insurgency in Thailand. He emphasised that the Thais were a peace-loving, Buddhist people, with a monarchy. Liao replied that was a domestic problem for Thailand but it was not quite accurate that Thailand was a peace-loving country:

> The Thai people were, but what of the Thai soldiers in Laos and Vietnam? Why was Thailand so afraid of China? In its long history, had China ever sent troops to Thailand?[68]

While China supported the peoples' revolution around the world, he stressed that revolution was not a 'product that can be exported'. According to Liao, a fear of China was 'pure nonsense'. Liao asked Prasit to 'tell the Thai people and government that we wish to be friendly with them. Let them come to China and see our country for themselves'. Liao suggested that the two countries could begin with trade relations, and take sports,

---

66 Sirin, *The Dragon's Pearl*, 303.
67 Warnwai, *Zhou Enlai: Pupluek maitri Thai-jeen*, 166.
68 Sirin, *The Dragon's Pearl*, 303.

cultural, medical and scientific diplomacy step by step.⁶⁹ Following the Liao–Prasit meeting, the Chinese Government and the Asian Table Tennis Union hosted a formal dinner at the Great Hall of the People to greet all ping-pong teams.⁷⁰

During similar meetings with other Chinese leaders, Prasit initiated trade and cultural contacts with China. On 2 September, at 16:00, Prasit had a two-hour meeting with Deputy Foreign Minister Han Nianlong at the Chinese Foreign Ministry. Han Nianlong informed Prasit that China sought peaceful relations with Thailand, and wished to restore the relationship. The only criteria for the establishment of diplomatic relations was the recognition of the One-China policy, meaning Thailand would have to terminate formal relations with Taiwan.⁷¹ He assured Prasit that if the Thai Government was not yet ready to establish formal diplomatic relations, China understood the situation, and could wait until their relations had matured further.⁷² In the meantime, any contact should be based on commercial relations and cultural exchange. Han emphasised that the Chinese respected the principles of sovereignty, territorial integrity and noninterference. In foreign relations, Chinese leaders emphasised that the relationship should be based on the Bandung's Five Principles of Peaceful Coexistence: mutual respect for sovereignty and territorial integrity; mutual non-aggression; noninterference in each other's internal affairs; equality and mutual benefit; and peaceful coexistence.⁷³

Prasit also asked about the issue of dual nationality of overseas Chinese in Thailand. Han Nianlong, and subsequently Zhou Enlai himself, confirmed that his government did not support dual nationalities, but instead urged the overseas Chinese to assimilate with the local population, to adopt the nationality of the country they reside, and respect the domestic laws.⁷⁴ Han assured Prasit that the PRC 'will not try to control overseas Chinese

---

69   Warnwai, *Zhou Enlai: Pupluek maitri Thai-jeen*, 167, 172.
70   Cheng Rui-sheng wrote later that there was a difficulty in the diplomatic protocol in arranging the table for Prasit because the latter was not the team leader, and should therefore not sit together with the host at the front. At the same time, if he were to sit with the Thai ping-pong team he would be too far back in the room. In the end, the Chinese, according to Cheng, decided to set a separate table for Prasit: 'Table No. 52'. This table was close to the front, and hosted independently by the ranking diplomat, Lu Wei-jao, Director-General of Asian Affairs from the Ministry of Foreign Affairs. Warnwai, Sirin, and Cheng joined the table too. Cheng, 'Karntoot ping-pong thai-jin', 108.
71   Apiwat Wannakorn, *Prasit Kanchanawat: Nakkanmuaeng si todsawat* [Prasit Kanchanawat: Four-decade Politician] (Bangkok: Matichon, 1996), 217.
72   Apiwat, *Prasit Kanchanawat*, 218.
73   Warnwai, *Zhou Enlai: Pupluek maitri Thai-jeen*, 167, 178.
74   Apiwat, *Prasit Kanchanawat*, 219–20.

in Southeast Asian countries'. He asserted that 'overseas Chinese should be loyal to the countries in which they live and obey the laws there'.[75] Han also suggested to Prasit that, as a friend with goodwill, Thailand should withdraw its troops from Indochina.[76] At the end of the meeting, Han reiterated that China could wait until such time that Thailand was ready for diplomatic relations, and that there was no obstacle from the Chinese side. In the meantime, Thai–Chinese contacts could be conducted on a step-by-step basis, starting with trade and sports exchanges.

On 4 September, at around 16:00, Prasit met Deputy Minister of Economic Affairs Li Qiang. In a one-hour meeting at the Ministry of Economic Affairs, Li told Prasit that China wanted to buy Thai products, such as rice, rubber, sugar, jute, burlap sacks, corn and sorghum, and officially invited Prasit and a Thai trade delegation to the Canton Trade Fair in October 1972. He said that the PRC was 'interested in trade with Thailand, on a government-to-government or government-to-people basis'. Prasit replied that 'trade with China should not be difficult'. He suggested that accounts could be opened in a bank in either country. After a year's trading, settlement could be made, with convertible currencies such as British pounds, US dollars or Swiss or French francs.[77]

The Thai delegation was anxious about the meeting with Zhou Enlai. There had been no confirmation until midnight on 5 September 1972, when Liao phoned Sirin to inform her that Zhou would receive Prasit in the Sichuan Province Reception Room of the Great Hall of the People.[78] During his 45-minute meeting with Zhou Enlai, Prasit discussed various Thai concerns. Zhou started the meeting by saying that the visit by Prasit and the Thai ping-pong team would be a good beginning for Sino–Thai relations and friendship. As he put it, 'it was a good omen that we are shaking hands. We have opened our doors, and you are the first to come in'. Prasit replied by admitting:

---

75 'Prasit Opens New Era With China', *Bangkok Post*, 15 September 1972, 1.
76 Warnwai, *Zhou Enlai: Pupluek maitri Thai-jeen*, 184.
77 'Prasit Opens New Era With China', 1.
78 Prasit had been advised to keep himself ready for 'an important occasion'. He had to keep dressed through the night in the hotel before he was summoned. Prasit acknowledged:

> I was accorded great honor. The Chinese most probably regarded our acceptance of the invitation to participate in the Asian Table Tennis Union championships as a sign of goodwill on our part, despite the fact that we don't have diplomatic relations.

'Prasit Opens New Era With China', 1.

> we feel somewhat awkward in our approach to you because of our long-term close relationship with Taiwan and the United States. We feel it will be difficult to cut off our relations with one side in order to improve our relations with the other.[79]

After reviewing the long history of Thai–Chinese relations, Zhou said that China understood Thailand's position and sympathised with it. At the present moment, Zhou went on, 'if there are obstacles to establish immediate diplomatic relations with us we are always patient, so we can wait'.

> But in the meantime, our two peoples can promote relations in other fields. Badminton and other sports teams may come. There may be exchange programs in the medical and scientific fields. We can also trade.[80]

During Sirin's translation, Zhou interrupted, pointing to both Sirin and Warnwai to say:

> they are part of the evidence for the existence of good relations between our two countries. They are now a sturdy bridge linking us together. Listen to her Chinese – she speaks Chinese with a better accent than mine.

He continued:

> So I hope that on your return you will inform your government that we understand its difficulty. And you know that in Indochina there must be peace. That war must end.[81]

In other words, Zhou strongly asserted that the Chinese wished to be friends with Thailand. As Prasit stated later, 'China has opened its door to us, Mr. Zhou told me'. Zhou welcomed 'friendship on a basis of equality with Thailand'.[82] However, China did not need to rush toward establishing formal diplomatic relations, and could wait until Thailand was ready. In the meantime, both countries could benefit from trade as well as cultural and sports exchanges.

---

79 'Prasit Opens New Era With China', 1.
80 Warnwai, *Zhou Enlai: Pupluek maitri Thai-jeen*.
81 Sirin, *The Dragon's Pearl*, 304.
82 'Prasit Opens New Era With China', 1.

5. INTERREGNUM – 1971

Prasit also inquired directly about China's alleged support for the CPT's activities. According to Prasit's biography, Zhou claimed that while China generally supported the people's struggle for independence and freedom against imperialism, it did not interfere in other states' internal affairs.[83] Likewise, Pote Sarasin, Assistant Chairman of the NEC, shared this topic with the US Secretary of Defense Melvin Laird, noting:

> Prasit told the Chinese that the Thais were worried about terrorists. The Thai people … assumed that the Chinese were supporting the insurgents. Zhou said 'we' had nothing to do with this but would continue to support freedom fighters.[84]

However, the Thai Government was 'not yet certain of Chinese motives'.[85] Last but not least, Pote confirmed that Premier Zhou sent warm regards to the Thai king, government leaders and to Prince Wan Waithayakon, the former foreign minister whom Zhou Enlai had met at the Afro-Asian Conference in Bandung in 1955.[86] Above all, Prasit's historic meeting with Zhou, Pote Sarasin said, 'was a correct and formal meeting'.[87]

After spending two weeks in Beijing, Prasit flew back to Bangkok on 10 September, while the remainder of the team continued the ping-pong competition.[88] At Don Mueang Airport, he boarded a car planeside to

---

83   Apiwat, *Prasit Kanchanawat*, 233–34.
84   'Memorandum of Conversation', 2 October 1972, in *Foreign Relations of the United States, 1969–1976, Vol. 20: Southeast Asia, 1969–1972* (Washington: Government Printing Office, 2010), Document 180.
85   'Memorandum of Conversation', 2 October 1972, in *Foreign Relations of the United States, 1969–1976, Vol. 20: Southeast Asia, 1969–1972*, Document 180.
86   Prince Wan praised Prasit's informal diplomacy as 'good policy', and Zhou Enlai as 'a man of great courtesy and acumen'. He welcomed the opening of China's door to Thailand, but he said that Zhou Enlai's statement that the Chinese did not interfere in the internal affairs of other countries and instead promoted the fight for freedom of various peoples should be made clear. As at Bandung, he insisted that peaceful coexistence should mean 'live and let live', in accordance with the formula set out in the Charter of the United Nations. Seventeen years after Bandung, Prince Wan realised that 'Asia-Africa is too vast a region for this purpose'. Rather, 'arrangements for peaceful coexistence should be made on a regional basis; the region concerned to be cohesive enough to maintain real solidarity'. After his trip to Beijing, Prasit called on Prince Wan to convey Zhou's best wishes. 'Beijing Peace "Hinges on Reduction of Red Support"', 3; 'Prasit Briefs Prince Wan on Results of Beijing Trip', *Bangkok Post*, 18 September 1972, 3.
87   'Memorandum of Conversation', 2 October 1972, in *Foreign Relations of the United States, 1969–1976, Vol. 20: Southeast Asia, 1969–1972*, Document 180.
88   According to Prasit, he spent a few days in Hong Kong before returning to Bangkok. He asked Warnwai to type the report for the Thai government. The typewriter was borrowed from the Consulate General there. Prasit Kanchanawat, 'Nueng Thosawad Mittaparp Thai-Jeen' [One Decade of Sino–Thai Friendship], in *Prasit Kanchanawat: Think, Speak, Write*, ed. Apiwat Wannakorn (Bangkok: Sukaparpjai, 1997), 100.

avoid reporters, choosing instead to report on his trip directly to Thanom and Praphas.[89] At a press conference at the NEC headquarters, Prasit announced the details of the meetings with the Chinese leaders, and provided his exotic and first-hand experiences of Beijing.[90] Some named Prasit 'Thailand's Kissinger'.[91]

In brief, Prasit's visit to China was perhaps the first, though informal, high-level meeting between Thai and Chinese leaders to begin exploring in earnest the possibility of improving relations since the 1955 meeting between Zhou Enlai and Prince Wan. Symbolically, it was a stepping stone to subsequent contacts and meetings between the Thais and the Chinese. However, no concrete agreements were concluded during the trip. As Henry Kissinger summarised for the US president:

> In August, talks in Beijing between a senior Thai official who accompanied the Thai ping-pong team and Zhou Enlai indicated that the PRC is now sufficiently interested in getting relations with Bangkok onto a different track to allow Bangkok to set the pace in moving the relationship in that direction … Thailand, however, intends to move slowly and prudently. The Government recently approved a small delegation to the Canton Trade Fair this fall.[92]

5.3.2. Toward Trade Diplomacy

The reaction of the Thai military elite to ping-pong diplomacy was mixed. For the first time, General Praphas Charusathien referred to Communist China as the 'People's Republic of China'. As he put it:

---

89   'Prasit Opens New Era With China', 1.
90   At a press conference Prasit said that he had taken Thai silk neckties with him to Beijing, but had to bring these ties back home because 'the Chinese do not accept gifts and there is no use for ties in China'. The Chinese people, said Prasit, wore ordinary shirts of blue, white or black: 'There are no red or green dresses'. The shirts 'do not have creases – they don't use iron'. He also mentioned that the People's Republic of China was 'trying to make it possible for the people to eat well. They don't care at present about modernizing or decorating their buildings'. Asked whether he enjoyed any nightlife, he replied, 'There are no night clubs and no neon signs. Electricity is used mainly for industry, none for decorative purposes'. 'Not Ready for These Ties', *Bangkok Post*, 15 September 1972, 1.
91   'Prasit to Put Thailand's Case', *Bangkok Post*, 3 August 1972, 1; Prasit, 'Sumphantamaitri Thai-Jeen korn por sor', 14.
92   'Memorandum from the President's Assistant for National Security Affairs (Kissinger) the President Nixon', 5 October 1972, in *Foreign Relations of the United States, 1969–1976, Vol. 20: Southeast Asia, 1969–1972*, Document 181.

> We accepted the invitation to send a ping-pong team to demonstrate that we are friendly to all who are friendly to us and that we do not want to have any enemy. Because we have had no communications for 20 years, we decided to send as adviser to the team someone who knows the Chinese language and culture and who has a sufficiently high position. [Prasit] was welcomed with honor and was received by Chinese leaders of top levels.[93]

'As a result', Praphas said he was 'satisfied' not only on 'the sports and cultural fields but also, unexpectedly, in the field of international politics. This is a good omen'.

> We are thankful to the Chinese for their welcome but we have to think carefully of what we do now. After 20 years of separation, we should be sure that we make a good beginning.[94]

However, Praphas pointed out that 'it is difficult to understand' Zhou's statement that China did not interfere in the internal affairs of other countries. He believed that 'Beijing may have been changing its policy since its admittance into the United Nations and is reducing its intervention in other countries'. Regarding trading with China, Praphas said:

> At present, Chinese goods are smuggled into this country but they are also being sold legally. This is because goods seized by the authorities are sold by auction and merchants resell them in the market … In future, it is likely that we will permit legal import of China goods and collect duty on them.[95]

In other words, despite the fact that the Thai military was taking a major step toward improving relations with China, it felt there was no rush to establish full diplomatic relations with China due largely to distrust of China's role in supporting the CPT insurgency. Nevertheless, the government expressed interest in developing sports and cultural exchanges as well as economic relations.

The ping-pong trip to Beijing was followed quickly by attendance at the Canton Trade Fair in October 1972. With Thanom and Praphas's approval, Prasit headed a 17-member delegation including Vicharn

---

93   'Trade Offer to Beijing', *Bangkok Post,* 19 September 1972, 3.
94   Likewise, Pote Sarasin said that the Zhou–Prasit meeting was 'a good beginning' for future cordial relations with the PRC: 'I welcome the information given by Mr. Prasit that China will not interfere in the internal affairs of other countries and I hope this will be carried out, both directly and indirectly, in our case'. 'Pote to Continue China Dialogue at UN Meet', *Bangkok Post,* 20 September 1972, 1.
95   'Trade Offer to Beijing', 3.

Nivatwongse, Permanent Secretary of the Ministry of Commerce, Pracha Gunakasem, Consul-General to Hong Kong, Wichian Pathommas, Trade Commissioner to Hong Kong, and key business representatives such as Ob Wasurat, the First Vice President of the Board of Trade, Kiat Srifuengfung (Thai Asahi Glass), Pongse Sarasin (Coca Cola Thailand), Kiat Vadhanavekin (Thai Sugar Producers Association), Thavorn Pornprabha (Siam Motors Group) and Prasert Prasart-thongosoth (Bangkok Mechanical Co.).[96] This time, Thanom clearly instructed the trade delegation to convey the message to Chinese leaders that the Thai people were not hostile towards China.[97]

Before its departure, the team met Praphas at his Sukhothai Road residence. Praphas praised the trade delegation members as 'the first group of merchants to visit the China mainland': 'After the Second World War, contacts were severed because of different ideologies and conflicts'. 'We have to move with the changing world situation', he said.

> With the easing of the world situation, we must adjust ourselves. We had made first contact with the Chinese through accepting an invitation of the Asian Table Tennis Union to participate in an international competition.[98]

As Praphas pointed out:

> We and the Chinese are turning our faces towards each other with peace as the prospect ... We felt that the atmosphere was good, and we saw the prospects of peace. The Chinese said that we could have peaceful coexistence if we have mutual trust and do not suspect or take advantage of each other. This is the way a dialogue should be.[99]

Praphas specifically asked the trade delegation to 'study the conditions for trade'. However, 'it's not yet time for actual transactions. China's trade is conducted by the state'. He also felt that establishment of diplomatic relations was not an urgent task: 'We had been in touch with the Chinese for 800 years. Though we did not have diplomatic relations, we traded

---

96 'Prasit Chosen to Lead 17-Man Trade Mission', *Bangkok Post*, 11 October 1972, 1.
97 'Prasit Chosen to Lead 17-Man Trade Mission', 1.
98 'Praphas: We Must Face Realities', *Bangkok Post*, 12 October 1972, 1
99 'Praphas: We Must Face Realities', 1, 3.

with each other'. Praphas highlighted Prasit's report in which Beijing said that 'diplomatic relations were not so very necessary at present. We should have contacts through sports, culture, education and trade first'.[100]

Prasit also told reporters, who asked when actual trade with China would begin, that

> it's too early to say. We have only been in contact with China for one month. The matter is under study. Whatever we do we must consider our national interest as more important than anything else.

Thailand, he cautioned, was 'a small country':

> We must work for survival. We will be friendly to those friendly to us, no matter whether they are a big power or small nation, or whether they have a different system from us.

'If the Chinese have goodwill towards us', continued Prasit, 'the opportunity for friendship and trade is great. We should not worry about losing in trade with China. Trade will have to go through a government organization'.[101] When Vicharn Nivatwongse was asked whether this trip to China would violate Revolutionary Proclamation No. 53 – which had banned trade with China since 1959 – he replied that the decree would be amended in the future so that trade could be carried out more easily.[102]

On 15 October, Prasit and his trade team attended the opening ceremony of the Canton Trade Fair, presided over by Chen Jia, Deputy Minister of Economic Affairs. According to Prasit, the ceremony was marked by 'firecrackers, with no speeches or ribbon-cutting', and the Thai delegation was given preferential treatment by the Chinese over other trade missions, including a banquet set up especially for the Thai trade members.[103] Prasit met with Cheng Su Fu, Assistant Minister of Commerce, and Peng Chin Po, Foreign Trade Director-General. The latter told him that 'the Chinese government is pleased to consider the purchase of Thai products available for export'.[104]

---

100 'Praphas: We Must Face Realities', 3.
101 'Trade Mission off to China', *Bangkok Post,* 14 October 1972, 1.
102 Kim, 'The Politics of Thailand's Trade Relations', 315.
103 According to Prasit, when the Thai delegation arrived at Canton, the Chinese authorities sent a fleet of eight new Toyota cars with a red pennant on the leading car to receive them. At the Trade Fair, 'all food and accommodation is being provided free, while other trade missions have to pay for themselves'. The trade delegation stayed at the Tong Fang Hotel. 'China Fetes Thais, Promised Trade', *Bangkok Post,* 21 October 1972, 1.
104 'China Fetes Thais, Promised Trade', 1.

After that, Prasit returned to Bangkok and Vicharn Nivatwongse continued to lead the remainder of the team to Beijing. Here he met with Li Xiannian, Deputy Prime Minister, on 22 October. Li said that the Chinese understood Thai difficulties in restoring diplomatic relations with China and did not wish to rush the process. For the time being, he instead urged for a move toward informal relations, including trade. Li suggested that the obstacle in establishing mutual trade did not originate with the Chinese, but with the Thais, largely because Thailand had not yet abolished Revolutionary Proclamation No. 53. Li therefore indicated to Vicharn that it was up to the Thai Government to make a decision, while the Chinese were ready to trade with Thailand based upon the principle of 'equality and mutual benefit'.[105] During this visit, the Chinese apparently indicated an interest in purchasing many items such as sugar, jute, rubber, hard wood and rice. For their part, the Thais indicated their interest in purchasing light manufactured items, fruit and medicines.[106]

After his trip to Canton, Prasit revealed that the Chinese were ready to trade with Thailand. But because China's government conducted its trade, Thailand would have to set up a counterpart government organisation for the same purpose. This would take at least two to three months to complete.[107] He acknowledged that trade with China would narrow Thailand's huge trade deficit, particularly with Japan.[108] Prasit also said in his conversation with the US ambassador in November 1972 that 'Thailand would begin trading with China as soon as arrangements for a formal mechanism could be worked out'.[109]

In an interview with the *Bangkok Post,* on 23 January 1973, Deputy Prime Minister General Praphas said that Thailand was willing to trade with China. 'The Chinese can now place orders for any Thai product they require', Praphas went on. 'All they have to do is to contact the Ministry of Commerce and place their order and make their offers'. However, Praphas emphasised that Thailand would not ask the Chinese to 'buy this and that'. He expressed hope that the easing of tensions through trade and informal contacts 'would lead to reduction or elimination of Beijing's material aid for the insurgents'.[110]

---

105 Warnwai, *Zhou Enlai: Pupluek maitri Thai-jeen,* 198–99.
106 'Team Back with China Trade List', *Bangkok Post,* 29 October 1972, 1.
107 Central Intelligence Agency, *Central Intelligence Bulletin,* 10 November 1972, 5.
108 'China Trade "Would Narrow Deficit"', *Bangkok Post,* 22 October 1972, 1.
109 Central Intelligence Agency, *Central Intelligence Bulletin,* 10 November 1972, 5.
110 General Praphas Charusathien's interview with the *Bangkok Post,* 23 January 1973, in *China and Thailand, 1949–1983,* ed. RK Jain (New Delhi: Radiant Publishers, 1984), 189–90.

With Praphas's endorsement, Commerce Minister Prasit encouraged applications from Thai firms to trade with China on 21 February. However, only two applications were submitted, largely because the private sector feared that, given the existence of the anticommunism act, they risked being accused of communist sympathisers. They also remained uncertain about the strength of the government's desire to establish commercial relations with China.

During a press conference on 22 March, Praphas asserted that the Thai Government was prepared to trade with Beijing and would consider amending Revolutionary Proclamation No. 53 in case the PRC made a request. However, he confirmed that, at this point, no proposal of this nature had yet been received from China: 'At present there is no trade between the two countries and thus no change in the law will be made'.[111]

Praphas later admitted that:

> we are carrying out our policy to be friendly to all who are friendly to us. We have no hostility towards China and we want to be friends with the Chinese people … However, their unfriendly action announcing support for communist insurgency makes us cautious about the People's Republic of China.[112]

He also suggested that 'if the Chinese on the Mainland want to buy from us they may approach us and we will respond accordingly'.[113]

Other developments in early 1973 helped facilitate Thai–Chinese rapprochement. On 20 March, for example, a Chinese medical team led by Professor Jang Wei-chun of Beijing Friendship Hospital had a 50-minute stopover at Don Mueang Airport. The delegation was comprised of seven physicians and one interpreter, and was en route from the World Health Organization (WHO) Convention in Geneva to a three-day WHO meeting in Manila. They met a team of Thai officials headed by Dr Somboon Vachrotai, the Deputy Permanent Secretary of Public Health, and Dr Veekij Viranuvat, who was the team doctor who

---

111 'Thai/Chinese Relations', 25 May 1973, Foreign and Commonwealth Office (FCO), FCO15/1788, the National Archives, London.
112 'Thai/Chinese Relations', 25 May 1973, FCO, FCO15/1788, the National Archives, London.
113 'Praphas: We Aren't Tied to Taiwan', *Bangkok Post*, 30 March 1973, 1.

visited Beijing during the first ping-pong delegation in August 1972. The MFA suggested to the government that 'medical diplomacy' might facilitate a détente with China.[114]

Another good signal was a commitment to initiate satellite communications between Shanghai and Bangkok by September, approved by the Thai Government on 28 March 1973. This request had been made to the Thai Ministry of Communication by Beijing in January, and the rapid move to set it up was viewed in the press as a part of the progressive easing of relations with the PRC, albeit without the precipitous abandonment of Taiwan.[115] Deputy Foreign Minister Chatichai Choonhavan even stated that 'Thailand will do everything to have normal relations with the PRC short of diplomatic ties'.[116] Chatichai also issued an invitation to the PRC to establish a permanent office at ECAFE in Bangkok.

At the same time, the Thai elite voiced a growing irritation with the new Taiwanese Ambassador Admiral Ma Chi-chuang, who arrived in Bangkok in August 1972. Ma persistently pressed both Thanom and Chatichai on the issue of whether Thailand was considering downgrading its level of representation in Taiwan (from ambassador to chargé d'affaires) and pursuing Thailand–PRC rapprochement.[117] This annoyed Chatichai, who publicly rebuked Ma:

> whether Thailand is going to establish relations with Mainland China or not is an internal affair of this country. Whether the Government will change ambassadors or transfer them from one post to another is also an internal affair. No envoy stationed here has the right to make any enquiry into such internal affair.[118]

---

114 'Thailand–People's Republic of China Relations', 23 June 1975, Library and Archives Division, MFA POL7/PM2518/4, at the Ministry of Foreign Affairs (MFA), Thailand, 3–4.
115 'Phone Link with China Agreed', *Bangkok Post*, 28 March 1973, 3.
116 'Thai Intelsat Link with China', 29 March 1973, RG59, 1973BANGKOK05014, National Archives and Records Administration (NARA) online database.
117 Ambassador Ma handed over a memorandum to Thanom and Chatichai expressing 'grave concern' over rumours suggesting that Thailand may downgrade the level of its representative in Taiwan in April 1973. In a press conference, Chatichai stated that he felt 'the Nationalist Chinese Ambassador was too anxious, active and over-concerned about the state of relations … They should be well aware of the changing trends of international politics'. After the 1973 student revolution, Ma was down at the Ministry of Foreign Affairs almost every day drawing the attention of the Foreign Minister to 'provocative' articles in the newspapers, and on 30 October, he even staged a three-hour sit-in at Government House while the Cabinet was in session and refused to go away. 'Thai/Chinese Relations', 25 May 1973, FCO, FCO15/1788, the National Archives, London; 'Thai/Chinese Relations', 9 November 1973, FCO, FCO15/1788, the National Archives, London.
118 'Thai/Chinese Relations', 9 November 1973, FCO, FCO15/1788, the National Archives, London.

There was no doubt that Taiwan's days of full diplomatic relations with Thailand were numbered.

By late 1972, therefore, the movement towards some kind of rapprochement with China had gained momentum, and the Thanom–Praphas Government had concluded that peaceful coexistence with the People's Republic of China was attainable. During this time, contact with Beijing increased in the fields of sports and trade, but there remained a reservation in terms of establishing formal diplomatic relations. As Praphas put it in March 1973, Thailand should 'not plunge headlong' into a dialogue with Beijing:

> It is like a case of a young boy and girl. The fact that the boy has sent one letter to the girl does not mean that the girl should give herself to him otherwise it would be too quick. The girl could be accused of being too easy. We have to maintain our posture.[119]

5.3.3. Behind Sports Diplomacy: The MFA Steps In

> I would contact China through diplomacy rather than ping-pong – though I am not bad at ping-pong.
> – Thanat Khoman, former foreign minister[120]

This section examines the diplomatic practices of the MFA, especially in relation to sports diplomacy with China. This reactivation of détente led to the formation of personal relationships between Thai and Chinese diplomats that helped pave the way for the formal normalisation of diplomatic relations in July 1975, to be discussed in Chapter 6.

Before the 1971 coup, the MFA under Thanat Khoman had proactively sought rapprochement with Beijing through back-channel diplomacy. Specifically, Anand Panyarachun, the Thai Ambassador to the UN and the US, had made personal contact with the Chinese ambassador, Huang Hua, at the UN. After the coup, the Foreign Ministry was initially marginalised in Thailand's foreign affairs, and this was particularly true in relation to policy towards China. However, after ping-pong diplomacy commenced, the Ministry resumed duties. By late 1972, Thai diplomats reactivated their contacts with their Chinese counterparts at the UN and in capitals around the world. Among others, the recently appointed

---

119 'Thai/Chinese Relations', 9 November 1973, FCO, FCO15/1788, the National Archives, London.
120 'Thanat Urges Contact with China', *Bangkok Post*, 7 January 1973, 1.

Deputy Foreign Minister, Major General Chatichai Choonhavan, who was personally in favour of closer relations with the PRC, became an ardent advocate of détente.[121]

By mid-1972, the Chinese Government clearly signalled its intention to move toward a dialogue with Thailand. The Chinese ambassadors in many other countries began to contact Thai ambassadors in order to promote friendly relations and build mutual trust. Thai officials initially remained vigilant and aloof due to having received no clear instruction from Bangkok. In September 1972, the Chinese Ambassador to Copenhagen, Denmark, even invited Thai leaders to make a visit to Beijing. But Prince Prem Purachatra, Thai Ambassador to Denmark, did not respond.[122]

On 5 October 1972, the Thai delegation to the UN, led by Deputy Prime Minister Pote Sarasin and Ambassador Anand, met Qiao Guanhua, Deputy Foreign Minister and head of the Chinese delegation at the Chinese Permanent Representative Office at the UN.[123] According to Anand, both sides were ready to progress in the realm of sport, trade and culture, with governmental visits to follow later. In their conversations, they laid out key issues that directly affected their relationship; namely the Vietnam War, the Kuomintang Army in Thailand and the communist insurgency in Thailand. Anand grasped the centrality of anti-Sovietism in the Chinese world view. By the end of the talks, they agreed that they would try to build a political atmosphere conducive to avoiding any verbal attacks on each other.[124]

In 1973, the Thai MFA made a decision to convey Thailand's readiness to initiate discussions with the PRC. MFA order No. 0100/371 was issued on 5 January instructing Thai ambassadors around the world to

---

121 In fact, when Chatichai returned from his post to be the Director-General of the Political Affairs Department at the Ministry of Foreign Affairs in 1972, he repeatedly emphasised contact with the PRC as a priority. Tej Bunnag praised the far-sighted Chatichai who would always remind his staff that the Communist world was not indivisible and monolithic, and Sino–Soviet tension was prevalent. Tej Bunnag, 'Satapana kwansumpan tai-jeen, 1 karakadakom 2518: prasobkarn kong nakkantud' [Establishing Thai–Chinese Relations, 1 July 1975: Diplomat's Experiences], *Warasan Asiatawanoak suksa* [East Asian Studies Journal] 3, no. 1 (July 1990): 28; Tej Bunnag, interview by author, 27 June 2016, Bangkok.

122 Anand Panyarachun, 'Pookmitr kub sataranaratprachachon jeen' [Befriending the People's Republic of China], in *Nayobai tangprated Thai bon tangpreng* [Thai Foreign Policy at the Crossroads], ed. Chantima Ongsuragz (Bangkok: Direk Jayanama Memorial Lecture Series, Thammasat University, 1990), 134.

123 Anand, 'Pookmitr kub sataranaratprachachon jeen', 133; Chulacheeb, 'Thai–Chinese Relations: Security and Strategic Partnership', 7.

124 Anand, 'Pookmitr kub sataranaratprachachon jeen', 133.

approach their Chinese counterparts and communicate a willingness 'to be friendly to every country that was friendly to Thailand'.[125] Thai diplomats in a variety of embassies including Stockholm, Tehran, Tokyo, Washington DC, Canberra, The Hague, Brussels and Madrid, and the Consular Office in Karachi, later telegrammed the MFA, reporting their various contacts with the Chinese diplomats. The Chinese Ambassador to The Hague announced that The Hague would be another contact point with Thailand and met with the Thai ambassador, assuring him of Chinese interest in expanding contacts and interactions, and expressing its wish to cooperate with Thailand at international economic conferences. The Chinese insisted that they would not interfere in the domestic affairs of other countries, and urged the overseas Chinese in Thailand to obey local laws.[126]

Both sides also met occasionally at international meetings such as the UN ECAFE meeting in Tokyo in April 1973. On 16 April, the head of the Thai delegation, Dr Boonrod Binson, Minister of University Affairs, met the Chinese delegation led by the Director-General of Department of International Organization, Treaty and Law, An Chih-yuan. The latter expressed interest in establishing a permanent mission in Bangkok. According to Boonrod, the Chinese 'asked how the Thai Government would feel if they were to send a mission to Bangkok'. Boonrod replied that 'ECAFE is a United Nations organization – this is not simply a matter between China and Thailand alone'. After the discussion, the Chinese explained that a Chinese study team would arrive in Bangkok 'sometime before September' to commence establishing a permanent mission to ECAFE.[127] They also discussed the possibility of exchange visits by economists and technicians. Both parties agreed to contact each other through the Chinese and Thai embassies in Japan. The Japanese would act as intermediaries with Suphat Thiensunthorn, Thai Ambassador to Japan, facilitating informal meetings.[128]

At that ECAFE meeting, Cheng Rui-sheng, then Deputy Director of the Southeast Asian Division of the Chinese Foreign Ministry, had a chance to meet Tej Bunnag, Director of the East Asian Division of the Thai MFA.

---

125 'Thai–PRC Relations', 23 June 1975, Library and Archives Division, MFA POL7/PM2518/4, MFA, Thailand, 3.
126 Anand, 'Pookmitr kub sataranaratprachachon jeen', 134–35.
127 'Red Chinese Team Due', *Bangkok Post*, 19 April 1973, 1.
128 'Red Chinese Team Due', 3.

Tej recalled: 'this is the beginning of friendship between Cheng and me, which led to a series of negotiations between both Ministries of Foreign Affairs in Sino-Thai rapprochement'. Tej called it 'corridor diplomacy'.[129]

This so-called 'corridor diplomacy' duly paved the way for the diplomatisation of sports by the MFA, so as to achieve peaceful coexistence and détente with the PRC. Deputy Prime Minister Praphas allowed the sports exchanges between Thailand and China: 'We do not regard sports as politics. We keep sports separate from politics.'[130]

The most important exchange was a Chinese ping-pong team led by Zhuang Zedong, a former three-time world table tennis champion who visited Bangkok between 17 and 24 June 1973. This was the first Chinese delegation to visit Thailand since 1949. Chinese high-ranking diplomat and Deputy Director of the Southeast Asian Division, Cheng Rui-sheng, accompanied the team as deputy head.[131] The team stayed at the Indra Regent Hotel at Pratunam, which was owned by Lenglert Baiyoke, the Chinese Thai business figure and close confidante of Chatichai's who would play a significant role as a liaison between Thailand and China over the next few years. The team was welcomed by members of the Thai Table Tennis Association, as well as the public, at Don Mueang Airport. Tej Bunnag also greeted Cheng Rui-sheng, who was said to be delighted to see his 'old friend'.[132]

On the evening of 17 June, a welcome party for the ping-pong team was hosted by the Table Tennis Association of Thailand at the hotel. Its chairman, General Tem Homsetthi, said 'this is a truly historic day. I welcome you most cordially on behalf of the Thai people'.[133] MFA officials including Arsa Sarasin, Secretary to the Foreign Minister, and Suthee Prasasvinitchai, the Deputy Director-General of the Political Affairs Department, and Tej Bunnag attended this party and met with Cheng Rui-sheng. According to Cheng, Lenglert Baiyoke informed him

---

129 Tej Bunnag, interview by author, 27 June 2016, Bangkok.
130 'Beijing Ping-Pong Trip Gets All Clear', *Bangkok Post*, 29 May 1973, 1.
131 Cheng Rui-sheng wrote later that at first the Chinese Ministry of Foreign Affairs had no plan to send him or any other officials with the ping-pong delegation. Yet when Zhuang Zedong was appointed as a team leader, he called Qiao Guanhua, Deputy Foreign Minister, and asked for Foreign Ministry official who had background knowledge about Southeast Asia to accompany the team. The Ministry of Foreign Affairs then assigned Cheng Rui-sheng. Cheng, 'Karntoot ping-pong thai-jin', 110.
132 Cheng, 'Karntoot ping-pong thai-jin', 111.
133 'Cheering Crowds Greet Chinese Team', *Bangkok Post*, 18 June 1973, 1.

that Major General Chatichai Choonhavan, Deputy Foreign Minister, wished to meet Cheng. Cheng readily agreed but stated he wanted the meeting to be informal, insisting that he should not go to the MFA itself.[134]

The following day, the ping-pong team visited a crocodile farm at Samut Prakarn. Cheng Rui-sheng did not join them, but instead met with Arsa Sarasin, Suthee Prasasvinitchai and Tej Bunnag at the Hotel. They had an informal working lunch, which lasted for three hours.[135] Both parties openly exchanged points of view, identifying key problems in Sino–Thai relations as well as discussing the general situation in Southeast Asia. The Thais said that Thailand and China had maintained good relations since ancient times, and the Thai Government was glad to restore and improve Sino–Thai relations. Cheng replied that in the past, Sino–Thai relations were interrupted due to the international and regional situation, but the contemporary international situation had rapidly changed. He hoped that both sides would grasp this opportunity to develop contacts, and gradually restore relations, step by step. Cheng also emphasised the Bandung five principles of peaceful coexistence, which respected territorial integrity, sovereignty and noninterference in the internal affairs of other countries. He suggested that while China and Thailand held differing views about the situation in Southeast Asia, rapprochement would be beneficial for both. Cheng recalled that the informal meeting was held in a 'friendly and sincere atmosphere'.[136]

That evening, Air Chief Marshal Dawee Chullasapya, Minister of Agriculture and Vice President of the Thai Olympic Association, hosted a formal dinner for the Chinese delegation at the Indra Hotel. He said that sports exchanges between the two countries would lead to friendly relations. Deputy Foreign Minister Chatichai Choonhavan was at the dinner and greeted Cheng Rui-sheng. According to Cheng, Chatichai was 'a diplomat with a military background, who was military-like open, straightforward and generous, and at the same time diplomat-like prudent with good humour'.[137]

The 18-member team did not meet Prime Minister Thanom, allegedly because he held no position in the sports associations. Yet, on 19 June, they did meet General Praphas, who was the President of the Thai

---

134   Cheng, 'Karntoot ping-pong thai-jin', 111.
135   Cheng, 'Karntoot ping-pong thai-jin', 112.
136   Cheng, 'Karntoot ping-pong thai-jin', 112.
137   Cheng, 'Karntoot ping-pong thai-jin', 112.

Olympic Association, at his Sukhothai Road residence. Praphas reiterated the Thai Government's position that ties with the PRC would begin if Beijing ended its support for communist insurgency as well as its radio attacks in Thailand.[138] However, Praphas said that the visit of the Chinese ping-pong delegation brought about closer relations between the two countries, and 'we will exchange other types of sports teams with China, if Beijing desires'.[139]

On 21 June, Cheng Rui-sheng was invited to a dinner with Deputy Foreign Minister Chatichai Choonhavan at his Soi Rajkru residence where they exchanged points of view. Chatichai put forward alleged Chinese support for the Thai insurgency, and Cheng Rui-sheng promised to take the issue back to the Chinese leaders.[140] Cheng also invited Chatichai to visit Beijing. Overall, 'the informal meeting', as the Thai MFA described it, was held in a 'friendly and understanding atmosphere'.[141]

This ping-pong visit was particularly significant for the MFA because this was the first time the ministry and its Foreign Deputy Minister were allowed to get to grips with the Chinese. For the Chinese leaders, relations were improving relatively fast, as there had been merely 10 months since the inaugural visit to Beijing.[142] The head of the Chinese delegation, Zhuang Zedong, told the *Bangkok Post* that the PRC and Japan took more than two decades to establish diplomatic relations. However, 'this does not mean that it will take such a long period of time to have ties between China and Thailand'. 'Far from it', he added.

> But we cannot forget the fact that first things come first. Through sport exchanges, we learn about each other. Cultural exchanges bind us in closer friendship and trade enables us to help each other. Once we have known each other well then we will be in a position to establish diplomatic ties.[143]

Thanom gave an interview in which he said:

> Thais and Chinese have had good relations since ancient times. My government is glad that the Chinese indicate friendliness towards us. Our policy calls for us to be friendly to every country [that was] friendly to us.

---

138 'Thai-Chinese Relations', 29 June 1973, FCO, FCO15/1788, the National Archives, London.
139 'China Policy Unchanged, But Relations Possible', *Bangkok Post*, 21 June 1973, 5.
140 Cheng, 'Karntoot ping-pong thai-jin', 113.
141 'Thai, Chinese Links Explored', *Bangkok Post*, 22 June 1973, 1.
142 'Thai-Chinese Relations', 29 June 1973, FCO, FCO15/1788, the National Archives, London.
143 'China Press Hails Ping-Pong Visit', *Bangkok Post*, 24 June 1973, 5.

5. INTERREGNUM – 1971

He went on to lay out the closer links between Thailand and China:

> Last year the Chinese invited us to send a ping-pong team and then a trade mission. This year we permitted a Chinese ping-pong team to come and play here. The exchange of sports delegations will improve understanding, beneficial to future relations.

Thanom was aware that 'there are some outstanding problems between the Chinese and ourselves. However, time, stability and mutual understanding will solve them'.[144] 'If informal relations are good', Thanom said pointedly, 'they may lead to official relations in the future'.[145]

Sports exchanges increased, particularly in 1973. For example, between 7 and 21 August 1973, a Thai badminton delegation led by the Deputy Minister of Interior, Police Lieutenant General Chumpol Lohachala, who had headed the first ping-pong visit the year before, went to Beijing. Now however, he was accompanied by two high-ranking diplomats from the Foreign Ministry, Phan Wannamethi, Director-General of the Political Affairs Department, and Tej Bunnag, Director of the East Asian Division.[146] On 13 August, Vice Premier Deng Xiaoping and Deputy Foreign Minister Han Nianlong received the Thai delegation.[147] Deng said that relations between China and Thailand had existed for as long as 2,000 years and that contact therefore ought to be continued in the future.[148]

Later, Tej Bunnag disclosed that Thai Foreign Ministry representatives had nine hours of cordial high-level conversations with Chinese Foreign Ministry officials in Beijing. The Chinese officials included Lu Wei-Jao, Director-General of the Asian Department, Cheng Rui-sheng, now Deputy Director-General of the Asian Department, Liu Yung-Chen, the desk officer for Thailand, and Li Mok from the Foreign Affairs Friendship Association as an interpreter.[149] Their talks were considered a 'presentation of points of views', rather than negotiations.[150] When the Thais brought up Chinese support for the Thai insurgency, the Chinese responded

---

144 'Closer Links with China Soon – PM', *Bangkok Post*, 21 June 1973, 1.
145 'China Policy Unchanged, But Relations Possible', 5.
146 Tej, 'Satapana kwansumpan tai-jeen, 1 karakadakom 2518', 25.
147 'China-Thailand', 15 August 1973, RG59, 1973HONGK08184, NARA.
148 Warnwai, *Zhou Enlai: Pupluek maitri Thai-jeen*, 213.
149 According to the Thai delegation, Liu Yung-Chen could 'read Thai but spoke it poorly'. 'Comments on Recent Visit to China', 6 September 1973, RG59, 1973BANGKO13889, NARA.
150 'Thai–PRC Relations', 23 June 1975, Library and Archives Division, MFA POL7/PM2518/4, MFA, Thailand 6.

that the Chinese Communist Party, not the Chinese Government, dealt with the insurgents. The latter then raised the issue of Thai support for Kuomintang operations against China in the northern part of Thailand, indicating that both sides were even.[151]

The Chinese brought up the alleged Thai Government order to Nationalist China to close down their 10 kilowatt radio station at Mae Jan in Chiang Rai in North Thailand, and what they presumed was an intelligence operation headquartered there. They then asked the Thais whether there might be a quid pro quo for the Chinese cessation of aid to the Thai insurgents. The Thai officials appeared unaware of the order, and said that they knew of no such intelligence operation.[152] The Chinese also reassured the Thais not to worry about a road construction that the Chinese had constructed in northern Laos.[153]

With regard to Thai–Chinese trade, Chinese officials noted that while they were interested in trading with Thailand, Revolutionary Proclamation No. 53 still hindered bilateral trade, and strongly urged that the law to be rescinded completely.[154] However, Thailand refused, claiming that they would be able to amend the law to permit China to trade with Thailand.

The Chinese informed Thai officials that the arrival of the PRC representative at the UN ECAFE in Bangkok in September, as originally discussed, would be delayed because of a shortage of qualified personnel at the Chinese MFA, many of whom were busy with other UN duties. According to the Chinese, the representation would be in the form of a study mission to be followed by the establishment of a permanent office in Bangkok. The Thai officials stated that they would use this office like an embassy, to establish direct communication with China.[155]

---

151 'Discussions of Thai Foreign Ministry Officials in China', 28 August 1973, RG59, 1973BANGKO13423, NARA.
152 'Comments on Recent Visit to China', 6 September 1973, RG59, 1973BANGKO13889, NARA.
153 According to Ross Terrill, a close confidante of the Australian prime minister on détente with the PRC and an Australian professor at Harvard who made various trips to Bangkok, Thai leaders no longer saw the Chinese road complex in North Laos as directed against Thailand, but rather as a way to achieve influence and bargaining leverage for China in Laos. 'Terrill comments on East Asia', 10 September 1973, RG59, 1973CANBER04986, NARA.
154 A rumour that 'secret' Sino–Thai trade negotiations were held in Hong Kong between the chief of the China Trade Office and a delegation of Thai businesspeople representing the Thai government was reported by the *Nation* on 25 August. However, it was a false report: the correspondent missed the badminton team and then fabricated the 25 August story after noticing several Thai business representatives in Hong Kong. 'Comments on Recent Visit to China', 6 September 1973, RG59, 1973BANGKO13889, NARA.
155 'Comments on Recent Visit to China', 6 September 1973, RG59, 1973BANGKO13889, NARA.

5. INTERREGNUM – 1971

The Thais were generally unimpressed with Chinese understanding of Thailand. According to them, the Chinese appeared to form their opinions from reading some newspapers such as *Phim Thai*, *Siam Rath* and *The Nation*. They suggested that the Chinese at least began reading *Prachathipatai* as well.[156]

Neither side raised the subject of the US military presence in Thailand.[157] After the trip, Thai Director-General Phan Wannamethi disclosed to the press that China had not expressed any uneasiness over the American military presence in Thailand.[158] Asked by the press whether Beijing objected to the US presence or indeed welcomed it as a counterweight to Soviet influence in the region, Phan said that such conclusions were unsubstantiated.[159] He also emphasised Thai diplomacy, which supported peaceful coexistence with all countries regardless of ideology.[160] According to Tej Bunnag, this meeting was 'the most comprehensive exchange of points of view between Thai and Chinese MFA officials, and the basis for a rapprochement with the PRC in 1975'.[161]

Shortly thereafter, between 26 August and 7 September 1973, another ping-pong team went to Beijing. The team was led by General Tem Homsetthi, Chairman of the Table Tennis Association of Thailand. He was accompanied by Suthee Prasasvinitchai, Deputy Director-General of the Political Affairs Department, and Kosol Sindhvananda, first secretary at the Foreign Ministry.[162] Both diplomats met Cheng Rui-sheng, Deputy Director-General of the Asian Department as well as Liu Yung-chen, and Zhang Jiuhuan, desk officers for Thailand. They further discussed a variety of international problems.[163] In Bangkok, meanwhile, on 26 August, General Pong Punnakanta, Minister of Transport, formally opened satellite communications services between Thailand and China. Via satellite services, Thai correspondents had an opportunity to interview General Tem Homsetthi, who was in Beijing.[164]

---

156 'Comments on Recent Visit to China', 6 September 1973, RG59, 1973BANGKO13889, NARA.
157 'Comments on Recent Visit to China', 6 September 1973, RG59, 1973BANGKO13889, NARA.
158 'Phan Reports: US Military Bases Don't Worry China', *The Nation*, 28 August 1973.
159 'Phan Reports: US Military Bases Don't Worry China'.
160 Vitthaya Vejjajiva, *Phan Pheua Phandin* [Phan for the Kingdom] (Bangkok: Post Publishing, 2014), 232.
161 Tej Bunnag, interview by author, 27 June 2016, Bangkok.
162 'Thai-Chinese Relations', 9 November 1973, FCO, FCO15/1788, the National Archives, London.
163 'Thai–PRC Relations', 23 June 1975, Library and Archives Division, MFA POL7/PM2518/4, MFA, Thailand 6–7.
164 Warnwai, *Zhou Enlai: Pupluek maitri Thai-jeen*, 216.

In short, between 1972 and 1973, sports exchanges became more frequent and normal. This sports diplomacy was accompanied with regular informal meetings between Thai and Chinese diplomats. The development of close working relationships helped further progress towards an easing of relations. As Thanom said in a press conference in late 1973, 'when people are able to visit one another, it creates good understanding, mutual sympathy, and compromises being reached in various matters both sides have joint interests in', and 'trade with the China Mainland will most probably be started in the near future'.[165]

5.3.4. Amending the Law

Following the trade and sports delegations to Beijing, the next step in improving Sino–Thai relations was to start trading with the PRC. The main technical obstacle was Revolutionary Proclamation No. 53, issued by Field Marshal Sarit Thanarat in 1959 to ban trade with communist countries, especially China. The Thanom Government repeatedly proclaimed its intention to revise or rescind this law, but by mid-1973 it had failed to act. In general, the benefits of trade with China seemed to be mutually recognised by leading power elites as well as by the Thai public. Charoon Sibunruang, former President of the Board of Trade, for example, said 'I welcome trade with China and I don't foresee any problems if trade is resumed'.[166] Likewise, Ob Wasurat, the current President of the Board of Trade, said in August 1973 that Thailand should have established trade relations with China much earlier. If Thailand traded directly with the country, Ob believed, Thailand would reduce its dependence on Hong Kong and Singapore.[167]

Within the business community itself, there was an internal debate between two factions over the best way to conduct trade with China. On the one hand, an idea described as state corporatism was spearheaded by Charoon Sibunruang and asserted that trade with China needed to be run by a state corporation. This idea was also represented by various factions within the government, including the military and the Ministry of Commerce. Prasit Kanchanawat, Commerce Minister, proposed that

---

165 'Prime Minister Thanom on Trade with China', 24 September 1973, RG59, 1973BANGKO14918, NARA.
166 'China Trade Move a Big Surprise: Business Community Welcomes Decision', *Bangkok Post*, 24 January 1973, 13.
167 Kim, 'The Politics of Thailand's Trade Relations', 317.

such a corporation should be set up with a budget of 2 million baht.[168] On the other hand, those who supported the idea of free trade liberalism saw a significant role for the private sector. The Thai Chamber of Commerce, headed by Ob Wasurat, wanted free enterprise and to open trade links with the PRC.[169]

However, further improvement in Sino–Thai trading relations was delayed largely because of the reluctance to trade with the PRC on the part of the military government. This was caused by the persistence of an anticommunist discourse within military thinking. The Thanom Government continued to favour caution in establishing trade with the PRC.[170] By 14 August 1973, the Thanom Government agreed in principle to amend, rather than abolish, Revolutionary Proclamation No. 53, only permitting government-to-government trade relations with China.[171] In his speech to the National Legislative Assembly on 6 September, Thanom briefly outlined government policy. While his government wished to trade with the Chinese Government, he insisted that only when his government was convinced trading with China posed no security danger to Thailand would he allow free trade to go ahead. Now, however, Thanom realised that it was inappropriate to trade freely with a country with which Thailand had no diplomatic relations. Scepticism of China had decreased, but remained intact due to China's alleged support for the CPT. Thanom felt that a cessation of Chinese assistance to communist subversion and insurgency, and an end to clandestine radio broadcasts from China against the Thai military government, would be necessary before formal relations between the two countries could be established.[172] By then, however, the idea of establishing diplomatic relations with the PRC had been tabled within the MFA.[173]

---

168 'Prasit to Query Cabinet on China Trade Policy', *Bangkok Post*, 27 February 1973, 13.
169 'Thai-Chinese Relations', 9 November 1973, FCO, FCO15/1788, the National Archives, London.
170 According to the British telegram, one cause of delay was in particular the reluctance of some members of the Cabinet, including Thanom himself, due to a security imperative: 'Thanom still felt anxious about the security implications and was strongly backed up by Sawaeng [Senanarong]', who was Secretary-General to the Prime Minister. The Thai Government would 'strictly control trade with China so as to minimize the risks of political "infection"'. Also, it showed the power plays in the government between two factions, namely the Praphas-Narong faction and the Sawaeng faction. Sawaeng, who had links with the Chinese and always thought that contact with China would benefit the faction, opposed efforts by Praphas and his group to 'monopolize the trade contacts'. Praphas occasionally used his influence with Thanom in favour of delay. The National Archives, London, FCO15/1788, 'Thai-Chinese Relations', 9 November 1973.
171 'Cabinet "Yes" to China Trade', *Bangkok Post*, 15 August 1973, 1.
172 *Bangkok Post*, 7 September 1973.
173 Tej Bunnag, interview by author, 27 June 2016, Bangkok.

In his meeting with US Deputy Secretary of Defense, William Clements, in Bangkok in September, Thanom said that Thailand must develop its relationship with China very carefully, and not 'jump in all at once'. He also permitted government-to-government trade relations with China, but emphasised that the government must avoid a situation in which the PRC could directly trade with individual Thai firms. Thanom made it clear that everything entering Thailand would be carefully checked, including financial transactions, to make sure that no funds went to the Thai communists.[174]

The Thai Government proposed three laws to establish the legal basis for trade with the PRC and communist countries in general, such as North Vietnam and North Korea. In order to permit goods from China to enter Thailand, the first law was to amend the decree by adding the words 'except as approved by the Ministry of Commerce' and to change 'the Land of the Chinese Communists' to 'the People's Republic of China'. The second law was to establish a state trading company with capitalisation of 2 million baht within the Ministry of Commerce, to trade directly with China.[175] The final law was to permit Thai civil servants to administer foreign trade with the People's Republic of China.

The proposal of these laws received an automatic first reading. The laws were then referred to the Legal Committee. In a press conference on 19 September, Thanom proclaimed that the amendment was readily passed in all stages by the National Assembly:

> The Ministry of Commerce is making preparations and this might take about 2–3 months, because it is necessary for preparations to be made in full to ensure smooth and satisfactory operation of trade when it is started.

'We must set up an organization or a unit to carry on trade at the government-to-government level'. As Thanom said, in order to preserve a proper balance of trade with China:

---

174 'Secretary Clements Discussing With Thai Prime Minister', 17 September 1973, RG59, 1973BANGKO14495, NARA.
175 Thailand followed the models of state trading corporations in the region, such as Malaysia's PERCAS and Singapore's INTRACO. NARA, RG59, 1973BANGKO15000, 'Thailand Decides to Trade Directly with the People's Republic of China', 25 September 1973.

under no circumstances must anybody be allowed to buy or sell anything as he pleases. All goods China offers to sell us will have to be considered by the Minister of Commerce first in order to decide whether we really need those respective goods quoted, as well as whether we could buy them elsewhere at lower prices. After the Minister of Commerce considers that any goods are suitable, of good quality, and at lower prices than quoted by other countries, as well as necessary for use in our country, then he will submit a report to the Cabinet for consideration and approval. He will not possess the authority to make any decision or reach any agreement on his own initiative. We are making all preparations in a careful and thorough manner; therefore, this will take time.[176]

This cautious road to trade with China aroused Chinese frustration. It was widely reported in the Thai newspapers that Chinese leaders were annoyed by the 'inadequate' amendment of decree 53. The amendment of the decree was 'not sufficient' since it continued to emphasise the requirement to be 'hostile' to Chinese communists.[177] According to Thai MFA staff, the Chinese wanted the Revolutionary Proclamation No. 53 abolished. The Thai Government desired to 'avoid giving in to every Chinese request without obtaining anything in return'. In short, 'the PRC had asked the [Thai Government] to abolish decree 53, the RTG compromised by merely amending it'.[178]

The Chinese Government was also annoyed by an incident that took place at the Dusit Thani Hotel in Bangkok on 19 September, when Thai representatives walked out of an Asian Games Federation executive committee meeting in protest against the expulsion of Taiwan. While the Thai Government had announced its support for the PRC admission, the Thai delegation, led by Luang Chattrakankson, staged a walkout just before the Iranian vote which admitted the PRC and terminated Taiwan's membership.[179] It was clear that the Thai delegation was instructed by the government to vote for PRC admission to the organisation and abstain on any resolution that admitted the PRC but expelled Taiwan. However, during his discussion with Chinese Deputy Foreign Minister Qiao

---

176 'Prime Minister Thanom on Trade with China', 24 September 1973, RG59, 1973BANGKO14918, NARA.
177 Theh Chongkhadikij, 'Beijing Détente Threatened', *Bangkok Post,* 2 October 1973, 1.
178 'Thailand Decides to Trade Directly with the People's Republic of China', 25 September 1973, RG59, 1973BANGKO15000, NARA.
179 'Sports and TRG Policies Toward China', 24 September 1973, RG59, 1973BANGKO14922, NARA.

Guanhua at New York a few months later, Chatichai was informed that the Chinese had taken no offence at the action of Thai sports administrators. The talks were going 'very well'.[180]

To sum up, by 1973, laws facilitating trade relations between Thailand and China were in the making, and the prospect of establishing diplomatic relations was now firmly on the radar of Thai leaders, or at least on the radar of the MFA. Rather than posing a 'go-slow' diplomacy, the Thanom Government to an extent continued the détente strategy with the communist powers that had been initiated by Thanat Khoman. Still locked in a Cold War mindset, Thanom, Praphas and the conservatives remained sceptical of Chinese motivations and pursued a cautious road to détente. Tej Bunnag, then a senior MFA official, recalled later that 'we [the Thai Foreign Ministry] spent nearly three years trying to convince security officials to agree to build normal ties with the People's Republic of China'.[181]

However, on 14 October 1973, the military regime under Thanom and Praphas fell following student-led demonstrations and internal conflict within elite circles.[182] The discourse of détente did not end. Rather, as the next chapter indicates, the process of democratisation expedited the process of détente and the normalisation of Sino–Thai relations, while the discourse of anticommunism appeared to fade away. At the same time, the tension between these two discourses persisted throughout the democratic interlude between 1973 and 1976.

5.4. Conclusion

'The crisis', as Gramsci put it, 'consists precisely in the fact that the old is dying and the new cannot be born; in this interregnum a great variety of morbid symptoms appear'.[183] In Thailand, the ensuing crisis of democracy and diplomacy, during the brief period of 1969 and 1971 brought about

---

180 The National Archives, London, FCO15/1788, 'Thai-Chinese Relations', 9 November 1973.
181 Tej Bunnag, interview by author, 27 June 2016, Bangkok.
182 Prajak Kongkirati, *And Then The Movement Emerged: Cultural Politics of Thai Students and Intellectuals Movements before the October 14 Uprising* (Bangkok: Thammasat University Press, 2005); Kullada Kesboonchoo Mead, 'The Cold War and Thai Democratization', in *Southeast Asia and the Cold War*, ed. Albert Lau (London and New York: Routledge, 2012), 215–40.
183 Antonio Gramsci, *Selections from the Prison Notebooks of Antonio Gramsci*, ed. and trans. Quintin Hoare and Geoffrey Nowell-Smith (London: Lawrence & Wishart, 1971), 276.

an interregnum of full-fledged authoritarianism between 1971 and 1973. Thanom and Praphas launched a coup against their own government, dissolved Parliament, dismissed Thanat from the position of foreign minister and deferred flexible diplomacy. At first, they appeared to pursue a 'go-slow' diplomacy with the communists. Subsequently, the changing dynamics of international politics, especially Nixon's historic visit to China in 1972, rendered the process of opening discussions with Beijing inevitable. This chapter has argued that there remained a persistence of the détente discourse with the PRC during this period of interregnum. Following the extraordinary ping-pong diplomacy, Thailand began the processes of negotiating trade links and developing other contacts. Throughout these processes, the MFA played an important role in negotiating with the Chinese, generating the increasingly close working relationship and acquaintance between the two ministries and diplomats. While the foreign policy of détente was deepening and the prospect of Sino–Thai rapprochement was nascent, the legitimacy of the military regime drastically waned. The student-led demonstrations of 14 October 1973 marked the end of the military regime and its role in foreign affairs. The old discourse of anticommunism was fading away, yet a new discourse of détente had not yet matured.

6

A Diplomatic Transformation: Chatichai, Kukrit and the Second Détente (1975–1976)

> Our [foreign] policy changes considerably. Now, we can go to Red China and to Russia.
>
> – Chatichai Choonhavan[1]

On 14 October 1973, the military regime of Thanom and Praphas was replaced with a civilian government. The 'democratic interlude' (October 1973 – October 1976) that followed facilitated a more open political climate where new realities could be acknowledged and put to the people. At the same time, the changing international environment made it possible for a culture of détente to flourish. Furthermore, the fall of US-backed regimes in Indochina in 1975 reduced American commitment to Southeast Asia. Meanwhile, the end of the Cultural Revolution and the deepening of the Sino–Soviet split saw China take a far less radical position in its diplomatic relations with Thailand. With the discourse of détente now deeply embedded in Thai politics, and with the Ministry of Foreign Affairs able to take a far more active role in shaping foreign policy, those who supported the shift in relations were able to act decisively. This culminated on 1 July 1975, when then prime minister, MR Kukrit Pramoj, and foreign minister, Major General Chatichai Choonhavan, established formal diplomatic relations with the People's Republic of China.

---

1   Quoted in 'Charunphan and Chatichai on Thai-US relations', 13 June 1974, RG59, 1974BANGKO09673, National Archives and Records Administration (NARA) online database.

This chapter elucidates how the normalisation of Sino–Thai relations and ongoing improvement in Thai–Soviet relations followed the same fundamental principle: that the communist powers could be friends rather than enemies. The first section argues that Thailand's relations with the People's Republic of China (PRC) continued to steadily improve, with ongoing petro- and sports diplomacy running alongside increasing trade. It closely examines a diplomatic revolution in Thai–Chinese relations, namely Kukrit's visit to Beijing and the restoration of diplomatic relations, in detail. The second section suggests that while Thailand had maintained diplomatic relations with the USSR since 1941, better trade relations and a cultural agreement signposted a new approach to relations with Moscow.

The chapter also recognises that these changes created deep anxiety within Thai elite circles. As Benedict Anderson has explained, this period saw Thailand experience 'withdrawal symptoms'.[2] US military withdrawal, changing class composition and ideological upheaval precipitated a crisis for the existing Thai elite in a topsy-turvy world. To this, I would add the 'symptom' of the changed diplomatic environment, in which détente with the communist powers gained momentum. On 6 October 1976, this anxiety would lead to mass violence and a subsequent coup, which led to the ultra-nationalist administration, underpinned by a radical anticommunist discourse.

6.1. Sino–Thai Rapprochement: Diplomatic Revolution

6.1.1. Building a Necessary Foundation: From Petro- to Trade Diplomacy

Following the 'October revolution' in 1973, King Bhumibol appointed the rector of Thammasat University, Sanya Dharmasakdi, as the new prime minister. To meet popular demands, Sanya, with a middle-of-the-road personality, pledged to promulgate a new constitution and set out a roadmap for elections within a year. In foreign affairs, he negotiated the gradual withdrawal of American troops and continued the détente strategy. In a speech to the National Assembly on 25 October, he made

---

2 Benedict Anderson, 'Withdrawal Symptoms: Social and Cultural Aspects of the October 6 Coup', in *Exploration and Irony in Studies of Siam over Forty Years* (Ithaca: Cornell University, 2014), 48–49.

clear that he would 'take steps to further good relations with all countries which are friendly towards Thailand, including countries with different political ideologies'.³ On the same day, the newly appointed Foreign Minister, Charoonphan Isarankhun Na Ayutthaya, stated that 'the government is opening the way for closer friendly contacts with the People's Republic of China'.⁴ This policy toward China was largely driven by Major General Chatichai Choonhavan, who remained in position as Deputy Foreign Minister.

Government policy was now constrained by both popular demands to distance Thailand from the US, and the changing international situation. Most pressing was the global oil crisis in October 1973, when the Organization of the Petroleum Exporting Countries (OPEC) drastically raised the oil price. It quadrupled by January 1974 to nearly US$12 a barrel. The oil crisis seriously hurt the Thai economy, not only due to the oil shortage, but also by pushing up domestic prices by up to 20 per cent.⁵ Yet this also provided new opportunities for improved Sino–Thai cooperation.

On 17 November 1973, the PRC approached the Thai Government with an offer to sell high-speed diesel oil to Thailand in return for Thai tobacco. By now, the Sanya Government was in urgent need of oil and welcomed the Chinese initiative. Subsequently, Anand Panyarachun, Thai Ambassador to the United Nations (UN), made direct contact with his Chinese counterpart in a bid to arrange the purchase of oil supplies.⁶ According to Anand, Huang Chen, head of the Chinese delegation to the UN, requested that Thailand end its aggressive attitude towards Cambodia's exiled government headed by Prince Sihanouk, in exchange for crude oil.⁷

---

3   Policy statement by Prime Minister Sanya Dharmasakdi to the National Assembly on 25 October 1973, *Foreign Affairs Bulletin* 13, no. 1 (August–October 1973): 28.
4   'Govt Sets Guidelines for Foreign Policy', *Bangkok Post*, 26 October 1973, 1.
5   Narongchai Akrasanee and Somsak Tambunlertchai, 'Thailand: Transition from Import Substitution to Export Expansion', in *Economic Development in East and Southeast Asia,* ed. Seiji Naya and Akira Takayama (Singapore: Institute of Southeast Asian Studies, 1980), 108.
6   'Beijing Offers Oil for Tobacco', *Bangkok Post,* 17 November 1973; Ministry of Foreign Affairs, 30 November 1973, in *120 Years Ministry of Foreign Affairs* (Bangkok: Ministry of Foreign Affairs, 1995), 239.
7   'Sihanouk Comes with the Oil', *Bangkok Post,* 30 November 1973, 1.

In early December, the Chinese Ambassador to the UN informed Anand that his government had agreed in principle to sell 50,000 tons of oil to Thailand. The Thai Foreign Ministry saw this quick and affirmative reply as a 'particular sign of good will' and thought it showed a 'desire to broaden relations'.[8] Chatichai's close confidante, Lenglert Baiyoke, a prominent Sino–Thai business figure and managing director of Sapanpla Cold Storage Industry, then made a secret arrangement with Beijing for Chatichai and himself to visit China. According to Lenglert, the main cause for Beijing's decision to open the door for Thailand was due to favourable reports to Premier Zhou Enlai about the friendliness of the Thai people during the Chinese ping-pong visit in 1973.[9]

Chatichai eagerly proposed that the Sanya Government abolish the controversial trade law of Revolutionary Proclamation No. 53. In the meantime, he accepted Beijing's invitation, and on 21 December 1973, departed for what was the first official visit by a Thai leader at ministerial level.[10] At an airport press conference, Chatichai announced that the government had decided to rescind Revolutionary Proclamation No. 53 but that this would need approval from the National Legislative Assembly.[11]

Upon his arrival in Beijing, Chatichai was welcomed by Chinese leaders at the airport. Over the next few days, he met with Wang Yao-ting, Chairman of the Council for Promotion of International Trade, and other prominent officials, including the Deputy Minister of Foreign Trade to negotiate the purchase of diesel oil. While the price of the oil remained in contention, Chatichai told the press later that 'all Chinese officials taking part in the negotiations … welcomed us warmly and held talks as if we were relatives and members of the same family'.[12]

---

8   'Chatichai: January Date in Beijing', *Bangkok Post*, 13 December 1973, 1; 'PRC as Source for Oil for Thailand', 14 December 1973, RG59, 1973BANGKO19363, NARA.
9   Lenglert later told the press that China 'has changed its policy to one of seeking every way to promote friendship with Thailand', including sports, trade, and even politics. Lenglert also claimed that the Chinese would not require Thailand to lift the anticommunist act, which they considered as 'an internal affair over which the Thai Government has sovereign right'. However, he also said they insisted on the abrogation of Revolutionary Proclamation No. 53, which had forbidden trade with the PRC since the late 1950s. 'Visits to China Under Review', *Bangkok Post*, 25 December 1973, 1.
10 'Chatichai in Beijing', *Bangkok Post*, 23 December 1973, 3.
11 'Readings of the Bangkok Political Barometer Through December 21', 21 December 1973, RG59, 1973BANGKO19786, NARA; 'China Team to Forge Official Trade Links', *The Nation*, 21 December 1973.
12 'Chatichai on Oil from China', 4 January 1974, RG59, 1974BANGKO00192, NARA.

On the last day of the visit, 28 December, Premier Zhou Enlai spoke with Chatichai for two hours in the Great Hall of the People, where they discussed Thai–Chinese relations, as well as the world situation with particular reference to events in Southeast Asia. Zhou assured Chatichai of China's desire for friendly relations with Thailand. Chatichai said that trade would be conducted normally through the Hong Kong office of the China Resources Corporation and that the Thai Government would control commerce only through licensing via the Ministry of Commerce. In other words, only specifically licensed businesses would be permitted to trade with China.[13] Zhou did not ask for a rapid withdrawal of American military forces from Thailand. According to Chatichai, Zhou was alarmed by Russia's expansionist strategy and naval presence in the Indian Ocean.[14] The PRC's main concern was thus to counter Soviet efforts to fill the power vacuum in Southeast Asia, making the US military withdrawal less of a priority.[15]

Finally, Zhou and Chatichai reached an agreement for the sale of 50,000 tons of diesel to Thailand. According to Chatichai, the diesel purchase was equivalent to a six-month supply, and after lengthy negotiations on price, Zhou intervened to offer the price Thailand had asked for in November (1 baht per litre). Zhou described this as a 'friendship price', and argued that it showed willingness to 'help each other mutually'.[16] Moreover, the Chinese did not require that Thailand recognise Prince Sihanouk's government or sever its relations with Taiwan.[17] Rather, Zhou invited Air Marshal Dawee Chullasapya, Defense Minister and the President of the National Olympic Committee of Thailand, to visit China.[18] For Chatichai, the visit demonstrated that the 'the People's Republic of China is a defensive nation and not aggressive'.[19]

---

13 'Beijing Throws the Door Wide Open', *Bangkok Post*, 29 December 1973, 1.
14 'Beijing Throws the Door Wide Open', 1, 3.
15 'China and Southeast Asia', 27 October 1973, RG59, 1973HONGK10771, NARA.
16 'Beijing Throws the Door Wide Open', 1; 'Chatichai on Oil from China', 4 January 1974, RG59, 1974BANGKO00192, NARA.
17 'Beijing Throws the Door Wide Open', 3.
18 The Chinese leaders were impressed with Dawee's speech during the first Chinese ping-pong visit. Officials of the ping-pong team reported the statements to the Chinese government. Dawee reportedly said:
> Communism is good for China. It has brought about unity of the largest nation in the world. It has brought about economic and social development. So long as the Chinese do not try to export this ideology by force or by subversion, they are welcome to it. I wish them well.

'Dawee Popular in Beijing', *Bangkok Post*, 5 January 1974, 1; 'Beijing Throws the Door Wide Open', 3.
19 'Zhou's Ideas for Southeast Asia', *Bangkok Post*, 30 December 1973, 1.

The visit provided reassurance that the Thai Government was committed to a policy of rapprochement with the PRC.[20] To show goodwill, shortly after the visit, the Thai Government for the first time officially advocated a 'One-China policy', reversing the long-term 'two-China policy' stance. As Chatichai reasoned, since the PRC was now the only member of the UN, Thailand thereby considered there to be only one China.[21]

This petro-diplomacy also provided a stepping stone toward the strengthening of Sino–Thai economic relations. The Sanya Government decided to allow imported goods from China to enter the country from 1 January 1974. In February, Commerce Minister Chanchai Leethawon announced that Thailand would allow the import of eight Chinese goods: machines and machine tools; chemicals for raw materials; steel and iron; raw silk; crude oil; petroleum products and coal; paper and newsprint; medicines and fertilisers.[22]

At the same time, the government facilitated sports relations with China. Defense Minister Dawee led the most important of these, in his capacity as the President of the Thai Olympic Committee. Arriving in Beijing on 7 February 1974 for a week-long visit, Dawee met with Zhou and other government ministers such as Wang Meng, Minister of the All-China Sports Federation, Li Qiang, Foreign Commerce Minister, and Han Nianlong, Deputy Foreign Minister.[23] The discussions ranged from sports to trade, as well as political and security issues. They discussed the Indochina situation, as well as Chinese support for Communist Party of Thailand (CPT) insurgents. Zhou reportedly reassured Dawee that since

---

20 'Thailand–People's Republic of China Relations', 23 June 1975, Library and Archives Division, MFA POL7/PM2518/4, Ministry of Foreign Affairs (MFA), 7.
21 'Chatichai on his China trip', 4 January 1974, RG59, 1974BANGKO00229, NARA.
22 'Rules on China Trade', *Bangkok Post,* 2 March 1974, 3.
23 At a banquet on 8 February 1974, Wang Meng spoke of the traditional friendship between the people of China and Thailand. He said that sports exchanges had been strengthened in the past few years, and this promoted the understanding and friendship between the sports teams and people of the two countries. Dawee said that Thailand and China should establish friendly relations and that these relations should be developed in the days to come. Speech by Wang Meng, at a banquet given in honour of a delegation led by Dawee Chullasapya, President of the Olympic Committee of Thailand, 8 February 1974, excerpted in *China and Thailand, 1949–1983,* ed. RK Jain (New Delhi: Radiant Publishers, 1984), 196.

the Thai military regime had gone, China had no reason to support the Thai communists, and that the Voice of the People of Thailand Radio was not located on Chinese territory.[24] As Dawee said:

> Zhou stressed that the PRC does not want to export Communism. He admitted that in the past, China had supported terrorists in Thailand to fight for freedom because the former (Thanom, Praphas) government was dictatorial and curtailed human rights.[25]

Dawee also emphasised that the Thai Government had already agreed to abrogate Revolutionary Proclamation No. 53, and was just waiting for the National Legislative Assembly to approve the decision. For Zhou, this should be a step toward opening 'the door for brotherly relationships based on good intentions towards each other'.[26] During the talks with the Chinese leaders, the old saying, 'the Thais and the Chinese are none other than brothers' was also highlighted. Furthermore, Zhou told Dawee that the Chinese realised how difficult it was for Thailand to establish diplomatic relations with the PRC and did not wish to rush the Thai Government into it. According to Dawee, the Chinese were concerned about the Soviet naval presence in the Indian Ocean, and Zhou asked him to 'tell your American friends' to 'watch the Russians'.[27]

China also agreed, in principle, to sell an additional 75,000 tons of diesel oil to Thailand.[28] As Dawee put it:

> [in] showing her goodwill, China is willing to buy all agricultural surpluses like rubber and gunny bags [burlap sacks] from Thailand in order to help us not to suffer heavy trade deficit from the purchase of diesel oil.[29]

---

24 'An MFA official who accompanied Dawee to China', or in fact Tej Bunnag, told the American Embassy in Bangkok that he believed that there could have been a 'communications problem' during the private meeting between Zhou and Dawee, with no other Thai officials present. He doubted that Zhou would have given Dawee 'such a categorical assurance about future Chinese non-involvement in the Thai insurgency as Dawee thought'. 'Marshall Dawee's Views on China', 21 February 1974, RG59, 1974BANGKO03050, NARA; 'Dawee's Meeting with Zhou Enlai and Deng Xiaoping', 22 February 1974, RG59, 1974BANGKO03050, NARA.
25 'China Ends Support for Local terrorists', *Bangkok Post*, 17 February 1974, 1.
26 'China Ends Support for Local Terrorists', 1.
27 Dawee recalled that in their private meeting, Zhou accused the Soviets of being 'liars', and of attempting to 'blackmail' China. The Chinese also stressed that the Soviets were no longer even Communists, but had become 'decadent capitalists', and regarded them as being far worse than 'US imperialists'. 'Marshall Dawee's Views on China', 21 February 1974, RG59, 1974BANGKO02958, NARA.
28 'Thailand-People's Republic of China Relations', 23 June 1975, Library and Archives Division, MFA POL7/PM2518/4, MFA, Thailand, 8.
29 'China Ends Support for Local Terrorists', 1.

Shortly after his visit, Dawee himself admitted to the press that he 'spent more time discussing politics than sports'.[30] As he later told the Deputy Chief of Mission (DCM) at the American embassy in Bangkok, Edward Masters, while he was 'not likely to recommend any sudden foreign policy departures', Dawee was 'convinced Thailand should move ahead rapidly to permit trade with the PRC, particularly since Chinese goods [were] freely entering Thailand anyway'.[31]

Throughout 1974, further sports exchanges became normal. For example, between 7 and 18 April, a Thai basketball team, led by Colonel Anu Romayanon, the President of the Football Association of Thailand, attended a friendship match in Beijing. The team was accompanied by Kobsak Chutikul from the Foreign Ministry, who met with Cheng Ruisheng, then Deputy Director of Southeast Asian Division of the Chinese Foreign Ministry. Between 15 and 30 May 1974, the Chinese badminton team, led by Chu Tze, attended the International Badminton Competition in Bangkok, while the Chinese football team arrived in Bangkok on 5 November. Between 4 and 10 December 1974, the Chinese basketball team returned the visit to Bangkok and played their Thai counterparts.[32] Thailand saw the Chinese outstanding performance in sports as helping to establish an image of China as a sports power.[33]

Underpinning this thawing of relations was an increased focus on improving trade links. On 6 December 1974, Revolutionary Proclamation No. 53 was finally lifted by the National Legislative Assembly. The Assembly also passed the State Trading Bill, which set up a state trading corporation under the supervision of the Ministry of Commerce to control direct trade with communist countries, including China.[34] Following the formal abrogation of Revolutionary Proclamation No. 53, Foreign Minister Charoonphan said, 'Thailand and the People's Republic of China will develop normal trade relations'.[35] In 1974, Thailand exported nearly US$113,000 worth of goods (mainly rice) to China, and imported goods worth around US$4.5 million (mostly crude and diesel oil).[36]

---

30 'Thai Aide Reports China's Assurance on Red Insurgents', *New York Times*, 17 February 1974, 9.
31 'Marshall Dawee's Views on China', 21 February 1974, RG59, 1974BANGKO02958, NARA.
32 'Thailand–People's Republic of China Relations', 23 June 1975, Library and Archives Division, MFA POL7/PM2518/4, MFA, Thailand, 8–9.
33 'Medical Team goes to Beijing in April', *Bangkok Post*, 22 February 1974, 7.
34 'Revolutionary Decree No. 53 Repealed: Assembly Opens Way for Trade with China', *Bangkok Post*, 7 December 1974, 1.
35 *Beijing Review*, commentary on Thai Government's repeal of Decree No. 53 on trade ban, 27 December 1974, excerpted in Jain, *China and Thailand*, 196.
36 Norman Peagan, 'Thailand Joins Beijing Ensemble', *Far Eastern Economic Review*, 11 July 1975, 21.

Shortly after the lifting of the law, Deputy Commerce Minister Prasong Sukhum and Ambassador Anand led the trade delegation to Beijing to negotiate and improve trade relations. Joining the delegation was Ob Wasurat, the pro-Beijing President of the Thai Board of Trade, and Tej Bunnag,[37] Director of the East Asian Division at the Foreign Ministry.

While there, Prasong and Anand met with the Chinese Deputy Vice-Premier Li Xiannian, who emphasised the importance of reciprocity and equality in Sino–Thai trade relations. Li made clear that the PRC intended to buy a substantial amount of rubber, tobacco and timber from Thailand,[38] while Prasong noted Thailand's decision to allow government-to-government direct trade, whereby private traders could trade with China after registering with the Commerce Ministry. This process was to 'assure that the good relationship established between the two countries is not destroyed by avaricious businessmen'.[39] As Prasong explained:

> There will be no barter but parallel trade … It will be to the mutual benefit of both countries, with each filling the other's needs. We will exchange lists of our exports and also of our import requirements.[40]

The Thai state corporation, supervised by the Ministry of Commerce, would act as a channel for working relations with China, especially the Bank of China, and the China Resources Company in Hong Kong.[41] According to Prasong, Chinese leaders also made it clear that a formal recognition of the One-China policy was a precondition for the PRC's diplomatic normalisation with Thailand.[42]

---

37 According to the US Embassy in Bangkok, Tej Bunnag had been 'its key working level action officer for dealings with the People's Republic of China ever since Thailand began exploring the possibilities of eventual diplomatic relations'. In other words, Tej was another strong détente proponent. He was 'an extremely bright and articulate Thai foreign service officer, who by virtue of his skill, motivation, and family prominence will almost certainly rise to the highest positions in the Thai Foreign Ministry'. 'Thai Trade Delegation to Beijing and Pyongyang', 11 December 1974, RG59, BANGKO19331, NARA.
38 'Thailand–People's Republic of China Relations', 23 June 1975, Library and Archives Division, MFA POL7/PM2518/4, MFA, Thailand, 10; Shee Poon Kim, 'The Politics of Thailand's Trade Relations with the People's Republic of China', *Asian Survey* 21, no. 3 (March 1981): 320.
39 'Prasong on China Trade', *Bangkok Post*, 9 January 1975, 3.
40 Theh Chongkhadikij, 'China Trade: Parallel Basis, Not Barter', *Bangkok Post*, 13 January 1975, 10.
41 Theh, 'China Trade', 10.
42 'Thai Trade Delegation to DPRK and PRC', 16 January 1975, RG59, 1975BANGKO00789, NARA.

In addition, Anand had a one-on-one hour-long conversation with the Chinese Foreign Minister, Qiao Guanhua. According to Anand, the Chinese were happy about the repeal of Revolutionary Proclamation No. 53, but remained reserved about the State Trading Bill. He reassured the Chinese that Thailand would treat all socialist countries equally.[43] Anand also stressed that his delegation was not empowered to negotiate the restoration of diplomatic relations. 'Whether the visit of the mission would lead to diplomatic relations', said Anand, depended on 'the attitudes of both governments'.[44] He defined his delegation as ostensibly a 'people-to-people mission'.[45]

On 16 December, Deputy Prime Minister Prakorb Hutasingh proclaimed that the Sanya Government would not 'hurry' to open diplomatic relations with the PRC, and so it would be left to the elected government to decide after the general election, scheduled for 26 January 1975.[46]

On 6 January, Chatichai led another Thai delegation to Beijing, primarily to discuss the further purchase of oil.[47] On this visit, he negotiated with Wang Yao-ting, Chairman of the China Council for the Promotion of International Trade. An agreement was reached only on 8 January, the last day of the trip, when an additional 75,000 tons of diesel oil were promised to Thailand at the friendship price. The dinner, hosted by Foreign Minister Qiao Guanhua, was followed by a meeting between Chatichai and Premier Zhou Enlai, who by then had been diagnosed with bladder cancer and therefore resided at Beijing Hospital. As he later explained to the press in Bangkok:

> When the car stopped in front of the hospital, Premier Zhou Enlai was standing at the door to welcome me, before I had even time to take off my overcoat. He took us into a reception room, reserved especially for his guests. We exchanged views on developments in the world situation, especially in the Indian Ocean, in the Middle East, in Laos and in Cambodia. The withdrawal of American military forces by gradual degrees from Thailand was also mentioned ... Though I was informed beforehand that I would

---

43 'Thai Trade Delegation to Beijing', 7 January 1975, RG59, 1975BANGKO00231, NARA.
44 'Team to China Will Initiate Trade Contacts', *Bangkok Post*, 12 December 1974, 3.
45 'Ambassador Anand's Interview with Dana Schmidt', 21 February 1975, RG59, 1975STATE032185, NARA.
46 'China "Ties" Left to New Govt', *Bangkok Post*, 17 February 1974, 1.
47 Quoted in 'Deputy Chatichai Choonhavan on his Trip to Beijing', 13 January 1975, RG59, 1975BANGKO00596, NARA.

be able to meet Premier Zhou Enlai for about 10 minutes only, he was so kind as to hold a conversation with me that lasted as long as 45 minutes.[48]

During their 45-minute discussion, Zhou and Chatichai agreed to support the Laotian Coalition Government, and leave the Cambodian people to solve their own problems. Zhou said that, in principle, China did not approve of foreign forces being based in Thailand, but expressed his understanding that it was necessary for Thailand to balance among great powers. Zhou also invited His Royal Highness Crown Prince Vajiralongkorn to visit Beijing.[49]

In Chatichai's view, the visit was only about oil. 'Diplomatic relations', he made clear, should be considered 'a totally different matter, which must be kept separate'. Yet, he also made clear that petro-diplomacy would 'help make relations between our two countries closer and create good mutual understanding'.[50] Shortly after returning, and as a clear demonstration of how the diplomatic mood had shifted, Chatichai announced to the newly established Chart Thai Party, of which he was Secretary-General, that after the coming election, a government led by his party would quickly establish diplomatic relations with Beijing.[51] Normalisation with the PRC thus became a foreign policy priority of Chatichai's political party.

To summarise, while the Sanya Government did not prioritise a diplomatic rapprochement with the PRC, it built a necessary foundation for the subsequent normalisation following elections. In other words, it pursued what Shee Poon Kim described as a 'slow thaw' in relations with Beijing.[52] While sports diplomacy and trade continued to increase the communications between the two countries, oil became a clear focus that helped to lubricate the process. Led by the Ministry of Foreign Affairs (MFA) and in particular by key détente proponents such as Chatichai, the change was normalised by emphasising the necessity of engaging in flexible diplomacy. As Chatichai explained in June 1974:

---

48   Quoted in 'Deputy Chatichai Choonhavan on his Trip to Beijing', 13 January 1975, RG59, 1975BANGKO00596, NARA.
49   'Prince Gets Invitation to China', *Bangkok Post*, 12 January 1975, 1.
50   Quoted in 'Deputy Chatichai Choonhavan on his Trip to Beijing', 13 January 1975, RG59, 1975BANGKO00596, NARA.
51   'Prince Gets Invitation to China', 1.
52   Shee Poon Kim, 'The Politics of Thailand's Trade Relations', 319. See also 'Quarterly Analysis of Developments and Trends in Thailand', 1 May 1974, RG59, 1974BANGKO07023, NARA.

[Thai] foreign policy has always changed. It is not necessary to be inflexible. On the contrary, our foreign policy must be revised according to changes and developments in the world situation.

'Our [foreign] policy', continued Chatichai, 'changes considerably. Now, we can go to Red China and to Russia'.[53]

6.1.2. Normalisation: The Restoration of Sino–Thai Diplomatic Relations

A Prelude to Diplomatic Relations

A new constitution was promulgated on October 1974, paving the way for a general election on 26 January 1975. Following the vote, no political party gained a majority. MR Seni Pramoj, the leader of the Democratic Party, failed to gain a vote of confidence from Parliament. This was because of the political manoeuvring of his younger brother, the leader of the Social Action Party (SAP), MR Kukrit Pramoj, who had strong support from the military.[54] Shortly thereafter, Kukrit formed a coalition government and became the new prime minister on 17 March.

Détente began in earnest with Kukrit's foreign policy statement to Parliament on 19 March. He announced that the objective of Thai foreign policy was 'to safeguard the national interests'. His government would pursue an 'independent policy' by considering 'national interests in line with the economic objective as well as the security of the nation'. Like his predecessors, Kukrit would promote 'peaceful coexistence' by befriending every country that demonstrated good intentions towards Thailand, regardless of differences in political ideology or governmental system.[55] What made him different, however, was that Kukrit indicated a strong endeavour (a) 'to recognize and normalize relations with the People's Republic of China', (b) 'to withdraw foreign troops from Thailand within one year through friendly negotiations keeping into consideration the

---

53   Quoted in 'Charunphan and Chatichai on Thai-US relations', 13 June 1974, RG59, 1974BANGKO09673, NARA.
54   We now know that the Commander-in-Chief of the Army, General Kris Srivara, had initially given the army's strong support to the Kukrit government. David Morell and Chai-Anan Samudawanija, *Political Conflict in Thailand: Reform, Reaction and Revolution* (Cambridge: Oelgeschlager, Gunn & Hain, 1981), 258–60.
55   Quoted in telegram from the Ministry of Foreign Affairs (Phan) to all Thai diplomatic and consular missions, 21 March 1975, Library and Archives Division, MFA POL7/PM2518/3, MFA, Thailand, 191.

situation in this region', and (c) 'to strengthen relations with neighboring countries and foster in every way close cooperation within ASEAN [Association of Southeast Asian Nations]'. This was in order 'to arrive at a balance in its relations with the superpowers'.[56] Alongside maintaining good relations with the USSR, Thailand explicitly pledged to establish diplomatic relations with the PRC and to negotiate the withdrawal of American troops by 20 March 1976.[57]

Chatichai, a staunch détente proponent and now foreign minister, continued to play a significant role too. In March, he gave an interview to *Newsweek*, confirming the Thai Government would seek the resumption of diplomatic relations with the PRC in the near future.[58] He asked Anand Panyarachun, Thai Ambassador to the UN and to the US, to contact the Chinese head of the delegation at the UN and inform him of these intentions. Also, Chatichai, through Anand, officially invited the Chairman of the International Trade Organization, Wang Yao-ting, to visit Thailand. He wished to conduct preliminary talks with the delegation, and regarded this invitation as the beginning of normalisation.[59] He also set up a task force at the MFA, chaired by Phan Wannamethi, the Permanent Secretary, in order to consider various problems which could arise. Of particular concern was the status of overseas Chinese in Thailand should normal relations between Thailand and Beijing be initiated.[60]

These diplomatic developments were accelerated by two key international events. The first was the communist victories in Indochina, starting with Vietnam and Cambodia in April 1975. Specifically, the subsequent fall of the Laotian monarchy in December shocked the ruling elite of Thailand, who perceived the monarchy as an intrinsic part of the nation.

---

56 Quoted in telegram from the Ministry of Foreign Affairs (Phan) to all Thai diplomatic and consular missions, 21 March 1975, Library and Archives Division, MFA POL7/PM2518/3, MFA, Thailand, 192.
57 Upon taking power, Kukrit summoned a meeting of the National Security Council on 21 March, where he made the decision of setting a deadline for the withdrawal of the remaining 25,000 US soldiers and 350 planes before 20 March 1976. He also called for an end to the US military supply airlift to Cambodia via air bases in Thailand. See R. Sean Randolph, *The United States and Thailand: Alliance Dynamics, 1950–1985* (Berkeley: Institute of East Asian Studies, University of California, 1986), Chapter 6.
58 Anand Panyarachun, 'Pookmitr kub sataranaratprachachon jeen' [Befriending the People's Republic of China], in *Nayobai tangprated Thai bon tangpreng* [Thai Foreign Policy at the Crossroads], ed. Chantima Ongsuragz (Bangkok: Direk Jayanama Memorial Lecture Series, Thammasat University, 1990), 140.
59 'Chatichai Invites China's Trade Chief', *Bangkok Post*, 6 April 1975, 3.
60 'Chatichai Told US Will Stand By Commitments', *Bangkok Post*, 29 April 1975, 3.

The idea that Thailand might be the 'next domino' and 'frontline state' became prevalent, with conservatives seeing the events as a direct 'threat' to Thailand's security and survival. This drastically changing situation furthered the desire to embrace Beijing in the hope that the PRC might prove vital in containing Hanoi and safeguarding Thai sovereignty.[61]

The second event was the *Mayaguez* incident in May. Without consulting the Thai Government, the US used the U-Tapao Airport for an operation to retrieve the US-flagged container ship, *Mayaguez*, which had been captured by Cambodia.[62] The Kukrit Government protested the US encroachment on Thailand's territorial sovereignty by presenting a protest memorandum. They also summoned the Thai Ambassador to the US, Anand, back to Bangkok for an indefinite period.[63] While delivering the protest note to Secretary of State Henry Kissinger, Anand told him that Thailand had no objection to the results of the operation to free the *Mayaguez* but did object to the procedures. He said that Kukrit was very 'upset' with the *Mayaguez* incident.[64] The incident not only indicated the challenge for Thai–US relations but also provided an opportunity for the government to speed up the policy of détente.[65]

In his session with a US National War College delegation on 1 May, Kukrit said that the Chinese were 'not really hostile to Thailand'. He speculated: 'China would not invade Thailand, but would prefer to revert to its historical role of "big brother"' – having a 'sort of influence in Thailand that the US exercised ten to fifteen years ago'. Moreover, he believed that

---

61 Sukhumbhand Paribatra, 'Dictates of Security: Thailand's Relations with the PRC since the Vietnam War', in *ASEAN and China: An Evolving Relationship*, ed. Joyce K Kallgren et al. (Berkeley: University of California, 1988), 293.

62 We now know that the Gerald Ford administration, bypassing the elected civilian government, got permission from the Thai military to launch the attack from the U Tapao air base. Daniel Fineman, *A Special Relationship: The United States and Military Government in Thailand, 1947–1958* (Honolulu: University of Hawai'i Press, 1997), 1.

63 'RTG Protest Memorandum Over the Mayaguez Affairs', 17 May 1975, RG59, 1975BANGKO08995, NARA.

64 'Delivery of Thai Protest Note Over Mayaguez Incident', 18 May 1975, RG59, 1975STATE115940, NARA.

65 In fact, the *Mayaguez* incident was not the decline of Thai–US military relations. According to Cheng Guan Ang, US congressional investigator Brady was informed by General Kriangsak that he approved of the US *Mayaguez* operation wholeheartedly. Cheng Guan Ang, 'Southeast Asian Perceptions of the Domino Theory', in *Connecting Histories: Decolonization and the Cold War in Southeast Asia, 1945–1962*, ed. Christopher E Goscha and Christopher F Ostenmann (Washington DC and Stanford: Woodrow Wilson Center Press with Stanford University Press, 2009), 112.

the Chinese preferred the US presence in Thailand in order to balance the increased Soviet influence in the region as well as its military presence in the Indian Ocean.[66]

Foreign Minister Chatichai asked Thai ambassadors around the world to contact their Chinese counterparts to explore possible ways to establish diplomatic relations. For example, on 5 May, Ambassador Anand had a conversation with the Chinese Ambassador to the UN, Huang Hua, in New York. The latter told Anand that the Chinese Government congratulated Prime Minister Kukrit on his statement to Parliament regarding his determination to establish diplomatic ties with Beijing. The Chinese leaders readily agreed to negotiate with the Thai Government.[67] The PRC had only one condition: that is, Thailand had to recognise one China and terminate its relations with Taiwan. According to Huang, the Chinese could not send the MFA officials to Bangkok to negotiate with their Thai counterparts, as requested from the Thai foreign minister, while the Taiwanese embassy remained in Thailand.[68]

By early May, the Chinese Government formally advised the Thai Foreign Ministry of its readiness to establish relations with Thailand.[69] By then, Chatichai repeatedly told the Thai public that the PRC had informed him that it was agreeable to opening diplomatic ties with Thailand. In his 19 May press conference, Chatichai said that Thailand would recognise the PRC before the UN General Assembly meeting in September. In the meantime, the Foreign Ministry drafted a bill to abrogate the law that set up a state trading organisation to trade with the communist countries. Since Anand's visit to Beijing in December 1974, the Chinese had repeatedly informed Thailand that it considered the law to be discriminatory.[70]

---

66 'Prime Minister Kukrit on RTG/PRC Relations', 1 May 1975, RG59, 1975BANGKO07843, NARA.
67 A conversation between Thai Ambassador to the UN and the Chinese Ambassador to the UN in New York, 26 May 1975, Ministry of Foreign Affairs Documents, (2) MFA 1.1/112, the National Archive of Thailand (TNA), Bangkok, 86.
68 Anand told Huang Hua he thought that since the Chinese trade delegation was about to be in Bangkok, the Thais should grasp the opportunity to discuss the preliminary talks with the Ministry of Foreign Affairs officials who accompanied the delegation. However, as the Chinese Ambassador informed Anand, the trade delegation led by Wang Yao-ting would not be in Bangkok until by the end of the year. Anand said those preliminary talks would thus be unnecessary and too late. His Chinese counterpart agreed with this observation. A conversation between Thai Ambassador to the UN and the Chinese Ambassador to the UN in New York, 26 May 1975, Ministry of Foreign Affairs Documents, (2) MFA 1.1/112, TNA, Bangkok, 86.
69 A conversation between Thai Ambassador and the Chinese Ambassador in Tokyo, 26 May 1975, Ministry of Foreign Affairs Documents, (2) MFA 1.1/112, TNA, Bangkok, 87.
70 'FM Pledges China Ties by September', *Bangkok Post*, 19 May 1975, 1.

Subsequently, Chatichai asked recently returned Ambassador Anand to handle the process in detail.[71] During his talks with Chinese counterparts, Anand recalled that 'the Chinese do not mention the term "*kanperd kwamsampan*" or "establishment of diplomatic relations" but use "*kanfeunfu kwamsampan*" or "restoration of diplomatic relations"' because 'they consider formal diplomatic relations with Thailand had never disappeared'.[72] Thus, the Thai term, '*kanfeunfu kwamsampan*', was promulgated in official language, though in general 'restoration' and 'establishment' were used interchangeably.

In his 21 May discussion with the US Ambassador to Thailand, Charles S Whitehouse (1975–1978), Chatichai was asked about Thailand's recognition of Communist China. He told Whitehouse that the PRC was 'agreeable to a visit by him at any time, but Thailand was not yet ready' because of the problem of resolving the status of the more than 310,000 Chinese with Taiwanese passports. 'These people must decide whether they want to become citizens of Thailand or Mainland China', Chatichai said. He stated further that the Thai Government was speeding up the process of the Chinese minority and would definitely recognise the PRC in the near future. Pracha Gunakasem, Director-General of the Information Department at the MFA, who accompanied Chatichai, said that one reason for Thailand's recognition of the PRC was to counter 'Sathorn Road [the site of the Soviet embassy in Bangkok]'.[73] For Chatichai, the search for Beijing ties was to counterbalance the North Vietnamese threat, and, possibly, the increased Soviet presence in the region.[74]

By the end of the month, Chatichai made public the fact that he officially received notice from the Chinese delegation to the UN that the PRC was willing to establish diplomatic relations with Thailand immediately. He planned to pay an official visit to Beijing probably in late June, and optimistically told reporters that if all went as planned, the establishment

---

71 Anand, 'Pookmitr kub sataranaratprachachon jeen', 140.
72 Anand Panyarachun, 'Patakata pised' [Special Lecture], in *Kwam sampan thai-jin* [Sino-Thai Relations: Past and Future Prospect], ed. Khien Theeravit and Cheah Yan-Chong (Bangkok: Chulalongkorn University, 2000), 16.
73 'Ambassador's Call on Foreign Minister Chatichai', 23 May 1975, RG59, 1975BANGKO09394, NARA.
74 'The Uncertain State of Thai/PRC Relations', 7 June 1975, RG59, 1975BANGKO10586, NARA.

of diplomatic ties would be announced during his visit.[75] The Thai chargé d'affaires in Taiwan, Khanit Sricharoen, was recalled back to Bangkok and on 26 May, Chatichai told Ma Chi-chuang, Taiwan's Ambassador to Bangkok, that he should prepare his embassy for departure in view of the imminent PRC arrival.[76]

In late May and early June, there was a flurry of further visits to Beijing, including a Democratic Party goodwill mission led by Pichai Rattakul, MP (Bangkok), followed by a parliamentary delegation led by Speaker of the House of Representatives, Prasit Kanchanawat, who had previously visited China twice. At the farewell banquet, Prasit said the visit 'had enhanced the friendship and mutual understanding' between the two peoples, and that 'Thailand was willing to live in friendship with China and all other countries in the world on the basis of the Five Principles of Peaceful Coexistence'. The Chinese Foreign Minister Qiao Guanhua expressed his wish that the two peoples would 'remain friends for generations to come'.[77]

To mid-June, the question of who would go to Beijing remained unclear. At first, it seemed that Chatichai would head the delegation, scheduled to begin on 27 June.[78] Initially, Prime Minister Kukrit was reluctant, wanting not to upstage Foreign Minister Chatichai, who had worked so hard for the opening of relations. However, Chatichai felt that he had done his bit and that the prime minister should now take the lead, similar to leaders of Japan, Malaysia and the Philippines.[79] According to reports, Kukrit made the decision to go having been persuaded by both pro-government and opposition MPs. He also consulted with Air Chief Marshal Dawee Chullasapya, the former Defense Minister who had visited China and met with Premier Zhou. Dawee strongly urged Kukrit to go.[80] At a press conference on 16 June, Kukrit hinted that the prime minister should go to China himself, but that the visit was still the preparatory stage, during which necessary steps were required at the level of officials.[81]

---

75 'Beijing Ties Likely on Chatichai Visit', *Bangkok Post*, 31 May 1975, 1. Anand Panyarachun called Chatichai's policy 'cha-cha-cha' diplomacy, and considered him as an idealist, rather than a realist. He observed that 'I think Mr. Chatichai had a romantic idea about China. He was not farsighted in seeing that regional geopolitics had changed'. See Anand, 'Patakata pised', 14.
76 'The Uncertain State of Thai/PRC Relations', 7 June 1975, RG59, 1975BANGKO10586, NARA.
77 'Delegation of Thai National Assembly Members Visits China', *Beijing Review* 18, no. 26 (June 1975), 3.
78 'Anand Off to Speed China Ties', *Bangkok Post*, 14 June 1975, 1.
79 Quoted in 'Kukrit on Thai/PRC Relations', 20 June 1975, RG59, 1975BANGKO11928, NARA.
80 'Kukrit on the Road to Beijing', *Bangkok Post*, 30 June 1975, 1.
81 Quoted in 'Kukrit on Thai/PRC Relations', 20 June 1975, RG59, 1975BANGKO11928, NARA.

In the meantime, Chatichai assigned Ambassador Anand Panyarachun to lead a five-man working group to travel to Beijing and negotiate the details of resumed diplomatic ties, and to prepare the arrangements for the visit. Before his departure to Beijing on 16 June, Anand told reporters:

> We are taking our own draft with us and we will study the Chinese draft in order to formulate a joint communiqué ... Then, should a satisfactory agreement be reached, the Minister of Foreign Affairs [Chatichai] will go to sign the treaty.[82]

Anand arrived in Beijing on 17 June. Key issues to be resolved included China's reservations over the Thai State Trading Corporation, the status of the 310,000 Chinese with Taiwanese passports in Thailand, the anticommunist law and the matter of how to handle large Taiwanese-controlled investments in Thailand. The stickiest issue was the dual nationality of the overseas Chinese in Thailand.

Anand had meetings with the Chinese Foreign Ministry officials led by Ko Hua, Director-General of Asian Affairs, and Cheng Rui-sheng, Deputy Director-General. The first informal meeting was held on 18 June at the Chinese Foreign Ministry. Thailand presented its draft joint communiqué to the Chinese, which had already been telegrammed prior to the visit.[83] The second meeting was on 20 June. This was the negotiation in detail. At China's insistence, the joint communiqué had an 'anti-hegemonic' clause, clearly directed toward the Soviet Union. The final draft was agreed upon by both sides.[84]

After that, Anand sent a cable to Bangkok asking whether and when the Thai delegation would go to China. In the cable, Anand reported that initial negotiations had been 'successful'. He also asked for details of the planned visit, including the duration of stay, and the number of

---

82   Quoted in 'Thai/PRC Relations', 19 June 1975, RG59, 1975BANGKO11750, NARA; 'A Plea to Beijing Before Ties', *Bangkok Post*, 16 June 1975, 3.
83   The joint communiqué followed the language of the Malaysian and Philippine joint communiqué in its recognition of the One-China policy, which required the termination of diplomatic relations with Taiwan. However, the Thai–Chinese communiqué contained a more detailed treatment and clarification of the status of overseas Chinese, which was also part of the Sino–Malaysian communiqué that was signed on 31 May 1974. It omitted the explicit pledge (included in the Sino–Philippine communiqué of 9 June 1975) for the two governments to cooperate to achieve certain expressed objectives. Following the Manila model, the document noted that China and Thailand would exchange ambassadors 'as soon as practicable'. It also included a long section on brotherhood and friendly relations between the two countries. 'Weekly Review of the People's Republic of China No. 27', 2 July 1975, RG59, 1975HONGK07399, NARA.
84   Anand, 'Pookmitr kub sataranaratprachachon jeen', 141.

people in the delegation, so that programs could be drawn up with the Chinese leaders. Chatichai replied that Prime Minister Kukrit would go to Beijing, and sign the official agreement, which could be made on 1 July as originally planned.[85]

On the last day, 21 June, Anand met with Foreign Minister Qiao Guanhua. The latter informed Anand that Premier Zhou formally extended an invitation to Thai Prime Minister Kukrit to visit Beijing between 30 June and 5 July 1975.[86] The joint communiqué was scheduled to be signed on 1 July. The exchange of ambassadors would be arranged later. Sunthorn Sathirathai, Deputy Director-General of the Protocol Department, who accompanied Anand from 17 June, remained in Beijing to continue planning.

Anand returned to Bangkok on the evening of 22 June, and reported on his trip to Chatichai. The following day, Chatichai and Anand presented the draft joint communiqué to the National Security Council (NSC) meeting, the first time that the MFA officially informed the Council regarding the issue. On 24 June, after receiving approval from the NSC, Kukrit presided over a Cabinet meeting, which approved the wording of the draft and the establishment of diplomatic relations.[87]

The full delegation consisted of Prime Minister Kukrit, Foreign Minister Chatichai and 38 high-ranking government officials and business representatives. These included Prakaipet Indhusophon, Secretary-General to the Prime Minister, Air Marshal Siddhi Savetsila, Secretary-General of the NSC, and six under-secretaries from the departments of Commerce, Defence, Finance, Agriculture, Interior and Industry. Foreign Ministry officials included, among others, Ambassador Anand Panyarachum, Nissai Vejjajiva (Ambassador attached to the Foreign Ministry), Kosol Sindhvananda (Director-General of the Department of Political Affairs), Manaspas Xuto (Consul-General in Hong Kong) and Tej Bunnag (Director of the Asian Division). The team also included

---

85 'Kukrit Will Lead Team to Beijing', *Bangkok Post,* 21 June 1975, 1; 'PM Ready to go to China Soon', 21 June 1975, *Daily News,* in Library and Archives Division, MFA POL7/PM2518/1, MFA, Thailand, 140.
86 'Zhou Enlai Sends Letter to Kukrit', *Bangkok Post,* 23 June 1975, 1; 'Delegation of Thai National Assembly Members Visits China', 3.
87 'Cabinet Approves China Ties Draft', *Bangkok Post,* 25 June 1975, 1.

a non-official 'China expert', Sarasin Viraphol from Faculty of Political Science at Chulalongkorn University.[88] Lenglert Baiyok also joined the team in Hong Kong.[89]

On 25 June, Chatichai summoned Admiral Ma Chi-chuang, Taiwan's Ambassador to Bangkok, to the Foreign Ministry where he informed him that after the signing of the joint communiqué with Beijing, formal diplomatic relations between Thailand and Taiwan would come to an end. The Taiwanese ambassador said he would leave Bangkok before 30 June.[90] In turn, the Thai chargé d'affaires in Taiwan, Khanit Sricharoen, would fly back to Bangkok before 1 July 1975.[91]

Prime Minister Kukrit met with US ambassador Charles Whitehouse on 27 June. In their discussion, Kukrit noted the increasing importance of China in regards to the security situation in Southeast Asia. He believed that the Sino–Soviet rivalry, which was one of the main reasons Beijing wanted to 'make friends' with Thailand, provided opportunities for manoeuvring by the countries in Southeast Asia including Thailand. The role of China would be significant in maintaining the balance with Hanoi, and perhaps the USSR.[92] Kukrit told Whitehouse that while he would sign the joint communiqué with Beijing in his upcoming visit, he had no intention of opening a Thai embassy in the near future. According to Kukrit, the Chinese may buy rice from Thailand for shipment to Cambodia where China was supporting the Khmer Rouge regime, which had come to power in 1975. He realised that 'China is a fact of life and Thailand must deal with it'. 'We don't', however, 'have to go to bed with them', he claimed. Kukrit presented the developments as part of a nuanced and pragmatic foreign policy. He did not believe that China would stop supporting the Thai communist insurgency merely because Thailand and China had diplomatic relations. For the US embassy,

---

88 'Memorandum from Foreign Minister to the Prime Minister on the Establishment of Diplomatic Relations with the PRC', 23 June 1975, in *120 Years Ministry of Foreign Affairs* (Bangkok: Ministry of Foreign Affairs, 1995), 244–48.
89 'Odd Guest at Beijing Banquet', *The Nation*, 1 July 1975, 1.
90 'Thai Note to Republic of China', 27 June 1975, RG59, 1975BANGKO12578, NARA.
91 'Establishing Thai–Chinese Relations in the First Week of July', *Prachathipatai*, 21 June 1975, in Library and Archives Division, MFA POL7/PM2518/1, MFA, Thailand, 142.
92 'Prime Minister Kukrit's Comments on his China Trip', 27 June 1975, RG59, 1975BANGKO12593, NARA.

Kukrit had 'a realistic assessment of Beijing': 'He is not about to rush into things but can be expected to approach Thailand's new relationship in a measured way'.[93]

On the evening of 28 June, the night before his departure, Kukrit explained in a televised speech to the nation the nature of the trip. 'In establishing ties with China', he said, 'we will not be at any disadvantages or suffer any adverse consequences'. He continued:

> It is only normal … that with the recognition of Beijing, Thailand's official ties with Taiwan will have to be broken. But this does not mean that all relations will stop because we still have trade relations with Taiwan.[94]

Kukrit asked the overseas Chinese in Thailand 'to choose whether to take up Thai or Chinese nationality'. He emphasised that under 'the changing world political situation', Thailand vitally needed 'more friends'.[95]

In short, by the end of June, Thai détente proponents such as Kukrit and Chatichai were ready to go to Beijing and establish diplomatic relations with the PRC. Although he realised that the establishment of diplomatic relations did not mean that the Chinese would stop supporting the Thai communist insurgency, Kukrit wished to promote 'friendly relations and good understanding' and strengthen trade relations with the PRC.[96] The next episode began with Kukrit's historic visit to Beijing.

Kukrit's Visit to Beijing and the Establishment of Diplomatic Relations

On Monday 30 June around 11:00, Kukrit and his entourage arrived by Thai Airways International flight TG5501 at Beijing airport, where the Chinese Government rolled out the red carpet to welcome him and his entourage. Deng Xiaoping, first vice-premier, Qiao Guanhua, foreign minister, and other high-ranking officials, welcomed and shook hands with the Thai delegates amid a crowd of several thousand ordinary people. A grand welcome ceremony took place at the airport, which flew the

---

93   'Prime Minister Kukrit's Comments on his China Trip', 27 June 1975, RG59, 1975BANGKO12593, NARA.
94   'Kukrit's Message: Stay Cool', *Bangkok Post*, 28 June 1975, 1.
95   'Kukrit's Message: Stay Cool', 1; 'Kukrit Asks Public for Good Wishes', *Bangkok World*, 28 June 1975, 1.
96   'Prime Minister Kukrit's Comments on his China Trip', 27 June 1975, RG59, 1975BANGKO12593, NARA.

national flags of China and Thailand. Big white posters were displayed from tall buildings saying 'A warm welcome to the Distinguished Guests from Thailand', 'Long live the friendship between the people of China and Thailand', and 'Long live the great unity of the people of the world'.[97]

On behalf of Premier Zhou, Deng extended a welcome to Kukrit, saying:

> The People of China and Thailand, which are close neighbours, enjoy a traditional friendship and have been widening the scope of friendly contact in recent years. Prime Minister Kukrit's official visit will see the normalization of the relations between the two countries and promote the traditional friendship between the two peoples.[98]

Accompanied by Deng, Kukrit reviewed a guard of honour from the Chinese People's Liberation Army, and the national anthems of Thailand and China were played.[99] As Kukrit recalled later:

> the reception was very grand indeed. I think they put on one of their grandest shows for us. It was so big that when I saw it from the airplane, it was quite frightening. [Deng Xiaoping] was there to meet me. Mr. Zhou Enlai at that time was in hospital. Of course, the Chairman [Mao Zedong] wasn't in a position to come to meet anybody.[100]

Upon his arrival in Beijing, the *Renmin ribao (People's Daily)* published an editorial entitled 'A Warm Welcome to the Distinguished Thai Guests'. It extolled Thailand's changing foreign policy as one that had 'won widespread appreciation', and reassured Thailand that China would not interfere in its internal affairs in the future.[101]

---

97 Telegram from the Thai Consulate-General, Hong Kong to the Ministry of Foreign Affairs, 30 June 1975, Library and Archives Division, MFA POL7/PM2518/3, MFA, Thailand, 174–75; 'What a Welcome!' *Bangkok World,* 30 June 1975, 1.
98 Telegram from the Thai Consulate-General, Hong Kong to the Ministry of Foreign Affairs, 30 June 1975, Library and Archives Division, MFA POL7/PM2518/3, MFA, Thailand, 175.
99 Telegram from the Thai Consulate-General, Hong Kong to the Ministry of Foreign Affairs, 30 June 1975, Library and Archives Division, MFA POL7/PM2518/3, MFA, Thailand, 190.
100 Kukrit Pramoj, interview by *Vilas Manivat,* 17 February 1980, in *M.R. Kukrit Pramoj: His Wit and Wisdom – Writings, Speeches and Interviews,* ed. Steve Van Beek (Bangkok: Duang Kamol, 1983), 151–52.
101 'A Warm Welcome to the Distinguished Thai Guests', *People's Daily,* 30 June 1975, in *News Bulletin,* The Embassy of the People's Republic of China, 2 July 1975, no. 1/7, 3–4.

After the welcoming ceremony, Deng led Kukrit and the Thai delegation to the *Daioyutai* State Guest House, where special foreign guests were received. Kukrit said that 'I think it was the same house that all the other heads of state including Mr. Nixon were taken to stay'.[102] The 30-member Thai press corps stayed at the Nationalities (*Minzu*) Hotel next to the Government Guest House. When Kukrit's motorcade passed the Nationalities Hotel, a Thai journalist from *The Nation* was asked: 'Is that your prime minister? He should have come here a long time ago'.[103]

In the afternoon, Kukrit, Chatichai and other delegates[104] held the first official talks with Deng Xiaoping and Foreign Minister Qiao Guanhua at the Great Hall of the People. The meeting started around 15:30 and lasted for an hour. They discussed a wide range of issues and challenges, including the Thai insurgency, US forces in Thailand, the situation in Indochina, trade and a return visit to Thailand. They focused more specifically on the joint communiqué to be signed the following day.[105]

After that, Kukrit and Chatichai went to meet Premier Zhou Enlai at Beijing Hospital. They had friendly talks for half an hour and discussed a wide range of issues. Later, Chatichai reported that Premier Zhou was very pleased that China would now have diplomatic relations with Thailand. Chatichai also said he was reassured that China would no longer interfere in Thailand's internal affairs by supporting the CPT. Zhou told Kukrit and Chatichai that his government would urge the overseas Chinese in Thailand to adopt Thai nationality. Zhou also congratulated Thailand on its decision to seek withdrawal of foreign troops within the definite deadline. In his opinion, there was no need for Thailand to have foreign troops for its defence.[106] Throughout the discussions, Chatichai felt that the Chinese leaders were concerned about the Soviet Union's increased influence in Southeast Asia. Lastly, Zhou sent warm regards to Prince Wan Waithayakon, a former Thai foreign minister.[107] According to one

---

102 Kukrit, interview by *Vilas Manivat*, 152.
103 'Thai Anthem Played Before Vast Parade', *The Nation*, 1 July 1975, 1.
104 They included Anand Panyarachun (Ambassador to the UN), Air Marshal Sitthi Sawetsila (Secretary-General of the National Security Council), Tej Bunnag (Director of the Asian Division), Nissai Vejjajiva (Ambassador attached to the Foreign Ministry) and Prakaipet Indhusophon (Secretary-General to the Prime Minister).
105 Banyat Tasaneeyavej, 'Kukrit, Zhou Make History Today', *Bangkok Post*, 1 July 1975, 1.
106 'Beijing Wants Chinese Here to Turn Thai', *The Nation*, 2 July 1975, 1.
107 'Chinese PM Advised Thai PM that Foreign Troop Unnecessary', *Prachathipatai*, 2 July 1975, 1 found in Library and Archives Division, MFA POL7/PM2518/1, MFA, Thailand, 77.

high-ranking official, the talks with Zhou, who looked 'healthy but slightly pale', were 'very encouraging': 'We got many points clarified. The meeting was ... very important to Thailand'.[108]

On 30 June, in the evening, Deng hosted a welcome banquet for Kukrit and the Thai delegation. After expressing a warm welcome, Deng began his speech by praising Thailand's long history and struggle to safeguard its national independence during the imperial era. Thailand's 'friendly relations with other Third World countries' and determination to stand for 'a peaceful and neutral Southeast Asia' and oppose 'power politics and hegemonism' was also noted. Then he blamed postwar tensions in Southeast Asia and the 'extremely abnormal' relationship with 'one of the superpowers' that 'persisted in a war of aggression in Indochina'. However, at present 'very favorable conditions' had been created because 'this superpower has finally suffered irrevocable defeat under the counter-blows of the Indochinese peoples and has to withdraw from Indochina'.[109]

While not mentioning the USSR directly, Deng also pointedly said that 'the other superpower with wild ambitions' sought 'new military bases in Southeast Asian countries' and sent 'its naval vessels to ply the Indian and West Pacific Oceans'. The 'specter of its expansionism', warned Deng, 'now haunts Southeast Asia'. It not only posed a 'menacing threat to the peace and security of the Southeast Asian countries' but also sought to convert 'this region into its sphere of influence some day'. Deng continued:

> Countries with different social systems ... can develop state relations on the basis of the five principles of mutual respect for sovereignty and territorial integrity, mutual non-aggression, noninterference in each other's internal affairs, equality and mutual benefit, and peaceful coexistence ... Foreign aggression and interference are impermissible and are doomed to failure.[110]

Deng condemned the 'unfortunate' interruption of contacts between Thailand and the PRC due to 'imperialist obstruction and sabotage'. However, he stressed that this should be seen as a 'brief interlude' in a 'long history of friendship between our two peoples', which were more than two thousand years old. Their friendship was a kind of traditional kinship.

---

108 'Kukrit Meets Zhou – Talks "Very Encouraging" ', *The Nation*, 1 July 1975, 1.
109 Telegram from the Thai Consulate-General, Hong Kong to the Ministry of Foreign Affairs, 1 July 1975, Library and Archives Division, MFA POL7/PM2518/3, MFA, Thailand, 131.
110 Telegram from the Thai Consulate-General, Hong Kong to the Ministry of Foreign Affairs, 1 July 1975, Library and Archives Division, MFA POL7/PM2518/3, MFA, Thailand 132.

He also highlighted the process of détente that led to the normalisation of relations: 'in recent years the traditional friendship of our two peoples has resumed and developed at a rapid pace. Cultural, athletic, scientific and commercial exchanges … have increased rapidly'. Kukrit's visit, he made clear, had turned 'a new page' in the history of Sino–Thai relations.[111]

Kukrit thanked the Chinese leaders and people for their hospitality, stating that it was a great pleasure to have 'the opportunity to take part in the revival and further strengthening of the traditionally close and friendly ties'. He also noted how this visit to Beijing was 'the result of efforts that had progressed step by step over the recent years'. All exchanges of sports teams, doctors, scientists, trade delegations and the visit by members of the National Assembly 'played an important role in drawing our two peoples close together'. In this process, 'both sides have cooperated with sincerity in the creation of mutual understanding'.[112]

He went on to state that his democratic government, which was 'elected by the Thai people and represents all the people of Thailand', would now pursue an 'independent course' in the conduct of its foreign policy, and that the normalisation of relations with the PRC was a 'high priority'. He reaffirmed that the people have the right to choose their own political, economic, and social system 'free from outside interference' and that the Southeast Asian nations would have to oppose 'all manner of subversion from outside'.[113] Referring to ASEAN, Kukrit defined the Kuala Lumpur Declaration on a zone of peace, freedom and neutrality (ZOPFAN) as an effort to free the region from great power rivalry, and welcomed PRC statements of support for ASEAN and its concept of ZOPFAN.[114] The banquet had a friendly atmosphere, and lasted until 21:30.

On Tuesday 1 July, from 8:30, Kukrit and his entourage were taken on a tour of Beijing, visiting the Central Institute for Nationalities, and then the Summer Palace. Wu Teh, Vice-Chairman of the Standing Committee of the National People's Congress, accompanied the Thai delegation. At the Central Institute for Nationalities, which was set up in 1951 by

---

111 Telegram from the Thai Consulate-General, Hong Kong to the Ministry of Foreign Affairs, 1 July 1975, Library and Archives Division, MFA POL7/PM2518/3, MFA, Thailand, 133.
112 Telegram from the Thai Consulate-General, Hong Kong to the Ministry of Foreign Affairs, 1 July 1975, Library and Archives Division, MFA POL7/PM2518/3, MFA, Thailand, 123.
113 Telegram from the Thai Consulate-General, Hong Kong to the Ministry of Foreign Affairs, 1 July 1975, Library and Archives Division, MFA POL7/PM2518/3, MFA, Thailand, 123–24.
114 Telegram from the Thai Consulate-General, Hong Kong to the Ministry of Foreign Affairs, 1 July 1975, Library and Archives Division, MFA POL7/PM2518/3, MFA, Thailand, 123.

Mao to train cadres of minority nationalities, they met with teachers and students from a variety of nationality groups. The students gathered on the campus and waved bouquets, streamers and the national flags of China and Thailand amid the beating of drums and gongs.[115] Kukrit enquired about the study and life of the students, and had a cordial conversation with students of Tai nationality from the southern province of Yunnan, who entertained the guests with Tai dances. A Tai student and a student of Chingpo nationality played a violin duet, 'I Love the Frontier'. Both the hosts and the visitors expressed their wish that the traditional friendship between the two peoples continue to grow.[116]

While at the Central Institute for Nationalities, Kukrit later recalled he was 'sitting in the hall looking at the entertainment and somebody came up to my chair and whispered in my ear: "The Chairman [Mao] will see you now"'. The Thai prime minister realised he was 'utterly unprepared'. Wearing a blue Thai-style *moh-hom* shirt, Kukrit went back to the Guest House to change and pick up the gift, a mirror box, 'a big one presumably to put cigars in though I don't think the Chairman smoked'.[117]

Just before noon, Kukrit, together with Chatichai, went into Chairman Mao's famous study in the Zhongnanhai compound: a room 'in a rather large round building with a dome', as Kukrit remembered.[118] When Kukrit arrived, the 81-year-old Chairman was already sitting prepared. Mao shook hands with Kukrit, and members of his party including Chatichai, Ambassador Anand and Prakaipet Indhusophon, Secretary-General to the Prime Minister. Kukrit later recalled that Mao got up all by himself and shook Kukrit's hand, while making 'a lot of noises'. Kukrit said he did not know what to do because he did not understand. Then, Chatichai 'went to him and he did the same thing, but he shook … Chatichai's hand with less noise'.[119] According to Chatichai, Mao greeted him, asking how many times he had visited China.[120] Then, Mao had a friendly conversation

---

115 Telegram from the Thai Consulate-General, Hong Kong to the Ministry of Foreign Affairs, 2 July 1975, Library and Archives Division, MFA POL7/PM2518/3, MFA, Thailand, 104.
116 Telegram from the Thai Consulate-General, Hong Kong to the Ministry of Foreign Affairs, 2 July 1975, Library and Archives Division, MFA POL7/PM2518/3, MFA, Thailand, 104.
117 Kukrit, interview by *Vilas Manivat*, 152.
118 Kukrit, interview by *Vilas Manivat*, 152.
119 Kukrit, interview by *Vilas Manivat*, 152.
120 *Prachathipatai*, 3 July 1975 found in Library and Archives Division, MFA POL7/PM2518/1, MFA, Thailand, 40.

with Kukrit and Chatichai, while Anand and Prakaipet waited outside. The meeting with Mao was scheduled to last for 10 minutes, but went on for an hour.[121]

They sat down and the interpreters came in. The main Chinese interpreter was Nancy Tang, but there were other interpreters because sometimes Nancy Tang could not catch everything Mao said. Mao suffered from undiagnosed Lou Gehrig's disease, which left his mental faculties intact but caused a gradual deterioration of the nerve cells controlling his muscles, leaving him with a speech impediment. As Kukrit put it:

> You had to watch the movement of his mouth to know what he was trying to say. There were very few people who could understand him. Sometimes they had to call in his nurse and sometimes even she didn't understand it all. When she didn't understand, they had to call in the old amah, the old lady who had served him personally. She would be the final authority.[122]

In an hour-long conversation, Mao sometimes got up and walked around while talking. Kukrit admired him greatly, commenting that 'there was no sign of physical weakness except for this speech impediment'.[123] First, Mao told Kukrit that he liked the interview the Thai premier had given in Hong Kong the night before the visit. The comment referred to Kukrit's response to a journalist who had asked why the visit was happening despite Chinese support for the communist insurgents in Thailand. Kukrit had claimed he didn't see the connection. 'I represent the Thai government and I was merely going to China to make friends with the government of a sovereign state.' Kukrit regarded communist support to Thai insurgents as party affairs, rather than a government affair, and therefore, he said he had nothing against the Chinese Government.[124] Mao's observation impressed Kukrit who 'knew what was happening all around'.[125]

Satisfied with Kukrit's answers, Mao wondered whether the Thai prime minister still wished to talk to him who was branded by the West as an aggressor. 'Aren't you afraid of me', asked Mao, 'since Chiang Kai-shek and the West have called me a bandit, a murderer?' Kukrit affirmatively

---

121 Telegram from the Thai Consulate-General, Hong Kong to the Ministry of Foreign Affairs, 1 July 1975, Library and Archives Division, MFA POL7/PM2518/3, MFA, Thailand, 127.
122 Kukrit, interview by *Vilas Manivat*, 152.
123 Kukrit, interview by *Vilas Manivat*, 153.
124 Kukrit, interview by *Vilas Manivat*, 153.
125 Kukrit, interview by *Vilas Manivat*, 153.

replied, 'No, not at all'.[126] The conversations went on, ranging from the world situation, to the Indochina crisis to the situation in Thailand. Mao also advised Kukrit what to do with the insurgency in Thailand:

> First of all, don't you go and condemn them. Don't say rude words about them, because they like it. They won't listen to you, they are thick-skinned, these people. Secondly, don't kill them, because these people want to become heroes, make martyrs of themselves. As soon as you kill one, another five will come. So there's no purpose in killing them. Third, don't send any soldiers against them because they'll run away. Soldiers can't stay in the jungle forever. They've got to go back to barracks. And when they do, the Communists come back again. There's no use. You waste time and money.[127]

Mao mocked, 'That's what I've been doing to Chiang Kai-shek, and look where he is now!'[128] Kukrit asked Mao, 'What to do?' He said:

> Do what you're already doing. Make people in the countryside happy. See that they are well fed, that they have work to do, they are satisfied with their work and their station. They won't join the Communists. Then the Communists cannot do anything.

He demurred disappointedly, 'I've been Chairman here for, well, so many years, and in all that time not one Thai Communist has come to see me'. Kukrit teased him back, 'Why didn't you say so at the beginning, Chairman! I'll send five of them over right away!'[129]

Following this, Mao complained that he was getting old and that he was not long for this world. Kukrit reassured him that, 'No, you can't be serious. You can't die at all, Chairman. The world cannot afford to lose its number one bad man as you know you are yourself'. Kukrit recalled how these words tickled him: 'He roared with mirth, he banged on his armchair and got up and shook hands all around. He liked that very much'.[130]

---

126 Kukrit, interview by *Vilas Manivat*, 153.
127 Kukrit Pramoj, interview by *Asiaweek Magazine*, 20 October 1976, in Van Beek, *M.R. Kukrit Pramoj: His Wit and Wisdom*, 143.
128 Kukrit, interview by *Asiaweek Magazine*, 143.
129 Kukrit, interview by *Asiaweek Magazine*, 143.
130 Kukrit, interview by *Vilas Manivat*, 153.

> Mao: Really, I'm getting old. Nowadays, I can do no work; I merely serve as a civil servant. I draw my salary and that's all.
>
> Kukrit: Are you really serious about that? Do you really work as a civil servant?
>
> Mao: Yes, or else how could I get any money to spend. I've got to have some salary.
>
> Kukrit: In that case, God save the Chinese civil servant.[131]

Kukrit's impression of Mao was that despite his old age, Mao could switch on and off. Sometimes, he was like an ordinary old man. But then he could turn on a switch and become 'very active', 'very intelligent, very well informed, [and] very powerful, at any moment'. Finally, Deng Xiaoping told Mao that it was time we should leave. When Kukrit got up to say goodbye, Mao had already switched off: 'When I shook hands he didn't even look at my face. He looked at the ceiling and was obviously ga-ga. He went back to his old age quite suddenly'.[132]

Overall, Kukrit was highly impressed by Chairman Mao: not only of his well-rounded knowledge about the world but also his kindness and good humour. As Kukrit put it, Mao 'knew everything, not only about Chinese affairs but about the world as well', and 'was a very, very kind, good-humored old gentleman who could talk with younger people and give them enjoyment in the conversation'.[133]

In the afternoon, around 15:30, Kukrit, Chatichai and other senior officials held another round of talks with Chinese leaders led by Deng. Deng was invited to visit Bangkok, and he readily accepted the invitation. During the discussions, Deng suggested that all overseas Chinese in Thailand should be allowed to take up Thai nationality because they had been living in the country for a long time, and had no intention of moving elsewhere.[134] The communist insurgency was not directly mentioned during the talks.

---

131 Kukrit, interview by *Vilas Manivat*, 154.
132 Kukrit, interview by *Vilas Manivat*, 155.
133 Kukrit, interview by *Vilas Manivat*, 155.
134 Telegram from Beijing Guest House to the Ministry of Foreign Affairs, 1 July 1975, Library and Archives Division, MFA POL7/PM2518/3, MFA, Thailand, 134; Banyat Tasaneeyavej, 'Kukrit Meets Mao as Relations Normalized', *Bangkok Post,* 2 July 1975, 1, 3.

Deng assured Kukrit that the China-built road in Laos near the Thai border would not threaten Thai security as it was being constructed for economic purposes only. Kukrit replied: 'We never questioned the road project. In fact, we think it could be useful for us'.[135] The Chinese vice-premier also described the Vietnam War as a 'bad mistake'. As he put it, 'the principle of solving a conflict is a three-step method of courting (talking), fighting, and killing. But the Americans reversed the process and started by killing first'. In Vietnam, Deng expressed discontent that a superpower was trying to impose hegemony in that country: 'it is highly possible that that superpower may request the use of bases in South Vietnam'.[136]

Deng told Kukrit that China was opposed to the stationing of American troops in Thailand. He dismissed claims by some in Thailand that Beijing would like Thailand to keep the American troops to deter Russian influence.[137] Throughout his talks on the world political situation, Deng mentioned Soviet expansionism several times. He reportedly warned the Thais to beware of the tiger (the Soviets) coming from the back door while pushing the wolf (the US) out of the front door. Deng also emphasised that China was a developing country and part of the Third World, rather than a part of any 'tripolar' superpower game.[138]

In the evening, Kukrit went to meet with Zhou at Beijing Hospital. At 19:00 on 1 July, Kukrit and Chatichai sat on the right-hand side of a long table while Zhou sat on the left. In the middle of the table was a small flag-stand with miniature Thai and Chinese flags, while other Thai and Chinese officials stood behind them. Beside Kukrit and Chatichai, there were 15 other Thai delegates, including Anand, Prakaipet, Nissai Vejjajiva and Tej Bunnag.

Kukrit and Zhou signed a 10-point joint communiqué, which formally established diplomatic relations between Thailand and the PRC, and agreed to exchange ambassadors 'as soon as practicable'. Endorsing the anti-hegemonic clause, the communiqué stated that the two countries opposed 'any attempt by any country or group of countries to establish hegemony or create spheres of influence in any part of the world'. It also endorsed the principle of noninterference by both countries in each other's internal affairs. The communiqué stated that Thailand

---

135 'China-Built Road in Laos Poses No Threat', *The Nation*, 3 July 1975, 1.
136 'China-Built Road in Laos Poses No Threat', 1.
137 'China-Built Road in Laos Poses No Threat', 1.
138 'China-Built Road in Laos Poses No Threat', 1.

'recognized the government of the People's Republic of China as the sole legal government of China', and had therefore decided 'to remove all its official representations from Taiwan within one month from the date of signature of this communiqué'.¹³⁹ In return, the PRC urged all 310,000 Chinese nationals living in Thailand 'to abide by the law of the Kingdom of Thailand, respect the customs and habits of the Thai people and live in amity with them'.¹⁴⁰ In Bangkok, the text of the joint communiqué was announced on Radio Thailand that very evening. Thailand became the third ASEAN nation and 102nd country to establish relations with the PRC.

During their toasts, Zhou apologised to Kukrit that he could not drink champagne to celebrate the signing of the official joint communiqué. 'My doctor forbids me to take any liquor so I will have to drink tea instead', as he told the Thai leaders who all broke into broad smiles.¹⁴¹ 'I have to get Deputy Premier Deng Xiaoping to work on my behalf', he continued.¹⁴²

With a cup of tea in his hand, Zhou clinked glasses with other Thai delegates. He praised the achievements and hard work of Chatichai and the Thai Foreign Ministry officials in opening the way for diplomatic relations:

> I am very happy over the signing of the joint communiqué. We have worked very hard. This is the result of the hard work of Foreign Minister Chatichai Choonhavan and his party.¹⁴³

In a toast, Kukrit wished Premier Zhou a 'long life', and gave a carved bronze cigarette case to him, telling him in English: 'although this is not very valuable. I am still very proud to give it to you'.¹⁴⁴ The entire ceremony lasted for seven minutes.

---

139 Taiwan issued a statement terminating diplomatic relations with Thailand, citing the 'most unfriendly act' by the Thai government, on 1 July 1975. 'GROC Statement on Establishment of RTG/PRC Relations', 2 July 1975, RG59, 1975TAIPEI03941, NARA.
140 Telegram from the Thai Consulate-General, Hong Kong to the Ministry of Foreign Affairs, 2 July 1975, Library and Archives Division, MFA POL7/PM2518/3, MFA, Thailand, 107–09.
141 'Almost Late for Mao', *Bangkok Post*, 2 July 1975, 1.
142 'Sihanouk Ready for Ties with Thailand – Zhou', *Bangkok Post*, 3 July 1975, 1.
143 'Zhou Sips Tea as PM has Champagne Toast', *The Nation*, 2 July 1975, 1.
144 'Almost Late for Mao', 3.

After the signing of the joint communiqué, the Thai delegation immediately went back to the Great Hall of the People to attend a soirée, in the company of Wu Teh, Vice-Chairman of the Standing Committee of the National People's Congress. The soirée was arranged by the Beijing Municipal Revolutionary Committee. The Thai delegation was entertained with a tour of the Great Hall of the People and a program of music and dance performances by Chinese musicians. The items were warmly received, and the performance of the Thai composition, 'Beautiful Moonlight', drew warm applause from the audiences. At the end of the performance, Kukrit and Wu Teh walked up to the stage, shook hands with the performers and presented them with a bouquet of flowers.[145] After the soirée, Foreign Minister Qiao Guanhua hosted a dinner for the Thai delegation at a famous Beijing restaurant, specialising in Beijing duck.[146]

On 2 July, Kukrit and the party left the Guest House at round 9:00 to visit the Great Wall at Ting Ling, which was an 80-minute ride by car. They were accompanied by Li Qiang, Minister of Foreign Trade, and Han Nianlong, Deputy Foreign Minister. This time, Kukrit wore a blue '*mohhom*' shirt to symbolise the dress worn by Thai farmers. Amid drizzling rain, the Thai delegates spent only 15 minutes at the Great Wall. Then they toured the Ming Tomb, and proceeded to the Summer Palace, which Kukrit had missed the previous day due to his impromptu summons to meet with Chairman Mao. They had lunch at the Summer Palace and in the afternoon toured the Forbidden City in Beijing.[147]

Meanwhile, Chatichai was relegated to dealing with the Chinese Foreign Minister, Qiao Guanhua, to arrange the finer details of the countries' diplomatic exchange. They held another meeting in the afternoon.[148] According to Deputy Foreign Minister Han Nianlong, Qiao asked Chatichai to help find a location for building the embassy in Bangkok and said their diplomatic staff would be less than 150. The Chinese Foreign Ministry would send an advance diplomatic mission, led by a chargé d'affaires, to Bangkok only one month after all staff of the

---

145 Telegram from the Thai Consulate-General, Hong Kong to the Ministry of Foreign Affairs, 2 July 1975, Library and Archives Division, MFA POL7/PM2518/3, MFA, Thailand, 103.
146 Telegram from the Thai Consulate-General, Hong Kong to the Ministry of Foreign Affairs, 2 July 1975, Library and Archives Division, MFA POL7/PM2518/3, MFA, Thailand, 113.
147 Telegram from the Thai Consulate-General, Hong Kong to the Ministry of Foreign Affairs, 2 July 1975, Library and Archives Division, MFA POL7/PM2518/3, MFA, Thailand, 64.
148 Telegram from the Thai Consulate-General, Hong Kong to the Ministry of Foreign Affairs, 2 July 1975, Library and Archives Division, MFA POL7/PM2518/3, MFA, Thailand, 64.

Taiwanese embassy had left Thailand.[149] Chatichai also held talks with Wang Yao-ting, Chairman of the China Council for the Promotion of International Trade.

In the evening, Kukrit conducted a live radio broadcast with Akom Makaranont, a spokesperson of the press.[150] Kukrit said that Sino–Thai relations would be closer in the future despite the differences between the two countries. He added that 1 July 1975 would be written in history as a 'special and important day' in relations between Thailand and China. He told the Thai people that Chairman Mao had talked to him for an hour and that Mao had emphasised that the Communist Party of Thailand was small and no serious danger to Thailand.[151] Kukrit also noted that the Chinese completely denied having aided the Thai insurgents or supported the Voice of the People of Thailand Radio.[152] Mao, he said, was:

> very kind to me. We had a long talk for about one hour and I learned a great deal from the Chairman and I don't think I'll ever be the same person again after that experience. It was such an outstanding experience to meet Chairman Mao.[153]

Kukrit noted that the Chinese were 'neutral' regarding the withdrawal of US forces and bases from Thailand, while the subject of increased Soviet influence in the region had not come up. He said the Chinese admitted they had sent soldiers to Laos 'to make roads' to assist the Laotian people, but that they had withdrawn when the projects were completed. On Cambodia, he said he had asked Zhou to convey a message to Sihanouk that Thailand would be happy to make friends. Kukrit also said a trade protocol would be signed in the next few months, and Deng had agreed in principle to make a return visit to Thailand.[154] Asked what the benefits of diplomatic relations with the PRC were, Kukrit replied, 'normal relationship, that is a benefit. People can come and go to see each other'.[155]

---

149 'Fewer than 150 Embassy Staff', *The Nation*, 4 July 1975, 1.
150 'Mao Tells Kukrit Not to Worry', *Bangkok Post*, 3 July 1975, 1.
151 'Mao Tells Kukrit Not to Worry', 1.
152 Quoted in 'Beijing News Conference of Kukrit Pramoj', 3 July 1975, RG59, 1975BEIJING01233, NARA.
153 Quoted in 'Beijing News Conference of Kukrit Pramoj', 3 July 1975, RG59, 1975BEIJING01233, NARA.
154 Quoted in 'Thai Prime Minister Kukrit's Visit to the PRC', 3 July 1975, RG59, 1975BEIJING01232, NARA.
155 Quoted in 'Beijing News Conference of Kukrit Pramoj', 3 July 1975, RG59, 1975BEIJING01233, NARA.

At the Great Hall of People on the evening of 2 July, Kukrit hosted the return banquet for Vice-Premier Deng Xiaoping and other Chinese leaders. The Thai football delegation led by Prachoom Ratanapien, which had just arrived in Beijing, and other diplomatic envoys of various countries to China were also present. On this evening, the national flags of China and Thailand were hung side by side in the banquet hall.

Both Kukrit and Deng gave speeches at the banquet. Kukrit called his conversations with the Chinese leaders 'straightforward and frank', but said they took place in a 'friendly atmosphere'. While there might have been differences of opinions, the 'close affinity' between the two countries would 'smooth out' and 'solve' these differences.[156] In his remarks, Deng Xiaoping rendered the talks rewarding on issues of common concern, and claimed that the visit to China by 'our Thai friends' had helped to increase 'our mutual understanding'. He called for friendly relations between the two countries to grow stronger and develop continuously. Deng also reiterated that the superpowers that wanted to assume the role of hegemon would be eliminated 'if we unite'.[157]

After their speeches, the band played the Chinese National Anthem and the Royal Anthem of Thailand. Xinhua News Agency reported on the friendly atmosphere of the banquet:

> The banquet was alive with a warm atmosphere of friendship. Hosts and guests warmly hailed the establishment of diplomatic relations between China and Thailand. They sincerely hoped that the Chinese and Thai people would live in friendship from generation to generation. Over the course of the banquet, the band played Chinese and Thai music.[158]

According to a telegram to the MFA from the Thai Consulate-General in Hong Kong, Kukrit's visit to China and its concomitant establishment of diplomatic relations between Thailand and China marked a 'new chapter of friendship'.[159]

---

156 Telegram from the Thai Consulate-General, Hong Kong to the Ministry of Foreign Affairs, 3 July 1975, Library and Archives Division, MFA POL7/PM2518/3, MFA, Thailand, 59–61.
157 Telegram from the Thai Consulate-General, Hong Kong to the Ministry of Foreign Affairs, 3 July 1975, Library and Archives Division, MFA POL7/PM2518/3, MFA, Thailand, 51–53.
158 Telegram from the Thai Consulate-General, Hong Kong to the Ministry of Foreign Affairs, 3 July 1975, Library and Archives Division, MFA POL7/PM2518/3, MFA, Thailand, 56.
159 Telegram from the Thai Consulate-General, Hong Kong to the Ministry of Foreign Affairs, 7 July 1975, Library and Archives Division, MFA POL7/PM2518/3, MFA, Thailand, 29–30.

6. A DIPLOMATIC TRANSFORMATION

The visit ended on 3 July when Chinese leaders, led by Deng Xiaoping, gave a farewell ceremony for Kukrit and his entourage at Beijing airport. Kukrit went to tour other provinces including Shanghai, Kunming and Guangzhou for the next four days.[160]

Kukrit returned to Bangkok on 6 July at around 14:00, and stated in his televised interview that, right from the start:

> the Chinese and ourselves made an agreement that despite different ideologies and systems … we can still get along together, can still be understanding friends with mutual respect, and can still talk to each other on an equal basis.[161]

He reported that the success of the establishment of diplomatic relations merely marked 'a first step': 'both sides must exchange various missions, such as military, educational, sports, and cultural'. Only this cooperation could pave the way to 'closer ties of friendship and good understanding'.[162]

He explained that was why 'political success must come first'. During this visit, Thai leaders had made personal acquaintance and built trust with Chinese leaders. Now, both sides would hold talks and negotiations on various subjects, especially economic relations, in a 'friendly and intimate manner … they will not be far apart as in the past'. Praising the Chinese leaders as 'sincere', Kukrit felt 'certain that China will have a much better attitude toward us than in the past, [and] that it will be friendly'.[163]

In retrospect, Kukrit's one-week trip to China marked a key turning point in Thai diplomacy in general and in Thai–Chinese relations in particular. Not only was this a diplomatic breakthrough: the process of normalisation also strengthened the narrative of détente. Thailand's discourse concerning 'China' shifted from enmity towards friendship. In the process, Hanoi was constructed as the common enemy and became the subject of Sino–Thai conversations thereafter. This emerging discourse

---

160 Telegram from the Thai Consulate-General, Hong Kong to the Ministry of Foreign Affairs, 3 July 1975, Library and Archives Division, MFA POL7/PM2518/3, MFA, Thailand, 57–58.
161 Press release, Department of Information, Ministry of Foreign Affairs, 10 July 1975, Library and Archives Division, MFA POL7/PM2518/3, MFA, Thailand, 74–78.
162 Quoted in 'Kukrit on China', 7 July 1975, RG59, 1975BANGKO13247, NARA; Press release, Department of Information, Ministry of Foreign Affairs, 10 July 1975, Library and Archives Division, MFA POL7/PM2518/3, MFA, Thailand, 74–78.
163 Quoted in 'Kukrit on China', 7 July 1975, RG59, 1975BANGKO13247, NARA; Press release, Department of Information, Ministry of Foreign Affairs, 10 July 1975, Library and Archives Division, MFA POL7/PM2518/3, MFA, Thailand, 74–78.

was of utmost importance because it not only symbolised the end of an era of confrontation, but also represented the advent of cooperation between the two countries. This historic event was described by *The Washington Post* as Thailand's policy of 'bending with the wind', a 'process that has been made even more urgent by the recent fall of the American-backed governments of South Vietnam and Cambodia'.[164]

Thai–Chinese Relations Thereafter: A 'Follow-up'

> This is only the beginning. There has to be a follow-up.
> – Anand Panyarachun, Ambassador to the UN[165]

The visit of Kukrit, and the resumption of Thai–Chinese diplomatic relations, paved the way for greater cooperation in a variety of spheres. First involved the expansion of trade. The Chinese made a friendly gesture by immediately buying 200,000 tons of Thai rice to help alleviate the rice crisis in Thailand. An official Thai trade delegation led by Commerce Minister Thongyot Cittawira went to Beijing between 17 and 21 August 1975 and completed a 50 million baht barter trade deal, exchanging Thai rice for Chinese oil. The Thais would supply the PRC with 200,000 tons of rice, while China would export 251,237 tons of gas and 312,129 tons of crude oil to Thailand at a 'friendly price'.[166] The delegation indicated that there would be follow-up trade discussions with the Chinese regarding other commodities, such as maize, tapioca, kenaf and tobacco.[167] Following Kukrit's visit to Beijing, this barter trade represented the first major deal between the two countries.

In December, Wang Yao-ting, the President of the China Council for International Trade Promotion, visited Thailand as a guest of Foreign Minister Chatichai. They agreed to hold a trade exhibition on the second floor of the Bangkok Bazaar, a new shopping centre complex behind Rajdamri Road, in March 1976.[168] Kukrit presided over the opening of the Chinese trade exhibition.

Second involved the conclusion of important diplomatic formalities. Upon their return, Kukrit and Chatichai sent messages of thanks by telegram to Chinese Premier Zhou Enlai, and Foreign Minister Qiao Guanhua,

---

164 'Bangkok "Bends with Wind" in Beijing Ties', *The Washington Post*, 2 July 1975.
165 'Kukrit Appeals for Trust, End to Fears', *Bangkok Post*, 7 July 1975, 1.
166 'Thai-PRC Rice-Oil Barter Trade', 25 August 1975, RG59, 1975BANGKO17760, NARA.
167 'Thai-PRC Rice-Oil Barter Trade', 25 August 1975, RG59, 1975BANGKO17760, NARA.
168 'Thai-PRC Trade', 5 February 1976, RG59, 1975STATE028179, NARA.

respectively. As the Permanent Secretary of the Foreign Ministry, Phan Wannamethi, said, this was the first time official messages were sent by telegram direct from Bangkok to Beijing through the ordinary telegraph service.[169] The Thais and the Chinese also agreed that before setting up embassies, they would make contact via the Thai and Chinese embassies in Laos. The Thais who wished to visit China could apply for a visa at the Chinese embassy in Laos.[170]

On 23 September, the Thai Foreign Ministry nominated MR Kasemsamosorn Kasemsri,[171] Thai Ambassador to Jakarta, to be the first Ambassador to Beijing, while the Chinese appointed Chai Zemin to be the Chinese Ambassador to Thailand.[172] Chai was an experienced Chinese diplomat whose previous posts included Hungary, Guinea and Egypt. According to Edward Masters, DCM of the American embassy in Bangkok, Chai's appointment as Ambassador to Thailand signified the importance that the PRC attached to its relationship with Bangkok:

> An interesting thread that runs through Chai's previous assignments is the presence of a strong and influential Soviet mission at each of his previous posts. This is also the case in Bangkok.[173]

In October, a 16-person advance team, led by Lu Tzu Po as chargé d'affaires, went to Bangkok to prepare for the establishment of the Chinese embassy in Bangkok. The advance party stayed at the third and fourth floors of the Ambassador Hotel. At the same time, the Guangzhou acrobatic troupe opened a performance in Bangkok. Lu also greeted King Bhumibol at the premier performance of the acrobats.[174] On 21 October, he met with Chatichai at the Foreign Ministry with a letter of introduction from the Chinese foreign minister, Qiao Guanhua. Chatichai officially welcomed the party, telling them that both countries had maintained good ties for

---

169 Telegram from the Ministry of Foreign Affairs to the Thai Consulate-General, Hong Kong, 9 July 1975, Library and Archives Division, MFA POL7/PM2518/4, MFA, Thailand, 286.
170 Telegram from the Ministry of Foreign Affairs to the Thai Embassy in Vientiane, 9 July 1975, Library and Archives Division, MFA POL7/PM2518/4, MFA, Thailand, 316.
171 MR Kasemsamosorn Kasemsri was a veteran diplomat. Before assuming his position in Jakarta in 1973, he had served as first secretary in the Philippines, chargé d'affaires in Canada, Thai representative on the SEATO Council, and Counsellor to the Thai Embassy in London. See 'PRC Ambassador to Thailand, Thai Ambassador to Beijing', 22 September 1975, RG59, 1975BANGKO19855, NARA.
172 'Memorandum from Foreign Minister to the Prime Minister on the Opening of the Chinese Embassy in Beijing', 2 October 1975, in *120 Years Ministry of Foreign Affairs*, 260–61.
173 'PRC Ambassador to Thailand, Thai Ambassador to Beijing', 22 September 1975, RG59, 1975BANGKO19855, NARA.
174 'Activity of the PRC Advance Team in Thailand', 10 November 1975, RG59, 1975BANGKO23600, NARA.

more than a thousand years and the sudden stoppage of relations for 25 years in the recent past was a 'passing cloud'. After a half-hour meeting, Chatichai disclosed that China would be free to make their choice on the location of their embassy in Bangkok.[175]

The advance team played a visible and active role in the diplomatic circles in Bangkok during their three-week visit, attending the official opening of the ESCAP building (the UN Economic and Social Commission for Asia and the Pacific, formerly the Economic Commission for Asia and the Far East, or ECAFE), and the Austrian, Iranian as well as Soviet National Day celebrations. On 8 November, a picture of the Chinese chargé and the Soviet ambassador shaking hands and smiling appeared on the front page of the *Bangkok Post*.[176] The new Chinese ambassador, Chai Zemin, arrived in Bangkok on 26 January 1976, while Thai ambassador MR Kasemsamosorn Kasemsri went to Beijing on 16 March. After presenting his credentials to King Bhumibol at Bhuping Palace in Chiang Mai on 21 March, Chai Zemin paid a courtesy call on Premier Kukrit.[177]

Third was in relation to clandestine radio broadcasts. In the weeks following the visit, the Voice of the People of Thailand shifted its propaganda towards a more anti-Soviet tone. For example, in a 29 July 1975 broadcast, it accused 'the Soviet social-imperialists' of 'rapidly expanding their aggressive influence in Thailand'. It charged the KGB with increasing its clandestine activity in Thailand and claimed that there were 100 KGB officers in Bangkok supported by another 150 Soviet officials.[178]

Fourth involved people-to-people contact. Aside from the trade delegation in August, various Thai leaders, groups and private individuals travelled to China, including a group of Thai journalists from the provinces, a group of high-ranking Thai nobility headed by Princess Siriratna Diskul, and a group from the Socialist Party of Thailand, led by its party deputy leader, Khaiseng Suksai, in October. All these parties were official guests of the PRC, and were escorted and hosted by its representatives.[179]

---

175 'Chinese Envoy Brings Message', *Bangkok Post*, 22 October 1975, 1.
176 'Activity of the PRC advance team in Thailand', 10 November 1975, RG59, 1975BANGKO23600, NARA.
177 'China Envoy Presents Credentials', *Bangkok Post*, 25 March 1976, 3.
178 Quoted in 'Stance of the Voice of the People of Thailand', 31 July 1975, RG59, 1975BANGKO15696, NARA.
179 'Thai Delegations to the PRC', 8 October 1975, RG59, 1975BANGKO21302, NARA.

Last but not least, the resumption of diplomatic relations paved the way for normalisation with Thailand's communist neighbours, the most notable of which was a rapprochement with Cambodia. As Kukrit said, 'Cambodia was handed to us on a silver tray, with ribbons, by Mr. Zhou Enlai'.[180] During his visit to Beijing, Zhou asked Kukrit of Thailand's policy toward Cambodia, Kukrit replied that Thailand would like to be friendly.

> Zhou: Even if Prince Sihanouk were to come back as Head of State?
>
> Kukrit: Yes, especially if Prince Sihanouk were to come back as Head of State.
>
> Zhou: Are you quite serious?
>
> Kukrit: I am very serious.
>
> Zhou: May I tell Prince Sihanouk that?
>
> Kukrit: Yes, by all means.[181]

According to Kukrit, Premier Zhou was very pleased with this conversation. Chatichai disclosed that on 3 September, Ambassador Anand Panyarachun met with Cambodian Vice Premier Ieng Sary at the UN, and said that Thailand was 'ready to supply Cambodia with necessary foodstuffs and other commodities on a government-to-government basis'.[182] Then in late October, the Kukrit Government received word from China that Ieng Sary would be landing at Don Mueang Airport in a Chinese plane, on his way to China on a goodwill mission. After the visit, Kukrit said that 'we were very friendly. And since then, very good things have been happening between Cambodia and this country … We are really very friendly toward Cambodia'.[183]

Overall, the formal normalisation of Sino–Thai relations marked a diplomatic revolution in Thai foreign policy. For Chatichai this had three important outcomes: 'One – mutual confidence. Two – noninterference in each other's affairs. Three – mutual benefits'.[184] Such a transformative event was also widely discussed during the meeting between Foreign Minister

---

180 Kukrit, interview by *Asiaweek Magazine*, 144.
181 Kukrit, interview by *Asiaweek Magazine*, 144.
182 'Historic Thai-Khmer Meeting in New York', *Bangkok Post*, 9 September 1975, 1.
183 Kukrit, interview by *Asiaweek Magazine*, 144.
184 'Chatichai: We Need Strong Independent Neighbors', *Bangkok Post*, 31 July 1975, 3.

Chatichai and US Secretary of State Henry Kissinger on 26 November 1975. Kissinger told Chatichai of the forthcoming presidential visit to Beijing and asked Chatichai about his visit to Beijing:

> Secretary: Do the Chinese support the insurgents [in Thailand]?
>
> Foreign Minister: They follow a two-track policy. The insurgents have moral support from the Chinese Communist Party.
>
> Secretary: Mao does not like foreign Communists at all. I am not sure that he likes Chinese Communists either. Did he form words when you met with him in Beijing?
>
> Foreign Minister: They used interpreters. There was a very nice-looking girl, Nancy Tang. When we came into the room, we did not see Mao at first. He was sitting in a chair. Then he stood up and greeted Prime Minister Kukrit. During the conversation, there was interpretation from Chinese to Chinese to English. Sometimes he would write things.
>
> Secretary: It was the same way when I saw him.[185]

They also discussed the situation in Indochina, and the role of China there. They agreed that 'the biggest threat in Southeast Asia at the present time is North Vietnam'. Chatichai added that the Chinese talked a lot about Vietnamese 'hegemony'. Kissinger said that US strategy was to 'get the Chinese into Laos and Cambodia as a barrier to the Vietnamese'. Chatichai told Kissinger that he 'asked the Chinese to take over in Laos. They mentioned that they had a road building team in northern Laos'. Kissinger said that 'we would support this'. He also asked Chatichai to 'tell the Cambodians that we will be friends with them. They are murderous thugs, but we won't let that stand in our way'. 'We are prepared to improve relations with them.' 'Tell them the latter part, but don't tell them what I said before'. Kissinger said that 'we bear no hostility towards them. We would like them to be independent as a counterweight to North Vietnam'. Also, the Secretary of State firmly noted, 'the Chinese fully support the Cambodians'.[186]

To sum up, Sino–Thai rapprochement was an integral part of a broader geopolitical realignment within the region, underpinned for the Thais by the changing discourse of friends and enemies. With the Chinese now

---

185 'Secretary's Meeting with Foreign Minister Chatichai of Thailand', 26 November 1975, RG59, 1975BANGKO24619, NARA.
186 'Secretary's Meeting with Foreign Minister Chatichai of Thailand', 26 November 1975, RG59, 1975BANGKO24619, NARA.

framed as a 'new friend', the Thais were able to offer help to the Cambodian 'thugs' (the Khmer Rouge) while the new arrangement helped reinforce their view of the Vietnamese as a threat and an aspiring subregional 'hegemonic power'.[187] This discursive change was to fundamentally shape the practices of diplomacy in the late 1970s and 1980s. Moreover, the shift also reflected the wish among some factions of Thai officials for greater balance or equilibrium in relations with the major powers, including the US, the USSR and the PRC. For Chatichai, Thailand's foreign policy was 'not to overemphasize relations with any single country'.[188] Rather, it necessitated a three-pronged and balanced strategy: 'we must stand out of balance, neither too close to one power nor too far from another power'.[189]

6.2. Thai–Soviet Relations: Resilience of Détente

6.2.1. Thai–Soviet Relations under Sanya

Under the Sanya Dharmasakdi Government, détente with the Soviet Union remained largely intact. One of his aims was to sustain the Thai–Soviet friendship. On the one hand, Sanya wished to develop closer trade and cultural exchanges between the two countries. On the other, he sought to achieve a balance of interests with the great powers in the region, thereby eschewing the Soviet Collective Security in Asia proposal.[190]

On 16 January 1974, Foreign Minister Charoonphan Isarankhun Na Ayutthaya explained to foreign correspondents that, for Thailand, the Soviet Union was

> [in] a strong position to contribute to the restoration of peace and harmony in the long suffering people living there (Indochina) and thereby contribute positively to the stability of the entire region.[191]

---

187 'Secretary's Meeting with Foreign Minister Chatichai of Thailand', 26 November 1975, RG59, 1975BANGKO24619, NARA.
188 'Chatichai: We Need Strong Independent Neighbors', 3.
189 'Chatichai: I Will Change the Image of Thailand', *Prachachatraiwan*, 13 July 1975, 2.
190 'Thai-Soviet Relations', 30 April 1974, RG59, 1974BANGKO07008, NARA.
191 Quoted in Leszek Buszynski, *Soviet Foreign Policy and Southeast Asia* (London: Croom Helm, 1986), 80.

It was a point he reiterated in a televised interview on 28 February:

> We would like to promote closer relations with [the Soviet Union], but we must create trust and confidence, mutual good understanding must exist, and there must be no interference. This is not meant for the Soviet Union or any other country, we do not want any interference in the internal affairs of our country ... The Soviet Union has the opportunity to play a role in finding a way to help restore peace and quiet to Southeast Asia, and especially to Indochina, since it desires to see peace restored.[192]

While Thailand under Sanya was not clear about how the USSR should contribute to the peace and stability of the region, it did not want the USSR to fill the power vacuum. In his speech to the Association for Asian Studies in Boston on 1 April, Ambassador to the US and the UN Anand Panyarachun endorsed Thailand's increased friendliness with Russia but confirmed that Thailand did not accept the Soviet proposal on Collective Security in Asia. As Anand stated:

> the Thai government rejects the Soviet Security Proposal as inappropriate and unnecessary, either to fill what some Thai see as a vacuum caused by an American withdrawal from Asia, or an anti-Chinese alliance.[193]

Despite Thailand's disapproval of the Soviet proposal on Asian Collective Security, there were key developments in three main areas. First, a series of people-to-people exchanges commenced. In November 1973, a ballet company of the Leningrad Opera and S Kirov Ballet Theater gave guest performances in Thailand. In February 1974, an education delegation visited Moscow to study the educational system in the USSR, and visit universities and institutions.[194] In the same month, Vladimir Promyslov, the Mayor of the Moscow City, visited Thailand. During his three-day visit, Promyslov met with Adth Visutyothapibal, the Governor of Bangkok. The latter voiced interest in expanding trade between the two countries, but raised 'domestic political sensitivities' as an impediment to improved political relations. Promyslov also invited Adth to visit Moscow.[195]

---

192 'Thai Foreign Minister on SEATO, Thai-US Relations, the USSR, and North Vietnam', 6 March 1974, RG59, 1974BANGKO03725, NARA.
193 'Thai-Soviet Relations', 30 April 1974, RG59, 1974BANGKO07008, NARA.
194 'A Diary of Soviet-Thai Cooperation', *Bangkok Post*, 7 November 1974, 1.
195 According to a diplomat at the Soviet Embassy in Bangkok, the Bangkok stopover was originally intended to be unofficial in order to provide the Promyslov party with an opportunity to rest following its busy schedule in Hanoi. The Thais requested it receive official status. 'Visit of Moscow Mayor', 15 February 1974, RG59, 1974BANGKO02586, NARA; 'Moscow's Lord Mayor Visits', *Bangkok Post*, 8 February 1974, 1.

In April, two Thai scientific officers of the Thai Industrial Standards Institute attended a four-month UN seminar for standards and metrology, organised by the State Committee of the USSR Council of Ministers for Standards in cooperation with the UN Industrial Development Organization in Moscow.[196]

The most important was a visit to the Soviet Union made by Princess Galayani Wattana, King Bhumibol's elder sister, in May 1974. She was received as a guest of the Presidium of the USSR Supreme Soviet. In Moscow, she called on a raft of Soviet leaders: Ivan Grushetsky, Vice-President of the Presidium of the USSR Supreme Soviet, Mikhail Georgadze, Secretary of the Presidium of the USSR Supreme Soviet, Alla Shaposhnikova, Deputy Ministry of Higher and Specialized Secondary Education, and other Soviet high-ranking officials.[197] As the head of the foreign languages department at Thammasat University, the Princess was interested in cultural exchanges and the Russian language. In her meeting with Vice-President Grushetsky, she said that Thammasat University would soon open Russian language as a major course, and that the instructors would be the two daughters of Yuad Lertrit, Thai Ambassador to Moscow. Yingboon and Yodboon Lertrit studied at Moscow State University.[198] Both started teaching Russian at Thammasat University on 1 August 1974.[199]

During her stay in the USSR, the Princess went to Moscow, Leningrad and Kiev. She observed the Soviet system of higher education and its achievements in the fields of science, technology and culture. When interviewed by a correspondent of the Novosti Press Agency, Princess Galayani pointed out that her visit to the USSR had been useful in many respects.

> This trip has convinced me [she said] of the Soviet people's friendly feelings for Thailand, its history and culture. Our countries are very different, and cultural exchanges between them would be

---

196 One scientist, Chalit Homhual, told a correspondent of the Novosti Press Agency:

The USSR has accumulated a wealth of theoretical and practical experience in the field of standardization, metrology and quality check-up. And, what is very important, it shares this experience with the developing countries. As far as we are concerned, the many things we have learnt while attending the course will be useful for the work done by our Institute.

'A Diary of Soviet-Thai Cooperation', 3.
197 'A Diary of Soviet-Thai Cooperation', 3.
198 'Visit of Thai Princess to Moscow', 17 May 1974, RG59, 1974BANGKO08082, NARA.
199 Yodboon Lertrit, interview by author, Bangkok, 23 June 2015.

very interesting ... I hope that contacts between our two countries in the field of culture and education will become closer with each passing year.²⁰⁰

Shortly after Princess Galayani's visit, Bangkok governor Adth Visutyothapibal paid a return visit. His delegation acquainted itself with the municipal economy of Moscow and the activities of the Moscow City Soviet, the legislative and executive organ of power in the city. They also visited Leningrad. In an interview with a correspondent of the Novosti Press Agency, Adth pointed out that he was impressed by the efficient functioning of Moscow's municipal economy, by the cleanliness and order prevailing in the streets of the city, by the rate of housing construction and by the Moscow public transport system. He hoped that 'friendship between Moscow and Bangkok will be strengthened and deepened'.²⁰¹

Three further visits were made by Thai writers and women's organisations between August and October.²⁰² In August, a group of Thai women arrived in the Soviet Union to present a gift of a sitting Buddha statue to the Soviet Buddhist community. Between August and September 1974, Ladda Thanathathankam, Vice-President of the Writers' Association of Thailand, and Subhat Sawasdivak, the editor of the *Sakulthai Weekly* magazine, met Russian journalists at the Novosti Press Agency. A delegation of the Women's Movement of Thailand, led by Mom Dusdi Boripat na Ayutthaya, visited the USSR between 26 September and 8 October. It was clear that by the mid-1970s, Thai–Soviet relations broadened to a series of people-to-people exchanges.

The second development came with increased cultural cooperation. The new Soviet Ambassador to Bangkok, Boris Ilyichev (February 1974 – June 1978), proactively supported further cultural exchanges and initiated a cultural agreement with Thailand, of which he claimed, there were no strings attached. As Ilyichev put it, 'One thing is certain, we will not export revolution anywhere'.²⁰³ His chargé d'affaires, Stanislav Semivolos, had a meeting with the Director-General of the Information Department of the MFA on 5 February 1974. In that meeting, he presented the Soviet proposal of a cultural agreement to the Thai Foreign Ministry. He said this agreement would help to promote good relations between Thailand

---

200 'A Diary of Soviet-Thai Cooperation', 3.
201 'A Diary of Soviet-Thai Cooperation', 3.
202 'A Diary of Soviet-Thai Cooperation', 3.
203 'Thai-Soviet Cultural Agreement', 8 May 1974, RG59, 1974BANGKO07468, NARA.

and the Soviet Union.²⁰⁴ The Soviet proposal included a wide range of cultural exchanges, including musicians, students and professors, football players and scientists. The Thai Foreign Ministry took the draft of the cultural agreement into consideration.

Ilyichev also broadened contacts with various groups of students, specifically offering scholarships – though this was never approved by the Thai Government. In March 1974, an exhibition on the Soviet Union was organised by students and faculty of Phrasanmit College, Bangkok. The exhibition included about 1,000 photographs showing the most diverse aspects of life in the USSR. Alexander Karchava, a staff member of the USSR embassy in Thailand, delivered a lecture, 'From the History of Russo-Thai Relations' on the occasion.²⁰⁵

In May, an exhibition was held at Thammasat University in connection with the International Day of Working People's Solidarity. The exhibition included photographs on the USSR: on the activities of Soviet trade unions, on the position of women in Soviet society and on working conditions in the USSR. Students who arranged the exhibition provided detailed texts to explain the photographs.²⁰⁶

The third development was in trade relations. After the trade agreement had been signed in December 1970, Thai–Soviet mutual trade relations gradually developed mainly due to increased Soviet purchases of rubber and fluorites from Thailand. In October, the Soviet Union informed the Thai Government that it wished to buy 50,000 tons of maize from Thailand. However, Thailand was not able to meet the Russian demand because of its prior commitments to supply Japan and Taiwan.²⁰⁷

Nevertheless, the Soviets remained concerned about the new State Trading Bill, which set up a state trading corporation to control direct trade with the communist countries. They felt that this law was 'discriminatory'.²⁰⁸ Thai Ambassador to Moscow, Yuad Lertrit, said that a state trading organisation would 'prove useful in promoting commerce with Soviet Russia and East

---

204 Memorandum between the Director-General of the Information Department of the Ministry of Foreign Affairs, and the Soviet chargé d'affaires to Bangkok, 5 February 1974, in Thailand's Ministry of Foreign Affairs, *Collected Volumes of Declassified Documents on Thai–Russian Relations, 1970–1991*, Vol. 3 (Bangkok: Ministry of Foreign Affairs, 2017), 9–11.
205 'A Diary of Soviet-Thai Cooperation', 3.
206 'A Diary of Soviet-Thai Cooperation', 3.
207 'Soviets Turn to Thailand for Maize', *Bangkok Post,* 10 October 1974, 10.
208 Sarasin Viraphol, *Directions in Thai Foreign Policy* (Singapore: Institute of Southeast Asian Studies, 1976), 28.

European countries'. He explained: 'at present our merchants are afraid of police surveillance if they trade with Socialist countries. If trading is done through a governmental enterprise then there is no such problem'.[209]

Between 2 and 22 December, a Soviet trade exhibition was held at Lumpini Hall in Bangkok. V Kulikov, trade representative of the Soviet Union in Thailand, expressed hopes that it would help expand trade between the two countries, and improve already good relations. At the exhibition, 12 foreign trade organisations from Soviet countries exhibited their products, such as new models of agricultural trackers, passenger cars, trucks, pumps and hydrofoil boats.[210]

All in all, Thailand under Sanya, while retaining closer military and economic linkages with the US, maintained friendship with the Soviet Union. Mutual trade, cultural and people-to-people exchanges were fostered, which became the basis for Kukrit's détente between 1975 and 1976.

6.2.2. Thai–Soviet Relations under Kukrit

Under Kukrit, with Sino–Thai rapprochement in the spotlight, changes to Thai–Soviet relations were relatively less radical. This was partly because of the changing geopolitical landscape in Southeast Asia, reflecting Sino–Soviet strategic competition, which in turn shaped the way in which the Thais sought to balance between the two powers. It culminated in equidistant diplomacy.

This section argues that despite these limitations, Thai–Soviet relations remained resilient. While an increase in the Soviet political and intelligence activities in Thailand raised scepticism, Thailand's discourse of détente with the USSR remained intact. It culminated in their mutual exchanges at various levels and the approval of the aforementioned cultural agreement.

Upon taking office in March 1975, Prime Minister Kukrit proclaimed that there were no issues of dispute with Moscow, and looked forward to closer ties between Thailand and the Soviet Union. As he remarked, 'we will maintain our friendship with the Soviets'.[211] As a superpower, the Soviet Union, Kukrit said:

---

209 Theh Chongkhadikij, 'Cultural Agreement Reached with USSR', *Bangkok Post*, 15 August 1974, 3.
210 'USSR Expo Boosts Hopes of More Trade', *Bangkok Post*, 30 November 1974, 10.
211 Quoted in Buszynski, *Soviet Foreign Policy and Southeast Asia*, 104.

obviously has interests here in this region as elsewhere around the globe. The great potential is there for the Soviets to play a significant role that would be consonant with interests of the regional countries themselves.[212]

One Soviet role, for example, could be to induce Vietnamese restraint. In the process of détente, the Thai Government regarded the USSR, like the PRC, as a friend, and Vietnam as an emerging threat that needed to be contained.

Ivan Shchedrov, the *Pravda* correspondent to Thailand, wrote his commentary praising Kukrit's new course of Thai foreign policy.[213] On 12 May, Shchedrov called upon Chatichai at the Foreign Ministry. They discussed Brezhnev's proposal for Collective Security in Asia, which had little traction in the region. Shchedrov also requested the establishment of a *Pravda* office in Bangkok, which Chatichai approved in principle. Later, on 25 June, Soviet ambassador Boris Ilyichev, in his speech at the Foreign Correspondent's Club in Bangkok, also highlighted Brezhnev's idea of Collective Security in Asia. He said that the proposal would benefit the countries in the region, including Thailand, due to the fact that it stood for:

> (1) the renunciation of force in orderly state relations (2) the respecting of each other's sovereignty and the principle of inviolability of national frontiers (3) noninterference in the state's internal affairs and (4) broad economic and other forms of cooperation on a basis of full equality and mutual benefits.[214]

Brezhnev's proposal came up again during an interview Shchedrov conducted with Kukrit in late June. Kukrit said that Thailand endorsed the neutralisation of Southeast Asia without military bases or blocs. As he put it, 'peace and security can only be established through the collective efforts of all countries of the region'. However, Kukrit stressed that Thailand's interest in the ZOPFAN resolution was a way of rejecting the Asian Collective Security proposal. Regardless of the proposal, the Thai premier strongly urged closer ties with the Soviet Union. [215]

---

212 Quoted in Buszynski, *Soviet Foreign Policy and Southeast Asia*, 104–05.
213 'Pravda on Thailand', 23 June 1975, RG59, 1975MOSCOW08708, NARA.
214 Quoted in Sarasin, *Directions in Thai Foreign Policy*, 26.
215 'Pravda on Thailand', 23 June 1975, RG59, 1975MOSCOW08708, NARA.

However, Sino–Thai normalisation deeply concerned Moscow. On 1 June, when the Soviet Deputy Foreign Minister, Nikolai Firyubin, hosted a luncheon meeting for the new Ambassador to Moscow, Arun Panupong (1974–1977), he raised the Soviet concerns. Firyubin warned that Thai relations with other countries should not affect Thai–Soviet relations in a negative way or discriminate against the Soviet Union. According to Arun, Firyubin emphasised the anti-Soviet Chinese policy. He claimed that China never stopped intervening in the internal affairs of other countries, and threatened to annex the territories of Vietnam in the South China Sea. At the same time, the Chinese leaked news that the Soviets wished to build a naval base there. For Firyubin, these Chinese attempts to discredit the Soviet Union were merely to conceal their own intentions in seeking influence in Cambodia, and in attempting to attack Vietnam. He also said that the Soviet Union was satisfied with Thailand's policy of American withdrawal.[216]

In bilateral relations, Firyubin stressed that the USSR wished to upgrade its relationship with Thailand. He told Ambassador Arun that despite their 'normal' relationship, the actual content of Thai–Soviet relations was at a 'standstill and too limited'. Firyubin suggested that there were effective technical and professional institutes that the Thai Government could consider sending students to as part of a student exchange or straight study (without being part of an exchange) in the Soviet Union. If Thailand had any problems or concerns, it was possible to have a straightforward and frank discussion. The Soviets would be pleased to listen and find a solution to alleviate scepticism. Arun replied that the Soviet Union, as one of the great powers, was of utmost importance to Thai foreign policy. He assured him that both countries did not have any significant problems or obstacles. Unlike Sino–Thai rapprochement, there was no exciting news in Thai–Soviet relations because the latter were normal. In his view, the Soviets were anxious that the Chinese were successfully establishing diplomatic relations with countries in Southeast Asia, and were dominating the headlines at the expense of the Soviet Union. They sought influence in the region, and therefore struggled with China's greater alignment with countries such as Thailand.[217]

---

216 Discussion between Thai Ambassador and Soviet Deputy Minister, 1 June 1975, Ministry of Foreign Affairs Documents, (2) MFA 1.1/112, TNA, Bangkok, 215.
217 Discussion between Thai Ambassador and Soviet Deputy Minister, 1 June 1975, Ministry of Foreign Affairs Documents, (2) MFA 1.1/112, TNA, Bangkok, 215–16.

When Kukrit returned from Beijing to Bangkok in early July 1975, he was asked by Thai reporters whether he would visit the Soviet Union anytime in the near future. Kukrit replied, 'No, not now. One play at a time'. He said that it was generally agreed that a visit to Moscow after the Beijing visit would be 'most disappointing' to the Chinese, who repeatedly spoke of their fear of Soviet expansionism. According to Kukrit, Thailand would consider closer, though more cautious ties with the Soviet Union in order to keep foreign policy options open.[218]

On 17 July, Thai Ambassador to Moscow Arun had a discussion with S Nemchina, Director of the Southeast Asian Department at the Soviet Foreign Ministry. While he understood that Thai rapprochement with the PRC was a readjustment to the regional reality, Nemchina warned that Mao and Chinese leaders had interfered with the internal affairs of other countries. He did not believe that in the event of Sino–Thai normalisation, the communist insurgency in Thailand would disappear. The Soviet Union, on the other hand, adhered to the principle of peaceful coexistence and détente and sought to promote peace in the region via the Asian Collective Security proposal, which, he felt, many Southeast Asian countries misunderstood. Adopting an anti-Soviet stance, the Chinese in particular deemed this proposal an anti-Chinese scheme. Nemchina praised Kukrit's diplomacy of independence and good neighbour policy. He also said that Thai–Soviet relations were normal, but wished to see an extension of the relationship based upon friendship and equality.[219]

Subsequently, the Soviet embassy in Bangkok directly complained to the Thai Foreign Ministry that the anti-hegemonic clause in the Thai–Chinese joint communiqué of 1 July was directed towards the Soviet Union. The Thais replied that they understood it differently, and that it meant hegemony by any power including the Chinese themselves.[220] It seemed that one of the Soviet aims was principally to counter increased Chinese influence in Thailand.

---

218 'Kukrit Appeals for Trust, End to Fears', 3.
219 Opinions of Soviet Director of Southeast Asian Department, 14 July 1975, Ministry of Foreign Affairs Documents, (2) MFA 1.1/112, TNA, Bangkok, 179.
220 'The Soviets in Bangkok: Undercover Diplomacy', *Far Eastern Economic Review*, 26 September 1975, 8.

Following Thailand's formal diplomatic relations with Beijing, Thai Foreign Ministry officials noticed a sharp increase in Soviet diplomatic activities.[221] Soviet Ambassador Ilyichev apparently broadened his contacts and influence at all levels of the Thai Government and bureaucracy. As Phirat Itsarasena, a press division chief of the MFA, observed, the Soviets were 'pushing very hard now, not only on the cultural exchange, but across the board'.[222]

First and foremost, the Soviet Union attempted to conclude the Thai–Soviet cultural agreement, which had originally been drafted by the Russians. By June, the Thai Foreign Ministry had taken the agreement into serious consideration. It found that the original draft was different from other cultural agreements that the Soviet Union had with other countries, and suggested some changes, such as the inclusion of a noninterference clause.[223] This revised draft was sent back to the Russians during the meeting between Soviet Ambassador Boris Ilyichev and Pracha Gunakasem, Director-General of the Information Department in the Foreign Ministry on 25 June. It was reported that a Thai mission would be dispatched to Moscow to work out the final details.[224]

By the end of July, Foreign Minister Chatichai reaffirmed the fact that Thailand did not 'have any dispute with Soviet Russia. We will soon sign a cultural agreement'.[225] On 1 August, at the Swiss National Day reception, Edward Masters, the US DCM, observed that Pracha Gunakasem carried an envelope to the Soviet ambassador with the remark, 'this is approved from our side'. Masters assumed that this referred to the cultural agreement.[226]

On 18 August, Soviet Ambassador Ilyichev held a meeting with Chatichai at the Thai Foreign Ministry. Chatichai told Ilyichev that the cultural agreement would be approved by the Cabinet on the next day, and if the Soviets wished to sign the treaty in Bangkok, he would like to invite the Soviet foreign minister to visit Thailand. No formal invitation would be issued until it was known that Gromyko could accept. Chatichai said

---

221 *Far Eastern Economic Review*, 22 August 1975, 5.
222 'Thai-Soviet Relations', 19 August 1975, RG59, 1975BANGKO17326, NARA.
223 'Thai Cultural Censorship Board', 18 June 1975, RG59, 1975BANGKO11545, NARA.
224 Discussion between Director-General of the Information Department and Soviet Ambassador to Bangkok, 25 June 1975 in Ministry of Foreign Affairs, *Collected Volumes of Declassified Documents on Thai–Russian Relations, 1970–1991*, Vol. 3, 15–16.
225 'Chatichai: We Need Strong Independent Neighbors', 3.
226 'Thai-Soviet Relations', 19 August 1975, RG59, 1975BANGKO17326, NARA.

that if the treaty could be signed sooner, the rumour of increased KGB activities would decrease. By the end of August, a draft had been approved by both countries.[227]

In September, Chatichai publicly announced that he would invite Soviet Foreign Minister Andrei Gromyko to Thailand for the formal signing of a Thai–Soviet cultural agreement.[228] He commented that 'we don't want the Soviets to feel that we are closer to China and the US than the Soviet Union' and that 'since we have established diplomatic ties with China, we should increase our contacts with the Soviet Union'.[229] The invitation was envisioned as a symbolic balance to the establishment of diplomatic relations with the PRC, with which the USSR had a heated political dispute. In general, Chatichai's ultimate aim was to deal with the USSR without offending Beijing. Although Gromyko did not plan to visit Thailand, the cultural agreement was approved by both sides.

Second, the Soviet Union stepped up its diplomatic and intelligence activities in Thailand. It increased its official presence from 70 officials in 1974 to 81 in 1975, working at the embassy, at the trade representation office and at ESCAP.[230] In July, a *Pravda* office was officially opened, and the Soviet embassy requested approval to station a Russian military attaché in Bangkok. While Chatichai denied any knowledge of such a Soviet request during his 31 July press conference, Nissai Vejjajiva, the Director-General of the MFA Information Department, stated that the request had been received from the Soviet embassy and forwarded to the Ministry of Defense for a final decision.[231]

---

227 Record of conversation between Thai Foreign Minister and Soviet Ambassador to Bangkok, 18 August 1975, in Ministry of Foreign Affairs, *Collected Volumes of Declassified Documents on Thai-Russian Relations, 1970–1991*, Vol. 3 (Bangkok: Ministry of Foreign Affairs, 2017), 17–18.
228 'Gromyko to Get Thai Invitation', *Bangkok Post*, 9 September 1975, 1. However, this invitation was a complete surprise to the Soviet Embassy in Thailand. Yuri Kuznetsov, Deputy Director of the Southeast Asia Division at the Soviet Ministry of Foreign Affairs, dismissed Chatichai's reported invitation for Gromyko to visit to Thailand as 'not serious', and portrayed Thai foreign policy as confused and uncertain about its direction. 'Invitation to Soviet Foreign Minister Gromyko to Visit Thailand', 5 September 1975, RG59, 1975BANGKO18721, NARA; 'Soviet View of Indochina and Thailand', 25 October 1975, RG59, 1975MOSCOW15406, NARA.
229 Quoted in Buszynski, *Soviet Foreign Policy and Southeast Asia*, 105.
230 'Reporting on Host Country Relations with Communist Countries', 15 November 1976, RG59, 1976BANGKO31296, NARA.
231 In late July, Foreign Minister Chatichai had directed a 'Russian Section' within the MFA, which was staffed with selected officers and designed to cultivate contacts with Soviet diplomats, to 'watch their activities and see what they want and how they see their prospects in Thailand'. It was reported that Chatichai wanted an organised effort 'to hold them off without seeming negative'. 'Thai-Soviet Relations', 19 August 1975, RG59, 1975BANGKO17326, NARA.

According to US Ambassador Whitehouse:

> the Soviet military attaché question appears a ploy to fend off the Soviets without bruising their feelings overmuch. The Thai military establishment remains overtly suspicious of the USSR, and the MFA can blame the Ministry of Defense in the event of a negative ... decision.[232]

However, by the end of 1975, the Thai Government agreed to accept a Soviet military attaché, while sending a Thai military attaché to Moscow too.

Third, following trade and aviation agreements in the early 1970s, the volume of Thai–Soviet trade increased through the 1970s, although it remained marginal. The Soviets focused their exports to Thailand on the sale of both fixed and moveable machinery, and provided large-scale financing to local purchases, through the Moscow Narodny Bank in Singapore.[233] They imported some Thai products, the most important of which was fluorite. However, the purchase of fluorite in 1975 decreased due to Soviet conditions that required Thai exporters to accept Soviet machinery as payment. In September 1975, Foreign Minister Chatichai accepted the Soviet offer to send a technical team of energy experts to Thailand to explore shale oil.[234]

Throughout 1975, the Russian Government repeatedly submitted formal complaints to the Thai Foreign Ministry regarding the State Trading Bill. The Soviets charged that the State Trading Bill targeted trade with both the USSR and the Eastern bloc, and would considerably affect the smooth functioning of trade relations. From the Soviet sides, the bill would hinder the original Thai–Russian trade agreement that facilitated free trade between the two countries. They said they would consider the abolishment of their trade agreement if Thailand insisted on implementing the State Trading Bill. According to an unnamed high-ranking Thai official, the Kukrit Government described this Russian intervention as a 'political issue', and it was believed that the Soviet move was aimed at checking the

---

232 'Thai-Soviet Relations', 19 August 1975, RG59, 1975BANGKO17326, NARA.
233 'Reporting on Host Country Relations with Communist Countries', 15 November 1976, RG59, 1976BANGKO31296, NARA.
234 *New York Times*, 28 September 1975. However, this acceptance of the Soviet offer was strongly opposed within the Cabinet, and the matter was dropped later.

growing Chinese trade influence in Thailand. In mid-September 1975, the Kukrit Government finally decided in principle to drop the law in order to maintain détente with Moscow.[235]

Fourth, the Soviets steadily increased their influence within Thai civil society, and in particular, with some labour leaders and students. On the one hand, they sponsored the visits of several Thai labour leaders to the USSR. For example, Soviet Ambassador Ilyichev invited five Thai labour leaders to visit industrial areas in the USSR in March 1976.[236] On the other hand, the Soviets sponsored Russian language courses offered at Ramkhamhaeng University. Also, Soviet cultural information officials, and in particular Mikhail A Romanov, a Second Secretary for Cultural Affairs, became frequent visitors to Thammasat University.[237] The Soviets attempted to offer scholarships to Thai students to study in the USSR and promote educational exchanges between Thailand and the USSR. However, these attempts were not particularly successful.[238]

Fifth, the Soviet Union sought increasing influence in mainland Southeast Asia. This was largely due to the Sino–Soviet rivalry, which, according to Prasong Suntsiri, Assistant Secretary-General of the Thai National Security Council, was 'intensifying since the normalization of relations between Thailand and China'.[239] The Soviets increasingly supported communist regimes in neighbouring countries. In particular, they began to provide Laos with advisors and material assistance.

In October, a series of border clashes along the Mekong River complicated relations between Thailand and the USSR further. The most notable border incident occurred when a Thai patrol boat was crippled and a Navy man killed by the Laotians on the Mekong River on 17 November. In response, the Thai Government ordered the closure of the border to 1 January 1976. Vietnam immediately announced its full support of Laos, while the USSR regarded Thailand's blockade as an act of intimidation. A *Pravda* commentary stated that an 'unnamed' country attempted to

---

235 'Russia Objects to State Trade Law', *Bangkok Post*, 16 September 1975, 1.
236 'Five Labor Leaders in Russia', 17 September 1976, RG59, 1976BANGKO25959, NARA.
237 'The Soviets in Bangkok: Undercover Diplomacy', 9.
238 'Reporting on Host Country Relations with Communist Countries', 15 November 1976, RG59, 1976BANGKO31296, NARA.
239 'Russians Vie for Control of Thai Reds', *Bangkok Post*, 26 February 1976, 1. Prasong even claimed that the Russians, working closely with Hanoi, sought to finance the activities of the CPT, while the PRC decreased its support. However, there was no evidence supporting this assertion. 'Soviet Relationship with the CPT', 26 February 1976, RG59, 1976BANGKO04354, NARA.

use Laos to expand its own influence or to interdict the process of social transformation in that country.[240] Moscow supplied Laos with basic needs such as fuel and rice through an airlift until the border closure was lifted.

Face-to-face diplomacy was used to manage the border conflict. On 23 November, Ilyichev had a luncheon meeting with Foreign Minister Chatichai at the latter's Soi Rajakru residence. In their three-hour meeting, they discussed the Thai–Laotian border incident. Chatichai told the Russian envoy that Thailand was very disappointed with Vietnam's action. He said that while Thailand had attempted to ease tension with Laos, Vietnam had intentionally made the situation worse. Chatichai also explained to Ilyichev that he did not mean to refer to the Soviet Union when he earlier mentioned a 'third country' that had prodded the Pathet Lao into taking aggressive action against Thailand. He emphasised that Thailand did not want the USSR or any other country to intervene in the incident 'which is strictly a Thai-Laotian affair'.[241] Lastly, citing the rapprochement with Cambodia as an example, Chatichai assured the Russian ambassador that Thailand was not an expansionist nation, but sincerely intended to coexist peacefully with neighbouring countries.

In conclusion, compared with Sino–Thai rapprochement, Thai–Soviet relations were relatively less transformative. Despite Soviet suspicion about the closer Thai–Chinese ties and the border conflicts along the Mekong River, the discourse of détente with Moscow remained intact during the Kukrit administration. A cultural agreement was signed while the business-as-usual relations in both trade and cultural exchanges continued. Further, the Kukrit Government eliminated the State Trading Bill, which the Soviets considered to be an obstacle to the bilateral trade, and approved a new position of Soviet military attaché and the opening of a *Pravda* office in Bangkok.

6.3. 'Withdrawal' or Diplomatic Symptoms? 'The Tiger Coming in the Back Door'?

By the mid-1970s, discursive anxiety that Thailand would become the 'next domino' in Southeast Asia dominated Thai politics. In his birthday speech on 5 December 1975, King Bhumibol observed:

---

240 Quoted in Buszynski, *Soviet Foreign Policy and Southeast Asia*, 106.
241 'FM Sees Russian Ambassador', *Bangkok Post*, 23 November 1975, 1, 3.

some people predicted that, by the end of this year, Thailand will not appear on the world map any more … Next year 'Thailand' would become 'Dieland' … It is a deliberate plan [he continued] to obliterate our country from the world map. We will not allow that to happen. I think that is a kind of intimidation plan. But if we all remain united and help each other, we will not die. And the proof is that everyone who is standing here is not yet dead. This is not yet 'Dieland'.[242]

This section discusses the deep anxiety within Thai elite circles and society following détente with the communist powers, especially the restoration of diplomatic relations with the PRC. It argues that the outburst of mass violence in 6 October 1976 and the return of dictatorship should be explained not only by what Benedict Anderson called 'withdrawal symptoms'[243] but also by diplomatic symptoms, or a clash of diplomatic discourses. Once again, the coup was symptomatic of a discursive tussle between anticommunism and détente.

Despite his diplomatic success, the Kukrit Government faced a domestic crisis. His coalition partners were restive, and a drastic cut in US economic assistance to Thailand and a drop in foreign direct investment caused an economic recession. The fall of Kukrit can be explicated by the discursive struggle. His détente strategy lost the support of the military, which were strongly anticommunist. In particular, General Kris Srivara, the powerful Commander-in-Chief of the Army, started to shift his support to the opposition Democratic Party.[244] Kris's protégé and the new Commander-in-Chief, General Boonchai Bumrungpong, hinted that 'a military coup could occur or other violence before the scheduled March 20 deadline for US withdrawal'.[245] On 11 January 1976, military leaders led by Kris called on Kukrit at his residence and sought his resignation. The following day, Kukrit dissolved Parliament and a new general election was announced to be held in April. At that election, Kukrit himself failed to get re-elected in Dusit, the military-dominated constituency in Bangkok, making the election a disaster for Kukrit.[246]

---

242 Quoted in Nicholas Grossman and Dominic Faulder, eds, *King Bhumibol Adulyadej: A Life's Work* (Bangkok: Editions Didier Millet, 2016), 133.
243 Anderson, 'Withdrawal Symptoms', 48–49.
244 Some also argue that Kukrit's negative policy toward the US resulted in his downfall. Marian Mallet, 'Causes and Consequences of the October '76 Coup', *Journal of Contemporary Asia* 8, no. 1 (1978): 88.
245 Quoted in *Far Eastern Economic Review*, 27 February 1976.
246 See Morell and Samudawanija, *Political Conflict in Thailand*, 262–66.

With the endorsement from General Kris, Prime Minister MR Seni Pramoj headed the newly formed Democrat-led coalition government (from April to October 1976). Pichai Rattakul was his foreign minister. Following the discourse of détente, Pichai, together with Anand Panyarachun, Permanent Secretary of the Foreign Ministry, maintained cooperation with the USSR and China, and sought rapprochement with Thailand's communist neighbouring countries. Although US Ambassador Whitehouse had presented Pichai with a proposal requesting continued American operations at Ramasun with a partial involvement of Thai technicians, the deal went nowhere and all US troops were eventually withdrawn from Thailand by the end of Seni's government.[247]

Meanwhile, General Kris, who was appointed as the new Defense Minister, died suddenly on 23 April. His mysterious death brought about tremendous instability within the military. The other faction within the military decided to invite two exiled 'tyrants', Field Marshals Thanom Kittikachorn and Praphas Charusathien, back to Bangkok. This incident precipitated mass demonstrations. Since the October 1973 uprising, right-wing and ultra-right movements, such as the *Krathing Daeng* (Red Gaurs), *Nawaphon*, and the village scouts, had emerged and increasingly used violence against students' and left-leaning movements. Several peasant leaders and intellectuals were assassinated, such as the socialist leader Boonsanong Punyodyana.[248] The most symbolic and spectacular event was the mass violence on 6 October 1976, when the rightists massacred students at Thammasat University. A military coup stepped in and the king appointed a staunch anticommunist judge, Thanin Kraivichien, as new prime minister (October 1976 – October 1977).

How can we explain these crises from within? In his provocative article, Benedict Anderson rendered this new kind of violence as 'nonadministrative, public and even mob character', and argued that violence and the concomitant U-turn back to dictatorship were 'symptomatic of the present social, cultural, and political crisis', which

---

247 Randolph, *The United Sates and Thailand*, 200, 204.
248 See Katherine A Bowie, *Rituals of National Loyalty: An Anthropology of the State and the Village Scout Movement in Thailand* (New York: Columbia University Press, 1997); Thongchai Winichakul, 'Remembering/Silencing the Traumatic Past: The Ambivalent Memories of the October 1976 Massacre in Bangkok', in *Cultural Crisis and Social Memory: Modernity and Identity in Thailand and Laos*, ed. Charles F Keyes and Shigeharu Tanabe (London and New York: Routledge, 2002), 243–83; Tyrell Haberkorn, *Revolution Interrupted: Farmers, Students, Law, and Violence in Northern Thailand* (Madison: University of Wisconsin Press, 2011).

he described as 'withdrawal symptoms'.[249] Anderson elucidates two structural setbacks, namely the process of class formation and ideological upheaval. On the one hand, Thailand's integration in the American world economic system and its involvement in the Vietnam War had brought about a period of rapid economic growth, which in turn produced a new stratum in Thai society. In particular, he pointed to the expansion of the education system, which had created a more self-aware bourgeoisie or middle class. Then, the mid-1970s saw a range of crises hit the country, ranging from the oil crisis and the prospect of American withdrawal, to the collapse of the Indochinese regimes amid the spectre of communism. These precipitated growing anger and anxiety among the emerging yet insecure middle class, which, in turn, targeted the radicalised students, their demonstrations and democracy itself. The latter were scapegoated. Anderson suggests that these explained why 'many of the same people', who 'sincerely supported the mass demonstrations of October 1973', provided 'the social base for a quasi-popular right-wing movement' that welcomed the return of a military dictatorship three years later.[250]

On the other hand, during the democratic interlude, between 1973 and 1976, an ideological polarisation emerged that pitted popular and democratic left-leaning ideas against the established conservative Thai ideology of nation–religion–king. The former questioned the legitimacy and authority of the latter, including the centrality of the monarchy.[251] Anderson traced the weak descent of so-called 'radical-populist, if not left-wing' nationalism in Thailand to the absence of a historical legacy of anti-colonialism. As Anderson puts it:

> A whole concatenation of crises in Thai society began to crystallize around the symbol of the monarchy. The end of the long economic boom, the unexpected frustrations generated by rapid educational expansion, inter-generational estrangement, and the alarm caused by the American strategic withdrawal and the discrediting of the military leadership – these linked crises were experienced most acutely of all by the insecure new bourgeois strata.[252]

These withdrawal symptoms set the stage for mass violence by the right-wing movements, which culminated in the orchestrated mob massacre on 6 October 1976.

249 Anderson, 'Withdrawal Symptoms', 48–49.
250 Anderson, 'Withdrawal Symptoms', 49, 62.
251 Anderson, 'Withdrawal Symptoms', 76.
252 Anderson, 'Withdrawal Symptoms', 73.

In this book, I add one more setback that fuelled the return of dictatorship: a diplomatic symptom. This diplomatic symptom can be understood within the framework of a discursive clash linked to contestation over who should hold the hegemonic position over Thai foreign policy. During the democratic interlude, the MFA played a pivotal role in the decision-making process in the realm of foreign and security policies, thereby marginalising the role of the military, which had dominated this field for so many years. For instance, the MFA's leading role in forbidding reconnaissance flights from U-Tapao airbase over the Indian Ocean was 'the salient episode' in its marginalisation of Supreme Command's former monopoly on Thai–US security relations.[253] More profound disagreements existed in relation to both the withdrawal of US forces and détente with the communist powers.

A telegram to the State Department written by US Embassy Minister Edward Masters captured this clash of discourses very well. According to Masters, Thailand in 1975 was in the midst of a foreign policy debate between two 'diverse tracks': 'quick accommodation' and 'heightened defense'.[254] On the one hand, those who supported 'quick accommodation', or what I call détente proponents, included 'some officials in the Ministry of Foreign Affairs'. They argued that 'Thailand must work out an arrangement with Communist Indochina' and the communist powers in general to 'permit peaceful coexistence without surrendering to the North Vietnamese'. 'Increasingly referring to their history books', détente proponents recalled that the Thais had been:

> forced to deal with hostile regimes ... on several occasions over the last 700 years. They have coped with the situation in the past and expect to do so in the future.

Highlighting continuity in Thai diplomacy, détente proponents strongly urged a rapid accommodation with the communists. They also found the US military presence in Thailand to be a 'hindrance'.[255]

---

253 'Changes in Thai Foreign Policy and their Effects on the US', 8 April 1975, RG59, 1975BANGKO05946, NARA.
254 'Changes in Thai Foreign Policy and their Effects on the US', 8 April 1975, RG59, 1975BANGKO05946, NARA.
255 'Changes in Thai Foreign Policy and their Effects on the US', 8 April 1975, RG59, 1975BANGKO05946, NARA.

On the other hand, those who favoured 'heightened defense', or what I call détente opponents, included 'senior generals in the Thai defense establishment'. They claimed that Thailand should 'strengthen itself enough militarily to withstand pressures from Hanoi and Beijing without giving them major concessions'. In other words, détente opponents favoured 'a more militant stand toward Hanoi and Beijing'. This position presupposed increased military spending, and a 'slowdown in the diplomatic approach' to Beijing and Hanoi. Enough military capability as a deterrent would 'convince' the communists of the military 'seriousness' and readiness of Thailand's posture. Thus, these groups rendered a continued US military presence in Thailand advantageous, both strategically and tactically. US presence benefited Thailand twofold: first, their presence served as a hedge against those communist countries. Second, the US presence helped guarantee continued military assistance for the Thai military, which was essential to strengthening the armed forces so as to address the communist insurgency and the growing external threat.[256] In brief, leading military leaders hoped for US military forces to 'stay, preferably indefinitely and preferably with enough force to do some good'.[257]

The military and conservatives viewed détente with China, and Kukrit's visit to Beijing in July, with scepticism. They recognised that 'rapprochement with the PRC' was 'advisable', but questioned 'the haste with which MFA is plunging ahead'. They feared that détente proponents, particularly the MFA, 'endangered' Thailand by 'making deals that are ill conceived and giving away too much in the bargaining process'.[258]

Views of Air Marshal Siddhi Savetsila, Secretary-General of the National Security Council, demonstrated the discourse of those détente sceptics. In his interview with Theh Chongkhadikij, the editor-in-chief of the *Bangkok Post*, on 7 September, Siddhi, who also accompanied with Prime Minister Kukrit to Beijing, said that the Chinese behaved like a 'mature adult'. He believed that 'the present leaders intend to let us solve our

---

256 'Changes in Thai Foreign Policy and their Effects on the US', 8 April 1975, RG59, 1975BANGKO05946, NARA.
257 'New Perceptions and Dilemmas in Thailand's Foreign Policy', 25 June 1975, RG59, 1975BANGKO12351, NARA.
258 'New Perceptions and Dilemmas in Thailand's Foreign Policy', 25 June 1975, RG59, 1975BANGKO12351, NARA.

internal problems. The Communist insurgency is a domestic problem'. However, he could not say what the situation would be like if the leadership in Beijing changed.²⁵⁹ Like Deng Xiaoping, Siddhi warned that

> while we drive the wolf away from our front door, we should be careful about the tiger coming in the back door. The tiger is not entering as an invasion force but is using subversion and other forms.²⁶⁰

Unlike Deng, the metaphor of 'tiger' left it unclear whether it referred to the USSR or China, or both.

We cannot explain the crisis only from exogenous or endogenous forces but must also consider the changing discourses and practices of Thai diplomacy. Once again, a clash of diplomatic discourses – between those of diplomats and those of the military – ended in a power contestation, which was ultimately expressed in the military coup after the 6 October 1976 massacre.²⁶¹ We can read the coup, and its concomitant ultra-conservative government under Thanin, as a last attempt to reinstate the anticommunist discourse.

6.4. Conclusion

In Thailand, what Chatichai once described as 'too much democracy'²⁶² gave way to a right-wing authoritarian government and a highly controlled society. Simultaneously, too much diplomacy was now replaced with a brief return to the discourse of a strict anticommunism, as espoused by the military and civilian conservatives. In the next chapter, I will demonstrate how the change in government left détente in disarray, only to be recovered under the guidance of General Kriangsak Chomanan.

---

259 *Bangkok Post*, 7 September 1975, quoted in 'Views of Air Marshal Siddhi', 8 September 1975, RG59, 1975BANGKO18841, NARA.
260 *Bangkok Post*, 7 September 1975, quoted in 'Views of Air Marshal Siddhi', 8 September 1975, RG59, 1975BANGKO18841, NARA.
261 In his New Year speech in 1977, King Bhumibol referred to the 6 October coup as 'a manifestation of what the people clearly wanted', and stated that 'such a manifestation leads us to our mutual understanding and helps us to construct what we desire and surmount all obstacles that might arise'. *Bangkok Post*, 1 January 1977. Quoted in Mallet, 'Causes and Consequences of the October '76 Coup', 91.
262 'Secretary's Meeting with Foreign Minister Chatichai of Thailand', 26 November 1975, RG59, 1975BANGKO24619, NARA.

7

Equidistance: Kriangsak and the Third Détente (1977–1980)

> If we balance the big powers properly, everything will hopefully come out all right.
>
> – General Kriangsak Chomanan, prime minister[1]

After the 6 October 1976 coup, the new prime minister, Thanin Kraivichien, put a halt to détente with the communist powers. His doctrinal anticommunism, in turn, alienated many Thai elites – most of whom by then were détente proponents. A year later, Thanin was ousted by the military groups led by General Kriangsak Chomanan, then Supreme Commander of the Armed Forces. Unlike the old military establishment, Kriangsak was a strong proponent of détente whose foreign policy position was not dissimilar to that of diplomats in the Ministry of Foreign Affairs. As Kriangsak stated, 'I see nothing wrong with being friends with the Soviets and the Chinese ... I want to treat all friendly countries on an equal basis and not discriminate against any friendly country'.[2] Kriangsak went to Beijing in March 1978 and to Washington DC in February 1979. He also became the first Thai prime minister to visit Moscow in March 1979.

By the late 1970s, Kriangsak's return to détente was an attempt to strike a balance between the great powers, or to develop what he described as equidistant relationships. The term became a buzzword in Thai foreign policy discourse.

---

1 *Bangkok World*, 7 October 1977.
2 Richard Nations, 'Thailand: Back in the Game', *Far Eastern Economic Review*, 10 November 1978, 22.

This penultimate chapter argues that despite the rhetoric of strict neutrality, equidistant diplomacy was in fact an alignment with the great powers in a more balanced and equal way. Despite some difficulties in rebalancing the relationship between the Soviet Union and the People's Republic of China (PRC), Kriangsak's Thailand achieved equidistance. However, this diplomacy generated another series of discursive struggles within Thai politics between balanced détente and unbalanced détente that ultimately precipitated the fall of Kriangsak in early 1980. Yet, the discourse of détente in general, and that of 'friendship' with the communist powers in particular, continued intact thereafter.

7.1. Anticommunist Strike-back: Thanin's Inflexible Diplomacy

The year 1976 marked a watershed in world politics which rendered Thai détente difficult to achieve. Mao Zedong's death on 9 September was a significant turning point. He was succeeded by Chairman Hua Guofeng. After eliminating the Gang of Four on 6 October, Hua attempted to build his ideological credentials by supporting Southeast Asian communist parties, including the Communist Party of Thailand (CPT). This was before Chinese foreign policy moved to a non-ideological or realist stance – culminating with the ascent of Deng Xiaoping as paramount leader from the end of 1978.[3]

For the USSR, 1976 marked the decline of détente, culminating with the deployment of SS20s, a medium-range missile, in Eastern Europe and expansion into Africa thereafter.[4] At the same time, the Soviet Union sought to expand its influence in Southeast Asia, especially in Vietnam. Coupled with the Sino–Soviet rivalry, the regional rise of Vietnam had an impact on the peace and stability of Indochina. Furthermore, in the US, the newly elected President Jimmy Carter focused on human rights and

---

3   Chen Jian, 'China and the Cold War after Mao', in *The Cambridge History of the Cold War, Vol. 3: Endings*, ed. Melvyn P Leffler and Odd Arne Westad (Cambridge: Cambridge University Press, 2010), 181–200.
4   Geoffrey Roberts, *The Soviet Union in World Politics: Coexistence, Revolution and Cold War, 1945–1991* (London and New York: Routledge, 1999), 80.

democracy promotion, which in turn complicated its own détente process with the Soviet Union.⁵ The Carter administration also reduced aid to Thailand and accused the Thai Government of human rights violations.

In late 1976, Thai détente was derailed not only by international but also domestic politics. The coup on 6 October 1976 ended the democratic interlude and installed an ardent anticommunist and royalist, Supreme Court justice Thanin Kraivichien, as prime minister (October 1976 – October 1977). His short-lived government was dominated by a form of civilian authoritarianism that attempted to re-establish 'democracy with the King as the Head of State'. Thanin promulgated a 12-year democracy development plan, reinstated a tougher anticommunist strategy, suppressed progressive dissidents and censored the press.⁶ In foreign affairs, he yearned for Cold War certainties. Détente declined accordingly and Thailand's relations with the communist countries returned to that of hostility. Trade decreased while state-sponsored cultural exchanges evaporated. This section provides a brief overview of Thanin's inflexible diplomacy.

Upon taking office, Thanin denounced communism as one of the 'major dangers' to the Thai nation, and demonised 'Communist imperialism'.⁷ His government launched a seminar on 'national security' aimed at indoctrinating bureaucrats on the dangers of communism.⁸ Thanin also advocated massive campaigns to suppress Thai communists, who had been joined by students in the jungle following the 6 October 1976 massacre. The all-out war against communism resulted in more confrontation, clashes and casualties. The CPT responded in kind, including by assassinating Princess Vipawadi Rangsit during her helicopter trip to the South in February 1977.

---

5   Daniel J Sargent, *A Superpower Transformed: The Remaking of American Foreign Relations in the 1970s* (Oxford: Oxford University Press, 2015), 264.
6   See John LS Girling, 'Thailand: The Coup and Its Implications', *Pacific Affairs* 50, no. 3 (1977): 387–405; Kobkua Suwannathat-Pian, 'Thailand in 1976', *Southeast Asian Affairs* (1977): 239–64; Frank C Darling, 'Thailand in 1976: Another Defeat for Constitutional Democracy', *Asian Survey* 17, no. 2 (1977): 116–32; Frank C Darling, 'Thailand in 1977: The Search for Stability and Progress', *Asian Survey* 18, no. 2 (1978): 153–63; Montri Chenvidyakarn, 'One Year of Civilian Authoritarian Rule in Thailand: The Rise and Fall of the Thanin Government', *Southeast Asian Affairs* (1978): 267–85.
7   Thanin had a long history of anticommunism, from his writings on anticommunism to the lectures he gave to the military institutes and universities on the subject. Together with Dusit Siriwan, Thanin also appeared on national radio preaching anticommunist narratives during 1975–1976. See Yos Santasombat, *Power, Personality and Thai Political Elite* (Bangkok: Thai Studies Institute, Thammasat University 1990), Chapter 3.
8   Kukrit Pramoj likened Thanin's schemes to the Red Guards' 'Cultural Revolution' in China. Kamol Somvichian, '"The Oyster and the Shell": Thai Bureaucrats in Politics', *Asian Survey* 18, no. 8 (1978): 835.

In foreign affairs, the Thanin Government pursued a more hostile diplomacy toward the communist regimes, including the USSR, the PRC and the neighbouring countries. Anand Panyarachun, Permanent Secretary of the Foreign Ministry, was relieved of his post, and accused of being 'pro-Communist' due to the role he had played in both establishing diplomatic contacts with communist countries and in negotiating the withdrawal of the American military.[9] Thanin, meanwhile, sought to improve Thailand's relationship with the US and non-Communist world and asserted the status of the Association of Southeast Asian Nations (ASEAN) as an anticommunist organisation. In his foreign visits, Thanin almost always lectured foreign leaders on the 'evils of Communism'. Thanin's orthodox anticommunism alienated many of them.[10]

As a consequence, Sino–Thai relations deteriorated rapidly. While the PRC sought to improve relations, it was frustrated by Thanin's anticommunist and pro-Taiwanese policies.[11] Thanin also prohibited Thai government officials from travelling to China. No Thai delegation visited Beijing until October 1977 when former prime minister Kukrit Pramoj made a private trip.[12] Cultural and sports exchanges were limited, with the exception of a Chinese martial arts troupe that visited in February and a football team in June.

The Chinese Ambassador to Bangkok, Chai Zemin, said that the PRC encountered a 'very difficult time' during the Thanin regime. In August 1977, he had one short meeting with Prime Minister Thanin, which he privately described as 'unproductive'.[13] Chinese influence over the local Sino–Thai community was restricted, but Chai still maintained contact with several Thai military leaders, including General Kriangsak Chomanan, then Supreme Commander of the Armed Forces. Chai also continued to promote visits to Beijing of Thai groups that did not require permission from the government.[14]

---

9   Anand Panyarachun, 'Patakata pised' [Special Lecture], in *Kwam sampan thai-jin* [Sino–Thai Relations: Past and Future Prospect], ed. Khien Theeravit and Cheah Yan-Chong (Bangkok: Chulalongkorn University, 2000), 20.
10 See Kobkua 'Thailand in 1976', 256–63.
11 Even ultra-rightist interior minister, Samak Sundaravej, attended an anticommunist meeting in Taiwan.
12 'Relations with Communist Countries', 17 November 1977, RG59, 1977BANGKO29844, National Archives and Records Administration (NARA) online database.
13 'PRC Ambassador Chai Zemin', 10 May 1978, RG59, 1978BANGKO13331, NARA.
14 'PRC Ambassador Chai Zemin', 10 May 1978, RG59, 1978BANGKO13331, NARA.

Relations between Thailand and the Soviet Union also cooled. The Thanin Government denied entry to at least nine Soviet officials. The vacant positions in the Soviet embassy then became an obstacle to improved Thai–Soviet relations. Ambassador Boris Ilyichev continued to broaden contacts and influence within the Thai elite at all levels, and officially expressed concern and displeasure over what the Soviets viewed as inferior treatment compared with the PRC.[15]

Trade between Thailand and the USSR remained modest. The Soviets continued to export machinery to Thailand, including tractors, textiles and mining equipment while they mainly imported fluorite. The majority of the 25 Soviet ships visiting the port of Bangkok per month were loaded with fluorite and run by Thasos, a joint Thai–Soviet shipping agency. Large-scale financing, provided by the Moscow Narodny Bank office in Singapore, decreased. According to the US embassy in Bangkok, 'the political climate during the past year did not favor growth, but neither was there any noticeable decrease'.[16]

While the Thai–Soviet cultural agreement had been accepted in principle, it had not yet been ratified, and was thus shelved following the 6 October coup. Moreover, there were no cultural or student exchanges during the Thanin Government. The absence of such exchanges meant the only outlet for cultural propaganda was the Soviet souvenir shop in Bangkok, which operated under the auspices of the Soviet Information Service.[17]

It is fair to say, therefore, that the processes of détente ceased under Thanin. Yet, his approach to diplomacy was to alienate many social forces in Thailand, including some factions within the military such as the so-called 'Young Turks'.[18] It was reported that top military leaders grumbled 'that the civilian leaders, particularly Thanin and his Interior

---

15 'Relations with Communist Countries', 17 November 1977, RG59, 1977BANGKO29844, NARA.
16 'Relations with Communist Countries', 17 November 1977, RG59, 1977BANGKO29844, NARA.
17 'Relations with Communist Countries', 17 November 1977, RG59, 1977BANGKO29844, NARA.
18 The 'Young Turks' military group was a group of young military officers and commanders, all of whom graduated from the Royal Chulachomklao Military Academy's Class 7. The members included Colonel Manoon Rupekajorn, Colonel Chamlong Srimuang and Colonel Prajak Sawangjit. See Chai-Anan Samudavanija, *The Thai Young Turks* (Singapore: Institute of Southeast Asian Studies, 1982).

Minister Samak Sudaravej, are too inflexible and too dogmatically obsessed with anticommunism'.[19] Thanin's programs were increasingly seen as short-sighted, counterproductive and detrimental to national security.

By now, important segments of the Thai elite – including both the military and civilians – saw the benefits of détente, particularly with the PRC. These détente proponents, the most important of which included Supreme Commander of the Armed Forces General Kriangsak and Foreign Minister Upadit Pachariyangkun, believed that the PRC occupied an important role as stabiliser in the region. This was due both to its influence in Cambodia and its strength as a counterbalance to Vietnamese expansionism. Following the coup, Kriangsak became good friends with the Chinese ambassador, Chai Zemin, and held numerous cordial talks with him, especially on the Vietnam problem.[20] While visiting Washington in March 1977, Kriangsak confirmed that anticommunism alone would not revive American aid.[21] In other words, Kriangsak, as a new détente proponent, used détente to counter Thanin's anticommunist regime.

In August, many of the Thai military attended the 50th anniversary of the Chinese People's Liberation Army Day celebration in Bangkok. They sought to appear moderate in their attitudes toward the Chinese.[22] In early October, Kukrit Pramoj went to Beijing on a 'personal visit'. Kukrit had meetings with Chinese leaders, including Chairman Hua Guofeng. In their 40-minute meeting on 12 October, Hua assured Kukrit that the PRC was committed to fostering 'firm' and 'friendly' relations with Thailand, and would seek to promote peace between Thailand and its neighbours, especially Cambodia. According to Kukrit, China wished to see a change in the direction of Thai foreign policy. If Thailand improved relations with the PRC, the problem with Cambodia could be easily solved. Kukrit claimed that this was because Cambodian leaders had a 'sensible talk with the Chinese leaders'. The latter strongly urged moderation on Cambodia, which could alleviate the Thai–Cambodian border conflict.[23] After his return to Bangkok, Kukrit revealed that Chairman Hua Guofeng

---

19   *Newsweek*, 10 October 1977, 11.
20   Michael R Chambers, '"The Chinese and the Thais are Brothers": The Evolution of the Sino-Thai Friendship', *Journal of Contemporary China* 14, no. 45 (2005): 612.
21   Richard Nations, 'The Military Muscle In', *Far Eastern Economic Review*, 4 November 1977, 14.
22   'Relations with Communist Countries', 17 November 1977, RG59, 1977BANGKO29844, NARA.
23   Nayan Chanda, 'The Two-year Solution', *Far Eastern Economic Review*, 4 November 1977, 12.

'was not too happy about the Thanin government's management of the relationship with China'. China's concern stemmed from Thanin's militant anticommunist stance.²⁴ While Kukrit was in Beijing, Foreign Minister Upadit met his Cambodian counterpart, Ieng Sary, at the United Nations (UN). Later, Upadit said he and Ieng Sary had 'frank and useful talks. We agreed our two countries should be friends and that the benefits would be immense'.²⁵

Such discursive tussles, between anticommunism and détente, deepened with the deteriorating civil–military relationship. For Thanin, civil–military relations were like an 'oyster-and-shell': if the government did not receive 'the strong support and protection' from the military, it would be like 'an oyster living outside its shell'.²⁶ By mid-1977, the analogy proved correct as Kriangsak increasingly stopped hiding his criticism of the Thanin regime.²⁷ On 7 October, at a press conference he stated:

> the military will not be a protective shell for any individual or group as it will become a worthless shell. In my opinion, the military will be a shell which protects larger things, namely, the Nation, Religion, Monarchy and the People.²⁸

Thus, Kriangsak concluded, 'the general situation had deteriorated to the point that it necessitated the military to beef up its strength for security reasons'.²⁹

The final showdown came when the 'Young Turks' called on the Thanin Government to resign before making an ultimatum that he reshuffle the Cabinet. When Thanin rejected their demands, his government was overthrown on 20 October 1977.³⁰ The coup-makers, led by Admiral

---

24   Kukrit Pramoj, interview, in Chanda, 'The Two-year Solution', 10.
25   Derek Davies, 'Thais Breathe a Sigh of Relief', *Far Eastern Economic Review*, 9 December 1977, 22.
26   Kamol, '"The Oyster and the Shell"', 829.
27   According to the US Embassy in Bangkok:

> at some point – probably around April or May 1977 – the dormant political ambitions of … Kriangsak Chomanan became fully awake, and it was clear that Kriangsak saw himself as a much more capable prime minster than Thanin would ever be. By his careful cultivation of Thailand's restive labour unions, beginning in October 1976, and through his growing and almost public criticism of Thanin to Thai and foreign visitors. Kriangsak steadily moved to establish himself as the logical successor to Thanin.

'Change of Government in Thailand: Developments and Prospects', 21 November 1977, RG59, 1977BANGKO30499, NARA.
28   *Bangkok Post*, 8 October 1977, 1.
29   *Bangkok Post*, 8 October 1977, 1.
30   Later, Thanin was appointed to the Privy Council on 16 December.

Sangad Chaloryu and Kriangsak, justified their action on a number of grounds. Politically, Thanin's 12-year democracy plan was unnecessarily 'long and not in accordance with the wishes of the people'. In terms of the economy, 'foreign investment has decreased and investors have been uncertain of the political situation'. Diplomatically, Thanin's approach was too rigid, and antagonised the communist states – both superpowers and neighbours.[31] With the strong support of the Young Turks, General Kriangsak Chomanan became the new prime minister. He adopted more liberal policies at home and a détente strategy abroad.

In sum, Thanin's diplomatic approach returned Thailand to the pre-1968 anticommunism, and thereby demolished détente. One of the key détente proponents, Kukrit, made a post-coup comment that the overthrow of the Thanin Government was 'long expected' as it was 'the most unstable government in human history', and 'a serious mistake on the part of Thailand'.[32] Kukrit said Thanin was 'so absorbed in fighting Communism that he does not know what he is doing. He has mixed up foreign affairs and foreign relations with doctrinal struggle'. Thanin had begun 'a Pinocchio of the army', but turned out to be 'Frankenstein's monster'.[33]

7.2. The Return of Détente: Kriangsak and the Strategy of Equidistance

This section examines General Kriangsak Chomanan's pivotal shift toward détente. It argues that détente in this period was characterised as equidistance – a position whereby the country pursued more flexible and relatively even-handed relations with the great powers. This culminated in Kriangsak's official visits to three major countries: the PRC in March 1978, the US in February 1979 and the USSR in March 1979. The section begins with a discussion of Kriangsak's politics and diplomatic approach in general, and then elucidates Thailand's relations with the PRC and the Soviet Union, respectively.

---

31 *Bangkok Post*, 21 October 1977, 3.
32 Kukrit, interview, in Chanda, 'The Two-year Solution', 11.
33 Kukrit, interview, in Chanda, 'The Two-year Solution', 12.

7.2.1. Politics and Diplomacy During the Kriangsak Administration: A 'Sigh of Relief'[34]

Within the military, the sudden and mysterious death of the powerful General Kris Srivara in April 1976 brought about a leadership crisis, and the mercurial rise to power of General Kriangsak Chomanan, Supreme Commander of the Royal Thai Armed Forces. While Kriangsak had a weak power base in the Army, he held key positions in the Supreme Command, which had worked closely with the US military leadership throughout the Vietnam War.[35] After Kris died, Kriangsak increasingly became the primary military 'power broker'.[36] Yet, he nevertheless remained on the periphery of the military establishment, while a part of the bureaucratic polity.[37]

Kriangsak was a key détente proponent, and thereby challenged Thanin's ultra-rightist anticommunism. With strong support from the Young Turks, Admiral Sangad Chaloryu and Kriangsak staged a coup on 20 October 1977. Sangad remained the chair of the National Policy Council, but was abruptly sidelined.[38] Kriangsak was his own prime minister, promoting liberalism at home and détente abroad.

In domestic politics, the Kriangsak administration consisted of technocrats that advocated more liberal policies.[39] Declaring himself a true believer in democracy, Kriangsak quickly scheduled elections for April 1979, and engaged in social and economic reforms. His first priority was to restore stability and order. He reinstated freedom of the press, adopted a more moderate and conciliatory position toward political dissidents, students

---

34 Davies, 'Thais Breathe a Sigh of Relief', 18.
35 According to *Newsweek:*
    Kriangsak has had a long working experience with the Americans. He served as a key link in such overt activities as the expansion of US bases facilities in Thailand and also in CIA covert activities, such as the use of Thai mercenaries in the 'secret war' in Laos.
Michael Hudson and Holger Jensen, 'Power Broker', *Newsweek,* 31 October 1977.
36 Marian Mallet, 'Causes and Consequences of the October '76 Coup', *Journal of Contemporary Asia* 8, no. 1 (1978): 87.
37 Girling, *Thailand: Society and Politics*, 219.
38 On the inter-military rivalry during the Thanin and Kriangsak administrations, see Krittin Suksiri, 'Political Conflict under the Government of General Kriangsak Chomanan' (MA thesis, Thammasat University, 2002).
39 Key technocrats included, inter alia, Sunthorn Hongladarom, the 'economic czar' as Deputy Prime Minister for Economic Affairs, Kasame Chatikavanij, Industry Minister, and Prok Amaranand, Deputy Commerce Minister. Sunthorn was a former Ambassador to the US and Secretary-General of SEATO.

and labour unions, and broadened his political base into rural areas.[40] Importantly, Kriangsak introduced an amnesty bill on 16 September 1978 to free 18 defendants, or the 'Thammasat 18', on charges of communist subversion and lèse majesté during the 6 October 1976 demonstrations at Thammasat University. He also granted amnesty to students and activists who went into the jungle to join the CPT.[41] As Kriangsak put it:

> I am convinced that most of [the students] have good intentions towards their country. We have opened the door and invited them all back. I hope they will accept that we have the same ideals, but experience has made us realize that it takes time.[42]

Nevertheless, the government inherited chronic problems from the Thanin Government. These included rising inflation, rising prices, trade deficits and declining foreign investment that haunted Kriangsak's prime ministership in the latter half of 1979.[43] With a more relaxed and pragmatic personality, Kriangsak sought to establish a more open society in Thailand.

In foreign affairs, Kriangsak's priority was to reverse Thanin's rigid anticommunist diplomacy. He instead promoted détente with the great powers, and sought a return to normalisation with communist neighbours. He declared that Thailand's goal was to be on good terms 'with all countries, regardless of ideology'.[44] 'Frustration with Thanin's evident inability to improve relations with Thailand's Communist neighbors', according to US Ambassador to Bangkok, Charles Whitehouse, was 'among the motives leading Kriangsak to advocate replacement of the Thanin government'.[45] As the prime minister put it, 'the government will adhere to a friendly policy toward neighboring countries and will not allow anyone to use Thailand's territory to harm our neighbors'.[46] The 'goal', explained Kriangsak, was:

---

40   See Khien Theeravit, 'Thailand: An Overview of Politics and Foreign Relations', *Southeast Asian Affairs* (1979): 302–4.
41   Ansil Ramsay, 'Thailand 1978: Kriangsak – The Thai who Binds', *Asian Survey* 19, no. 2 (1979): 110.
42   'An Optimistic Kriangsak', *Far Eastern Economic Review*, 21 April 1978, 31.
43   See Vichitvong na Pombhejara, 'The Kriangsak Government and the Thai Economy', *Southeast Asian Affairs* (1979): 312–22.
44   Nations, 'Thailand: Back in the Game', 21.
45   'Kriangsak Government Rounds Out First Six Months in Office', 19 April 1978, RG59, 1978BANGKO11275, NARA.
46   Quoted in Girling, *Thailand: Society and Politics*, 245.

to discourage the Communist Party of Thailand (CPT) from clinging to the Khmer Rouge as their resort. If we could isolate the CPT and make them lose their backing, border problems would be diminished.[47]

Kriangsak believed that friendly relations between communist and non-communist states would not only 'stop the flows of aid to the Communist movement in Thailand', but also 'weaken the Communist united front'. With peace at the frontiers, the government could concentrate its armed forces on communist suppression at home.[48] Kriangsak reassured the public that 'we combat Communists in our country. We are not fighting Communism in Vietnam', or other neighbours.[49]

Once in office, Kriangsak sent letters to the leaders of Vietnam, Cambodia and Laos, inviting them to visit Bangkok. A series of exchange visits between the leaders of Thailand and the neighbouring countries followed. In January 1978, Vietnamese Deputy Foreign Minister, Nguyen Duy Trinh, visited Bangkok. On 31 January, Foreign Minister Upadit held a long meeting in Phnom Penh with Ieng Sary, Cambodian Deputy Prime Minister and Foreign Minister.[50] Lao Deputy Prime Minister and Foreign Minister, Phoun Sipaseuth, visited Bangkok in late March. On 14–17 July, Ieng Sary paid a visit to Bangkok.[51] In early September, during his tour of five ASEAN countries, Vietnamese Premier Pham Van Dong visited Bangkok, and promised that 'Vietnam would not support Communist insurgents in Thailand directly or indirectly'.[52]

---

47 *Bangkok World,* 1 February 1978, 1.
48 Khien, 'Thailand: An Overview of Politics', 306.
49 *Bangkok Post,* 26 October 1976.
50 Drawing from Chinese sources, Christopher Goscha convincingly explains that the Khmer Rouge began to improve its relations with Thailand only in early 1978, as the confrontation with Vietnam was approaching: 'Presumably, the Khmer Rouge understood the need to have peace on their western flank in order to concentrate on the Vietnamese in the east'. Goscha, 'Vietnam, the Third Indochina War and the Meltdown of Asian Internationalism', in *The Third Indochina War: Conflict between China, Vietnam and Cambodia, 1972–1979,* ed. Odd Arne Westad and Sophie Quinn-Judge (London and New York: Routledge, 2006), 175.
51 Richard Nations, 'Only a Morsel from Sary: An Offering, But Little Substance from Bangkok's Visitor', *Far Eastern Economic Review,* 28 July 1978, 11–12.
52 We now know that shortly after his return to Hanoi, Pham told the East German ambassador that he was not bound by pledges given to the Kriangsak Government that he would stop the Vietnamese support to the CPT. As Pham announced, Vietnam would continue 'to contribute to the cause of revolution … in Southeast Asia and the world'. Lorenz M Luthi, 'Strategic Shifts in East Asia', in *The Regional Cold Wars in Europe, East Asia, and the Middle East: Crucial Periods and Turning Points,* ed. Lorenz M. Luthi (Washington DC: Woodrow Wilson Center Press, 2015), 226.

Kriangsak also asked Thai diplomats to make bilateral contact with their counterparts in neighbouring countries.[53] A Vietnamese embassy was opened in Bangkok on 28 February and the first Vietnamese Ambassador to Thailand, Hoang Ban Son, arrived in Bangkok in April.[54] The Kriangsak Government now began to view its communist neighbours as promising markets. Bangkok and Hanoi signed a trade, economic and technical cooperation agreement in January 1978 and Thai trade delegations visited Laos and Vietnam in June. During the visit, Thailand and Laos signed a trade treaty and an overland transit agreement. In Hanoi, a Thai trade delegation worked out trading details with the Vietnamese. As well as offering a US$5 million credit line, Thailand signed a communications agreement restoring telephone and telegraph links with Hanoi.[55] Overall, Thai delegates hoped that increased trade would provide an incentive for neighbouring countries to seek friendly relations.[56]

With the great powers, the Kriangsak Government pursued what it described as an equidistant relationship. That is, while it often described its posture as neutral nonalignment,[57] equidistance was in fact a more flexible, balanced and even-handed diplomatic engagement and alignment with the US, the USSR and the PRC. Referring to the US, Kriangsak said: 'we cannot forget old friends, but we do not anticipate the return of American troops'. Contrary to Thanin, he argued that Thai policy toward the USSR and China had not changed from the period prior to the 1976 coup.[58] Foreign Minister Upadit Pachariyangkun stated:

> Thailand doesn't balance one power off against another ... Our policy is simply to contribute to the conditions for peace and stability in which both our country and the region can prosper.[59]

---

53 Khien, 'Thailand: An Overview of Politics', 305.
54 'Kriangsak Government Rounds Out First Six Months in Office', 19 April 1978, RG59, 1978BANGKO11275, NARA.
55 Richard Nations, 'The Makings of Friendship', *Far Eastern Economic Review*, 22 September 1978, 29.
56 Richard Nations, 'The Indochina Initiative', *Far Eastern Economic Review*, 9 June 1978, 32.
57 For example, Kobkua Suwannathat-Pian claims that the policy of equidistance was 'a more flexible stand on neutrality', which was 'the key in Thailand's dealings with the three great powers'. 'Implicit in the policy of equidistance', she continued, 'was the nonaligned pose which rejected any military pact with any power and the withdrawal of all foreign troops from Thai soil'. See 'Thailand in 1976', 256–57.
58 *Bangkok Post*, 26 October 1976.
59 Richard Nations, 'At Home to an Old foe', *Far Eastern Economic Review*, 15 September 1978, 23.

7. EQUIDISTANCE

Kriangsak's equidistance was constituted by the changing situation in the region. The late 1970s marked a watershed in global and regional politics: The Cold War was fought not only between the democratic and communist regimes but also among the communists themselves. From 1978, conflict in Indochina between Cambodia and Vietnam precipitated skirmishes along the Thai–Cambodian border and fuelled a subsequent refugee crisis, especially at Aranyaprathet in Thailand. This deteriorated into the so-called Third Indochina War when Vietnam invaded Cambodia on Christmas Day in 1978. Within weeks, Vietnamese forces ousted Pol Pot's Khmer Rouge from power and installed the Heng Samrin regime in Phnom Penh. Khmer Rouge guerrillas continued to fight jungle warfare along the Thai border.[60]

This Indochina tragedy was fuelled by a change in the international balance of power. On the one hand, the PRC and the US supported the Khmer Rouge, while, on the other, the Soviet Union backed the Vietnamese. Shortly before the Vietnamese intervention in Cambodia, Hanoi became a member of the Council for Mutual Economic Assistance (COMECON) in June 1978. The Soviet–Vietnamese treaty of friendship and cooperation was signed in November shortly before Hanoi's intervention into Cambodia.[61] Vietnam's January 1979 occupation of Phnom Penh infuriated China, which in turn launched a punitive war against Hanoi a month later. Although the US under Jimmy Carter, who promoted a human rights policy, appeared neutral, its ultimate aim was to contain Vietnam. In so doing, the US prioritised closer relations with China, culminating with the establishment of diplomatic relations on 1 January 1979.[62] At the same time, the Soviet invasion of Afghanistan

---

60 See Goscha, 'Vietnam, the Third Indochina War and the Meltdown of Asian Internationalism', 152–86; and Sophie Quinn-Judge, 'Victory on the Battlefield; Isolation in Asia: Vietnam's Cambodia Decade, 1979–1989', in Westad and Quinn-Judge, *The Third Indochina War*, 207–30.
61 We now know that the treaty with the Soviet Union was a limited agreement. As Sergey Radchenko asserts, 'the assumption that the Soviet Union blessed or even encouraged Vietnam's invasion of Cambodia had no factual basis'. The evidence indicates that 'the Vietnamese leaders did not share their plans with Moscow'. Sergey Radchenko, 'Vietnam's Vietnam: Ending the Cambodian Quagmire, 1979–89', in *Unwanted Visionaries: The Soviet Failure in Asia at the End of the Cold War* (Oxford: Oxford University Press, 2014), 127.
62 See Enrico Fardella, 'The Sino-American Normalization: A Reassessment', *Diplomatic History* 33, no. 4 (September 2009): 545–78; Cecile Menetrey-Monchau, 'The Changing Post-War US Strategy in Indochina', in Westad and Quinn-Judge, *The Third Indochina War*, 65–86; R Sean Randolph, *The United Sates and Thailand: Alliance Dynamics, 1950–1985* (Berkeley: Institute of East Asian Studies, University of California, 1986), Chapter 7.

on 25 December 1979 fundamentally damaged US–Soviet détente, and accelerated Sino–US normalisation.[63] Thailand was thus caught in the middle of this changing global security complex.

More generally, Jimmy Carter's shifting policy toward Southeast Asia was initially driven by the situation in Indochina, including the refugee humanitarian crisis. Thailand now became a focal interest of the US. In early May 1978, US Vice President Walter Mondale paid an official visit to Bangkok to guarantee continued US commitment and military aid. The US also appointed Morton Abramowitz, a China expert and Deputy Assistant Secretary of Defense, as the new Ambassador to Thailand. He arrived in Bangkok in August.[64]

Further US focus on Thailand was fuelled by the Vietnamese military intervention in Cambodia. During Kriangsak's visit to Washington in February 1979, Carter confirmed America's security commitment to Thailand and extended military aid as well as assistance for refugee relief programs. In mid-1979, Kriangsak opened Thai borders to Indochinese refugees on humanitarian grounds. However, the US remained reluctant to become militarily involved in Southeast Asia. Only after the Soviet invasion of Afghanistan in December 1979 did the US begin to feel that the Soviet Union, which threatened to gain strategic predominance in the Indian Ocean, had to be contained and isolated. As a result, the US under President Carter sought to normalise relations with Hanoi. This was a departure from the previous US position and placed the administration at odds with Kriangsak's diplomacy of equidistance, which will be discussed below.

In sum, Kriangsak was a prime minister who, as US Ambassador Whitehouse summed up, was 'a less vocal opponent to Communism', and 'willing to adopt a more flexible approach in dealing with internal dissent as well as external relations'.[65] Kriangsak's diplomatic strategy was thus driven by equidistance as a balanced form of détente with both the Western and communist powers. According to political scientist Khien Theeravit, Thailand now entered a 'new age of enlightenment in foreign affairs'.[66]

---

63   See Odd Arne Westad, ed., *The Fall of Détente: Soviet-American Relations During the Carter Years* (Oslo: Scandinavian University Press, 1997).
64   See Randolph, *The United Sates and Thailand*, Chapter 7.
65   'Kriangsak Government Rounds Out First Six Months in Office', 19 April 1978, RG59, 1978BANGKO11275, NARA.
66   Khien, 'Thailand: An Overview of Politics', 311.

7.2.2. Thai–Chinese Relations: Toward Tacit Alliance

> China has become cooperative, more friendly – especially with Thailand – and we regard this as a stabilizing role.
>
> – Upadit Pachariyangkun, foreign minister[67]

Unlike the Thanin regime, Kriangsak deepened détente with the PRC, culminating with a visit to Beijing in March 1978 and a return visit by Deng Xiaoping in November. Trade and technical cooperation were expanded and relations were strengthened through a realisation of shared security interests in Indochina. This closeness became a priority to contain the Soviet-backed Vietnamese regime, particularly following the Vietnamese invasion of Cambodia in December 1978. By then, the Chinese leadership under Deng had even ended their support to the CPT. While Thailand formally upheld a policy of strict neutrality, it developed a Sino–Thai quasi-alliance, which was part and parcel of an equidistant policy.

During 1977, Kriangsak's détente with the PRC was accelerated by the transformation of Chinese diplomatic practices in Indochina. The Sino–Vietnamese alliance broke down for reasons including increased clashes along their border where Vietnamese maltreatment of ethnic Chinese, or Hoa, in northern Vietnam saw many flee Vietnam. This precipitated a regional refugee crisis, largely composed of the 'boat people'. In response, China terminated aid to Vietnam in mid-1977, which in turn pushed the Vietnamese toward Moscow for economic and military assistance.[68] More broadly, Beijing was increasingly convinced that the Soviet Union intended to move into the power vacuum in the region and seek dominance. This appeared evident by the Soviet–Vietnamese treaty of 3 November 1978. As Chairman Hua Guofeng told the Khmer Rouge leader, Pol Pot, on 30 September 1977, the worsening of the Sino–Vietnamese alliance was due to the 'hand of the USSR' and 'connivance' between the USSR and Vietnam.[69]

---

67 Davies, 'Thais Breathe a Sigh of Relief', 23.
68 Xiaoming Zhang, *Deng Xiaoping's Long War: The Military Conflict between China and Vietnam, 1979–1991* (Chapel Hill: The University of North Carolina Press, 2015).
69 Goscha, 'Vietnam, the Third Indochina War and the Meltdown of Asian Internationalism', 174.

Worried about Sino–Soviet rivalry and the rising Vietnamese threat in Indochina, Chinese leaders led by Deng Xiaoping decided to protect the Khmer Rouge regime at all costs. In so doing, it was necessary for China to strengthen its relationship with Thailand, which had a long border with Cambodia. By then, the Cambodian question – of how to support the Khmer Rouge and block Vietnam's tentative occupation of Cambodia – was central to Chinese foreign policy, and by extension, to Sino–Thai relations.

On 8 December 1977, the PRC officially invited Kriangsak to visit Beijing: the visit took place a few months later, between 29 March and 4 April 1978. In Bangkok, Kriangsak told Chinese ambassador Chai Zemin that 'while Thailand makes its own sincere efforts to be friendly with Cambodia, China could also make a valuable contribution'.[70] He told Chai that the Chinese could play a significant role in smoothing Thai–Cambodian relations.

Before the visit, the Kriangsak Government set a clear agenda for discussions with Chinese leaders. First, Cambodia was the top priority in negotiating with China. As Kriangsak told US Ambassador Whitehouse, China was 'very helpful and friendly', but would try to get clarification regarding Chinese policy toward Thailand.[71] Second, Kriangsak intended not to press the insurgency matter or directly raise the question of China's two-tier policy on foreign relations: while maintaining friendly government-to-government relations, the Chinese Communist Party maintained party-to-party relations with communist parties in Southeast Asia.[72] Kriangsak later told the press that the 'question of Communist insurgency' was an 'internal problem' for which Thailand 'did not look to other countries for a solution'.[73] Third, the Thai Government wished to strengthen its economic relations with Beijing in order to manage the unbalanced payments, and find an alternative source of oil. They wanted the Chinese to buy more products from Thailand and sell crude oil at

---

70 'Thai Prime Minister Kriangsak to Visit China and Soviet Union', 9 December 1977, RG59, 1977BANGKO33681, NARA.
71 'Discussion with Prime Minister Kriangsak Chomanan', 13 March 1978, RG59, 1978BANGKO07547, NARA.
72 Memorandum, Department of Political Affairs, 20 March 1978, Library and Archives Division, MFA POL2/PRC2521/2, Ministry of Foreign Affairs (MFA), Thailand, 199.
73 Quoted in 'Thai Prime Minister Kriangsak Chomanan's Visit to PRC', 4 April 1978, RG59, 1978SINGAP01507, NARA.

a favourable price (see Table 7.1). The drafts of the trade agreement and the agreement on scientific and technical cooperation had been discussed by the two sides in detail.[74]

Table 7.1: Thailand's trade volume with the People's Republic of China (million baht).

Year	Volume	Export	Import	Trade balance
1972	0.0	0.0	0.0	–
1973	0.0	0.0	0.0	–
1974	94.4	2.5	91.9	–
1975	735.3	391.4	343.9	+
1976	2,728.0	1,266.0	1,462.0	–
1977	3,452.0	2,082.0	1,371.0	+
1978	3,201.0	1,498.0	1,704.0	–
1979	6,511.0	1,572.0	4,939.0	–
1980	11,066.0	2,531.0	8,535.0	–

Source: Thai Ministry of Commerce.

In general, Kriangsak's diplomatic aim was to preserve Thailand's sovereignty and promote a more even-handed approach toward the three superpowers. He announced that following his trip to Beijing, he would pay visits to both Moscow and Washington. Kriangsak also authorised the stationing of a Chinese military attaché in Bangkok, following his approval of a Soviet military attaché several months ago.[75] As a goodwill gesture to the Chinese Government, Kriangsak permitted two Chinese-language newspapers, namely *Chung Hua Jit Pao* and *Hsin Chung Yuan*, previously banned during the Thanin regime, to reopen.[76]

For Foreign Minister Upadit, the main objective of the trip was 'to strengthen the good relationship between Thailand and the People's Republic of China'. 'We just want', he continued, 'to exchange views with the Chinese leaders on the general political situation around the world and the region'. Upadit characterised Sino–Thai relations as 'excellent'.[77]

---

74 Memorandum, Department of Economic Affairs, 20 March 1978, Library and Archives Division, MFA POL2/PRC2521/2, MFA, Thailand, 204.
75 'A Bridge to China', *Asiaweek*, 14 April 1978, 30.
76 'Weekly Highlights – March 24-30, 1978', 30 March 1978, RG59, 1978BANGKO09427, NARA.
77 'Proposed Schedule for Thai Prime Minister Visit to China', 29 March 1978, RG59, 1978BANGKO09217, NARA.

On 29 March, Kriangsak was greeted by Chairman Hua Guofeng and Vice-Premier Deng Xiaoping as he arrived at Beijing airport. His 27-member delegation included, inter alia, his wife, Khunying Virat Chomanan, Foreign Minister Upadit Pachariyangkun, Industry Minister Kasame Chatikavanij, Secretary-General of National Security Council Air Marshal Siddhi Savetsila, and Director-General of Political Department of Foreign Ministry, Opart Suthiwart-Narueput. Chinese newspapers reported on Kriangsak's visit positively. In its editorial, the New China News Agency praised Thailand's independent foreign policy and its 'friendly exchanges with Third World countries'. Xinhua also noted the improvement in relations with neighbouring countries, adding:

> These policies, and the righteous stand taken by the Thai government, are beneficial to the common cause of the peoples of Asian countries in uniting against hegemonism, and they have received wide support and admiration.[78]

After the welcoming ceremony at the airport, Deng accompanied Kriangsak on a car journey to Beijing, where they engaged in erudite repartee. Deng mentioned their historical relationship and the greatness of the ancient Thais. In his first formal speech, Kriangsak decided to focus on the historical relationship that Deng had begun. It went on for almost an hour, most of it off-the-cuff. At the end, the Thai prime minister described Deng Xiaoping as not only a great leader but also a great historian, who mastered the knowledge of history.[79] He also urged for the recognition of each nation's institutions. In the Thai case, he meant the monarchy. For Kriangsak, true peace and stability 'can be obtained only if the traditional institutions of each country are respected'.[80]

At the banquet in the Great Hall of the People that night, Deng gave a speech praising the Kriangsak Government for his 'determination to pursue an independent foreign policy'. He expressed that the Chinese supported ASEAN's aims to achieve a 'zone of peace, freedom and neutrality' (ZOPFAN), and opposed hegemonism in the region. He stressed the friendly relations between China and Thailand. 'Since

---

78 'A Bridge to China', 30.
79 At one point, Kriangsak mentioned that the Thais and the Chinese long ago fought a common enemy, namely the Mongols. That did not please the Mongolian ambassador, who was present. 'A Bridge to China', 27.
80 'A Bridge to China', 26–27.

the establishment of diplomatic relations', Deng went on, 'our traditional friendship has been enhanced'. He concluded that Kriangsak and his visit had made 'positive efforts' in strengthening closer ties.[81]

Kriangsak replied by highlighting 'an opportunity' in bilateral relations while praising the Chinese Government for 'adhering to the principles of equality among nations, whereby the big shall not bully the small nor shall the powerful impose its will on the weaker states' as well as its 'stand against interference in internal affairs and violation of sovereignty of others'. Emphasising that ASEAN was not a 'military organization', he believed that Thailand and China had 'common aspiration' with regard to 'peace, stability, and other major issues' in Indochina.[82]

The following day, Kriangsak had his first formal meeting with Deng, who repeatedly emphasised his support for ASEAN and readiness to discuss the establishment of full diplomatic relations with Singapore and Indonesia. Regarding Indochina, their main agenda was the Vietnamese threat to the region. Deng wondered why Vietnam had developed a closer relationship with Moscow, despite its historic ties with Beijing. He then complained that some 90 per cent of Chinese supplies sent to Cambodia via Vietnam 'never turned up'. In their discussions, both leaders agreed on their mutual interest in peace and stability in Indochina, especially their opposition to Vietnamese expansionism.[83] Kriangsak asked Deng to persuade the Khmer Rouge to halt armed incidents on the Thai border. The Chinese vice-premier agreed to help because the security of China, Thailand and Cambodia was interrelated and 'whatever happens to one will affect the others'.[84] When Kriangsak raised the question of Thailand's concern over communist insurgents, Deng reassured him that Beijing would not interfere in Thailand's internal affairs.

On 31 March, Kriangsak had a friendly talk with Chairman Hua Guofeng. Hua appreciated Kriangsak's foreign policy and stressed that the Sino–Thai relationship had broad prospects for development and friendly relations.[85] After that, Kriangsak held a second meeting with

---

81 'State Council Gives Grand Banquet for Thai Prime Minister', *Xinhua General News Service*, 30 March 1978.
82 'State Council Gives Grand Banquet'.
83 Chambers, '"The Chinese and the Thais are Brothers"', 612.
84 'A Bridge to China', 26.
85 'Chairman Hua Meets Thai Prime Minister Kriangsak Chomanan', *Xinhua General News Service*, 1 April 1978.

Deng, which lasted for one and a half hours. The Chinese leader noted his displeasure for hegemonism in the region, by which he meant the Soviet Union, and defined the US as a 'defensive' superpower and the Soviet Union an 'offensive' one. For Deng, the US adopted a weak posture following the Vietnam War, while the Russians became more expansionist. He described the Americans as 'tolerable' while the Russians were 'intolerable'.[86] Concerning the overseas Chinese in Thailand, Deng, according to Kriangsak, reaffirmed that:

> 1) overseas Chinese should adopt the nationality of the country of their residence; 2) if they are not willing or unable to do so, they should strictly adhere to the local laws and customs; and 3) the Chinese government does not, and will not, recognize dual nationality.[87]

On the same day, Kriangsak and Deng signed two agreements: one on trade and the other on scientific and technical cooperation. For trade, they agreed to expand their relations. China would export petroleum products, chemicals, machinery, metal products, agricultural implements, construction materials and general merchandise. In return, Thailand would export sugar, rubber, maize, kenaf (also known as ambary), chemical fibre, fabrics, medicinal herbs, tapioca products, tobacco and mung beans to China. Importantly, Beijing promised to sell 60,000 tons of high-grade diesel fuel at 'friendship' prices.[88] On scientific and technical cooperation, the two countries agreed to exchange know-how and technicians and set up a joint Thai–Chinese committee under ministerial level co-chairmanship to facilitate cooperation.

After the signing ceremony, Kriangsak made remarks at a press conference. His visit to Beijing, he believed, would 'lead to expansion of the base of cooperation and good understanding', and marked 'the start of a new era of cooperation and close and warm friendship' between Thailand and the PRC. The two agreements were, according to Kriangsak, 'a symbol of our firm intention to further develop and expand our bilateral relations'.[89]

---

86 'A Bridge to China', 27.
87 'Kriangsak Comments on China', 10 April 1978, RG59, 1978BANGKO04411, NARA.
88 'An Optimistic Kriangsak', 31; Nations, 'The Makings of Friendship', 30.
89 'Thai Prime Minister Speaks of Success of Visit to China at Beijing Press Conference', *Xinhua General News Service,* 1 April 1978.

That night, the Thai Government hosted a return banquet for the Chinese. Premier Kriangsak gave a speech deeming this visit a 'complete success'. Kriangsak stressed that both sides concurred in 'several important matters relating to peace and stability in our region' and their mutual cooperation and continued dialogue at the policy level.[90]

Deng asserted that Kriangsak's visit to Beijing was 'a major event in the history of Sino-Thai relations'. He highlighted that Thailand and the PRC shared 'identical views on a number of important international issues', and supported 'one another in the task of combatting hegemonism and building up their countries'.[91] The Chinese leaders, including Chairman Hua Guofeng and Vice-Premier Deng Xiaoping were invited for reciprocal visits to Bangkok. The Chinese leaders also extended their invitation to the King and Queen of Thailand to visit Beijing.

On 1 April, Kriangsak and his entourage left Beijing for tours in Shanghai, Guilin and Guangzhou, before catching the train to Hong Kong on 4 April. The following day, Kriangsak addressed the Hong Kong Foreign Correspondents' Club. He said that 'the horizontal base for cooperation' between Thailand and the PRC 'has been expanded and consolidated' and sought to build 'permanent vertical structures in the form of concrete and substantive exchanges and joint efforts'.[92] Through his 'frank and sincere' and 'straight-forward' talks with the Chinese leaders, he believed that they would support Thailand's diplomatic approach, especially its efforts to normalise relations with Indochinese neighbours.[93] For Kriangsak, the PRC was a 'peace-loving country' as 'the Thai and Chinese peoples have been in contact with each other for centuries', and 'never been at war with one another'. Both countries shared 'similar interests' in the region.[94]

Regarding relations with the great powers, the Thai prime minister said he welcomed the constructive participation of the great powers if their aims were beneficial to the region. As he put it:

---

90 Speech by H.E. General Kriangsak Chomanan at the banquet in honour of H.E. Chairman Hua Guafeng, Premier of the People's Republic of China, March 1978, Library and Archives Division, MFA POL7/PM2521/1, MFA, Thailand, 26–30.
91 'Thai Prime Minister and Mrs. Chomanan Give Grand Banquet in Beijing', *Xinhua General News Service,* 1 April 1978.
92 'Kriangsak Comments on China', 10 April 1978, RG59, 1978BANGKO04411, NARA.
93 'Kriangsak Addresses Hong Kong Foreign Correspondents' Club on China Trip', 7 April 1978, RG59, 1978BANGKO10242, NARA.
94 'Kriangsak Comments on China', 10 April 1978, RG59, 1978BANGKO04411, NARA.

> We cannot prevent rivalry among the major powers, but we hope that for Southeast Asia, this rivalry will be in the nature of who can do more to better the lives of the peoples of this region and not who can gain military or strategic advantage.[95]

Kriangsak said he was also prepared to visit both the US and the USSR. The Thai prime minister reiterated that the government 'will establish good and friendly relations with all countries, irrespective of their economic, social or administrative systems'.[96]

After returning to Bangkok, Kriangsak hosted a dinner for the Chinese ambassador, Chai Zemin, who was seen by the Thai Government as a key person in fostering Sino–Thai relations.[97] Chai was subsequently promoted to head the Chinese Liaison Office in Washington and replaced by Chang Wei-lieh, former Ambassador to the Mongolian People's Republic in Ulan Bator.[98]

Following Kriangsak's eight-day visit to the PRC, the Thais and the Chinese had thus moved toward a sort of tacit alliance. For its part, China envisioned Thailand as a pivotal state both to check Soviet influence in the region and improve relations with ASEAN. The Chinese hoped that the Thais would encourage Indonesia and Singapore to establish full diplomatic ties with Beijing. On the other hand, Kriangsak's heavy tilt toward Beijing was built upon the aspiration for better relations with Cambodia, and to contain Soviet-backed Vietnam. Over the long term, warmer Sino–Thai relations would isolate the domestic communist insurgents. In order to alleviate pressing economic problems, the Thais also strived for stronger trade relations, especially the import of Chinese oil. Above all, both countries shared common concerns, namely the possibility of the Vietnamese domination of Cambodia, and Soviet–Vietnamese collusion in Southeast Asia.

---

95 'Kriangsak Addresses Hong Kong Foreign Correspondents' Club on China Trip', 7 April 1978, RG59, 1978BANGKO10242, NARA.
96 'Kriangsak Comments on China', 10 April 1978, RG59, 1978BANGKO04411, NARA.
97 Chai also presented the formal invitation for the Thai king and queen to visit Beijing, but Kriangsak indicated that the king would not visit the PRC in the foreseeable future. 'PRC Ambassador Chai Zemin's Return to Thailand', 17 April 1978, RG59, 1978BANGKO10979, NARA; and 'Sino-Thai Relations', 8 May 1978, RG59, 1978BANGKO13097, NARA.
98 'PRC Ambassador Chai Zemin', 10 May 1978, RG59, 1978BANGKO10979, NARA.

Thai–Chinese relations continued to broaden with an increase in both Thai delegations to Beijing, and Chinese counterparts to Bangkok. This included, for example, a 24-member private trade delegation led by Major General Pramarn Adireksarn, President of the Association of Thai Industries, which left Bangkok on 2 June to attend an organising meeting for the eighth Asian Games, to be held in Bangkok in December 1978. Also in June was an 18-member Thai press delegation, headed by Phongsak Phayakkawichian, President of Reporter's Association and a 24-member trade delegation led by Commerce Minister Nam Phunwatthu.[99] The group of Thai–Chinese Friendship Association, presided over by former foreign minister Major General Chatichai Choonhavan,[100] met with Vice-Premier Deng Xiaoping on 15 June. In the evening, Chatichai, who was in Beijing, telephoned Prime Minister Kriangsak to report his meeting with Deng, and confirmed that Cambodian Deputy Prime Minister Ieng Sary would visit Bangkok in July.[101]

The first Chinese trade delegation to Thailand, headed by Hu Fu-hsing, arrived in Bangkok in early August 1978. They went to the rice demonstration station in Rangsit, where they observed the assembly and demonstration of two paddy planting machines, given to Thailand by China during the Kriangsak visit.[102] On 31 August, a Thai National Assembly delegation, headed by General Tawit Seniwong Na Ayuthaya, met with Vice-Premier Deng Xiaoping in Beijing. While Deng emphasised Soviet expansionism in Southeast Asia and Vietnam's role as a Soviet pawn, Tawit raised the issue of Chinese support for Thailand's communist insurgency. The latter said he understood China's two-tier policy between state and party policies, but found it unconvincing. Deng replied that Chinese support for the CPT was rooted in history, and was a complicated question. It was part of the international communist

---

99 Royal Thai Embassy in Beijing to the Ministry of Foreign Affairs, 15 May 1978, Library and Archives Division, MFA POL2/PRC2521/3, MFA, Thailand, 83; 'Sino-Thai Relations', 7 June 1978, RG59, 1978BANGKO16246, NARA.
100 The Thai-Chinese Friendship Association was established on 22 December 1975. It was intended to promote friendship and mutual understanding between the peoples of the two countries. It served as a focal point for cultural exchanges. Former Foreign Minister Chatichai Choonhavan was the first president.
101 'Thai-PRC Relations and Ieng Sary Visit', 16 June 1978, RG59, 1978BANGKO17347, NARA.
102 'Sino-Thai Scientific and Technical Cooperation Treaty Ratified', 21 August 1978, RG59, 1978BANGKO24054, NARA.

movement in general, and could not be treated simply as a bilateral matter. He particularly focused on the competition between the PRC and the USSR for loyalty of communist groups throughout the world.[103]

As relations between China and Vietnam worsened, and following the signing of the Soviet–Vietnamese treaty in November, Thailand became increasingly central to China's regional strategy. In private talks with Thai leaders, the Chinese now referred to the possibility that the Khmer Rouge may be forced to resort to guerrilla warfare against the Vietnamese.[104] Yet they remained cautious about becoming involved militarily and instead settled on offering support to the Khmer Rouge. With the prospect of a Vietnamese conquest of Cambodia looking ever more likely, the Chinese increasingly anticipated supporting the Khmer Rouge in a campaign fought from the western mountain ranges. In such a case, it would be unavoidable that the Chinese would wish to send weapons and food via Thailand.

Vice-Premier Deng Xiaoping began his ASEAN tour by arriving in Bangkok on 5 November for a five-day official visit. Coincidently, his visit occurred two days after the Soviet–Vietnamese treaty was signed in Hanoi. At Don Muaeng Airport, he was received by Kriangsak and representatives of the Chinese community. In his arrival statement, Deng stated that the purpose of the visit was:

> [to] strengthen and develop the traditional friendship between our two peoples and the cooperation between the two governments and to learn and benefit from the experiences of the Thai people in building up their country.[105]

Accompanying Deng were his wife, Jjo Lin, and a total party of 40 including Foreign Minister Huang Hua.

Following a warm and friendly reception at the airport, Deng went to meet with King Bhumibol, Queen Sirikit and Princess Maha Chakri Sirindhorn at the Royal Palace. He asked for and was given royal permission to attend the 7 November ordination ceremony for His Royal Highness Crown Prince Vajiralongkorn at the Temple of the Emerald Buddha.[106]

---

103 'Deng Xiaoping Meeting with Thai General: Thai Insurgency', 1 September 1978, RG59, 1978BEIJING02759, NARA.
104 'Deng Meeting with Thai Journalists', 6 October 1978, RG59, 1978BEIJING03225, NARA.
105 'Vice-Premier Deng Visits to Thailand', *Beijing Review,* 10 November 1978, 3.
106 See 'The Marxist and the Monarchy', *Far Eastern Economic Review,* 17 November 1978, 10–12.

This gesture indicated Deng's sensitivities towards the symbolism of both the Thai monarchy and Buddhism, which the Thai Government believed demonstrated his support for the key institutions of the country.[107]

The following day, Deng held a meeting with Kriangsak. Besides bilateral relations, the Cambodian question was central to their discussion. According to Kriangsak, Deng admitted in private talks that 'China was giving moral, political and strong material support to the present Cambodian government to maintain its stability in fighting against Vietnamese invasion'. Deng felt that Cambodia was 'fighting against Soviet–Vietnamese ambitions in the area, which will contribute to peace and security to this region and serve our national interests as a whole'. He said that every country including the US, 'should give Cambodia at least moral support'. The Chinese vice-premier also urged Thailand and other ASEAN countries to make 'some political gestures' if Vietnam launched a military invasion.[108] For Deng, the Chinese response would be 'guided and gauged by steps which Vietnam is taking'. While the Chinese would 'not be afraid to lose some of her manpower for Cambodia', Deng refused to 'say definitely at present how China would use her manpower or commit her troops to the fighting'.[109]

Kriangsak supported 'the idea to keep Cambodia independent and free from outside influence'. He asked Deng to pass his 'assurance to Pol Pot or Ieng Sary that Thailand will not allow anyone to use our territory to create troubles for Cambodia'. Kriangsak asked that Cambodia send its ambassador to Thailand 'as soon as possible', and wished to 'help Cambodia economically'.[110] According to Kriangsak, Deng also made a strong criticism of the closer Soviet–Vietnamese relations. 'Vietnam will be more ambitious and aggressive after signing the new pact with the USSR', and become the 'Cuba' of Asia.[111]

---

107 'Arrival of PRC Vice-Premier Deng Xiaoping', 6 November 1978, RG59, 1978BANGKO32603, NARA.
108 These quotations are from Prime Minister Kriangsak's written debrief on the Deng Xiaoping visit, prepared for his 14 November meeting with US Ambassador to Thailand, Morton Abramowitz. 'Ambassador's Call on Prime Minister – Discussion of Refugees and Visit to the US', 15 November 1978, RG59, 1978BANGKO16246, NARA.
109 'Ambassador's Call on Prime Minister – Discussion of Refugees and Visit to the US', 15 November 1978, RG59, 1978BANGKO33743, NARA.
110 'Ambassador's Call on Prime Minister – Discussion of Refugees and Visit to the US', 15 November 1978, RG59, 1978BANGKO33743, NARA.
111 'Ambassador's Call on Prime Minister – Discussion of Refugees and Visit to the US', 15 November 1978, RG59, 1978BANGKO33743, NARA.

Both leaders reached an agreement on the sale of Chinese crude oil and high-speed diesel oil to Thailand at the friendship price. Thailand granted permission for the Chinese to overfly Thailand on a weekly Kunming–Rangoon–Phnom Penh flight. Deng also suggested the establishment of a direct Bangkok–Beijing civil air link. Kriangsak said his government would take the proposal into consideration. Thailand asked for Chinese assistance in getting permission to fly to Angkor Wat. Deng told Kriangsak that a delegation of a Civil Aviation Authority of China would be dispatched to Bangkok to discuss the civil aviation agreement in detail later.[112]

In the evening, the Kriangsak Government hosted a banquet for Deng and his entourage at Government House. Kriangsak said that during Vice-Premier Deng's stay in Bangkok, he

> will have an opportunity personally to see and learn about Thailand and her people, thus increasing your understanding of our country. This understanding is an important foundation for the further development of relations and cooperation between our two nations.

The steadily growing bilateral relationship, for Kriangsak, would contribute to 'the maintenance of peace, stability and progress in this region'.[113]

Vice-Premier Deng appreciated the Thai policy of independence and its interest in developing friendly relations with countries regardless of their sociopolitical systems. Deng highlighted a 'highly turbulent' international system with 'hegemonism' that posed 'a serious threat to world peace and security'. These hegemonists, he continued, had 'stepped up their expansionist activities in Asia, particularly in Southeast Asia'. He praised ASEAN, which was 'farsighted when it adheres to the proposal for establishing a zone of peace, freedom and neutrality', and Thailand, which had an increasingly important role in the region.[114]

On 7 November, Deng held informal talks with former prime minister Kukrit Pramoj, and former foreign minister Chatichai Choonhavan, now the President of Thai–Chinese Friendship Association. Then he attended

---

112 'Deng Xiaoping's Visit to Thailand – An Overview', 11 November 1978, RG59, 1978BANGKO33207, NARA.
113 'Vice-Premier Deng Visits to Thailand', 3.
114 'Vice-Premier Deng Visits to Thailand', 3.

a religious ceremony to witness Crown Prince Vajiralongkorn enter into the monkhood for a fortnight. Being allowed into this intimate ceremony signified to the Thai people that the relationship with China was going to a new level.[115] After that, Deng, together with Kriangsak, went to watch the final game of the First World Badminton Championships, organised by the World Badminton Federation. Kriangsak then hosted and cooked a dinner at his residence.[116]

The next day, Deng gave a speech to a press conference expressing his satisfaction with his visit, and stressed the accelerating development of diplomatic, political, economic, scientific and cultural ties with Thailand. He also reiterated the Chinese Government's stance toward the overseas Chinese, maintaining that they should adopt Thai citizenship and respect Thai laws, while reaffirming China's two-tiered policy, which made the distinction between state-to-state and party-to-party relations. Referring to Chinese support for the CPT, he recognised that the problem had historical antecedents and could not be solved overnight. The vice-premier assured the Thais that the Chinese would be frank and sincere in discussing this problem with Thailand.[117]

Deng directly criticised Vietnamese Premier Pham Van Dong's pledge of noninterference during his September visit in Bangkok. As he put it, 'if the Chinese people do just what Pham Van Dong said, it will bring disaster to Asia and the Pacific'. 'If anyone tells a lie, deceives, or sells out his soul', continued Deng, 'he will not win friendship. Therefore, I will not learn from Pham Van Dong'. He denounced Vietnam as the 'Cuba of the Orient', involved in 'hooliganism' in Southeast Asia.[118] Deng strongly opposed the 'hegemonists', including the 'big hegemonist', and the 'small hegemonist', which demonstrated ambitious aggression against Southeast Asia, in particular against Cambodia: a clear reference to the Soviet Union and Vietnam. He went on, 'we are waiting to see how far they advance into Cambodia before deciding on countermeasures'.[119]

---

115 See Chambers, '"The Chinese and the Thais are Brothers"', 599–629.
116 'Deng Xiaoping's Visit to Thailand – An Overview', 11 November 1978, RG59, 1978BANGKO33207, NARA.
117 'PRC Deputy Premier Deng Xiaoping's Press Conference', 9 November 1978, RG59, 1978BANGKO33056, NARA.
118 'PRC Deputy Premier Deng Xiaoping's Press Conference', 9 November 1978, RG59, 1978BANGKO33056, NARA.
119 'PRC Deputy Premier Deng Xiaoping's Press Conference', 9 November 1978, RG59, 1978BANGKO33056, NARA.

After his press conference, Deng flew to the Thai military centre at Lop Buri where he was given a two-hour demonstration by the Thai military. The live-fire show included mock attacks by Thailand's newly acquired F5-Es, delivering Thai manufactured ordnance, helicopter-borne infantry assault and artillery bombardment. In a show of friendly relations, Thai parachutes exploded in a shower of Chinese-language banners stating Thai–Chinese friendship and welcoming the vice-premier.[120]

On 9 November, the two foreign ministers, Huang and Upadit, signed three protocols, the first of which was the establishment of the joint trade committee. This provided for annual meetings to decide on trade schedules, to review implementation of the trade agreement, to study and explore measures to expand bilateral trade, to seek solutions to problems, and to make appropriate recommendations. The second protocol was on the importation and exportation of commodities. The third referred to technical and scientific cooperation, providing a total of 29 projects. There were 12 Chinese projects, such as research into potash deposits, sugar manufacture, rubber planting and processing, aquaculture of fish and prawns, horticulture, grape development, rice seed hybridisation, prevention and control of disease, and Thai language training for three students. The 17 Thai projects included education in herbal medicine, rural health service, silk production, petrochemical industry, reforestation, irrigation, pig rearing, flower planting and hydrological data from the upper Mekong.[121]

Deng's five-day visit to Bangkok marked a significant turning point in Thai–Chinese relations amid the deteriorations of Sino–Vietnamese relations and Vietnamese–Cambodian relations. In early December, Hanoi publicly announced its aim for regime change in Phnom Penh and on 25 December, its troops intervened in Cambodia. On 7 January 1979, the Pol Pot regime collapsed, and a guerrilla war commenced along the Cambodian–Thai border. The international community, including ASEAN, condemned Vietnam.[122] After his visit to Washington to meet

---

120 'Deng Xiaoping's Visit to Thailand – An Overview', 11 November 1978, RG59, 1978BANGKO33207, NARA.
121 'Deng Xiaoping's Visit to Thailand – An Overview', 11 November 1978, RG59, 1978BANGKO33207, NARA.
122 'ASEAN Unites in Anger', *Far Eastern Economic Review*, 19 January 1979, 12–14. See Lee Jones, *ASEAN, Sovereignty and Intervention in Southeast Asia* (Hampshire: Palgrave Macmillan, 2012), Chapter 4.

with President Jimmy Carter in late January, Deng assumed he had been given a green light from the US to launch punitive attacks against Hanoi in mid-February.[123]

Wishing to avoid the attention of the Soviet embassy in Bangkok, Deng led a secret military delegation to Thailand, landing at U-Tapao Airport on 13 January. He was accompanied by Deputy Foreign Minister Han Nianlong and an interpreter. Deng met with Kriangsak the following day. While the meeting did not last long, it laid the foundations for a Sino–Thai quasi-alliance during the Third Indochina War. Kriangsak agreed to provide the Chinese with logistic support and transport facilities to supply the Khmer Rouge, and to allow Khmer Rouge leaders to cross the Thai borders.[124]

During their meeting, Deng told Kriangsak that the Chinese were going to support the Khmer Rouge at all costs. He also asked the Thai Government to cooperate with the Chinese, and allow them to use Thai territory to supply the Khmer Rouge forces. The Chinese vice-premier also asked Thailand to use its influence in ASEAN not to recognise the Vietnam-installed Hang Samrin regime in Cambodia. According to Deng, Kriangsak replied that 'currently we do not recognize them'.[125]

In return for any sort of Thai help, Kriangsak insisted that the Khmer Rouge halt supporting the Thai communist insurgency. Deng replied that the Chinese had already instructed Ieng Sary while he was in Beijing. He reassured Thai leaders that from now on, the communist insurgency would be an internal affair rather than an inter-communist one. Also, Deng asked Kriangsak to help Ieng Sary to transit through Thailand on his return to Khmer Rouge zones, and to meet with Ieng 'to discuss or negotiate directly the problems of your two countries'. 'Ieng Sary', said Kriangsak, 'can come. I'll do all I can to get him back through'. However, Kriangsak said he would not meet with Ieng Sary once he arrived in

---

123 Zhang, *Deng Xiaoping's Long War*.
124 Nayan Chanda, *Brother Enemy: The War after the War – A History of Indochina since the Fall of Saigon* (New York: Collier Books, 1986), 348–49. The Deng-Kriangsak secret meeting was discussed in details when Deng met with Ieng Sary in Beijing on January 15, 1979. See Goscha, 'Vietnam, the Third Indochina War and the Meltdown of Asian Internationalism', 178–80.
125 Goscha, 'Vietnam, the Third Indochina War and the Meltdown of Asian Internationalism', 178.

Thailand because of his public stance of strict neutrality. According to Deng, Ieng Sary could contact the Thai Government via the Chinese embassy in Bangkok or through Chatichai Choonhavan.[126]

Finally, Deng asked how the Chinese could transport material assistance to the Khmer Rouge areas. Deng said that Kriangsak suggested three ways. First, the Chinese could send arms to Koh Kong, a Cambodian island close to the Thai border, and then transport them to Khmer Rouge areas by small boats flying foreign flags. Kriangsak recommended that the Khmer Rouge should defend these areas, so as to receive Chinese aid. Second, the Chinese could supply arms and merchandise camouflaged as commercial goods in large boats flying foreign flags. When they arrived in Thailand, the Thai Army would unload them and the Chinese could parachute these arms by plane into northern Cambodia. Third, Beijing could sell oil to Thailand at favourable prices and during the shipping to Bangkok, the Chinese could stock arms in the cargo. Upon arrival, the Thai Army would unload them, and later transport them by truck from Bangkok to Cambodia.[127]

From the secret meeting with Deng, Kriangsak, while still maintaining a façade of neutrality, committed to help Chinese resupply operations to the Khmer Rouge. As Han Nianlong put it:

> the most important problem is to maintain links to Thailand based on a common matter: oppose [Vietnam]. When it comes to the [Vietnamese] occupation of Cambodia and its threat to Thailand, the Thai support Cambodia. They say they are neutral, but it is only officially so. In reality they intend to aid Cambodia.[128]

Particularly following the Vietnamese invasion of Cambodia, the Cambodian question became the focus of closer Thai–Chinese relations. The Thais viewed China's punitive war against Vietnam in neutral or positive ways. Yet, in public Kriangsak maintained strict neutrality. At a press conference on 18 February, Kriangsak stated that 'we would rather see them negotiate than use force against each other. We don't want

---

126 Goscha, 'Vietnam, the Third Indochina War and the Meltdown of Asian Internationalism', 178–79.
127 Goscha, 'Vietnam, the Third Indochina War and the Meltdown of Asian Internationalism', 179.
128 Quoted in Goscha, 'Vietnam, the Third Indochina War and the Meltdown of Asian Internationalism', 180.

the war to intensify because we want to have peace and stability in the region'. 'There is only one thing I must say', he continued, 'just don't get us involved. It's a matter for other people to fight about'.[129]

In addition, Thailand and the PRC also deepened trade and technical cooperation, which can be seen from the surge in visits between the two countries. Between 10 and 15 January 1979, Deputy Prime Minister Sunthon Hongladarom led a Thai delegation to Beijing to negotiate additional oil supplies for Thailand.[130] On 14 January, both Thai and Chinese leaders signed a five-year protocol on the purchase of crude oil at favourable prices. According to Prok Amaranand, Deputy Minister of Commerce, the PRC would sell Thailand 600,000–800,000 tons of crude oil in 1979, 800,000 tons in 1980 and 1,000,000 tons per year between 1981 and 1983. The Thais would use Chinese crude oil to produce high-speed diesel fuel, which had been in short supply.[131]

The Chinese also dispatched seven trade-related visits, culminating in the March visits by Minister of Foreign Trade, Li Qiang, and Minister of Communications, Zeng Cheng. Out of five cultural delegations to Thailand, the highlight was a tour by the Eastern Music and Dance Ensemble between 19 December and 29 January, and a visit by the Chairman of the Chinese People's Association for Friendship with Foreign Countries, Wang Pingnan, during March.[132]

As the US Ambassador to Bangkok, Morton Abramowitz summed up, Thailand's objective was 'to enlist PRC support for easing of tension with' Cambodia, while China's intention was to 'strengthen its influence with Thailand', especially as the Soviet Union and Vietnam attempted to extend their influence over Indochina. The Thais, according to Abramowitz, seemed 'more and more willing to accommodate the PRC'.[133] Thailand's main objective was to get Vietnam out of Cambodia.[134]

---

129 Thai newspapers expressed much the same line. *The Nation* presented a more favourable editorial, noting that 'however much we may want the tensions to ease, there is inevitably a certain warmth in our heart that there is somebody who is not allowing Vietnam to run amuck in Southeast Asia'. *The Nation*, 19 February 1979, 'Thai Reaction to Sino-Vietnamese Hostilities', 19 February 1979, RG59, 1979BANGKO13097, NARA.
130 See also Krajang Phantumnavin, 'Negotiating to Buy Sheng Li Oil', in *Learn from the Teacher, Know from the Boss, and Gain from Work* (Bangkok, 2016), 182–99.
131 'Thailand and China Sign Oil Protocol', 19 January 1979, RG59, 1979BANGKO02188, NARA.
132 'Trends in Sino-Thai Relations', 20 March 1979, RG59, 1979BANGKO09309, NARA.
133 'Trends in Sino-Thai Relations', 20 March 1979, RG59, 1979BANGKO09309, NARA.
134 See Gregory V Raymond, 'Strategic Culture and Thailand's Response to Vietnam's Occupation of Cambodia, 1979–1989 A Cold War Epilogue', *Journal of Cold War Studies* 22, no. 1 (Winter 2020): 4–45.

As Sino–Vietnamese hostilities increased and Soviet military activities in Cambodia swelled, it seemed natural for China to move closer to Thailand in many ways. First, the Chinese leaders sought to offer a certain form of security commitment to Thailand. On 4 April, the new Chinese Ambassador to Thailand, Chang Wei-lieh, made a statement saying the Chinese would support the Thai people should the Vietnamese 'hegemonists' attack.[135] In May, Deputy Foreign Minister Song Zhiguang reportedly said that the Chinese would support Thailand in the face of any acts of aggression by the Vietnamese over the Cambodian conflict.[136]

The Chinese moves prompted Kriangsak to inform the press on 9 May that Thailand would not accept any military aid from China in the event of Vietnamese aggression. He stressed his policy of equidistance by saying that 'neither do we want Russian or American troops to be rushed to our country to our rescue'. That, he claimed, would be an embarrassment:

> The Thai were capable of defending themselves, and Thailand would not allow itself to be pushed or dragged by other countries into the Cambodian conflict.[137]

While it was necessary for the prime minister to publicly deny any military cooperation with the PRC, Kriangsak began to take this option seriously. In early June, he asked his close confidante, Lieutenant General Tuanthong Suwannatat, the Deputy Chief of Staff of the Supreme Command, to convene a small meeting, later known as the 'War Council', to discuss this option in detail.[138]

After the meeting, Kriangsak dispatched a secret military mission to Beijing to raise the issue of China's military commitment to Thailand. The delegation included three military officials, including Lieutenant General Phin Gaysorn, Colonel Pat Akkaniput and Colonel Chavalit Yongchaiyudh. On 24 June, they provided Vice-Premier Deng Xiaoping with briefings on the situation in Thailand and Thai concerns over the

---

135 Kriangsak found the current Chinese Ambassador to Thailand 'inflexible' and 'difficult to deal with'. He told the US Ambassador to Thailand that he wished he could have got back Chai Zemin, who now led the Chinese Liaison Office in the US. 'Ambassador's Meeting with Kriangsak', 28 September 1979, RG59, 1979BANGKO39760, NARA.
136 'Chinese Commitment to Thailand', 10 May 1979, RG59, 1979BANGKO15682, NARA.
137 The US Embassy in Bangkok did not take Kriangsak's words at face value. It was believed that they were merely rhetoric in order to reassure the public. 'Chinese Commitment to Thailand', 10 May 1979, RG59, 1979BANGKO15682, NARA.
138 Pat Akkaniput, interview, in *Cremation Volume In Honor of General Pat Akkaniput* (Bangkok, 2016), 43; *Biography of General Chavalit Yongchaiyudh* (Bangkok, 2004), 112.

Vietnamese strategy. Deng first promised that, in the event of a Vietnamese invasion of Thailand, the Chinese Army would launch military operations against Hanoi. Second, the PRC would gradually decrease its support to the CPT. Both sides agreed to establish military cooperation.[139]

Although this Sino–Thai military cooperation was covert, the Chinese leaders reassured the Thai leaders of their security commitment on several occasions. For example, when Deputy Prime Minister Dawee Chullasapya led a delegation to Beijing in June, he said he was convinced that China would attack Vietnam if Vietnamese forces made any serious incursion into Thailand.[140]

The second Chinese move was to deal with the refugee crisis, both the boat people from Vietnam and the Cambodian refugees. Initially, the PRC had failed to respond to the refugee crisis. Kriangsak said he had sent messages to the Chinese Government asking them to take 8,000 ethnic Chinese refugees from Indochina, but received no response.[141] On 20 July, the Chinese Red Cross gave 200,000 renminbi (approximately US$130,000) to the Thai Government to aid Indochinese refugees in Thailand. This was the first donation the Chinese made toward the refugee relief program in Thailand. Chinese chargé d'affaires, Wang Buyun, presented the donation to Prime Minister Kriangsak. Wang later told reporters that he expressed sympathy with the Thai Government for carrying the burden of the refugee problem. He regretted Hanoi's expulsion of its people, and reiterated that the root cause was Vietnam's expansionism. Wang also called for the Vietnamese to withdraw from Cambodia, and halt mistreatment of its own people. He said that the Chinese had already accepted more than 250,000 refugees.[142] By November, the PRC decided to take more refugees from Thailand, up to an overall limit of 10,000.[143]

Third, the inter-Communist war brought about the de-ideologisation of the Cold War in Indochina. Some even argue that this marked the end of Cold War antagonism in the region.[144] Emblematic of this was the

---

139 Pat, interview, in *Cremation Volume In Honor of General Pat Akkaniput*, 45–46; *Biography of General Chavalit Yongchaiyudh*, 116–17.
140 'RTG Deputy PM Comments on PRC Intentions Re SRV', 12 July 1979, RG59, 1979BANGKO23877, NARA.
141 'Discussion with Prime Minister', 16 June 1979, RG59, 1979BANGKO20696, NARA.
142 'China Donates Dols 130,000 to Aid Refugees in Thailand', 24 July 1979, RG59, 1979BANGKO25321, NARA.
143 'Thai Comments on Sino-Thai Affairs', 23 November 1979, RG59, 1979BEIJIN08459, NARA; 'PRC Refugee Program for 10,000', 28 November 1979, RG59, 1979BANGKO48817, NARA.
144 Luthi, 'Strategic Shifts in East Asia', 223.

PRC's move to cut support for Southeast Asian insurgents in order to focus on the Cambodian question, which necessitated support from non-Communist Southeast Asian countries. This was largely due to a shift in Chinese foreign policy, spearheaded by the paramount leader, Deng Xiaoping. Deng not only had informed the communist parties in the region, including the CPT, that they were now on their own, but also relayed this changing policy to the Kriangsak Government.[145] The Chinese subsequently terminated the CPT's Voice of the People of Thailand radio station. Together with internal disagreement within the CPT, aggravated by the Sino–Soviet split, the lack of Chinese support put a final nail in the coffin of the communist insurgency in Thailand. During Deputy Prime Minister Dawee Chullasapya's visit to Beijing in June, the Chinese told Dawee that the insurgents were a Thai internal affair, which did not have anything to do with the Chinese Government.[146] This was confirmed when in late October Thai parliamentarians went to China and met with Ji Pengfei, Vice-Premier. The latter told them that the Voice of the People of Thailand had stopped broadcasting.[147]

Fourth, the Chinese attempted to conclude a civil aviation agreement with Thailand. This topic had been raised during Deng's visit in November 1978. On 21 June 1979, Shen Tu, the President of the Civil Aviation Administration of China, met with the new Thai Ambassador to the PRC, Sakol Vanabriksha, in Beijing to ask about the progress of the air agreement. Shen informed Sakol that the Chinese had signed a similar agreement with the Philippines, and began negotiations with Singapore. He said this agreement would be a stepping stone for further economic and cultural cooperation between the two countries.[148]

When Deputy Foreign Minister Arun Panupong visited Beijing in late August, he met with Vice Foreign Minister, Han Nianlong, who pushed for a Sino–Thai air agreement. As Arun later told the American Ambassador to Thailand, the Thai Government would not move very

---

145 'China Further Reduces Support for Southeast Asian Insurgents', 24 July 1976, RG59, 1979BEIJIN04839, NARA; Goscha, 'Vietnam, the Third Indochina War and the Meltdown of Asian Internationalism', 176.
146 'China Further Reduces Support for Southeast Asian Insurgents', 24 July 1979, RG59, 1979BEIJIN04839, NARA.
147 'Chinese Comments on Relations with Thai Communist Party', 5 November 1979, RG59, 1979BEIJIN07897, NARA.
148 Ministry of Foreign Affairs to Ministry of Transport, 'Negotiation of Aviation Agreement with the People's Republic of China', 23 July 1979, Library and Archives Division, MFA POL2/PRC2521/3, MFA, Thailand, 4.

fast on this agreement because of the lucrative Taiwan air connection and because Thai Airways International did not have enough planes for the China route.[149] A Thai delegation led by the Permanent Secretary of Communications arrived in Beijing on 26 November to negotiate the second round of a civil aviation agreement, though with little progress.[150]

Last but not least, Chinese leaders were increasingly dependent on Kriangsak's leadership. As the Chinese military attaché to Thailand, Mao Xianqi, told a senior US embassy official, the Chinese considered Thai cooperation essential to Chinese aims in the region, and in particular, to the survival of the Pol Pot forces. Deeming Kriangsak's political survival strategically important, they became concerned over his position in Thai politics. This was largely because the Chinese leaned on Kriangsak and his tacit support for Chinese supplies to the Khmer Rouge. As the US embassy in Bangkok reported, 'the PM runs the Chinese assistance operation out of his hip pocket with few of his advisors aware of it'.[151] In other words, the Sino–Thai quasi-alliance was built on Chinese understandings with Prime Minister Kriangsak. US Ambassador Abramowitz even claimed that 'Thai cooperation with the Chinese could diminish significantly should Kriangsak fall from power'.[152]

Amid the political decline of Kriangsak in early 1980, the Chinese stepped up their pressures on the Thai Government to publicly side with China and the Khmer Rouge regime. During her visit to Bangkok, Deng Yingchao, the National People's Congress Vice-Chairperson and Zhou Enlai's wife, gave a speech reassuring Kriangsak of Chinese support for Thailand against Vietnam in the event of the latter's attack on Thailand. Her speech, given at a lunch attended by senior Thai officials, caused some uneasiness and embarrassment to Kriangsak.[153]

Overall, while not all Thai leaders were enthusiastic about military cooperation with Beijing, the Third Indochina War undoubtedly rendered Sino–Thai relations ever closer. In short, Thai–Chinese relations during the Kriangsak administration were developed and strengthened through

---

149 'Ambassador's Meeting with Deputy Foreign Minister', 8 September 1979, RG59, 1979BANGKO35310, NARA.
150 'Thai Comments on Sino-Thai Affairs', 23 November 1979, RG59, 1979BEIJIN08459, NARA.
151 'PRC Military Attaché Comments Further on Indochina', 20 September 1979, RG59, 1979BANGKO37975, NARA.
152 'Sino-American Relations in Cambodia', 2 December 1979, RG59, 1979BANGKO49427, NARA.
153 Nayan Chanda, 'A Bid to Hold the Middle Ground', *Far Eastern Economic Review*, 7 March 1980, 27.

economic and technical cooperation. Although the Third Indochina War contributed to an unlikely alliance between Thailand, China, the US and the Khmer Rouge, the closer ties between Thailand and China were a part of Kriangsak's equidistance, which sought to rebalance all the great powers.

7.2.3. Thai–Soviet Relations: Correct but Distant?

> I see nothing wrong with being friends with the Soviets ... I want to treat all friendly countries on an equal basis and not discriminate against any friendly country.
>
> – Kriangsak Chomanan[154]

While behind the scenes, Kriangsak was working ever closer with the Chinese, his government nevertheless attempted to maintain a semblance of equal and balanced relations with both communist powers. Compared with Sino–Thai relations, Thai–Soviet relations were correct but distant, especially following the Soviet-backed Vietnamese invasion of Cambodia in late 1978. However, both countries continued functioning relationship, culminating in Prime Minister Kriangsak's visit to Moscow in March 1979. Despite the difficulties, discourses of détente remained intact.

Since entering office, Kriangsak's aim was to maintain a policy of even-handedness with both the USSR and the PRC. In his speech to Foreign Correspondents' Club of Thailand in 1978, Kriangsak said:

> we want to have friendly relations with China [and] the USSR ... I hope for expansion of trade with these countries. Regarding the USSR, we need their friendship. It is important to any concept of neutrality in Southeast Asia.[155]

As he put it, 'I see nothing wrong with being friends with the Soviets ... I want to treat all friendly countries on an equal basis and not discriminate against any friendly country'.[156] However, Thai diplomacy toward Moscow was constrained by Sino–Soviet rivalry and the Soviet aspiration to consolidate its relations with Hanoi.[157]

---

154 Nations, 'Thailand: Back in the Game', 22.
155 'Prime Minister Kriangsak Speaks to Foreign Correspondents' Club of Thailand', 20 January 1978, RG59, 1978BANGKO02150, NARA.
156 Nations, 'Thailand: Back in the Game', 22.
157 Leszek Buszynski, *Soviet Foreign Policy and Southeast Asia* (London: Croom Helm, 1986).

Bilaterally, the Soviet Union sought to strengthen its ties with Vietnam and, to a lesser extent, Laos. Moscow also echoed Vietnamese criticism of the Khmer Rouge regime in Phnom Penh, and regarded the Chinese as the source of Vietnamese–Cambodian border conflicts.[158] It publicly condemned the Chinese role in the regional communist insurgency. Mikhail Kapitsa, head of the Far Eastern Department of the Soviet Foreign Ministry, criticised China for cultivating relations with the smaller nations in Southeast Asia, and in particular Thailand, at the state-to-state level while continuing to support communist insurgencies against these governments at the people-to-people level.[159]

At the regional level, the Soviet Union did not develop close relations with ASEAN. Brezhnev's idea of Collective Security in Asia was largely ignored by the non-Communist states in ASEAN. Rather than endorsing ASEAN's zone of peace, freedom and neutrality, the Soviet Union expressed support of the Vietnamese proposal for 'a zone of peace, independence and neutrality'.[160]

In Thailand, the Russian embassy in Bangkok sought to play a more proactive role within the détente environment. Bilateral relations improved, while trade continued at a steady pace. Shortly after the Chinese invitation of Kriangsak to Beijing on 8 December 1977, Soviet Ambassador in Bangkok, Boris Ilyichev, extended an invitation to the Thai prime minister to visit Moscow, and Kriangsak agreed in principle.[161] In the same month, the position of the Soviet military attaché, Colonel Anatoli Gouriev, who was suspected of belonging to GRU (Soviet military intelligence), was approved by the Thai Government. Later, the Thai Government appointed Colonel Wanchai Chitchamnong as Thai military attaché to Moscow.[162]

---

158 'Background Information for Prime Minister Kriangsak', 23 March 1978, RG59, 1978STATE075406, NARA.
159 'MFA's Kapitsa Discusses East Asian Issues', 7 March 1978, RG59, 1978MOSCOW03846, NARA.
160 Soo Eon Moon, 'Importance of ASEAN in Soviet Foreign Policy: An Evaluation of Soviet Policy toward Southeast Asia in the Post-Vietnam War Era' (PhD thesis, Claremont Graduate School, 1984).
161 'Thai Prime Minister Kriangsak to Visit China and Soviet Union', 9 December 1977, RG59, 1977BANGKO33681, NARA.
162 'Thailand Selects Military Attaches for Beijing and Moscow', 22 May 1978, RG59, 1978BANGKO14463, NARA.

Ilyichev also pushed the Thai Government to sign the pending cultural agreement, which had been drafted during the Kukrit era and left unsigned under Thanin.[163] At the same time, cultural and sports exchanges increased. For example, the Soviet sports delegation led by Vladimir L Avilov visited Bangkok in early November 1978 and met with the Sports Organization of Thailand. They agreed in principle to conclude protocol on sports cooperation for 1979.[164]

There were also high-level visits, the most important of which were Soviet Deputy Foreign Minister Nikolai Firyubin's two visits to Bangkok in March and October, respectively. Prior to the Vietnamese invasion, in March 1978, Firyubin called on Foreign Minister Upadit at the Ministry of Foreign Affairs (MFA). The purpose, according to a Soviet embassy official, was to 'establish friendly relations with present Thai leadership'. Upadit asked Firyubin about the Soviet position on ASEAN's principle of a zone of peace, freedom and neutrality (ZOPFAN). The Soviet counterpart replied that the Soviet Union supported any proposals for peace in Southeast Asia and similar proposals in other parts of the world. He did not say directly that the USSR supported the ASEAN concept of ZOPFAN. However, his response was not negative.[165] He went on to thank the Thai Government for supporting Soviet actions for peace such as nuclear nonproliferation and other UN resolutions.

According to the Soviet embassy official, both sides agreed that a settlement to the Vietnamese–Cambodian border conflict was desirable. The Soviet Union desired a ceasefire, 'something along the lines of the Vietnamese proposal, although it doesn't necessarily have to follow their exact points'. Firyubin also observed that the Thais were nervous about the fighting in the region. The long-pending Thai–Soviet cultural agreement was not brought up during Firyubin's visit. However, the Soviets wanted it ratified.[166]

---

163 *Far Eastern Economic Review*, 3 March 1978.
164 Sports Organization of Thailand to the Ministry of Foreign Affairs, 'The Soviet Sports Delegation in Thailand', 30 November 1978, in Thailand's Ministry of Foreign Affairs, *Collected Volumes of Declassified Documents on Thai–Russian Relations, 1970–1991*, Vol. 3 (Bangkok: Ministry of Foreign Affairs, 2017), 24–27.
165 'Visit of Soviet Deputy Foreign Minister Nikolai Firyubin', 20 March 1978, RG59, 1978BANGKO08261, NARA. According to one of Soviet Embassy official, the Thai newspaper misunderstood Firyubin's comments. See, for example, 'Russia "Evasive" on ASEAN Peace Zone Scheme', *The Nation*, 14 March 1978.
166 'Visit of Soviet Deputy Foreign Minister Nikolai Firyubin', 20 March 1978, RG59, 1978BANGKO08261, NARA.

In June, the incoming Soviet Ambassador to Thailand, Yuri Kouznetzov (June 1978 – October 1984), arrived in Bangkok. It was reported that he was under orders from the Kremlin to take a tougher line with the Thai Government. He held a press conference even before his credentials ceremony with the king. Press releases were sent to local newspapers, and Soviet officials asked the editors to publish the Soviet viewpoint.[167]

On 27 September, Kouznetzov met with Deputy Foreign Minister, Wongse Polnikorn, at the MFA to discuss Kriangsak's state visit to Moscow. He asked the Thai Foreign Ministry to support the Soviet initiative on nuclear nonproliferation, the 'International Convention on Strengthening of Guarantee of Security of Non-Nuclear States', at the UN General Assembly. Kouznetzov expressed the Soviet intention to expand embassy activities by increasing personnel at the embassy. Wongse requested that the Soviet ambassador help to facilitate other official visits to Moscow.[168]

In late October 1978, Soviet Deputy Foreign Minister, Nikolai Firyubin, visited the Philippines, Indonesia and Thailand. He met with Prime Minister Kriangsak. After his talks with Firyubin, Kriangsak disclosed that the possibility of opening a formal dialogue between the Soviet Union and ASEAN had not been discussed. During the visit, the Soviet Ambassador to Thailand, Yuri Kouznetzov, told the press in an interview that the Soviet Union was 'on the Vietnamese side' and 'ready to render not only economic but also military aid to Vietnam'. This aroused concern in the region.[169]

The Soviets signed a treaty with Vietnam on 3 November, just two days before Chinese leader Deng Xiaoping visited Bangkok. At both receptions for Deng, at the airport and at Government House, Soviet Ambassador Kouznetzov was noticeably absent.[170] During Deng's visit, the Soviets were active in Thailand. Two delegations of Soviet tennis and basketball players came to Bangkok. Kouznetzov also asked the Kriangsak Government to

---

167 John McBeth, 'Suspicion and Non-involvement', *Far Eastern Economic Review*, 24 August 1979, 28.
168 Record of conversation between Thai Deputy Foreign Minister and Soviet Ambassador to Thailand, 27 September 1978, in Ministry of Foreign Affairs, *Collected Volumes of Declassified Documents on Thai–Russian Relations, 1970–1991*, Vol. 3, 20–23.
169 'Soviet Vice-Foreign Minister Visits ASEAN Countries', *Xinhua General News Service*, 3 November 1978.
170 'Arrival of PRC Vice-Premier Deng Xiaoping', 6 November 1978, RG59, 1978BANGKO32603, NARA.

go on live television and mark the anniversary of the Bolshevik Revolution on 7 November. The Thai authorities unsurprisingly turned down his request.[171] Shortly after Deng left Bangkok, the Soviet ambassador presented a strong verbal protest to the Thai Foreign Ministry, claiming that there were unwarranted attacks in local Chinese-language newspapers against Soviet interests in the region.[172]

At the end of the year, Soviet-backed Vietnamese forces intervened in Cambodia. The Vietnamese deployed troops along the Thai–Cambodian border, having a direct impact on Thailand. The Soviets repeatedly reassured the Thais that the Vietnamese would neither attack Thailand nor cross the Thai border. The Soviet Ambassador to Bangkok, in his talks with the US Ambassador Abramowitz, said 'I can guarantee Vietnamese forces will not go into Thailand'.[173] In his interview with the Thai-language *Daily News* in January 1979, Soviet Deputy Chief of Mission, Olek Gershov, denied press reports that the Soviet Union had 4,000 military personnel in Cambodia supporting Vietnamese forces. He insisted that the Soviet Government considered the new Heng Samrin regime the legal government, and only helped it politically and diplomatically. Gershov argued that Thailand was not endangered 'because of its wise policy towards Cambodia'.[174]

Despite the Vietnamese military intervention in Cambodia in December 1978 and corresponding Soviet support of Hanoi, Kriangsak continued to pursue a friendly relationship with the Soviet Union, and emphasised his commitment to an equidistant strategy. His state visit to Moscow was a major turning point. In his dinner remarks at the Dutch embassy in late January 1979, Prime Minister Kriangsak reiterated Thailand's stance on Indochina. Underlining his position, he said that following his visit to his 'good friend Jimmy Carter', he would visit the Soviet Union in March.[175] While détente proponents such as Foreign Minister Upadit supported the trip, some factions within the military, including Interior Minister, General Lek Naeomali, Commander of Royal Thai Army, General Prem

---

171 'The Marxist and the Monarchy', 11.
172 McBeth, 'Suspicion and Non-involvement', 28.
173 'Vietnamese Incursion into Thailand', 5 January 1979, RG59, 1979BANGKO00653, NARA.
174 Quoted in 'Soviet Diplomat's Remarks on Cambodia', 31 January 1979, RG59, 1979BANGKO03368, NARA.
175 On the following day, Thailand presented a plan to visit Moscow in March. This was confirmed during a conversation between General Phon Thanaphum, Secretary-General of the Prime Minister and one of Kriangsak's closest aides, and the American chargé d'affaires to Bangkok. 'Possible Kriangsak Visit to Soviet Union', 31 January 1979, RG59, 1979BANGKO03389, NARA.

Tinsulanonda, and National Security Council (NSC) Secretary-General, Air Marshal Siddhi Savetsila, disagreed with Kriangsak's decision.[176] According to the American documents, they urged the US ambassador to advise the prime minister to call off the Moscow visit. They reasoned that Thailand would gain nothing from the trip, and it was unnecessary for the prime minister to call on the Soviet Union as it supported the Vietnamese expansionism in Indochina.[177] The Chinese also viewed Kriangsak's visit with discomfort. The Chinese Ambassador to Moscow mildly complained to his counterpart, Sathit Sathian-Thai, about the timing of the visit.[178] However, Kriangsak publicly and privately insisted that his Moscow visit was important in order to sustain a more even-handed Thai diplomacy toward the great powers.[179]

Shortly before Kriangsak's visit to the USSR, Moscow vetoed an ASEAN resolution on the Indochina conflicts, which proposed the withdrawal of foreign troops in Cambodia, at the UN Security Council. This had a negative impact upon Kriangsak's upcoming trip. In his conversation with the US Ambassador to Thailand, Kriangsak said that he had no illusions about his Soviet visit. He would grasp this opportunity to clarify ASEAN views on Indochina situations, and emphasised Thai diplomatic ties with ASEAN and the US.[180]

Upon the departure of the Kriangsak delegation to the Soviet Union, the Soviet embassy in Bangkok placed a paid advertisement in *The Nation* newspaper to present its alternative picture of Thai–Soviet relations. The lengthy article, written by A Olenin, suggested that talks between the Thai and Soviet leaders would 'play a major role in promoting friendship and mutual understanding'. It went on to compliment the Kriangsak Government for taking steps to extend relations with the Soviet Union and other socialist countries. It praised the wisdom and realism of Thai leaders. According to Olenin, Thai–Soviet relations were based on principles of peaceful coexistence, regardless of the different sociopolitical

---

176 For example, Air Marshal Siddhi Savetsila, Secretary-General of National Security Council, said that 'he disagreed' with the visit to Moscow and what he called Kriangsak's strategy of 'balance of power with the three major powers. Siddhi Savetsila, *Pan Rorn Pan Nao* [Through Thick and Thin] (Bangkok, 2013), 78.
177 'Pressures to Postpone Visit by PM Kriangsak to USSR', 13 March 1979, RG59, 1979BANGKO08520, NARA. See also 'Call Off Visit to Russia', *Bangkok Post,* 8 March 1979.
178 'Kriangsak Visit to USSR', 10 April 1979, RG59, 1979MOSCOW08847, NARA.
179 'Pressures to Postpone Visit by PM Kriangsak to USSR', 13 March 1979, RG59, 1979BANGKO08520, NARA.
180 'Conversations with Prime Minister Kriangsak', 19 March 1979, RG59, 1979BANGKO09194, NARA.

systems. Highlighting trade, cultural and sports cooperation, the article concluded that these relationships would gain new impetus during the Kriangsak trip.[181]

Kriangsak arrived in Moscow on 21 March, and was warmly greeted by the Soviet leaders led by Prime Minister Alexei Kosygin and Foreign Minister Andrei Gromyko at the airport. Kriangsak's party included, inter alia, his wife, Khunying Wirat Chomanan, Deputy Prime Minister Sunthorn Hongladarom, Foreign Minister Upadit Pachariyangkun, Interior Minister General Lek Naeomali, Deputy Commerce Minister Prok Amaranand, and NSC Secretary-General Air Marshal Siddhi Savetsila. Kriangsak stayed in Moscow for three nights, and spent another three days in Leningrad before returning to Bangkok.

In the afternoon, Kriangsak met with Soviet Prime Minister Alexei Kosygin for two hours and 40 minutes at the Kremlin. The Indochina situation was the central issue. After greetings, Kriangsak asserted that Thailand pursued a policy of independence and self-reliance, and wished to be friends with any country regardless of sociopolitical differences. Kosygin asked in an aggressive manner whether, in the event that one country invaded another, Thailand would be friends with it. Kriangsak responded with a firm exposition of Thai attitudes. He said that Thailand was neutral in relation to the Indochina conflicts.[182] As Kriangsak put it, 'Thailand will adhere to its position of strict neutrality and will not incline toward any side of the present conflict'.[183]

While Thailand would not interfere in the internal affairs of other countries, Kriangsak told Kosygin that Thailand would not fear defending itself against foreign aggression. Domestically, Thailand would continue to fight communist terrorism. Despite Thailand's respect for the monarchy and Buddhism, Kriangsak said the Thai Government could be friends with communist states. Kosygin reacted by asserting that 'the Communist terrorists were Chinese', which, for him, were the genuine threat to Thailand.[184]

---

181 A Olenin, *The Nation*, 22 March 1979; 'Soviets Advertise Thai-Soviet Relations', 22 March 1979, RG59, 1979BANGKO09559, NARA.
182 Record of conversation between General Kriangsak Chomanan, Thai Prime Minister, and Alexei Kosygin, Soviet Prime Minister, 21 March 1979, in Ministry of Foreign Affairs, *Collected Volumes of Declassified Documents on Thai–Russian Relations, 1970–1991*, Vol. 3, 98–104.
183 *Pravda*, 22 March 1979.
184 'Conversation with Prime Minister on Soviet Trip', 30 March 1979, RG59, 1979BANGKO09194, NARA.

The Thai prime minister stated that his government strongly supported the ASEAN peaceful principle, and the principle of inviolability of international frontiers. Thailand was opposed to any violations of the principle, and asked aggressors to withdraw their troops. He asked whether Vietnam had violated the Thai frontier. Kosygin assured the Thai prime minister that it was impossible that Vietnam would invade Thailand. On the contrary, it was very possible that the PRC, which had invaded Vietnam, would someday decide to 'teach Thailand and the other ASEAN states a lesson'.[185]

Throughout their meeting, Kosygin strongly condemned the Chinese. According to Kriangsak, the Soviet prime minister told him that 'in fact, President Carter sanctioned the Chinese aggression against Vietnam'. Deng Xiaoping had announced his intentions in the US, and the US was aware of Chinese plans to launch a punitive attack on Hanoi. The Soviet leader stressed that the Soviet Union would supply the Vietnamese anything they needed militarily.[186]

Maintaining a firm distinction between the Chinese invasion of Vietnam and the situation in Cambodia, Kosygin did not deny that Vietnamese troops were in Cambodia but treated the issue as settled. He encouraged the Thai Government to recognise the Heng Samrin regime. He said the Pol Pot regime was finished, and contended that Thailand should recognise the new government which stood for neutrality and peaceful relations with its neighbours. Kriangsak reacted by commenting that he heard only two persons, Heng Samrin and Hun Sen, and two persons could not constitute a government. He told the Soviet premier that he did not consider the Heng Samrin group a legitimate government. His government would have to consult with the ASEAN leaders, he went on, but in the meantime, Thailand would not recognise any regime. Commenting on Pol Pot's murderous regime, Kriangsak said that neither Thailand nor his ASEAN partners supported Pol Pot personally. However, he emphasised that there was a clear difference between the nature of a regime and a regime change by external forces.[187] On this matter, their interests and opinions diverged,

---

[185] 'Conversation with Prime Minister on Soviet Trip', 30 March 1979, RG59, 1979BANGKO09194, NARA.
[186] Record of conversation between General Kriangsak Chomanan, Thai Prime Minister, and Alexei Kosygin, Soviet Prime Minister, 21 March 1979, in Ministry of Foreign Affairs, *Collected Volumes of Declassified Documents on Thai–Russian Relations, 1970–1991*, Vol. 3, 98–104.
[187] 'Conversation with Prime Minister on Soviet Trip', 30 March 1979, RG59, 1979BANGKO09194, NARA.

> Kriangsak: We consider any invasion of another country wrong.
>
> Kosygin: What about the government killing its own people? Is it right? The Cambodian people did not kill each other, but it results from the Chinese influence.
>
> Kriangsak: I do not accept that action either, but they are different stories.
>
> Kosygin: They are much interrelated.
>
> Kriangsak: But I consider that it is unacceptable for any country to invade another country.[188]

Kosygin mentioned the charges by Hun Sen, foreign minister of the Heng Samrin regime, that Thailand was permitting Chinese resupply operations to Pol Pot's forces. Kriangsak replied that Pol Pot's forces supplied themselves by seizing them from their opponents. Showing the Soviet leader with maps, Kriangsak pointed out the Cambodian coastline from Koh Kong to Kompong Som, and suggested that the Chinese could resupply very easily by the sea. Kosygin did not press the issue further.[189]

Kosygin moved to the existence of large ethnic Chinese communities in Southeast Asia, which, he claimed, posed a serious threat to their security. He informed Kriangsak that in its borderland areas, the Soviet Union had been forced to expel those ethnic Chinese. He recommended that Thailand and other ASEAN states should do the same, especially the approximately 310,000 stateless Chinese in Thailand. Kriangsak objected to the Soviet proposal.[190]

Kriangsak mentioned the behaviour of the Soviet embassy in Thailand, claiming that for many years it had acted like a security force. Kosygin expressed surprise but promised to look into the matter. The Soviet leader also offered Thailand weapons, such as tanks. Kriangsak responded by saying he had supply relationships with the US, Britain, France and Italy, which he planned to maintain. He told Kosygin that prior to his Moscow trip, he held talks with Suharto of Indonesia, and Hussein Onn of Malaysia, and they had mentioned difficulties dealing with the Russians.

---

188 Record of conversation between General Kriangsak Chomanan, Thai Prime Minister, and Alexei Kosygin, Soviet Prime Minister, 21 March 1979, in Ministry of Foreign Affairs, *Collected Volumes of Declassified Documents on Thai–Russian Relations, 1970–1991*, Vol. 3, 98–104.
189 'Conversation with Prime Minister on Soviet Trip', 30 March 1979, RG59, 1979BANGKO09194, NARA.
190 'Conversation with Prime Minister on Soviet Trip', 30 March 1979, RG59, 1979BANGKO09194, NARA.

While Malaysia experienced the Soviet failure to finance Malaysian electrical projects, Indonesia could not acquire necessary spare parts from the Soviet Union. Kriangsak said he advised Kosygin to follow through better.[191] They discussed the expansion of trade, cultural, scientific and sports exchanges. Although Kosygin said at the outset that the Soviets would not push or impose any agreements on the Thais, one of Thai diplomats revealed that at lower levels, the Soviets tried very hard to obtain Thai approval for an economic and technical agreement.[192]

In the evening, the Soviet premier hosted a formal dinner for Kriangsak. Speaking on behalf of Vietnam, Kosygin said that Hanoi came 'out actively for developing peaceful and friendly ties' with its neighbours. Kriangsak replied that Thailand was 'seriously concerned over the situation that has developed in Indochina'. He said that Thailand's policy was one of 'strict neutrality', and would not be swayed into supporting anyone's side in any conflict. He denied that Thai territory was used to transport arms or material to the Chinese-backed forces of Pol Pot in Cambodia.[193] After the dinner, Kosygin escorted Kriangsak and his entourage to the Bolshoi ballet performance.

On the following day, 22 March, Kriangsak met with Soviet Secretary-General, Leonid Brezhnev, whom Kriangsak described as a 'good man, healthy, but not strong'. He occasionally slurred his speech, and appeared to have difficulty swallowing.[194] According to the Russian News Agency, Tass, Brezhnev told Kriangsak that Moscow fully supported Vietnam. Referring to China, he said that 'reliable security' in Asia must be based on the absence of force or the threat of force. In other words, Brezhnev reiterated the threat to peace posed by Chinese ambitions. He called for a 'deepening of the process of détente' in Asia.[195] Kriangsak informed Brezhnev that the Chinese did not use Thai soil to supply Pol Pot's force. He stressed that Thailand did not recognise the newly installed Heng Samrin regime, and did 'not want the presence of foreign troops' in neighbouring countries.[196] He also brought up the matter of the Soviet

---

191 'Conversation with Prime Minister on Soviet Trip', 30 March 1979, RG59, 1979BANGKO09194, NARA.
192 'Kriangsak Visit to USSR', 10 April 1979, RG59, 1979MOSCOW08847, NARA.
193 Miles Hanley, 'All Smiles from the Soviets', *Far Eastern Economic Review,* 6 April 1979, 34.
194 'Conversation with Prime Minister on Soviet Trip', 30 March 1979, RG59, 1979BANGKO09194, NARA.
195 Hanley, 'All Smiles from the Soviets', 34.
196 'Kriangsak Visit to USSR', 10 April 1979, RG59, 1979MOSCOW08847, NARA; 'Thai Prime Minister Ends Visit to Soviet Union', *Xinhua General News Service,* 29 March 1979.

veto in the UN Security Council against the ASEAN resolution, proposing the withdrawal of foreign forces from Vietnam and Cambodia. According to Kriangsak, 'on this matter, we have differences of opinion'.[197]

In his single 55-minute session with Brezhnev, Kriangsak urged the Soviet leader to recognise ASEAN and deal with the organisation as a grouping. He noted that failure to do so would create suspicion in ASEAN countries. According to Kriangsak, Brezhnev listened attentively, and asked Kriangsak whether there were military features of ASEAN. Kriangsak replied that ASEAN was not a military pact. Brezhnev promised that 'a dialogue between the Soviet Union and ASEAN would take place in the future'.[198] However, the Soviet leader warned that ASEAN should avoid association with the Chinese, who would endanger regional cooperation. According to Kriangsak, Brezhnev also stressed the importance of reaching the Strategic Arms Limitation Talks (SALT) II agreement with the US for Soviet domestic economic reasons.[199]

On the same day, there were other meetings at the ministerial level. For instance, Deputy Prime Minister Sunthorn Hongladarom held talks with Soviet Deputy Prime Minister, Vladimir A Kirillin. They discussed a proposed agreement covering full economic and technical cooperation, including an exchange of technicians. The Soviets suggested that the Thais should negotiate separate technical agreements on specific issues. The Thais also requested academic cooperation on oil shale development. Soviet expertise on energy, especially on nuclear power plants, hydro energy, gas and coal, would benefit Thailand. Sunthorn suggested that both sides should exchange their technicians.[200]

At the same time, Deputy Minister of Commerce Prok Amaranand and his Soviet counterpart, MP Kuzmin, Deputy Minister of Foreign Trade, discussed future trade cooperation. They noted how, in 1978, the trade balance between the two countries was in favour of the Soviets. The value of Thai imports from Moscow was 222.8 million baht, while exports were 148.3 million baht. The leading exports from Thailand were rubber

---

197 'Thai Prime Minister Ends Visit to Soviet Union'.
198 *Bangkok Post*, 24 March 1979.
199 'Conversation with Prime Minister on Soviet Trip', 30 March 1979, RG59, 1979BANGKO09194, NARA.
200 Conclusion of negotiations between Sunthorn Hongladarom, Thai Deputy Prime Minister, and Vladimir A Kirillin, Soviet Deputy Prime Minister, 22 March 1979, in Ministry of Foreign Affairs, *Collected Volumes of Declassified Documents on Thai–Russian Relations, 1970–1991*, Vol. 3, 52–53.

and fluorite. In 1978, Thailand earned 115.9 million baht from rubber sales to Moscow. Prok suggested that the Soviets could cut the Thai trade deficit by buying canned pineapple, but Kuzmin was reluctant because of alternative supplies from Cuba and Vietnam. The Thai Deputy Commerce Minister also complained about unpredictable rubber purchases from the Soviets. Prok said that the Thais wished to sell more rubber and textiles to Moscow, and buy products such as fertiliser, paper and cement. They signed no agreement on trade because they believed a trade agreement signed on 25 December, 1970 provided sufficient basis for cooperation. Both sides agreed to increase trade between the two countries, and to exchange more trade delegations.[201]

On 23 March, Kriangsak gave a press conference. Referring to the situation in Indochina, Kriangsak said that 'we wish to see all sides cease hostility and withdraw to their former boundaries'. He repeatedly emphasised Thailand's strict neutrality in Indochina conflicts. 'We wish to preserve peace and neutrality in this region of the world', he continued.

> We do not think we should take sides. We cannot sit idly by while the situation is getting serious in this region. We expressed our concern over the settlement of this region's disputes by force. We do not wish to see a state invade others.[202]

The Kriangsak party spent three days negotiating the joint communiqué. Kosygin called on Kriangsak for three additional half-hour unscheduled meetings on 23 March. For Kriangsak, Kosygin was 'very tough'.[203] Thai Foreign Minister Upadit assigned Permanent Secretary of the Foreign Ministry Arun Panupong to the negotiations on the wording of the communiqué. Arun was a former Thai Ambassador to Moscow and knew how to deal with the Russians. His Soviet counterpart was Deputy Foreign Minister Nikolai Firyubin. He became indignant when Arun insisted on deleting huge chunks from the Soviet-proposed draft. At one point, Firyubin threatened to abandon the communiqué altogether, to which the Thai side responded by showing their willingness to do the same. The Soviets however resumed negotiations.[204] In the end, they agreed on

---

201 Record of conversation between Prok Amaranand, Deputy Commerce Minister, and MP Kuzmin, Deputy Minister of Foreign Trade, 22 March 1979, in Ministry of Foreign Affairs, *Collected Volumes of Declassified Documents on Thai–Russian Relations, 1970–1991*, Vol. 3, 54–61.
202 'Thai Prime Minister Visits Soviet Union', *Xinhua General News Service*, 25 March 1979.
203 'Conversation with Prime Minister on Soviet Trip', 30 March 1979, RG59, 1979BANGKO09194, NARA.
204 'Kriangsak Visit to USSR', 10 April 1979, RG59, 1979MOSCOW08847, NARA.

a compromised version of a joint communiqué. Kriangsak did not yield at all on the Indochina-related questions and as a result, the communiqué did not mention Vietnam, Cambodia or China.[205]

The communiqué was promulgated on the last day of the visit, 27 March, during Kriangsak's visit to Leningrad. It began by saying that 'a broad exchange of views on various aspects of bilateral relations and on major international problems of mutual interest was held' during talks between Thai and Soviet leaders. The communiqué continued:

> The Prime Minister of Thailand expressed the determination of the Thai Government to carry through an independent foreign policy, based on the principle of peaceful coexistence and aimed at strengthening friendly relations with all countries, irrespective of their political, economic and social order, for the sake of peace, progress and prosperity ... The Thai side gave an account of ASEAN [which was] aimed at the development of regional economic, social and cultural cooperation of its member-countries.

'The Soviet sides', on the other hand, 'emphasized that it consistently opposed mutually exclusive military-political and economic blocs', and 'expressed its readiness to deepen mutually advantageous contacts' in relations with the ASEAN member states. On this matter, the Soviet Union did not go beyond its earlier positions on ASEAN. As indicated in the communiqué, it stated its readiness to deal with the member states bilaterally.[206] Lastly, the communiqué indicated the intentions of Thailand and the Soviet Union to maintain mutual contact, hold consultations and continue to develop relations 'as extensively as possible'.

Symbolically, Kriangsak's visit to Moscow marked the first time that the Thai prime minister visited the Soviet Union. Despite the warm Soviet welcome and cordiality, it was not an easy visit. Nevertheless, Kriangsak characterised his visit as a 'pleasure trip'. He was pleased with the visit, having given nothing and maintained firm positions protecting Thai and ASEAN interests. There was no treaty signed between the two countries during this visit.[207] Kriangsak was assured by the Soviet leaders that the Vietnamese would not invade Thailand. Overall, the trip represented Kriangsak's strategy of equidistance toward the contending powers.

---

205 'Kriangsak Visit to USSR', 10 April 1979, RG59, 1979MOSCOW08847, NARA.
206 'Kriangsak Visit to USSR', 10 April 1979, RG59, 1979MOSCOW08847, NARA.
207 'Conversation with Prime Minister on Soviet Trip', 30 March 1979, RG59, 1979BANGKO09194, NARA.

Following his trip, Kriangsak attempted to maintain a good friendship with Moscow. First, the Thai Government allowed Soviet cargo flyovers from Bombay to Hanoi. This was partly because of the criticism that the Thais had supported Chinese resupply operations to Cambodia. The Soviets presented these flights as 'innocent' air traffic in conformity with international conventions. During March and May, reports of 79 Soviet flyovers to Vietnam were intercepted. Kriangsak told reporters that Thailand had permitted the Soviet Union to increase its flyovers on a temporary basis, but he said he had no idea what the aircrafts were carrying to Vietnam.[208] In September, the Soviets incessantly asked Thai permission that Soviet flyovers increase to 20 per day.[209] The Thais reportedly suspected that the heavy Soviet cargos contained components that assembled T-45 tanks, MiG-21s and helicopters at the former American airbase at Danang.[210]

Kriangsak asked the Thai NSC, chaired by Air Marshal Siddhi, to review the flyover issue, and take steps to reduce the number of flights. Thai authorities told the Soviet ambassador that from now on all flyover requests would be handled by the NSC.[211] In September, the Soviet Union also requested permission for a 'goodwill visit' by two military vessels to call at Bangkok's port, including the 4,000-ton guided missile destroyer *Gnevny*, and the 7,000-ton training ship *Borodino*. Thailand refused to grant Soviet warships permission. Requests by Aeroflot, the Soviet airline, to increase the number of flights to Bangkok, were turned down, too.[212]

Second, mutual visits increased. Soviet Prime Minister Kosygin was invited to Bangkok. In late May, Soviet Ambassador to Bangkok, Yuri Kouznetzov, invited Thailand to send an observer to the Genny Council for Mutual Economic Assistance (COMECON) meeting in Moscow.[213]

---

208 'Soviet Airlift Reported', *The Washington Post*, 25 May 1979; *The Associated Press*, 24 May 1979.
209 'Soviet Overflights across Thailand', 4 May 1979, RG59, 1979BANGKO14913, NARA.
210 Richard Nations, 'Bangkok Tries a New Tack', *Far Eastern Economic Review*, 28 September 1979, 12.
211 'Ambassador's Meeting with Kriangsak', 28 September 1979, RG59, 1979BANGKO39760, NARA; Victoria Butler, 'Soviets Irk Thailand in Sport and Politics', *The Globe and Mail*, 1 November 1979.
212 General Prem Tinsulanonda told visiting US Commander-in-Chief in the Pacific that the Thai military would not support Soviet warship visits. 'Soviet Fleet Visits to Thailand', 20 September 1979, RG59, 1979BANGKO38115, NARA; 'Asians Reject Soviet Ship Visits', *The Washington Post*, 19 September 1979.
213 It was reported that the communist states in Eastern Europe wished to broaden their trade relations with Thailand. However, it seemed this was not approved by the Soviet government. According to Sompong Faichampa, MFA chief of the European Division, 'three days later, the [Soviet] ambassador told us to forget about [the invitation letter]; that it was a mistake'. 'FORMIN Upadit Explains COMECON Invitation', 13 June 1979, RG59, 1979BANGKO20291, NARA; McBeth, 'Suspicion and Non-involvement', 28.

On 20–26 August, Air Marshal Harin Hongsakul led an eight-member delegation of the Thai National Assembly to the Soviet Union. He gave an interview to the Russian News Agency, Tass, stating that ideological differences were not an obstacle to friendly Thai–Soviet relations. The Soviets sent their sports delegation to Bangkok, including boxing and tennis teams.[214]

Third, Thai–Soviet trade relations increased significantly. In April, the Bangkok Metropolitan Administration bought trucks from the Soviets costing 13 million baht. The Soviets also opened a trade exhibition in Nakornprathom province, close to Bangkok. The organiser, Min Sen Machinery, which acted as an agent for importing machinery from the Soviet Union, sold a number of tractors.[215] In July, a newly elected President of the Board of Trade and the Thai Chamber of Commerce, Kijja Vadhanasindhu, led a five-man delegation to Moscow. He signed a private sector agreement on trade, economic, scientific and technological cooperation. The Soviets placed an order with Thai Hua for 50,000 tons of maize worth about 176 million baht to be shipped to Vietnam.[216] Under the International Trade State Corporation Act of 1974, requiring trade with the communist countries to have official approval, Thai exporters applied to the Commerce Ministry for a routine export license. The ministry supported their sales to Moscow. It was reported that Thai exporters regularly met with trade representatives in the Soviet embassy on Sathorn Road. In December, the Soviets started lining up 100,000 tons of high-quality Thai rice, due to be shipped in January 1980.[217]

However, Thai sales of grain to the Soviets were viewed by the Americans with disapproval, because it was inconsistent with President Jimmy Carter's partial grain embargo against Moscow, imposed in January following the Soviet invasion of Afghanistan. The US embassy in Bangkok privately warned Kriangsak that the US would retaliate if Thailand went ahead with its sales. Prok Ammaranan, Deputy Commerce Minister, said 'we have never had any commitment with the US that we would have to fall in line with its embargo'. He stressed:

---

214 Alexander A Karchava, *Kaewsip pee kwam sampan tang karntoot Russia–Thai* [Ninety-Year Russian–Thai Diplomatic Relations] (Bangkok: Bapith Printing, 1988), 119.
215 Karchava, *Kaewsip pee kwam sampan tang karntoot Russia–Thai*, 136.
216 K Sonsomsook, 'Goodwill Has Its Limits', *Far Eastern Economic Review*, 7 September 1979, 51.
217 Ho Kwon Ping, 'The Thais Defy the Grain Embargo', *Far Eastern Economic Review*, 15 February 1980, 9.

> We are not a satellite of the US ... The US is trying hard to get Thailand to fall in line as far as rice exports to the Soviet Union are concerned ... If a grain embargo became a United Nations resolution, we would certainly abide by it.

'But until then', Prok explained, 'we are friends with both sides'.[218]

While Kriangsak condemned the Soviet invasion of Afghanistan, he approved the sale of grain to the Soviet Union. He declared that the Soviet action was 'considered a threat to the security, peace and stability of Asia and the world'. He asked 'the Soviet Union to withdraw its troops and stop infringing on the sovereignty of Afghanistan so that the Afghan people can determine their fate by themselves'.[219] With regard to Thailand's grain sales to Moscow, Kriangsak said his government would make its own trade decisions. 'We are an independent country', he said, 'and no one can tell us what to do'.[220]

In short, the Kriangsak administration to a certain extent pursued détente with the Soviet Union. Thai–Soviet relations were friendly to the extent that they had a stable, yet distant relationship. They were not merely bilateral relations but, more importantly, part and parcel of the broader strategy of equidistance, based on the balancing of the Sino–Soviet rivalry in the region. It can be argued that Kriangsak's equidistance policy was a discourse of balanced détente. On the one hand, it was fairly successful in maintaining flexibility and even-handedness with the great powers. On the other, this policy generated discursive disagreement with the military and security forces within Thai politics: a fact that eventually led to the fall of Kriangsak.

---

218 Ho, 'The Thais Defy the Grain Embargo', 9, 11.
219 'Thai Prime Minister Denounces Soviet Invasion of Afghanistan', *Xinhua General News Service*, 3 January 1980.
220 *The Associated Press*, 8 February 1980.

7.3. The Fall of Kriangsak: Intra-Discursive Struggle?

The existing literature explains the fall of Kriangsak as related to either endemic economic problems, a legitimacy crisis or the lack of support from the monarchy and military, especially from the Young Turks.[221] It also pinpoints the year 1979 as the turning point in the gradual decline of the Kriangsak administration. According to this argument, the promulgation of the Constitution in December 1978 and a subsequent parliamentary election on 22 April 1979 served to weaken rather than strengthen Kriangsak, who decided not to run in the election. The reason was twofold: first, the election was won by a group of opposition parties led by Kukrit Pramoj. Second, Kriangsak was able to remain prime minister, largely due to the votes of the appointed Senate. He therefore lacked support in the elected House of Parliament and his Cabinet consisted largely of non-elected technocrats. The government was further delegitimised by pressing economic problems, including high inflation, widening deficits and price rises, in particular of oil. Amid the global oil crisis, Kriangsak's decision to raise energy prices was the final straw, sparking a series of anti-government demonstrations. Economic mismanagement not only made it difficult for Kriangsak to broaden his support but also exacerbated military factionalism. The Young Turks finally shifted their support from Kriangsak to the new Army Commander-in-Chief and Defense Minister, General Prem Tinsulanonda.[222]

However, this economic explanation is flawed. As Vichitvong na Pombhejara has pointed out, 1979 was in fact a year of 'relative stability'. The Thai economy was not doing 'too badly' and despite the persistent inflation and trade imbalances, Thailand maintained economic growth. 'On the macro level', observed Vichitvong, the economy was 'satisfactory':

---

221 David Morell and Chai-Anan Samudavanija, *Political Conflict in Thailand: Reform, Reaction, Revolution* (Cambridge: Oelgeschlager, Gunn & Hain Publishers, 1981), 280; Krittin, 'Political Conflict under the Government of General Kriangsak Chomanan'; Larry Niksch, 'Thailand in 1980: Confrontation with Vietnam and the Fall of Kriangsak', *Asian Survey* 21, no. 2 (1981): 223–31.
222 Ansil Ramsay, 'Thailand 1979: A Government in Trouble', *Asian Survey* 20, no. 2 (1980): 112–22.

> Trade deficits are not expected to adversely affect the rate of economic growth as long as export expansion continues satisfactorily. Also, as long as the economy continues to grow at a high rate, the investment climate is likely to remain favorable. Investment, in turn, helps sustain economic growth.[223]

More importantly, this approach largely ignores the diplomatic dimension. This chapter argues that the fall of Kriangsak can be understood through the lens of the discursive struggles over détente. By the end of the 1970s, it was no longer a struggle between the discourses of anticommunism versus détente, but between détente proponents about how détente should work. In other words, it was the intra-discursive struggle between balanced détente and unbalanced détente. In this version, it was the latter's proponents that brought down Kriangsak. The major turning point was Kriangsak's visit to Moscow in March 1979.

The intra-discursive struggle that set the stage for Kriangsak's downfall was fought on two fronts. The first was the domestic struggle between those balanced and unbalanced détente proponents. As was clear during the militant anticommunist regime of Thanin, most factions within the military had by then become détente proponents or sympathisers. The same was true of civilians, especially those based at the MFA. It was not surprising, therefore, that both groups supported the coup in October 1977, and subsequently endorsed Kriangsak's policy of equidistance toward the contending powers, and détente with the communist powers in general. Key détente proponent Upadit remained foreign minister in the Kriangsak Government.

However, the Soviet-backed Vietnamese invasion of Cambodia in November 1978 gradually changed the perception and identity of military elites. They became sceptical of the policy of equidistance and many disagreed with Kriangsak's decision to visit the Soviet Union – particularly security and military détente proponents.

Generally, military and security elites supported détente, believing that Thailand should bend with the emerging Sino–American relationship or quasi-alliance. In turn, they advocated a set of policies in neighbouring Indochina, including (1) explicitly denouncing the Vietnamese threat or expansionism; (2) implicitly supporting the Khmer Rouge forces along the

---

223 Vichitvong na Pombhejara, 'Thailand in 1979: A Year of Relative Stability', *Southeast Asian Affairs* (1980), 321. See also Vichitvong, 'The Kriangsak Government and the Thai Economy', 312–22.

Thai border; and (3) distancing from the Soviet Union, which politically and militarily supported Hanoi. We can call those who followed this course 'unbalanced détente proponents'.

As noted earlier, these unbalanced détente proponents such as Interior Minister General Lek Naeomali, Commander of Royal Thai Army General Prem Tinsulanonda, and NSC Secretary-General Air Marshal Siddhi Savetsila, disapproved of Kriangsak's decision to visit Moscow, and even asked the US ambassador to encourage Kriangsak to call off the visit.[224] In his interview, Siddhi said that he totally 'disagreed' with the Soviet visit.[225] Despite their support for détente in general, their stance was unbalanced in the sense that they promoted détente with the PRC, while remaining aloof with the Soviet Union.

Even the *Bangkok Post* newspaper, which had advocated détente, printed an editorial on 8 March entitled 'Call Off Visit to Russia'. It urged that rather than making an unproductive Moscow trip, the Thai prime minister should remain in Thailand to protect national interests, and exert strong and sensible leadership in dealing with urgent domestic problems, such as oil shortages. The editorial pointed to the lack of Soviet interest in Thailand, noting that Soviet Prime Minister Kosygin departed for India at the same time as Kriangsak's visit was initially scheduled.[226]

Those proponents of unbalanced détente formed a new power configuration, leading to a struggle within the Thai military, and it was this that saw Kriangsak begin to lose control of the Army. After the April 1979 election, Prem became a new locus of power, succeeding Kriangsak as Defense Minister, and retaining his position of Commander-in-Chief of the Royal Thai Army. Through his dual positions, Prem also consolidated power within the military. Kriangsak's power base was limited to the Supreme Command, while his supporters, such as General Tuanthong Suwannatat, were marginalised from commanding battalions.[227]

Despite their continued support for Kriangsak, the Young Turks started to raise concerns over the situation in Indochina, and Kriangsak's equidistance policy. Its key member, Colonel Prajak Sawangjit said:

---

224 'Pressures to Postpone Visit by PM Kriangsak to USSR', 13 March 1979, RG59, 1979BANGKO08520, NARA.
225 Siddhi, *Pan Rorn Pan Nao*, 78.
226 'Call Off Visit to Russia', *Bangkok Post*, 8 March 1979.
227 Ramsay, 'Thailand 1979', 112–13.

we are the class of 1960. At the outbreak of the war in Laos in 1961, we went to fight in Laos and [later on] in the jungle with the [Thai] communist terrorists. Our feelings while fighting in the jungle were that the country was decaying and degenerating because the mechanisms in the city were bad. We therefore decided to get together and do something so that our union can survive. We were closely united, all of us determined in our pursuit of the same objective: to solve the nation's problems … We don't want anything more than to save the Nation, the Religion, and the Monarchy.[228]

The Soviet invasion of Afghanistan in December 1979 confirmed that the rhetoric of strict neutrality was not a viable option. In January 1980, the radical right-wing Red Gaur movement, which had massacred students outside Thammasat in October 1976, staged a demonstration outside the Soviet embassy to protest the Soviet invasion of Afghanistan and to attack Kriangsak's foreign policy.[229] In mid-January, General Prem began to distance himself from Kriangsak. He gave an address to a students' debating club at Chulalongkorn University on the security situation in Thailand. On 22 February 1980, he opened an economic seminar at Thammasat University by saying 'if people suffer, the government should do something to solve the problem'.[230]

The situation worsened when, in early February, amid the global energy crisis, Kriangsak made the decision to raise energy prices. This brought about mass urban unrest, spearheaded by rightist political forces, and sparked political manoeuvring within the military.[231] With few options, Kriangsak reshuffled his Cabinet on 12 February in an attempt to balance the internal struggle. He replaced balanced détente proponents with those anti-Soviet or unbalanced détente proponents. Air Marshal Siddhi took the portfolio of Foreign Minister, while Upadit and Prok Amaranand, Deputy Commerce Minister, were dismissed. Yet it was too little, too late and Kriangsak was forced to resign on 29 February. General Prem, with the king's support, was made the new prime minister on 3 March, and formed what he called 'the government of His Majesty'.[232]

---

228 Chai-Anan, *The Thai Young Turks*, 35–36.
229 John McBeth, 'The Government under Siege', *Far Eastern Economic Review*, 8 February 1980, 15.
230 John McBeth, 'Enter Prem, the Reluctant General', *Far Eastern Economic Review*, 14 March 1980, 11.
231 Niksch, 'Thailand in 1980', 229.
232 McBeth, 'Enter Prem, the Reluctant General', 10; John McBeth, 'Kriangsak Government – Mark III', *Far Eastern Economic Review*, 22 February 1980, 8–9.

On the second front, US policy shifts exacerbated the discursive struggle. While there are no documents that directly point to US involvement in the downfall of Kriangsak, the US policy shift towards Indochina, and a corresponding disapproval of Kriangsak's policy, did help those unbalanced détente proponents oust Kriangsak from power.[233] The Soviet invasion of Afghanistan encouraged a shift in American policy toward Vietnam. Carter's close advisors, in particular Zbigniew Brzezinski, National Security Advisor, and Richard Holbrooke, Assistant Secretary of State for East Asia, believed that a normalisation with Vietnam would diminish Soviet influence in the region, weakening its control of the Indian Ocean. American and Thai interests diverged. This became obvious during a meeting in Bangkok on 13 February 1980 between Kriangsak and Holbrooke. US Ambassador to Thailand Abramowitz, and Admiral Robert J Long, a new US Commander-in-Chief in the Pacific, also attended the meeting. It ended with tense discussions and disagreement.

During the meeting, the Americans emphasised the paramount importance of the Indian Ocean to their geopolitical interests, and underlined their anxiety that the Soviet Union sought access to Vietnamese port facilities such as in Cam Ranh. They thus wished to adopt a policy of normalising relations with Hanoi in order to distance Vietnam from Moscow. For Kriangsak, any Western attempt to concede to Vietnam would jeopardise ASEAN's regional diplomacy, rather than weaken the Soviet position in the region. Kriangsak reportedly stated that 'after that, ASEAN could never stand up to Hanoi with the strength and determination of the past year'.[234] For Kriangsak, Thailand's objective was to secure a withdrawal of Vietnamese troops from Cambodia. Kriangsak criticised the US for its failure to provide for the security needs of Thailand, and said he believed that US security in the region was dependent on a strong ally like Thailand. The Americans told Kriangsak that building up Thailand militarily would only aggravate regional tensions and obstruct US normalisation with Hanoi.[235] In his view, Kriangsak believed that one of the reasons his government fell two weeks later was the withdrawal of American support.[236]

---

233 Richard Nations, 'Thai Sources say Washington's Disfavor Helped Kriangsak's Ouster', *Far Eastern Economic Review*, 4 April 1980, 8.
234 Nations, 'Thai Sources say Washington's Disfavor Helped Kriangsak's Ouster', 9.
235 Nations, 'Thai Sources say Washington's Disfavor Helped Kriangsak's Ouster', 10.
236 Randolph, *The United Sates and Thailand*, 220.

In sum, Kriangsak's downfall fundamentally emerged from the intra-discursive struggle between the balanced détente discourse and emerging unbalanced détente discourse, which shaped the way in which military elites and commanders shifted their support away from Kriangsak. An increase in energy prices was merely a pretext that precipitated the mass demonstrations against the Kriangsak Government. While Washington's disfavour did not directly cause Kriangsak's downfall, the former rendered the latter possible.

7.4. Conclusion

By the late 1970s, a 'fear of communism', said Carter's National Security Advisor, Zbigniew Brzezinski, was 'no longer the glue that holds our foreign policy together'.[237] So too was the case in Thailand. Prime Minister's Order No. 66/2523, which was promulgated by Prime Minister Prem Tinsulanonda in April 1980, was just such an example. It has become conventional wisdom that the order marked the end of communism in Thailand. It not only used political means to defeat communism but also pardoned the former Thai communists, thereby allowing them to return from the jungle.

This conventional wisdom is problematic. Strictly speaking, the prime minister's order was not the move that ended communism, but rather one of the products of the détente discourse. Resulting from a long discursive struggle between anticommunism and détente in the long 1970s, détente ended communism in Thailand. The end of the Cold War in Thailand was thus marked by closer Sino–Thai relations, normal Thai–Soviet relations, Chinese withdrawal of support from the CPT, and the CPT's anticipated decline.

'Whether or not there is peace in this region', as one Thai military officer close to Kriangsak put it, 'depends entirely on how Beijing reacts to what it sees as direct or indirect Soviet threats', and perhaps vice versa.[238] Kriangsak recognised these changing power realities in the midst of the emerging Third Indochina War in the late 1970s. His policy of equidistance was a flexible and equal approach to diplomacy with the ultimate aim of balancing the intense Sino–Soviet rivalry in the region. Equidistance

---

237 Quoted in Sargent, *A Superpower Transformed*, 263.
238 Nations, 'The Makings of Friendship', 29.

could be a de jure policy but proved to be extremely difficult to execute in practice. By that time, anticommunism was no longer a viable discourse, partly because of the de-ideologisation of the Cold War, and partly because of the establishment of Sino–American diplomatic relations. Yet it was also fading because of the simultaneous construction of Thai détente as the decisive characteristic of Thai foreign policy.

8

Conclusion: The End of 'Bamboo' Diplomacy? Back to the Future

> With regard to foreign policy, Thailand should be committed to following a policy of equidistance. Thailand should try to keep on the best possible terms with Major Powers – the United States, the Soviet Union, China … If we allow one Power to station troops here, we may get into trouble with another large Power or one of the smaller Powers. I do not want the United States forces to leave and the Soviets to come in place of them. I do not think we should have any at all. We should not ask any Major Powers to involve themselves too deeply.
>
> – Thanat Khoman, 1975[1]

'The age of "bending with the wind", a metaphor commonly used to describe Thailand's foreign policy, had come to an end', proclaimed Prime Minister Chatichai Choonhavan in December 1988.[2] His business-oriented diplomacy, culminating in the catchy slogan of 'turning Indochina from battlefield to marketplace', significantly redefined the framing of Thailand's national interest. It in turn deemphasised national security to affirm Thailand's status as an aspiring regional economic power.

---

1   Michael Morrow, 'Thanat's Interview', *Far Eastern Economic Review* 88, no. 25 (June 1975): 34.
2   Leszek Buszynski, 'Thailand's Foreign Policy: Management of a Regional Vision', *Asian Survey* 34, no. 8 (1994): 724.

However, in reality, Chatichai continued to follow the recently constructed bamboo strategy. Thailand still believed in maintaining a flexible relationship with the great powers, and in moving toward a closer alignment with China. We can say that it is easier to imagine the end of the Cold War in Asia – the Vietnamese withdrawal from Cambodia, the end of Third Indochina War, and the peace settlement in Cambodia – than to imagine the end of bamboo diplomacy. Since then, the metaphor of bamboo diplomacy endures. As one scholar summarised, bamboo diplomacy has been 'the norm in Thai foreign policy'.[3]

This book is first and foremost a genealogy of Thai détente and the concomitant narrative of bamboo diplomacy. It asserts a diplomatic discursive framework to understand and explicate the (trans)formation of Thai diplomacy toward the Soviet Union and the People's Republic of China between 1968 and 1980. I argue that a genealogy of Thai détente can be explicated as a history of rupture and history of the present in order to reassess and reinterpret changing diplomatic discourses and practices. On the one hand, a history of rupture indicates how the discourse of détente emerged in the late 1960s, and developed in three main episodes, namely under Thanat Khoman, Chatichai Choonhavan and Kukrit Pramoj, and Kriangsak Chomanan. It also emphasises that the ascent of détente happened within discursive struggles with the hegemonic discourse of anticommunism. On the other hand, a history of the present demonstrates the knowledge production of bamboo diplomacy. It argues that bamboo diplomacy was recently produced during the détente era in Thailand. Rather than forming a long diplomatic tradition, it was the making of détente that produced the invented tradition of bamboo diplomacy. This chapter concludes with these two contributions, on which the book has sought to shed light.

8.1. Genealogy as a History of Rupture

The book argues that during the Cold War, Thailand did not have a continuity of diplomacy, but rather experienced a rupture in diplomatic practices. From the late 1950s, the dominant discourse in Thailand was anticommunism. It rendered communism – both as an ideology

---

3   Leszek Buszynski, 'New Aspirations and Old Constraints in Thailand's Foreign Policy', *Asian Survey* 29, no. 11 (1989): 1057.

and a political struggle with the communist powers – a vital 'threat' to body politic and to the survival of the nation. The emergence of détente discourse marked a rupture in Thai diplomacy in the late 1960s when the communist powers began to be considered 'friends'. To put it dialectically, détente can be counted as an antithesis of the anticommunist discourse, which was the predominant thesis.

Crucially, I argue that détente began even before the declaration of the Nixon Doctrine in 1969 and that the key proponent, Foreign Minister Thanat Khoman, initiated the concept of 'flexible diplomacy' and later 'détente' in order to seek rapprochement with the PRC and to readjust Thai–Soviet relations, hence bending before the wind. Kukrit Pramoj and Chatichai Choonhavan continued with détente in the democratic period. They established diplomatic relations with the PRC on 1 July 1975 and concluded a cultural agreement with the Soviet Union. From then, the discourse developed into balanced détente, which culminated in Kriangsak Chomanan's stated policy of 'equidistance' toward the three great powers and was exemplified in his visits to three capitals, namely Beijing, Washington and Moscow. Air Marshal Siddhi Savetsila called this balanced détente a 'balance-of-power' or realist strategy.[4]

A genealogy of Thai détente reconceptualises diplomacy in various ways. Firstly, diplomacy as knowledge production constituted a new form of diplomatic knowledge, framed by the notion of 'bamboo' diplomacy. Second, diplomacy as subject formation formed the subject positions of détente proponents, whose identity and interests were shaped by the discourse of détente. The strength of leading détente proponents such as Thanat, Kukrit and Kriangsak was partly due to the fact that they were formerly known as staunch anticommunists. With clear records of anticommunism, they were not vulnerable to any accusations of sympathising with the communists. Just as we say only Nixon could have gone to China, so we can say only Kukrit and Kriangsak could go to the PRC or the Soviet Union.

Third, diplomacy as institutionalisation. Détente rendered the Ministry of Foreign Affairs (MFA) an independent source of foreign policy formulation. When anticommunism was the hegemonic discourse, military and security elites dominated Thai foreign policy decision-making while marginalising the MFA. During the 1970s, however,

---

4 Siddhi Savetsila, *Pan Rorn Pan Nao* [Through Thick and Thin] (Bangkok, 2013), 78, 191.

foreign affairs for the first time became a sphere where the MFA would be the sole institution and legitimate actor, while Thai diplomats began to protect their own turf.

Fourth, diplomacy as a power struggle. The discourse of détente did not prevail without a fight. Those anticommunists incessantly sought to strike back, which led to showdowns including the coups in November 1971 and October 1976. However, the 1971 coup did not terminate détente. Instead, slow détente was pursued through sports and petro-diplomacy with the PRC. The 1976 coup, which installed the militant anticommunist regime of Thanin Kraivichien, lasted only a year and was replaced by Kriangsak in late 1977. The détente discourse was once again strengthened, although subtly reformulated to maintain what was described as equidistance or balanced détente with the communist powers. By the end of the 1970s, anticommunism gradually faded from the discursive struggle in Thai politics, and everyone was to an extent a détente proponent.

The fall of Kriangsak in early 1980 was the result of another discursive struggle, or what I call 'intra-discursive struggle'. This time it was between two versions of détente. On the one hand, proponents of balanced détente argued for Thailand to keep an equal and balanced relationship with the great powers while seeing détente with Vietnam as a possibility. On the other, proponents of unbalanced détente promoted a closer alliance with the PRC and saw détente with Vietnam as unnecessary or even dangerous. The unbalanced form of détente prevailed.

Those who supported unbalanced détente, especially the conservative military elites, became the key actors in the Prem Government in the 1980s. This was the beginning of a shrewdly pro-Chinese Thai foreign policy, which Pongphisoot awkwardly terms as a 'bamboo swirling in the wind'[5]. Despite the Sino–Thai quasi-alliance, the discourse of détente remained intact in a double sense. First, the discourse of anticommunism no longer existed in Thai diplomatic discourses and practices with the communist powers. Second, flexible diplomacy and its corresponding languages of friendship towards the communist powers endured up to the end of the Cold War. In other words, Thailand adhered to the pro-Chinese stance, while maintaining a correct but distant relationship with Moscow.

---

5   Pongphisoot Busbarat, 'Bamboo Swirling in the Wind: Thailand's Foreign Policy Imbalance between China and the United States', *Contemporary Southeast Asia* 38, no. 2 (2016): 233.

8. CONCLUSION

The new discursive struggle between balanced and unbalanced détente has continued to dominate Thai diplomacy since the détente period. Three examples are, as follows:

First, Prem Tinsulanonda's diplomacy was ruled by unbalanced détente. Prem's foreign minister, Air Marshal Siddhi Savetsila, called it 'omnidirectional foreign policy'. In his 1985 article, 'The Future of Thailand's Foreign Policy', Siddhi claimed:

> Five years ago you will recall that we lived in a period of great anxiety … All this forced us to confine the conduct of our foreign policy mostly within the political and security fields. There was no time to think of foreign policy as an instrument to enhance the national well-being, much less creating new initiatives in other fields … We were in the process of becoming mired by the prudent, the tactical, or the expedient. The tendency was more toward solving the crisis of the day.[6]

'For the first time', Siddhi continued, 'I think it is fair to say that our sense of direction has returned. So have our self-confidence and pride. We have adapted well to the changing circumstances'. He laid out the new omnidirectional foreign policy, stating:

> it is therefore obvious that we need now, more than ever, to conduct our foreign policy with perseverance, persistence, subtlety, and flexibility. We must also be prepared to accept the fact that what has been achieved at one point may lost its significance as conditions change and that it may not always completely satisfy our principles … With our expanded role we must build a new set of foreign policy principles, similar in scope but different in content.[7]

To put it differently, Siddhi suggested that this novel 'omnidirectional' diplomacy was 'similar in scope' but 'different in content' from the traditional 'bamboo' diplomacy: unbalanced détente. For Siddhi, the outline of this new foreign policy was based on four principles: (1) active diplomacy provides the best guarantee for Thai national security; (2) solidarity with ASEAN (the Association of Southeast Asian Nations) is an overriding priority; (3) strengthening Thailand's relations with great powers is necessary; and (4) the conduct of foreign affairs is inextricably

---

6   Siddhi Savetsila, 'The Future of Thai Foreign Policy', *Bangkok Post*, 18 January 1985.
7   Siddhi, 'The Future of Thai Foreign Policy'.

linked to the well-being of the Thai people, and every diplomatic tool should be used for Thai socio-economic development.[8] Regarding relations with the great powers, the Prem Government moved toward a closer alignment with China, while to a lesser extent maintaining friendly relations with the Soviet Union.

Second, the discursive struggle can be found across society, especially within the academic community. In the 1980s, a debate emerged at Chulalongkorn University between the Institute of Asian Studies (IAS) and the Institute of Strategic and International Studies (ISIS Thailand).[9] It was a debate between unbalanced and balanced détente discourses. On the one hand, the IAS, led by its Director and Professor in International Relations, Khien Theeravit, firmly supported the Foreign Ministry's position that the PRC was the natural counterweight to Vietnam, and Thai foreign policy should endorse the Khmer Rouge regime. According to Khien:

> The question for us as a neighbor to the 'Big' Vietnam is whether we would allow the big fish (Vietnam) to swallow the small fish (Cambodia), which is now struck in the big fish's throat; whether we should stay idle and let a few leaders in Hanoi brutalize innocent Cambodians and Vietnamese; whether we should tolerate threats and shoulder the displaced people who escaped the killing by the ruthless people. I think we should not stay idle. We cannot accept it, not because we hate Vietnam, but because Cambodia's independence is our problem too. Man is not a wild animal, which tends to resort to violent means and ignore what is right or wrong. Even Vietnam itself doesn't want to be a wild animal because she is trying to be a member of the United Nations. However, Vietnam only wants to obtain rights, not the duty and obligations of the UN resolution. Therefore, we must oppose Vietnam's aggression and expose its deception and real goal.[10]

---

8   Eric Teo Chu Cheow, 'New Omnidirectional Overtures in Thai Foreign Policy', *Asian Survey* 26, no. 7 (1986): 747.
9   I argue elsewhere that this debate generated the 'first great debate' in the discipline of international relations in Thailand. See Jittipat Poonkham, 'Why is there no Thai (Critical) International Relations Theory? Great Debates Revisited, Critical Theory, and Dissensus of IR in Thailand', in *International Relations as a Discipline in Thailand: Theory and Sub-fields*, ed. Chanintira na Thalang, Soravis Jayanama and Jittipat Poonkham (London: Routledge, 2019), Chapter 2.
10   Khien Theeravit, *The Kampuchean Problem in Thai Perspective: Positions and Viewpoints* (Bangkok: Institute of Asian Studies, 1985).

On the other hand, the Institute of Strategic and International Studies promoted the discourse of balanced détente with the great powers. The Institute's Director, MR Sukhumbhand Paribatra, criticised Prem's foreign policy. In an interview, he argued:

> the Thai government, among others, takes a rather complacent attitude towards this problem, at most admitting that the Khmer Rouge issue can be tackled as a part of the political settlement or after that political settlement has been reached. This is partly due to conceptual naivety, partly to fear of antagonising Thailand's Chinese patron, partly to continuing distrust of Vietnam and partly to the existence of bureaucratic vested interests in the Khmer Rouge connection ... The point is that there can never be a stable, durable and just political solution in Kampuchea as long as the Khmer Rouge is allowed to retain its present leadership or maintain its present level of military strength.[11]

Sukhumbhand recommended that 'what is needed here is flexibility, vision, and a willingness to re-examine past assumptions. Without these, the best we can hope for is a continuing stalemate – with all its implications'.[12] First:

> Thailand should perhaps consider ASEAN as an end in itself and strive to create within that organization a regional order whose purpose would go beyond common solidarity against one specific threat, toward a more distant (yet more self-fulfilling) horizon of idealism ... Without this change in Thailand's security perception, no modus vivendi can be found on mainland Southeast Asia.[13]

Second, the ASEAN countries, together with the Western powers, needed to promote cross-linkages and offer economic incentives and aid to Vietnam and Kampuchea.[14] During the Chatichai Choonhavan Government (August 1988 – February 1991), Sukhumbhand was appointed as a key advisor to the prime minister.

---

11 Quoted in Puangthong Pawakapan, 'Thailand's Response to the Cambodian Genocide', in *Genocide in Cambodia and Rwanda: New Perspectives*, ed. Susan E Cook (New Brunswick: Transaction Publishers, 2009), 100.
12 Sukhumbhand Paribatra, 'Can ASEAN break the stalemate?', *World Policy Journal* 3, no. 1 (1985): 104.
13 Sukhumbhand Paribatra, 'Strategic Implications of the Indochina Conflict', *Asian Affairs* 11, no. 3 (1984): 44.
14 Sukhumbhand, 'Can ASEAN break the stalemate?', 103.

The third example of the intra-discursive struggle was the foreign policy of Chatichai Choonhavan, the first elected prime minister since 1976. This was a return to balanced détente discourse. At the outset, Chatichai sought to control foreign policy formulation under his newly established policy advisors at Ban Phitsanulok, two of which were Sukhumbhand and Kraisak Choonhavan, his own son and lecturer in political science at Kasetsart University. This caused a major conflict between Chatichai's foreign policy advisors and Siddhi's Foreign Ministry: once again instigating a power struggle between balanced and unbalanced détentes. Both Sukhumbhand and Kraisak strongly criticised Siddhi's foreign policy, which largely depended on the great powers. They advocated greater independence in foreign policy, were opposed to Thailand's support for the Khmer Rouge, and urged economic interdependence among the neighbouring countries. The latter culminated in Chatichai's notion of 'turning Indochina from battlefield to marketplace', and 'Suwannabhumi' (golden peninsula), which focused on Thailand's economic leverages to link Vietnam into a regional network of economic interdependence.[15]

'Rapprochement with Vietnam', Chatichai asserted at a December 1988 speech before the Foreign Correspondents' Club, was 'one of my top priorities'. He added that 'Indochina must be transformed from a war-zone to a peace-zone linked with Southeast Asia through trade ties, investment, and modern communications'. 'Politics', stressed Chatichai, 'will take second place to economics'.[16] While he publicly supported the idea of developing trade relations with Indochina, Foreign Minister Siddhi Savetsila argued that it should be done only after the resolution of the Cambodian issue. Chatichai's foreign policy advisors made statements challenging Siddhi's position and contesting the right of the foreign minister to define priorities in foreign affairs. Sukhumbhand also revealed that the prime minister intended to visit Vietnam and to assume a greater role in foreign policy.[17]

The discursive clash between balanced and unbalanced détente worsened. The Foreign Ministry officials regarded the prime minister's advisors as essentially illegitimate diplomats or upstarts. Warning against what he called 'sensational diplomacy', Siddhi, who was also the leader of the Social

---

15 See Sunai Phasuk, 'Thai Foreign Policy: A Case Study on the Policy Formulation Process of General Chatichai Choonhavan's Government on the Cambodian Problem (4 August 1988 to 23 February 1991)' (MA thesis, Chulalongkorn University, 1986).
16 Buszynski, 'New Aspirations and Old Constraints', 1059.
17 Buszynski, 'New Aspirations and Old Constraints', 1062.

Action Party, insisted that changes to Thai foreign policy ought to be introduced gradually to achieve consensus. In an effort to reduce tension without conceding his position, Chatichai made a distinction between government-sponsored trade with Vietnam and private trade. While the former was dependent on Vietnam's withdrawal from Cambodia, the latter could come prior.[18] While Sukhumbhand resigned in August 1989, the discourse and policies of balanced détente continued in Chatichai's foreign policy and Thai diplomacy thereafter. These three examples have illustrated the persistence of the détente discourse and the intra-discursive struggle after the long 1970s.

By tracing a genealogy of détente, it is therefore possible to fully understand a discontinuity in Thai diplomacy from the late 1960s. Proponents of Thai détente not only contested the anticommunism discourse but established détente itself a new hegemonic idea in the foreign policymaking process. At the onset of its hegemonic status, détente encountered conceptual contradictions from within. A dual form of détente emerged by the end of the decade: balanced and unbalanced détente with the communist powers. This dual track lent itself to an intra-discursive struggle. Prem and Siddhi's 'omnidirectional' foreign policy was neither a reversal of détente nor a return to the discourse of anticommunism. Rather, it was a modified détente discourse – a synthesis of an unbalanced détente. It was guided by the formation of a quasi-alliance with the PRC and the US in the Third Indochina War. Nevertheless, the emphasis on détente with the Soviet Union faded but did not vanish. Thailand and the Soviet Union remained what they called 'friends'.

8.2. Genealogy as a History of the Present

'The myth of the success of Thai foreign policy due to its flexibility to "bend with the prevailing wind"', asserts Pavin Chachavalpongpun, 'needs a serious reinterpretation'.[19] Following this proposition, the book goes one step further: to historically problematise or genealogise the narrative of bamboo diplomacy. It has demonstrated how bamboo diplomacy narrative was constructed only in the 1970s.

---

18 Buszynski, 'New Aspirations and Old Constraints', 1062–63.
19 Pavin Chachavalpongpun, *Reinventing Thailand: Thaksin and His Foreign Policy* (Singapore: Institute of Southeast Asian Studies, 2010), 5.

The narrative of bamboo diplomacy was, and remains, powerful in both policymaking and academic communities. Yet, few have stopped to ask why it is so dominant, especially within academia, and how it became a metanarrative, which cannot be easily transcended. Even those self-reflexive and critical-minded scholars, such as, inter alia, Arne Kislenko, Sutayut Osornprasop, Pavin Chachavalpongpun, Thitinan Pongsudhirak and Pongphisoot Busbarat share a certain common ground. Namely, they see bamboo diplomacy as a tradition, while recognising its continuity. It thus becomes a flawless strategy and/or heuristic device for evaluating the success or failure of Thai foreign policy at any given time.

In the most oft-cited article, entitled 'Bending with the Wind: The Continuity and Flexibility of Thai Foreign Policy', Arne Kislenko asserts:

> whatever new winds blow in the region, Thailand will undoubtedly try to accommodate them. With an emphasis on flexibility, and a remarkable history of continuity, Thai foreign policy – like a bamboo – faces the 21st Century with solid roots.[20]

In his thesis, Kislenko also conceptualises Thai foreign policy during the Cold War as 'the bamboo in the wind', which was 'always solidly rooted, but flexible enough to bend whichever way it had to in order to survive'. In other words, bamboo diplomacy was a key to national survival. It does not reflect 'mere pragmatism' but more importantly 'a long-cherished, philosophical approach to international relations', which is deeply rooted in Thai culture and religion. He claims:

> although the Thais had in the past entered into diplomatic pacts with foreign powers, they were extremely careful to avoid anything more than temporary arrangements. Formal alliances of any kind were infrequent in Thai history, and Thais considered the stationing of even friendly foreign troops on their soil a serious affront to their independence.[21]

However, Kislenko's proposition largely contradicts his main argument that in the 1960s, the special relationship forged with the US 'seemed only logical, and entirely consistent with the "bamboo" nature of Thai diplomacy'. He contends that these closer ties were not 'a fundamental

---

20 Arne Kislenko, 'Bending with the Wind: The Continuity and Flexibility of Thai Foreign Policy', *International Journal* 57, no. 4 (Autumn 2002): 561.
21 Arne Kislenko, 'Bamboo in the Wind: United States Foreign Policy and Thailand during the Kennedy and Johnson Administrations, 1961–1969' (PhD thesis, University of Toronto, 2000), 8.

digression from its traditional and renowned foreign policy flexibility'.²² He even holds that by the end of the 1960s, when it became apparent that the US military was losing in Vietnam, Thailand changed course in line with bamboo diplomacy. As Kislenko put it, Thailand 'bent its foreign policy with the new winds in Southeast Asia towards a peaceful accommodation with China and Vietnam'.²³ In his final analysis, 'the bamboo bent, but it never did break'.²⁴

Likewise, in his multi-archival dissertation on Thailand's covert military intervention in Laos during 1960–1974, Sutayut Osornprasop concludes that the emerging Sino–Thai alliance against Hanoi's expansionism since the late 1970s was 'Thailand's traditional foreign policy of "bending as bamboo and never breaking"', rather than 'a hawkish, military-oriented policy'.²⁵ As he put it:

> Interestingly, Bangkok had formed a close alliance with Washington against Beijing during the 1960s and the early half of the 1970s in order to obstruct Chinese expansion southwards. But with the American departure from mainland Southeast Asia, the Thais were successful in turning an old threat into an opportunity, and formed a new alliance with Beijing to deter Hanoi.

Bamboo diplomacy, according to Sutayut, 'had helped preserve Thailand's security and sovereignty throughout the country's history. It would protect Thailand's interests throughout the tumultuous decades of the Cold War'.²⁶

Even one of the most critical intellectuals in Thai studies, Pavin Chachavalpongpun, implicitly adopts this traditional view of Thai diplomacy without questioning its emergence. In an approach similar to the mainstream conservative narrative, he suggests that bamboo diplomacy is dubbed the accommodation policy, where the logic is simple: 'to go with the flow of the wind, to align with hegemons of the day and to use this alliance to strengthen the power position of the Thai elites at home'. Its ultimate aim was to 'maintain national sovereignty and territorial integrity'.²⁷ While he

---

22 Kislenko, 'Bamboo in the Wind', 9, 320.
23 Kislenko, 'Bamboo in the Wind', 14.
24 Kislenko, 'Bamboo in the Wind', 330.
25 Sutayut Osornprasop, 'Thailand and the American Secret War in Indochina, 1960–1974' (PhD thesis, University of Cambridge, 2006), 237.
26 Sutayut, 'Thailand and the American Secret War', 237.
27 Pavin, *Reinventing Thailand*, 85–86.

traces this concept in Thai diplomatic history, Pavin only reiterates bamboo diplomacy as a 'traditional' or 'classic' Thai diplomacy. That is, what he envisions is the continuity and persistence of bamboo diplomacy – 'since Siam's old days up to Thailand's modern era'.[28]

Second, rather than reinterpret bamboo diplomacy, as he initially aims, Pavin evaluates the success of Thaksin's foreign policy based on the key criterion of bamboo diplomacy, which, for him, was guided by flexibility, pragmatism and opportunism. He claims that Thaksin's diplomacy was no longer bending with the wind, but instead sought to 'set' or 'manipulate' the direction of the wind.[29] A deviation from bamboo diplomacy, therefore, rendered Thaksin's foreign policy 'unsuccessful' and 'unsustainable'.[30] Pavin contends:

> the old bamboo policy may have no longer been desirable in the eyes of Thaksin since he embarked on a new process of reinventing Thailand and reinventing himself as a prominent regional leader. But what has remained intact ... is the adoption of the accommodation approach in Thai foreign policy.[31]

In other words, for Pavin, bamboo diplomacy remains intact, and sets the gold standard for evaluating Thai diplomacy.

Pongphisoot Busbarat follows this same line of argument. In a recent article, he claims that Thailand since the early 2000s has encountered difficulties in maintaining 'its time-honored diplomatic tradition of flexibility and pragmatism'. Contemporary Thai foreign policy was shrewdly pro-Chinese. Pongphisoot labelled this policy 'bamboo swirling in the wind'. For him, it increasingly deviates from the 'conventional "bending with the wind" diplomacy that tends to reflect a better-calculated strategy to balance Great Power influence'.[32]

Even when scholars criticise the current Prime Minister Prayut Chan-o-cha's diplomacy, they tend to employ a lens of 'bamboo diplomacy'. As Thitinan Pongsudhirak, political scientist at Chulalongkorn University, puts it, Thailand is

---

28 Pavin, *Reinventing Thailand*, 63–64, 274.
29 Pavin, *Reinventing Thailand*, 34–36.
30 Pavin, *Reinventing Thailand*, 272–76.
31 Pavin, *Reinventing Thailand*, 274.
32 Pongphisoot, 'Bamboo Swirling in the Wind', 233.

demonstrably famous for its foreign policy balancing. From the era of imperialism and two World Wars through the Cold War, Thailand's gifted geography and diplomatic finesse and skill shepherded the country's sovereignty and independence through the thick and thin of geopolitical headwinds.[33]

According to Thitinan, 'whatever happens out there, the Thais (and their Siamese forebears) had a way to diplomatically navigate and geopolitically balance their national interests to stay out of harm's way'. 'Centuries of diplomatic ingenuity and geographic luck' is however undermined by 'quick and careless acts of injudicious leadership'.[34]

Until now, bamboo diplomacy serves not only to narrate transhistorical diplomatic practices but also to make a judgment on the achievement of respective Thai foreign policies. This in turn assumes that 'great' foreign policy is the product of a 'great' leader's far-sightedness, diplomatic flexibility and pragmatism. They must demonstrate an understanding of Thailand's geographically strategic location and the sustainability of so-called 'national interests'. Arguably, even the most critically engaged scholar of Thailand in the modern era, Benedict Anderson has extolled 'bamboo diplomacy' as a 'uniquely Thai' blend of realism and flexibility.[35]

However, what is mystified by this mainstream explanation is the making of the bamboo diplomacy. It lacks two historical problematisations. First, this existing literature neglects the way in which the knowledge of bamboo diplomacy was constructed within historical time, and was a very recent conceptual lexicon. Knowledge production of bamboo diplomacy was, as argued here, the result of the changing diplomatic discursive practices or détente in the long 1970s. It was at this point, and not before, that bamboo diplomacy arose. The introduction of 'bamboo diplomacy' was thus not continuity, but the product of rupture or discontinuity. It rather emerged as a direct result of an epistemological break and a shift in diplomatic practices related explicitly and only to détente.

---

33 Thitinan Pongsudhirak, 'Thai Geopolitical Balancing Compromised', *Bangkok Post*, 6 July 2018.
34 Thitinan, 'Thai Geopolitical Balancing Compromised'.
35 Benedict Anderson, 'Withdrawal Symptoms: Social and Cultural Aspects of the October 6 Coup', in *Exploration and Irony in Studies of Siam over Forty Years* (Ithaca: Cornell University, 2014), 48–49.

While there may have been previous mention of bamboo diplomacy before the 1970s, it was only then that the term became accepted knowledge, epistemically. It did so within academic and policy-producing communities for whom the notion had become of clear use. In academia, pioneering works, led by Likhit Dhiravegin, Sarasin Viraphol and Thamsook Numnonda, only appeared in the 1970s, and began to narrate Thai foreign policy through the lens of 'bamboo diplomacy' (as indicated in Chapter 1). This not only explained contemporary Thai foreign policy,[36] but was also the first time that the conceptual lexicon was employed to explicate Thai diplomacy in the past, such as to describe Siam's approach during the colonial period in the nineteenth century, and again, to explain (or more accurately to obscure) Thailand's position during the Second World War.[37]

Normatively, bamboo diplomacy justified the emerging discourse of flexible diplomacy and the technocratic role of the MFA in formulating foreign policy and relations with other countries. In other words, it legitimised the détente strategy and the practices of those détente proponents during and since the long 1970s. A genealogy of détente thus sheds light on the birth of bamboo diplomacy in terms of knowledge and practices transformation.

Secondly, the mainstream literature also naturalises and essentialises the conventional wisdom and wit of the bamboo diplomacy narrative. It treats bamboo diplomacy as if it is a 'tradition' of Thai diplomacy. If anything, however, this is an invented tradition.[38] Moreover, the essentialising of bamboo diplomacy led to some setbacks. First, the literature ignores the fact that bamboo diplomacy emerged out of a discursive struggle linked to contested power politics. It was neither a neutral nor value-free concept: it was inherently political and developed to overtly oppose the bipolar anticommunism of the early Cold War and to realign with a changed geopolitical reality.

---

36   Sarasin Viraphol, *Directions in Thai Foreign Policy* (Singapore: Institute of Southeast Asian Studies, 1976).
37   Likhit Dhiravegin, 'Thailand Foreign Policy Determination', *The Journal of Social Sciences* 11, no. 4 (1974); Likhit Dhiravegin, *Siam and Colonialism (1855–1909): An Analysis of Diplomatic Relation* (Bangkok: Thai Wattana Panich, 1975); Thamsook Numnonda, *Thailand and the Japanese Presence, 1941–1945* (Singapore: Institute of Southeast Asian Studies, 1977).
38   I borrow the term from Eric Hobsbawm and Terence Ranger, eds, *The Invention of Tradition* (Cambridge: Cambridge University Press, 1983).

The second drawback is that given its status as a 'classic' or 'traditional' policy, bamboo diplomacy is a powerful heuristic device that determines how particular governments or periods of time are judged or deemed successes or failures. In turn, it can legitimise one set of foreign policy approaches while delegitimising others. The risk here is of determinism in Thai foreign policy, which overemphasises realism or profits at the expense of neglecting universal or cosmopolitan principles as motives for Thailand's foreign relations.[39]

The third drawback is that bamboo diplomacy is cast as a unique characteristic of the Thai nation in two senses. First, Thailand is accordingly viewed as an exceptional country that maintained independence and integrity in the midst of colonialism in the nineteenth century – due to its successful policy. This indicates the flawless continuation of Thai foreign policy and the far-sightedness of the elites, either the king or the military. Bamboo diplomacy tends to be nationalistic and chauvinistic. Second, Thailand is unique in the sense that it cannot be compared with other countries. This tends to cause hubris in Thai foreign policy.

The final drawback is that despite its status as an innovation in the 1970s, bamboo diplomacy is first and foremost a conservative project. It serves the status quo, dominated by the predominant role and position of the MFA. It is presumed to be an art adopted entirely by the Thai elites, and suggests a lack of any participation from the public in determining foreign policy. As long as this metanarrative exists, therefore, it remains difficult to imagine an alternative means to conduct Thai diplomacy, let alone of democratizing it. Given these impediments, Thai diplomacy needs to be emancipated from the dominant perspective in order to adopt a genuinely balanced, equal and people-oriented approach.

Concurring with Pavin's proposition, I therefore argue that bamboo diplomacy is a myth that needs to be fundamentally reinterpreted, reassessed and rewritten. Moving beyond that, it should be genealogised or historically problematised in order to trace its emergence as a conceptual lexicon within historical time. Bamboo diplomacy, which is constituted by and constitutive of détente, is a novel knowledge that was recently produced in the 1970s and was reproduced thereafter. It was a by-product of Thailand's shift in diplomacy toward détente with the communist

---

39 See Kusuma Snitwongse, 'Thai Foreign Policy in the Global Age: Principle or Profit?' *Contemporary Southeast Asia* 23, no. 2 (2001).

powers. Since then, bamboo diplomacy praxeologically shapes the way in which Thailand balances its position within global politics, and in particular its relationship with the great powers. It epistemically narrates or explicates Thai diplomatic discourses and practices in the past, and determines foreign policymaking processes in the present and the future. Bamboo diplomacy is an invented tradition of Thai diplomacy.

Bibliography

Primary Sources

Archival Sources

The Ministry of Foreign Affairs (MFA), Library and Archives Division, Bangkok, Thailand
  POL2/PM2517/9
  POL7/PM2518/1
  POL7/PM2518/2
  POL7/PM2518/3
  POL7/PM2518/4
  POL2/PRC2521/2
  POL2/PRC2521/3

The National Archives of Thailand (TNA), Bangkok, Thailand
  (2) MFA 1.1/112
  (2) MFA 1.2/35
  (2) MFA 1.2/36
  (9) MFA 1.1/107

The National Archives, London, UK
  Foreign and Commonwealth Office Files (FCO)

Online Databases

National Archives and Records Administration (NARA) online database
  Record Group (RG) 59, General Records of the Department of State, Central Foreign Policy Files

Central Intelligence Agency (CIA) online database

Official Documents in Edited Volumes

120 Years Ministry of Foreign Affairs. Bangkok: Ministry of Foreign Affairs, 1995.

Collected Interviews of H.E. Dr. Thanat Khoman, Minister of Foreign Affairs of the Kingdom of Thailand, Vol. 1: 1967. Bangkok: Department of Information, Ministry of Foreign Affairs, 2014.

Collected Interviews of H.E. Dr. Thanat Khoman, Minister of Foreign Affairs of the Kingdom of Thailand, Vol. 2: 1968. Bangkok: Department of Information, Ministry of Foreign Affairs, 2014.

Collected Interviews of H.E. Dr. Thanat Khoman, Minister of Foreign Affairs of the Kingdom of Thailand, Vol. 3: 1969. Bangkok: Department of Information, Ministry of Foreign Affairs, 2014.

Collected Statements of H.E. Dr. Thanat Khoman, Minister of Foreign Affairs of the Kingdom of Thailand, Vol. 4, October 1967–October 1968. Bangkok: Department of Information, Ministry of Foreign Affairs, 2014.

Collected Statements of H.E. Dr. Thanat Khoman, Minister of Foreign Affairs of the Kingdom of Thailand, Vol. 5, November 1968–October 1969. Bangkok: Department of Information, Ministry of Foreign Affairs, 2014.

Devawongse-sarn [Devawongse Journal]. Bangkok: Ministry of Foreign Affairs, 2010.

Jain, RK, ed. *China and Thailand, 1949–1983.* New Delhi: Radiant Publishers, 1984.

Thailand's Ministry of Foreign Affairs, *Collected Volume of Soviet Archival Documents, 1941–1970.* Bangkok: Ministry of Foreign Affairs, 2016.

Thailand's Ministry of Foreign Affairs, *Collected Volumes of Declassified Documents on Thai–Russian Relations, 1970–1991.* 3 vols. Bangkok: Ministry of Foreign Affairs, 2017.

US Department of State. *Foreign Relations of the United States* (FRUS). Washington DC: US Government Printing Office.

Newspapers and Periodicals

Asiaweek
The Associated Press
Bangkok Post
Bangkok World

Beijing Review
Daily News
Far Eastern Economic Review
Foreign Affairs
Globe and Mail (Toronto)
The Nation
New York Times
News Bulletin (China)
Newsweek
Phim Thai
Prachachatraiwan
Prachathipatai
Pravda
Siam Rath
Strait Times
Thai Rath
Times (London)
Washington Post
Xinhua General News Service

Interviews by the author

Sarasin Viraphol
Surapong Jayanama
Tej Bunnag
Warnwai Phathanothai

Secondary Sources

Adler, Emanuel and Vincent Pouliot. 'International Practices'. *International Theory* 3, no. 1 (2011): 1–36.

Adler-Nissen, Rebecca and Vincent Pouliot. 'Power in Practice: Negotiating the International Intervention in Libya'. *European Journal of International Relations* 20, no. 4 (2014): 889–911. doi.org/10.1177/1354066113512702.

Algie, Jim, Denis Gray, Nicholas Grossman, Jeff Hodson and Wesley Hsu. *Americans in Thailand*. Singapore: Editions Didier Millet, 2014.

Anand Panyarachun. 'Negotiating Readjustment in Thai–Vietnam Diplomatic Relations'. Presented in seminar 'Thai–Vietnam Relations in the Contemporary Decade and Towards Cooperation in the Future', Faculty of Political Science, Thammasat University, 2 August 1996.

Anand Panyarachun. 'Patakata pised' [Special Lecture]. In *Kwam sampan thai-jin* [Sino–Thai Relations: Past and Future Prospects], edited by Khien Theeravit and Cheah Yan-Chong, 7–23. Bangkok: Chulalongkorn University, 2000.

Anand Panyarachun. 'Pookmitr kub sataranaratprachachon jeen' [Befriending the People's Republic of China]. In *Nayobai tangprated Thai bon tangpreng* [Thai Foreign Policy at the Crossroads], edited by Chantima Ongsuragz, 128–44. Bangkok: Direk Jayanama Memorial Lecture Series, Thammasat University, 1990.

Anderson, Benedict. *Exploration and Irony in Studies of Siam over Forty Years*. Ithaca: Cornell University, 2014. First published 1978.

Anderson, Benedict. *In the Mirror: Literature and Politics in Siam in the American Era*. Bangkok: Duang Kamol, 1985.

Anderson, Benedict. 'Withdrawal Symptoms'. In *The Spectre of Comparisons: Nationalism, Southeast Asia, and the World*, 139–73. London and New York: Verso Books, 1998.

Ang Cheng Guan. 'Southeast Asian Perceptions of the Domino Theory'. In *Connecting Histories: Decolonization and the Cold War in Southeast Asia, 1945–1962*, edited by Christopher E Goscha and Christopher F Ostenmann, 301–34. Washington DC and Stanford: Woodrow Wilson Center Press with Stanford University Press, 2009.

Anuson Chinvanno. *'Brief Encounter': Sino–Thai Rapprochement after Bandung, 1955–1957*. Bangkok: Institute of Foreign Affairs, 1991.

Anuson Chinvanno. *Thailand's Policies towards China, 1949–54*. Hampshire: Macmillan, 1992.

Apichart Chinwanno. 'Thailand's Search for Protection: The Making of the Alliance with the United States, 1947–1954'. PhD thesis, University of Oxford, 1985.

Apiwat Wannakorn. *Prasit Kanchanawat: Nakkanmuaeng si todsawat* [Prasit Kanchanawat: Four-decade Politician]. Bangkok: Matichon, 1996.

Aree Pirom. *Buanglang kan sathapana samphanthaparp yukmai thai-jeen* [Background to the Establishment of Sino–Thai Relations in the Modern Period]. Bangkok: Mitnara Press, 1981.

Asadakorn Eksaengsri. 'Foreign Policy-Making in Thailand: ASEAN Policy, 1967–1972'. PhD thesis, State University of New York, 1980.

Batson, Benjamin. *The End of the Absolute Monarchy in Siam*. Oxford: Oxford University Press, 1985.

Beek, Steve Van, ed. *M.R. Kukrit Pramoj: His Wit and Wisdom – Writings, Speeches and Interviews*. Bangkok: Duang Kamol, 1983.

Berenskoetter, Felix. 'Friends, There Are No Friends? An Intimate Reframing of the International'. *Millennium: Journal of International Studies* 35, no. 3 (2007): 647–76. doi.org/10.1177/03058298070350031501.

Bhansoon Ladavalya. 'Thailand's Foreign Policy under Kukrit Pramoj: A Study in Decision-Making'. PhD thesis, Northern Illinois University, 1980.

Bowie, Katherine A. *Rituals of National Loyalty: An Anthropology of the State and the Village Scout Movement in Thailand*. New York: Columbia University Press, 1997.

Buszynski, Leszek. 'New Aspirations and Old Constraints in Thailand's Foreign Policy'. *Asian Survey* 29, no. 11 (1989): 1057–72. doi.org/10.1525/as.1989.29.11.01p0321o.

Buszynski, Leszek. *Soviet Foreign Policy and Southeast Asia*. London: Croom Helm, 1986.

Buszynski, Leszek. 'Thailand: The Erosion of a Balanced Foreign Policy'. *Asian Survey* 22, no. 11 (1982): 1037–55. doi.org/10.2307/2643978.

Buszynski, Leszek. 'Thailand's Foreign Policy: Management of a Regional Vision'. *Asian Survey* 34, no. 8 (1994): 721–37. doi.org/10.2307/2645260.

Campbell, David. *Writing Security: United States Foreign Policy and the Politics of Identity*. Minneapolis: University of Minnesota Press, 1992.

Casella, Alessandro. 'US–Thai Relations'. *The World Today* 26, no. 3 (March 1970): 118–25.

Chai-Anan Samudavanija. *The Thai Young Turks*. Singapore: Institute of Southeast Asian Studies, 1982.

Chambers, Michael R. '"The Chinese and the Thais are Brothers": The Evolution of the Sino-Thai Friendship'. *Journal of Contemporary China* 14, no. 45 (2005): 599–629. doi.org/10.1080/10670560500205100.

Chanda, Nayan. *Brother Enemy: The War after the War – A History of Indochina since the Fall of Saigon*. New York: Collier Books, 1986.

Chantima Ongsuragz. 'Thai Perceptions of the Soviet Union and Its Implications for Thai-Soviet Relations'. In *The Soviet Union and the Asia-Pacific Region: Views from the Region,* edited by Pushpa Thambipillai and Daniel C Matuszewski, 122–33. New York: Praeger, 1989.

Chavalit Yongchaiyudh. *Biography of General Chavalit Yongchaiyudh.* Bangkok, 2004.

Cheng Rui-sheng. 'Karntoot ping-pong thai-jin' [Sino-Thai Ping-pong Diplomacy], translated by Vasin Ruengprathepsang, *Saranrom Journal* 63 (February 2006): 106–13.

Cheow, Eric Teo Chu. 'New Omnidirectional Overtures in Thai Foreign Policy'. *Asian Survey* 26, no. 7 (1986): 745–58. doi.org/10.1525/as.1986.26.7.01 p0396g.

Chulacheeb Chinwanno. *Sam sib har pee kwam sampan tang karntoot thai-jin, 2518–2553: Aded pajupan anakod* [Thirty-five Years of Diplomatic Relations between Thailand China, 1975–2010: Past Present and Future]. Bangkok: Openbook, 2010.

Chulacheeb Chinwanno. *Sam sib pee kwam sampan tang karntoot thai-jin: kwam ruammue rawang kalayanamitr, 2518–2548* [Thirty Years of Diplomatic Relations between Thailand and China: Cooperation between Truthful Friends, 1975–2005]. Bangkok: Ministry of Foreign Affairs, 2005.

Chulacheeb Chinwanno. *Siam, Russia, Thai: Karntootkarnmuang Karnmuangkarntoot, Aded pajupan anakod* [Siam, Russia, Thailand: Diplomatic Politics, Politics of Diplomacy, Past Present and Future]. Bangkok: Thammasat University Press, 2013.

Chulacheeb Chinwanno. 'Thai-Chinese Relations: Security and Strategic Partnership'. Working Paper No. 155. S Rajaratnam School of International Studies, Singapore, 24 March 2008.

Chulacheeb Chinwanno. 'Thai Foreign Policy during the Cold War'. In *A Collection of Articles and Speeches on Thai Foreign Affairs from the Past to the Present,* Vol. 1, edited by Corrine Phuangkasem, Komgrit Varakamin, Prapat Thepchatree and Siriporn Wajjawalku, 72–99. Bangkok: Faculty of Political Science, Thammasat University, 1999.

Ciorciari, John D. *The Limits of Alignment: Southeast Asia and the Great Powers since 1975.* Washington DC: Georgetown University Press, 2010.

Corrine Phuangkasem. 'Thai Foreign Policy: Four Decades since the Second World War (1945–1989)'. In *A Collection of Articles and Speeches on Thai Foreign Affairs from the Past to the Present,* Vol. 1, edited by Corrine Phuangkasem, Komgrit Varakamin, Prapat Thepchatree and Siriporn Wajjawalku. Bangkok: Faculty of Political Science, Thammasat University, 1999.

Corrine Phuangkasem. *Thailand's Foreign Relations, 1964–80.* Singapore: Institute of Southeast Asian Studies, 1984.

Darling, Frank C. *Thailand and the United States.* Washington DC: Public Affairs Press, 1965.

Darling, Frank C. 'Thailand: De-escalation and Uncertainty'. *Asian Survey* 9, no. 2 (February 1969): 115–21.

Darling, Frank C. 'Thailand in 1976: Another Defeat for Constitutional Democracy'. *Asian Survey* 17, no. 2 (1977): 116–32. doi.org/10.1525/as.1977.17.2.01p02672.

Darling, Frank C. 'Thailand in 1977: The Search for Stability and Progress'. *Asian Survey* 18, no. 2 (1978): 153–63. doi.org/10.1525/as.1978.18.2.01p0385c.

de Beer, Patrice. 'History and Policy of the Communist Party of Thailand'. *Journal of Contemporary Asia* 8, no. 1 (1978): 143–57.

Der Derian, James. *On Diplomacy.* Oxford: Blackwell, 1987.

Dikotter, Frank. *The Cultural Revolution: A People's History, 1962–1976.* London: Bloomsbury, 2016.

Epstein, Charlotte. *The Power of Words in International Relations: Birth of an Anti-Whaling Discourse.* Cambridge, Massachusetts: The MIT Press, 2008. doi.org/10.7551/mitpress/9780262050920.003.0010.

Epstein, Charlotte. 'Who Speaks? Discourse, the Subject and the Study of Identity in International Politics'. *European Journal of International Relations* 17, no. 2 (June 2011): 327–50. doi.org/10.1177/1354066109350055.

Fardella, Enrico. 'The Sino-American Normalization: A Reassessment'. *Diplomatic History* 33, no. 4 (September 2009): 545–78. doi.org/10.1111/j.1467-7709.2009.00799.x.

Fineman, Daniel. 'Phibun, the Cold War, and Thailand Foreign Policy Revolution of 1950'. In *Connecting Histories: Decolonization and the Cold War in Southeast Asia, 1945–1962,* edited by Christopher E Goscha and Christopher F Ostenmann, 275–300. Washington DC and Stanford: Woodrow Wilson Center Press with Stanford University Press, 2009.

Fineman, Daniel. *A Special Relationship: The United States and Military Government in Thailand, 1947–1958.* Honolulu: University of Hawai'i Press, 1997. doi.org/10.1515/9780824864415.

Flockhart, Trine. 'The Problem of Change in Constructivist Theory: Ontological Security Seeking and Agent Motivation'. *Review of International Studies* 42, no. 5 (2016): 799–820. doi.org/10.1017/s026021051600019x.

Foucault, Michel. *The Archaeology of Knowledge.* Translated by AM Sheridan Smith. London and New York: Routledge, 1972.

Foucault, Michel. *Discipline and Punish: The Birth of the Prison.* Translated by Alan Sheridan. London: Vintage Books, 1995.

Foucault, Michel. 'Lecture on Nietzsche: How to Think the History of Truth with Nietzsche without Relying on Truth'. In *Lectures on the Will to Know: Lectures at the College de France, 1970–1971 and Oedipal Knowledge.* Translated by Graham Burchell, 202–23. Hampshire: Palgrave Macmillan, 2013.

Foucault, Michel. 'Nietzsche, Genealogy, History'. In *The Foucault Reader: An Introduction to Foucault's Thought.* Edited by Paul Rabinow. London: Penguin Books, 1991.

Foucault, Michel. 'The Order of Discourse'. In *Language and Politics.* Edited by Michael J Shapiro. New York: New York University Press, 1984.

Foucault, Michel. 'Politics and the Study of Discourse'. In *The Foucault Effect: Studies in Governmentality.* Edited by Graham Burchell, Colin Gordon and Peter Miller, 76–100. Chicago: University of Chicago Press, 1991.

Funston, John. 'The Role of the Ministry of Foreign Affairs in Thailand: Some Preliminary Observations'. *Contemporary Southeast Asia* 9, no. 3 (December 1987): 229–43. www.jstor.org/stable/25797961.

Ghebhardt, Alexander O. 'The Soviet System of Collective Security in Asia'. *Asian Survey* 13, no. 12 (December 1973): 1075–91.

Girling, John LS. 'The Guam Doctrine'. *International Affairs* 46, no. 1 (January 1970): 48–62.

Girling, John LS. *Thailand: Society and Politics.* Ithaca: Cornell University Press, 1981.

Girling, John LS. 'Thailand: The Coup and Its Implications'. *Pacific Affairs* 50, no. 3 (1977): 387–405. doi.org/10.2307/2757168.

Girling, John LS. 'Thailand's New Course'. *Pacific Affairs* 42, no. 3 (Autumn 1969): 346–59. doi.org/10.2307/2753903.

Goh, Evelyn. *Constructing the US Rapprochement with China, 1961–1974: From 'Red Menace' to 'Tacit Ally'*. Cambridge: Cambridge University Press, 2005. doi.org/10.1002/j.1538-165x.2007.tb00595.x.

Gordon, Bernard. 'Thailand: Its Meaning for the US'. *Current History* 52, no. 305 (1967: 16–21, 53–54.

Goscha, Christopher E. *Thailand and the Southeast Asian Networks of the Vietnamese Revolution, 1885–1954*. London and New York: Routledge, 1999. doi.org/10.4324/9780203036716.

Goscha, Christopher E. 'Vietnam, the Third Indochina War and the Meltdown of Asian Internationalism'. In *The Third Indochina War: Conflict between China, Vietnam and Cambodia, 1972–1979*, edited by Odd Arne Westad and Sophie Quinn-Judge, 152–86. London and New York: Routledge, 2006. doi.org/10.4324/9780203968574-14.

Gourevitch, Peter. 'The Second Image Reversed: The International Sources of Domestic Politics'. *International Organization* 32, no. 4 (1978): 881–912. doi.org/10.1017/s002081830003201x.

Grossman, Nicholas and Dominic Faulder, eds. *King Bhumibol Adulyadej: A Life's Work*. Bangkok: Editions Didier Millet, 2016.

Haberkorn, Tyrell. *Revolution Interrupted: Farmers, Students, Law, and Violence in Northern Thailand*. Madison: University of Wisconsin Press, 2011.

Hanhimäki, Jussi M. *The Rise and Fall of Détente: American Foreign Policy and the Transformation of the Cold War* Washington DC: Potomac Books, 2013.

Hansen, Lene. *Security as Practice: Discourse Analysis and the Bosnian War*. London and New York: Routledge, 2006.

Heidegger, Martin. *Being and Time*. Translated by J Macquarrie and E Robinson. New York: Harper and Row, 1967.

Hobsbawm, Eric and Terence Ranger, eds. *The Invention of Tradition*. Cambridge: Cambridge University Press, 1983.

Horelick, Arnold L. 'The Soviet Union's Asian Collective Security Proposal: A Club in Search of Members'. *Pacific Affairs* 47, no. 3 (Autumn 1974): 269–85. doi.org/10.2307/2755766.

Jha, Ganganath. *Foreign Policy of Thailand*. New Delhi: Radiant Publishers, 1979.

Jian, Chen. 'China and the Cold War after Mao'. In *The Cambridge History of the Cold War*. Vol. 3: *Endings*, edited by Melvyn P Leffler and Odd Arne Westad. Cambridge: Cambridge University Press, 2010.

Jittipat Poonkham. 'Détente Studies in Cold War International History: Questions (Un)Marked?' *Interstate – Journal of International Affairs* 3 (2015/2016).

Jittipat Poonkham. 'Why is there no Thai (Critical) International Relations Theory? Great Debates Revisited, Critical Theory, and Dissensus of IR in Thailand'. In *International Relations as a Discipline in Thailand: Theory and Sub-fields*, edited by Chanintira na Thalang, Soravis Jayanama and Jittipat Poonkham, 19-46. London: Routledge, 2019. doi.org/10.4324/9781351180887.

Jittipat Poonkham. *Withet Panid Sampan su Songkram Yen: Kwam sampan rawangprathet Thai–Russia (1897–1991)* [Foreign Economic Relations to the Cold War: Thai–Russian Foreign Relations (1897–1991)]. Bangkok: Chulalongkorn University Press, 2016.

Jones, Lee. *ASEAN, Sovereignty and Intervention in Southeast Asia*. Hampshire: Palgrave Macmillan, 2012.

Jory, Patrick. 'Republicanism in Thai History'. In *A Sarong for Clio: Essays on the Intellectual and Cultural History of Thailand*, edited by Maurizio Peleggi, 97–117. Ithaca: Cornell Southeast Asia Program Publications, 2015.

Kamol Somvichian. '"The Oyster and the Shell": Thai Bureaucrats in Politics'. *Asian Survey* 18, no. 8 (1978): 829–37. doi.org/10.1525/as.1978.18.8.01p04422.

Karchava, Alexander A. *Kaewsip pee kwam sampan tang karntoot Russia–Thai* [Ninety-Year Russian–Thai Diplomatic Relations]. Bangkok: Bapith Printing, 1988.

Kasian Tejapira. *Commodifying Marxism: The Formation of Modern Thai Radical Culture, 1927–1958*. Australia: Trans Pacific Press, 2001.

Khien Theeravit. *The Kampuchean Problem in Thai Perspective: Positions and Viewpoints*. Bangkok: Institute of Asian Studies, 1985.

Khien Theeravit. 'Thailand: An Overview of Politics and Foreign Relations'. *Southeast Asian Affairs* (1979): 299–311. www.jstor.org/stable/27908383.

Kierkegaard, Soren. *The Concept of Anxiety*. Princeton: Translated by Reidar Thomte. Princeton University Press, 1981.

Kim, Shee Poon. 'The Politics of Thailand's Trade Relations with the People's Republic of China'. *Asian Survey* 21, no. 3 (March 1981): 310–24. doi.org/10.2307/2643727.

Kislenko, Arne. 'Bamboo in the Wind: United States Foreign Policy and Thailand during the Kennedy and Johnson Administrations, 1961–1969'. PhD thesis, University of Toronto, 2000.

Kislenko, Arne. 'Bending with the Wind: The Continuity and Flexibility of Thai Foreign Policy'. *International Journal* 57, no. 4 (Autumn 2002): 537–61. doi.org/10.2307/40203691.

Kobkua Suwannathat-Pian. 'Thailand in 1976'. *Southeast Asian Affairs* (1977): 239–64.

Krajang Phantumnavin. 'Negotiating to Buy Sheng Li Oil'. In *Learn from the Teacher, Know from the Boss, and Gain from Work*, 182–99. (Bangkok, 2016).

Krittin Suksiri. 'Political Conflict under the Government of General Kriangsak Chomanan'. MA thesis, Thammasat University, 2002.

Kullada Kesboonchoo Mead. 'The Cold War and Thai Democratization'. In *Southeast Asia and the Cold War*, edited by Albert Lau, 215–40. London and New York: Routledge, 2012. doi.org/10.4324/9780203116616-21.

Kullada Kesboonchoo Mead. *Kanmueng Thai yuk Sarit–Thanom phaitai khrongsang amnat lok* [Thai Politics during Sarit–Thanom Regimes under Global Power Structure]. Bangkok: 50 Years Foundation, The Bank of Thailand, 2007.

Kullada Kesboonchoo Mead. 'A Revisionist History of Thai-US Relations'. *Asian Review* 16 (2003): 45–67.

Kusuma Snitwongse. 'Thai Foreign Policy in the Global Age: Principle or Profit?' *Contemporary Southeast Asia* 23, no. 2 (2001): 189–212. www.jstor.org/stable/25798542.

Lacan, Jacques. *Anxiety: The Seminar of Jacques Lacan, Book X*. Translated by AR Price. Cambridge: Polity Press, 2014.

Laing, RD. *The Divided Self: An Existential Study in Sanity and Madness*. New York: Penguin, 1990.

Lebow, Richard Ned. *A Cultural Theory of International Relations*. Cambridge: Cambridge University Press, 2008.

Leffler, Melvyn P and Odd Arne Westad, eds. *The Cambridge History of the Cold War.* Vol. 2: *Crises and Détente*. Cambridge: Cambridge University Press, 2010).

Likhit Dhiravegin. *Siam and Colonialism (1855–1909): An Analysis of Diplomatic Relations*. Bangkok: Thai Wattana Panich, 1975.

Likhit Dhiravegin. 'Thailand Foreign Policy Determination'. *The Journal of Social Sciences* 11, no. 4 (1974): 37–65.

Likhit Dhiravegin. 'Thailand's Relations with China, the US, and Japan in the New Political Environment'. In *A Collection of Articles and Speeches on Thai Foreign Affairs from the Past to the Present*, Vol. 1, edited by Corrine Phuangkasem, Komgrit Varakamin, Prapat Thepchatree and Siriporn Wajjawalku, 357–76. (Bangkok: Faculty of Political Science, Thammasat University, 1999).

Lobo-Guerrero, Luis. 'Archives'. In *Research Methods in Critical Security Studies: An Introduction*, edited by Mark B Salter and Can Mutlu, 121–24. London and New York: Routledge, 2012.

Luthi, Lorenz M. 'Strategic Shifts in East Asia'. In *The Regional Cold Wars in Europe, East Asia, and the Middle East: Crucial Periods and Turning Points*, edited by Lorenz M Luthi, 223–44. Washington DC: Woodrow Wilson Centre Press, 2015. doi.org/10.1111/1468-2346.12577.

MacMillan, Margaret. *Nixon in China: The Week That Changed the World*. New York: Random House, 2007.

MacMillan, Margaret. 'Nixon, Kissinger, and the Opening to China'. In *Nixon in the World: American Foreign Relations, 1969–1977*, edited by Fredrick Logevall and Andrew Preston, 107–25. Oxford: Oxford University Press, 2008.

Mallet, Marian. 'Causes and Consequences of the October '76 Coup'. *Journal of Contemporary Asia* 8, no. 1 (1978): 80–103. doi.org/10.1080/00472337885390051.

Mastny, Vojtech. 'The New History of Cold War Alliances'. *Journal of Cold War Studies* 4, no. 2 (Spring 2002): 55–84. doi.org/10.1162/152039702753649647.

McLane, Charles B. *Soviet–Asian Relations*. London: Central Asian Research Centre, 1973.

Menetrey-Monchau, Cecile. 'The Changing Post-War US Strategy in Indochina'. In *The Third Indochina War: Conflict between China, Vietnam and Cambodia, 1972–1979*, edited by Odd Arne Westad and Sophie Quinn-Judge, 65–86. London and New York: Routledge, 2006. doi.org/10.4324/9780203968574-10.

Mezey, Michael L. 'The 1971 Coup in Thailand: Understanding Why the Legislature Fails'. *Asian Survey* 13, no. 3 (1973): 306–17.

Milliken, Jennifer. 'The Study of Discourse in International Relations: A Critique of Research and Methods'. *European Journal of International Relations* 5, no. 2 (June 1999): 225–54. doi.org/10.1177/1354066199005002003.

Montri Chenvidyakarn. 'One Year of Civilian Authoritarian Rule in Thailand: The Rise and Fall of the Thanin Government'. *Southeast Asian Affairs* (1978): 267–85. www.jstor.org/stable/27908352.

Moon, Soo Eon. 'Importance of ASEAN in Soviet Foreign Policy: An Evaluation of Soviet Policy Toward Southeast Asia in the Post-Vietnam War Era'. PhD thesis, Claremont Graduate School, 1984.

Morell, David. 'Thailand: Military Checkmate'. *Asian Survey* 12, no. 2 (1972): 156–67. doi.org/10.2307/2643077.

Morell, David and Chai-Anan Samudawanija. *Political Conflict in Thailand: Reform, Reaction and Revolution.* Cambridge: Oelgeschlager, Gunn & Hain, 1981.

Murashima, Eiji. *The Early Years of Communism in Thailand (1930–1936).* Bangkok: Matichon, 2012.

Narongchai Akrasanee and Somsak Tambunlertchai. 'Thailand: Transition from Import Substitution to Export Expansion'. In *Economic Development in East and Southeast Asia,* edited by Seiji Naya and Akira Takayama, 104–20. Singapore: Institute of Southeast Asian Studies, 1980.

Naruemit Sodsuk. *Sampantaparp tang karntoot rawang thai jeen* [Diplomatic Relations between Thailand and the People's Republic of China]. Bangkok: Thai Wattana Panich, 1981.

Natthaphon Jaijing. 'Kanmueng Thai samai rattaban Chomphon Po Phibun Songkhram phaitai rabiap lok khong Saharat America (2491–2500)' [Thai Politics under Field Marshal Phibun in US World Order (1948–1957)]. PhD thesis, Chulalongkorn University, 1999.

Nealon, Jeffrey T. *Foucault Beyond Foucault: Power and Its Intensification since 1984.* Stanford: Stanford University Press, 2008.

Neher, Arlene Becker. 'Prelude to Alliance: The Expansion of American Economic Interest in Thailand During the 1940s'. PhD thesis, Northern Illinois University, 1980.

Neher, Clark D. 'Thailand: The Politics of Continuity'. *Asian Survey* 10, no. 2 (February 1970): 161–68.

Niksch, Larry. 'Thailand in 1980: Confrontation with Vietnam and the Fall of Kriangsak'. *Asian Survey* 21, no. 2 (1981): 223–31. doi.org/10.1525/as.1981.21.2.01p0247v.

Noranit Setabutr. *Kwam sampan tang prathet rawang Thai–Russia* [Thai–Russian Foreign Relations]. Bangkok: Sukhothai Thammathirat Open University Press, 1985.

Nuechterlein, Donald E. *Thailand and the Struggle for Southeast Asia.* Ithaca: Cornell University Press, 1965.

Pat Akkaniput. Interview. In *Cremation Volume In Honor of General Pat Akkaniput.* Bangkok, 2016.

Pavin Chachavalpongpun. *Reinventing Thailand: Thaksin and His Foreign Policy.* Singapore: Institute of Southeast Asian Studies, 2010.

Peera Charoenwattananukul. 'Beyond Bamboo Diplomacy: The Factor of Status Anxiety and Thai Foreign Policy Behaviors'. In *Routledge Handbook of Contemporary Thailand,* edited by Pavin Chachavalpongpun, 408–19. New York: Routledge, 2020. doi.org/10.4324/9781315151328-32.

Pensri Duke. *Karntangprated kub aekkarat lae attippatai kong thai* [Foreign Affairs and Thailand's Independence and Sovereignty, since King Rama V to the Phibun Government]. Bangkok: The Royal Institute, 1999.

Phillips, Matthew. *Thailand in the Cold War.* London and New York: Routledge, 2016.

Pongphisoot Busbarat. 'Bamboo Swirling in the Wind: Thailand's Foreign Policy Imbalance between China and the United States'. *Contemporary Southeast Asia* 38, no. 2 (2016): 233–57. doi.org/10.1355/cs38-2c.

Pouliot, Vincent. *International Pecking Orders: The Politics and Practice of Multilateral Diplomacy.* Cambridge: Cambridge University Press, 2016.

Prajak Kongkirati. *And Then the Movement Emerged: Cultural Politics of Thai Students and Intellectuals Movements before the October 14 Uprising.* Bangkok: Thammasat University Press, 2005.

Prasit Kanchanawat. 'Nueng Thosawad Mittaparp Thai-Jeen' [One Decade of Sino–Thai Friendship]. In *Prasit Kanchanawat: Think, Speak, Write,* edited by Apiwat Wannakorn, 94-103. Bangkok: Sukaparpjai, 1997.

Prasit Kanchanawat. 'Sumphantamaitri Thai-Jeen korn por sor' [Sino–Thai Friendship before 1975]. *Warasan Asiatawanoak suksa* [East Asian Studies Journal] 3, no. 1 (July 1990): 13–22.

Puangthong Pawakapan. 'Thailand's Response to the Cambodian Genocide'. In *Genocide in Cambodia and Rwanda: New Perspectives,* edited by Susan E Cook, 79–126. New Brunswick: Transaction Publishers, 2009. doi.org/10.4324/9780203790847-4.

Puangthong Pawakapan. *Truth in the Vietnam War: The First Casualty of War and the Thai State.* Bangkok: Kobfai, 2006.

Quinn-Judge, Sophie. 'Victory on the Battlefield; Isolation in Asia: Vietnam's Cambodia Decade, 1979–1989'. In *The Third Indochina War: Conflict between China, Vietnam and Cambodia, 1972–1979,* edited by Odd Arne Westad and Sophie Quinn-Judge, 207–30. London and New York: Routledge, 2006. doi.org/10.4324/9780203968574-16.

Radchenko, Sergey. 'Vietnam's Vietnam: Ending the Cambodian Quagmire, 1979–89'. In *Unwanted Visionaries: The Soviet Failure in Asia at the End of the Cold War,* 124–58. Oxford: Oxford University Press, 2014. doi.org/10.1093/acprof:oso/9780199938773.003.0004.

Ramsay, Ansil. 'Thailand 1978: Kriangsak – The Thai who Binds'. *Asian Survey* 19, no. 2 (1979): 104–14. doi.org/10.2307/2643776.

Ramsay, Ansil. 'Thailand 1979: A Government in Trouble'. *Asian Survey* 20, no. 2 (1980): 112–22. doi.org/10.2307/2644015.

Randolph, R. Sean. *The United States and Thailand: Alliance Dynamics, 1950–1985.* Berkeley: Institute of East Asian Studies, University of California, 1986.

Rapeeporn Lertwongweerachai. 'The Role of Thanat Khoman in Thai Foreign Affairs during 1958–1971'. MA thesis, Chulalongkorn University, 2002.

Raymond, Gregory V. 'Strategic Culture and Thailand's Response to Vietnam's Occupation of Cambodia, 1979–1989 A Cold War Epilogue'. *Journal of Cold War Studies* 22, no. 1 (Winter 2020): 4–45. doi.org/10.1162/jcws_a_00924.

Reynolds, Craig J. *Thai Radical Discourse: The Real Face of Thai Feudalism Today.* Ithaca: Cornell Southeast Asia Program Publications, 1987.

Reynolds, Craig J and Hong Lysa. 'Marxism in Thai Historical Studies'. *Journal of Asian Studies* 43, no. 1 (1983): 77–104. doi.org/10.2307/2054618.

Roberts, Geoffrey. *The Soviet Union in World Politics: Coexistence, Revolution and Cold War, 1945–1991.* London and New York: Routledge, 1999. doi.org/10.4324/9780203983461.

Saichon Sattayanurak. *Kukrit kap praditthakam 'Khwam pen Thai', lem 2* [Kukrit and the Construction of 'Thainess', Book 2]. Bangkok: Silapawatthanatham, 2007.

Saiyud Kerdphol. *The Struggle for Thailand: Counter-insurgency, 1965–1985.* Bangkok: S. Research Center, 1986.

Sarasin Viraphol. *Directions in Thai Foreign Policy.* Singapore: Institute of Southeast Asian Studies, 1976.

Sarasin Viraphol. 'The Soviet Threat: Development of the Thai Perception'. *Asian Affairs: An American Review* 11, no. 4 (Winter 1985): 61–70. doi.org/10.1080/00927678.1985.10553704.

Sargent, Daniel J. *A Superpower Transformed: The Remaking of American Foreign Relations in the 1970s.* Oxford: Oxford University Press, 2015.

Schmitt, Carl. *The Concept of the Political.* Chicago and London: The University of Chicago Press, 1996.

See, Jennifer W. 'An Uneasy Truce: John F. Kennedy and Soviet–American Détente, 1963'. *Cold War History* 2, no. 2 (2002): 161–94. doi.org/10.1080/713999948.

Shirk, Paul R. 'Thai–Soviet Relations'. *Asian Survey* 9 (September 1969): 682–93.

Siddhi Savetsila. *Pan Rorn Pan Nao* [Through Thick and Thin]. Bangkok, 2013.

Singh, Bilveer. *Soviet Relations with ASEAN, 1967–1988.* Singapore: Singapore University Press, 1989.

Sirin Phathanothai. *The Dragon's Pearl.* New York and London: Simon & Schuster, 1994.

Smart, Barry. *Michel Foucault.* Sussex: Ellis Horwood, 1985.

Soymook Yingchaiyakamon. 'Thailand's Foreign Policy towards the People's Republic of China during Field Marshal P. Phibulsonggram's Government (1948–1957)'. MA thesis, Chulalongkorn University, 2001.

Stanton, Edwin F. *Brief Authority: Excursions of a Common Man in an Uncommon World.* New York: Harper, 1956.

Steele, Brent. *Ontological Security in International Relations: Self-Identity ad the IR State.* London and New York: Routledge, 2008.

Steiner, Zara. 'On Writing International History: Chaps, Maps and Much More'. *International Affairs* 73, no. 3 (1997): 531–46. doi.org/10.2307/2624271.

Stowe, Judith. *Siam Becomes Thailand: A Study of Intrigue*. Honolulu: University of Hawai'i Press, 1991.

Strate, Shane. *The Lost Territories: Thailand's History of National Humiliation*. Honolulu: University of Hawai'i Press, 2015. doi.org/10.21313/hawaii/9780824838911.003.0004.

Suchit Bunbongkarn. 'The Role of Social Science in Foreign Policy Making of Thailand'. In *Social Sciences and National Development: The Southeast Asian Experience*, edited by Shou-sheng Hsueh, 115–34. New Delhi: Abhinav Publications, 1977.

Suhrki, Astri. 'Smaller-Nation Diplomacy: Thailand's Current Dilemmas'. *Asian Survey* 11, no. 5 (May 1971): 429–44. doi.org/10.2307/2642980.

Sukhumbhand Paribatra. 'Can ASEAN Break the Stalemate?' *World Policy Journal* 3, no. 1 (1985): 85–106.

Sukhumbhand Paribatra. 'Dictates of Security: Thailand's Relations with the PRC since the Vietnam War'. In *ASEAN and China: An Evolving Relationship*, edited by Joyce K. Kalgren, Noordin Sopiee and Soedjati Djiwandono, 297–316. Berkeley: University of California, 1988.

Sukhumbhand Paribatra. *From Enmity to Alignment: Thailand's Evolving Relations with China*. Bangkok: Institute of Security and International Studies, Chulalongkorn University, 1987.

Sukhumbhand Paribatra. 'Strategic Implications of the Indochina Conflict'. *Asian Affairs* 11, no. 3 (1984): 28–46. doi.org/10.1080/00927678.1984.10553698.

Sunai Phasuk. 'Thai Foreign Policy: A Case Study on the Policy Formulation Process of General Chatichai Choonhavan's Government on the Cambodian Problem (4 August 1988 to 23 February 1991)'. MA thesis, Chulalongkorn University, 1986.

Surachai Sirikrai. 'Sino–Thai Relations: A Thai Perception'. In *China–ASEAN Relations: Political, Economic and Ethnic Dimensions*, edited by Theresa C Carino, 42–59. Manila: De La Salle University, 1991.

Surachai Sirikrai. 'Thai Perceptions of China and Japan'. *Contemporary Southeast Asia* 12, no. 3 (December 1990): 247–65.

Surachart Bamrungsuk. *United States Foreign Policy and Thailand Military Rule, 1947–1977*. Bangkok: Duang Kamol, 1988.

Sutayut Osornprasop. 'Thailand and the American Secret War in Indochina, 1960–1974'. PhD thesis, University of Cambridge, 2006.

Tej Bunnag. 'Satapana kwansumpan tai-jeen, 1 karakadakom 2518: prasobkarn kong nakkantud' [Establishing Thai–Chinese Relations, 1 July 1975: Diplomat's Experiences]. *Warasan Asiatawanoak suksa* [East Asian Studies Journal] 3, no. 1 (July 1990): 23–30.

Terrill, Ross. 'Reports and Comment – Thailand'. *The Atlantic Monthly*, October 1972.

Thak Chaloemtiarana. *Thailand: The Politics of Despotic Paternalism*. Ithaca: Southeast Asia Program Publications, Cornell University, 2007. First published 1979. doi.org/10.7591/9781501721106.

Thamsook Numnonda. *Thailand and the Japanese Presence, 1941–1945*. Singapore: Institute of Southeast Asian Studies, 1977.

Thongchai Winichakul. 'Prawatisat thai baep rachachatniyom: Jak yuk ananikhom amphrang su rachachatniyom mai rue latthi phor khong kradumphi thai nai patchuban' [Royalist Nationalist History: From the Colonial Era to the New Royalist Nationalism], *Silapawatthanatham* 23, no. 1 (November 2001): 43–52.

Thongchai Winichakul. 'Remembering/Silencing the Traumatic Past: The Ambivalent Memories of the October 1976 Massacre in Bangkok'. In *Cultural Crisis and Social Memory: Modernity and Identity in Thailand and Laos*, edited by Charles F Keyes and Shigeharu Tanabe, 243–83. London and New York: Routledge, 2002. doi.org/10.4324/9781315027906-22.

Thongchai Winichakul. *Siam Mapped: A History of the Geo-Body of a Nation*. Honolulu: University of Hawai'i Press, 1994.

Tuck, Patrick. *The French Wolf and the Siamese Lamb: The French Threat to Siamese Independence, 1858–1907*. Bangkok: White Lotus Press, 1995.

Ukrist Pathmanand. 'Saharat America kap nayobai sethakit Thai' [The US and Thai Economic Policy]. MA thesis, Chulalongkorn University, 1983.

Vichitvong na Pombhejara. 'The Kriangsak Government and the Thai Economy'. *Southeast Asian Affairs* (1979): 312–22.

Vichitvong na Pombhejara. 'Thailand in 1979: A Year of Relative Stability'. *Southeast Asian Affairs* (1980): 311–24.

BIBLIOGRAPHY

Vieira, Marco A. 'Understanding Resilience in International Relations: The Non-Aligned Movement and Ontological Security'. *International Studies Review* 18 (2016): 290–311. doi.org/10.1093/isr/viw002.

Vitthaya Veljajiva. *Phan Phuea Phandin* [Phan for the Kingdom]. Bangkok: Post Publishing, 2014.

Waltz, Kenneth N. *Theory of International Politics*. New York: McGraw-Hill, 1979.

Warnwai Phathanothai. *Zhou Enlai: Pupluek maitri Thai-jeen* [Zhou Enlai: The Man Who Planted Thai-Chinese Friendship]. 2nd ed. Bangkok: Prakonchai, 2001. First published 1976.

Westad, Odd Arne, ed. *The Fall of Détente: Soviet–American Relations during the Carter Years*. Oslo: Scandinavian University Press, 1997.

Wiwat Mungkandi. 'The Security Syndrome (1941–1975)'. In *A Century and a Half of Thai–American Relations*, edited by Wiwat Mungkandi and William Warren, 61–114. Bangkok: Chulalongkorn University, 1982.

Wiwat Mungkandi and William Warren, eds. *A Century and a Half of Thai–American Relations*. Bangkok: Chulalongkorn University, 1982.

Wong, John. *The Political Economy of China's Changing Relations with Southeast Asia*. London: Macmillan Press, 1984.

Wyatt, David. *Thailand: A Short History*. New Haven: Yale University Press, 1984.

Yos Santasombat. *Power, Personality and Thai Political Elite*. Bangkok: Thai Studies Institute, Thammasat University 1990.

Young, Kenneth. 'Thailand's Role in Southeast Asia'. *Current History* 56, no. 330 (1969): 94–99, 110–11.

Zagoria, Donald S and Sheldon W Simon. 'Soviet Policy in Southeast Asia'. In *Soviet Policy in East Asia*, edited by Donald S Zagoria, 153–73. New Haven and London: Yale University Press, 1982.

Zehfuss, Maja. 'Constructivism and Identity: A Dangerous Liaison'. *European Journal of International Relations* 7, no. 3 (September 2001): 315–48. doi.org/10.1177/13540661010070030002.

Zhang, Xiaoming. *Deng Xiaoping's Long War: The Military Conflict between China and Vietnam, 1979–1991*. Chapel Hill: The University of North Carolina Press, 2015.